To Improve the Academy

To Improve the Academy

Resources for Faculty, Instructional, and Organizational Development

Volume 22

Catherine M. Wehlburg, Editor
Texas Christian University

Sandra Chadwick-Blossey, Associate Editor
Rollins College

Anker Publishing Company, Inc.
Bolton, Massachusetts

To Improve the Academy
Resources for Faculty, Instructional, and Organizational Development

Volume 22

ISBN 1-882982-65-7

Composition by Deerfoot Studios
Cover design by Boynton Hue Studio

Anker Publishing Company, Inc.
176 Ballville Road
P.O. Box 249
Bolton, MA 01740-0249 USA

www.ankerpub.com

To Improve the Academy

To Improve the Academy is published annually by the Professional and Organizational Network in Higher Education (POD) through Anker Publishing Company, and is abstracted in ERIC documents and in Higher Education Abstracts.

Ordering Information

The annual volume of *To Improve the Academy* is distributed to members at the POD conference in the autumn of each year. To order or to obtain ordering information, contact:

Anker Publishing Company, Inc.
P.O. Box 249
Bolton, MA 01740-0249
Voice (978) 779-6190
Fax (978) 779-6366
Email info@ankerpub.com
Web www.ankerpub.com

Permission to Copy

Instructions to Contributors for the Next Volume

Anyone interested in the issues related to instructional, faculty, and organizational development in higher education may submit manuscripts. Manuscripts are submitted to the current editors in December of each year and sent through a blind review process. Correspondence, including requests for information about guidelines and submission of manuscripts for Volume 23, should be directed to:

Sandra Chadwick-Blossey
Director, Christian A. Johnson Institute for Effective Teaching
Rollins College
1000 Holt Avenue, Box 2636
Winter Park, FL 32789
Voice (407) 628-6353
Fax (407) 646-1581
Email schadwick@rollins.edu

Mission Statement

Approved by the Core Committee on April 11, 2003:

The Professional and Organizational Development Network in Higher Education encourages the advocacy of the ongoing enhancement of teaching and learning through faculty and organizational development. To this end, it supports the work of educational developers and champions their importance to the academic enterprise.

Vision Statement

During the 21st century, the Professional and Organizational Development Network in Higher Education will expand guidelines for educational development, build strong alliances with sister organizations, and encourage developer exchanges and research projects to improve teaching and learning.

Values

The Professional and Organizational Development Network in Higher Education is committed to:

- Personal, professional, instructional, and organizational development.
- Humane and collaborative organizations and administrations.
- Diverse perspectives and a diverse membership.
- Supportive educational development networks on the local, regional, national, and international levels.
- Advocacy for improved teaching and learning in the academy through programs for faculty, administrators, and graduate students.
- The identification and collection of a strong and accessible body of research on development theories and practices.

- The establishment of guidelines for ethical practice.
- The increasingly useful and thorough assessment and evaluation of practice and research.

Programs, Publications, and Activities

The Professional and Organizational Development Network in Higher Education offers members and interested individuals the following benefits:

- An annual national conference designed to promote professional and personal growth, nurture innovation and change, stimulate important research projects, and enable participants to exchange ideas and broaden professional networks.
- An annual membership directory and networking guide.
- Publications in print and on the web.

Membership, Conference, and Programs Information

For information contact:

Frank and Kay Gillespie, Executive Directors
The POD Network
P.O. Box 9696
Fort Collins, CO 80525
Voice (970) 377-9269
Fax (970) 377-9282
Email podnetwork@podweb.org

Chapter Contributors

Ashleah Bechtel, United States Military Academy

Phyllis Blumberg, University of the Sciences in Philadelphia

Timothy W. Bothell, Brigham Young University

Corly Brooke, Iowa State University

Marjorie H. Carroll, United States Military Academy

Nancy Van Note Chism, Indiana University–Purdue University Indianapolis

Jacqueline K. Coffman, California State University, Fullerton

Peter Felten, Vanderbilt University

Doug Foster, Abilene Christian University

Kenneth France, Shippensburg University

Bo Green, Abilene Christian University

Scott E. Hampton, United States Military Academy

Tom Henderson, Washington State University

Ellen N. Junn, California State University, Fullerton

Jennifer Karlin, South Dakota School of Mines and Technology

Kevin Kecskes, Portland State University

Ellen Kottler, California State University, Fullerton

Karen Krupar, Metropolitan State College of Denver

Paul Lakey, Abilene Christian University

Raye Lakey, Abilene Christian University

David J. Langley, Indiana State University

Devorah Lieberman, Portland State University

Deandra Little, Vanderbilt University

Kathleen McKinney, Illinois State University

Barbara J. Millis, U. S. Air Force Academy

Pamela M. Milloy, Iowa State University

Foy Mills, Abilene Christian University

Craig D. Morrow, United States Military Academy

Sue E. Neeley, University of Houston–Clear Lake

Terence W. O'Connor, The College of New Jersey

Chris O'Neal, University of Michigan

Pamella H. Oliver, California State University, Fullerton

Mathew L. Ouellett, University of Massachusetts, Amherst

Allison Pingree, Vanderbilt University

Marlene M. Preston, Virginia Polytechnic Institute and State University

Fred Ramirez, California State University, Fullerton

Margaret K. Snooks, University of Houston–Clear Lake

Amy Spring, Portland State University

D. Lynn Sorenson, Brigham Young University

Christine A. Stanley, Texas A&M University

Michele M. Welkener, Indiana State University

Carol Williams, Abilene Christian University

Debbie Williams, Abilene Christian University

Kathleen M. Williamson, University of Houston–Clear Lake

Deborah Willis, Victoria University of Wellington

Table of Contents

Section IV: Faculty Development Tools

Section V: Student Learning and Faculty Development

Section VI: Faculty Development With Part-Time Instructors

Preface

The continued high quality of *To Improve the Academy* requires that thoughtful and comprehensive manuscripts are submitted; focused and knowledgeable reviewers give of their time; and authors are open to edits and modifications of their work. This volume attests to all of these things. I would like to thank the authors for their dedication to the sharing of knowledge and to the continuing improvement of teaching and learning in higher education. I would also like to thank the reviewers: Danilo M. Baylen, Donna C. Bird, Phyllis Blumberg, Tuesday L. Cooper, Darcey Cuffman, Cynthia Desrochers, Michele DiPietro, Ruby Evans, Peter Felten, Marne George Helgesen, Eileen M. Herteis, Patricia Kalivoda, Kathleen McKinney, Roberta McKnight, Jennifer McLean, Eric T. Metzler, Edward Nuhfer, Karen Marie Peters, Ronald E. Pitt, Douglas Reimondo Robertson, Karen E. Santos, David Starrett, Margaret K. Snooks, Laurel Warren Trufant, Patricia Valley, Peggy A. Weissinger, and Dina Wills. Their role in this process is crucial and the selection of excellent manuscripts is largely due to their competence and energy.

This volume was edited during my first year as Director of the Center for Teaching Excellence (CTE) at Texas Christian University. I would like to thank my colleagues at CTE (Romana Hughes, Arrion Howard, and Cathy Vahrenkamp) for their support of my work with POD and *To Improve the Academy.* All took on additional tasks so that I could focus on the work for this volume. I would like to especially thank Cathy Vahrenkamp for her wonderful editing skills. Her reading and rereading of manuscripts was a very important part of this work. Leo Munson, Associate Vice Chancellor for Academic Support, also gave support to my work on this volume. Finally, no amount of thanks can express my appreciation adequately for Sandra Chadwick-Blossey, Associate Editor. She will take over the editing for Volumes 23 and 24, and I can assure readers that the next two volumes will be exemplary.

My family played a large part in the completion of this volume. George, Trevor, and Brooke were all supportive and gave me the time that I needed to focus on this work. Brooke (three years old at this writing) tried very hard to help with the typing—I hope that I have removed most of her efforts, as her typing skills need a little work.

Catherine M. Wehlburg
Texas Christian University
Fort Worth, TX
April 2003

Introduction

Volume 22 of *To Improve the Academy* contains articles that speak to the widespread influence of faculty, organizational, and instructional development. In times of budget and staff cuts and enrollment drops, the need for quality, effective higher education can only increase. As postsecondary institutions look to become more efficient, faculty development professionals must help to ensure excellence in education. In order to do this, there must be high quality and meaningful data.

Section I: Past, Present, and Future of SoTL includes only one chapter, written by Kathleen McKinney, and provides an overview of the history of the scholarship of teaching and learning. She calls for additional research in many areas of faculty development, including appropriately increasing the legitimacy of research on the scholarship of teaching and conducting this research in an ethical manner.

Section II: Assessment and Faculty Development focuses on methods used to assess student learning and the impact of faculty development. In Chapter 2, D. Lynn Sorenson and Timothy W. Bothell share a needs assessment that was conducted in conjunction with a qualitative study. These study results (and additional data) more clearly described the needs of faculty and how these needs might be met.

Faculty needs do not focus only on teaching, as Phyllis Blumberg points out in Chapter 3. This chapter describes a Document of Innovations that has been used to highlight faculty innovations in the classroom and bring innovative thinking into higher regard at the University of the Sciences in Philadelphia.

In Chapter 4, Timothy W. Bothell and Tom Henderson discuss how they used return on investment (ROI) with a Freshman Seminar Program and student retention.

Chapter 5, by Pamela M. Milloy and Corly Brooke, describes a needs assessment project that was used at Iowa State University and how its results helped to guide appropriate and meaningful direction for the faculty development center.

In Section III: Curriculum Design and Evaluation, three chapters focus on how faculty development can use different tools to redesign curriculum to improve student learning. In Chapter 6, Marlene M. Preston describes a color-coded course design that she uses to help faculty "see" what their course will look like before it begins. This graphic method of designing a course can be very helpful to faculty.

Chapter 7, by Margaret K. Snooks, Sue E. Neeley, and Kathleen M. Williamson, describes the Bare Bones Questions (BBQ) process that is a streamlined midterm evaluation. Faculty can be trained to use this process with colleagues (called "collegial training"), thus opening the discussion of teaching to an even broader audience.

Chapter 8, by Barbara J. Millis, describes a focus group process that can gather student perceptions to help faculty modify their courses to improve student learning.

Section IV: Faculty Development Tools provides several models for enhancing what is currently being done in faculty development. In Chapter 9, David J. Langley, Terence W. O'Connor, and Michele M. Welkener describe a model for professional and organizational development with an individual/public dimension and a reflection/performance dimension. This may give a different framework to discuss programming that meets the needs of faculty.

Scott E. Hampton, Craig D. Morrow, Ashleah Bechtel, and Marjorie H. Carroll describe a systematic, hands-on, reflective, and effective (SHORE) approach to faculty development in Chapter 10, demonstrating that this SHORE method may help instructors meet teaching goals, feel like a part of the department, and encourage them to continue to improve their teaching.

In Chapter 11, Peter Felten, Deandra Little, and Allison Pingree discuss Michel Foucault's theories of power and how they are related to faculty development and teaching. Power is an important (and often unseen) variable in faculty development and education. Institutions are often hierarchial with untenured faculty having much less power, individually and collectively, than administrators or tenured faculty.

Chapter 12, by Ellen N. Junn, Ellen Kottler, Jacqueline K. Coffman, Pamella H. Oliver, and Fred Ramirez, describes a faculty support program for untenured faculty and full-time lecturers. This organization (the ULO) provides activities and programs specifically designed for those who are untenured.

Mathew L. Ouellett and Christine A. Stanley describe in Chapter 13 the travel and internship grants that POD has offered over the past nine years. A survey of the recipients was conducted and the results are presented here.

In Chapter 14, Nancy Van Note Chism outlines how collaboration with other departmental units can strengthen academic development centers and work toward a more inclusive educational process.

Section V: Student Learning and Faculty Development focuses more on helping faculty to work with students to enhance and improve student learning. In Chapter 15, Kenneth France shares results from three psychology courses that used problem-based service learning. These results demonstrate how this type of pedagogy can be used to help students better understand a topic and increase their learning.

Chapter 16, by Debbie Williams, Doug Foster, Bo Green, Paul Lakey, Raye Lakey, Foy Mills, and Carol Williams, reviews some of the learning team and peer evaluation literature. They also describe results of how peer evaluation can be used formatively and summatively to increase learning.

Deborah Willis and Barbara J. Millis discuss in Chapter 17 the value of group work and how it can enhance student learning. This chapter describes some of the research and policy in several countries to help the reader focus on the need for an integrated approach to using group work.

In Chapter 18, Kevin Kecskes, Amy Spring, and Devorah Lieberman describe Portland State University's recent Hesburgh recognition for their work with service learning and community-university partnerships.

The final section, Section VI: Faculty Development With Part-Time Instructors, provides information and ideas concerning adjunct faculty and graduate students. Chapter 19, by Karen Krupar, discusses adjunct faculty and their lack of general integration into the life of an institution. The chapter further describes the program at Metropolitan State College of Denver, which seeks to provide support and innovation for adjunct faculty.

Graduate students, too, often are left out of the integration "loop" at many institutions. Chris O'Neal and Jennifer Karlin present in Chapter 20 a program of Graduate Student Mentors to try and bridge this gap. This program seeks to train graduate student instructors and continue that training as the graduate student progresses through school.

Section I

Past, Present, and Future of SoTL

1

The Scholarship of Teaching and Learning: Past Lessons, Current Challenges, and Future Visions

Kathleen McKinney
Illinois State University

This chapter reviews the complex history of the scholarship of teaching and learning (SoTL) including SoTL as a social movement and various conceptualizations of the term. Based on extant work, I also discuss past lessons, current challenges, and future directions for SoTL. Additional theorizing and research are needed in many areas. Suggestions related to faculty and organizational development and change are imbedded in this discussion.

Introduction

Formal ideas about the scholarship of teaching and learning (SoTL) and related concepts have been discussed in the field of higher education for over a dozen years. Yet SoTL work has existed, in many disciplines in higher education, for decades. Consider, for example, the many college-level, disciplinary teaching journals with long histories. In my discipline, this journal is *Teaching Sociology*, which has been in existence for about 30 years. Though Boyer's (1990) work on the scholarship of teaching concept has received the most attention, others contributed to this early discussion. For example, Shulman coined the phrase pedagogical content knowledge (Shulman, 1987). Pellino, Blackburn, and Boberg (1984) discussed multiple forms of scholarship including the scholarship of pedagogy. Activities and products such as course content and activities were seen as a form of scholarship in Braxton and Toombs's (1982) research. In the discipline of sociology, Goldsmid and Wilson (1980) grappled with the similarities of and standards for research and teaching, and argued "collaborative inquiry is at the heart of both activities" (p. 32). In addition, Baker (1980, 1985, 1986) discussed ideas about the relationships among what we know about teaching as sociologists, and our work and writing about teaching.

The increased prominence of the SoTL in the national higher education arena can be seen through efforts such as the Carnegie Academy for the Scholarship of Teaching and Learning, or CASTL, program; the Carnegie Scholars program; a growing number of local, regional, and national conferences on college teaching and/or SoTL (e.g., sessions at Lilly Conferences; the American Association for Higher Education pre-conference, Rockhurst University's annual SoTL conference); and new SoTL journals, both online and traditional, both general and discipline based (e.g., *Journal of Scholarship of Teaching and Learning, Journal of Active Learning, Journal of Student Centered Learning*). National disciplinary societies are also showing more interest in supporting SoTL work as seen in cooperative efforts between these societies and the CASTL program. For example, with help from the CASTL program, the American Sociological Association (ASA) brought together about 40 sociologists in the summer of 2000 to discuss and develop position papers on the status of knowledge and research on teaching and learning in the discipline. Finally, a significant number (12 of 50 using a narrow definition; 27 of 50 using a broader definition) of the institutional social change projects at the 2002 American Association for Higher Education (AAHE) Summer Academy in Vermont focused on promoting the SoTL. For example, projects dealt with SoTL development opportunities, increasing the quantity and quality of SoTL work, changes in reward structures to recognize SoTL, and involving more students in SoTL work.

Why the growing emphasis on SoTL? Due to changes in the higher education climate we have been reminded that we need to know much more about how, why, and when our students learn. These changes include a renewed focus on teaching across all types of institutions, increasing diversity of the student body, rapid adoption of new instructional technologies, new knowledge about learning and the brain, and additional pressures for the use of assessment data to determine student learning outcomes. In addition, many of us have come to realize that we cannot afford what Shulman (2001) called the great tragedy of teaching—the collective amnesia about what works and why in teaching and learning. SoTL is the primary treatment for preventing this amnesia and creating an up-to-date knowledge base that can be used to improve student learning and development.

We can look at this growing interest in and support for SoTL as a social movement—not one that is integrated into society as a whole but rather one that is limited in scope and somewhat specific to the institution of higher education (sometimes called an alternative social movement). Over 15 years ago, Mauksch and Howery (1986) articulated the notion of the teaching movement in sociology as a social change movement. A similar argument can be made today for the national/international SoTL movement.

Based on the deprivation/frustration (e.g., Smelser, 1963) and resource mobilization (McCarthy & Zald, 1977) approaches to social movements, there are a variety of factors that influence and characterize social movements: frustration over a problem or a needed reform, a sense that the problem or change is possible, an ideology, use of networks to recruit members, mobilization of resources including leaders and finances, a sense that the movement has legitimacy, increased awareness of the issues and movement, the ability to fend off counter-movements, existence of allies from outside the movement, and the development of organizations to support the movement.

As we look at recent trends in and the status of SoTL today, we can see many of these same characteristics. There has been increasing concern about the lack of knowledge and insufficient use of such knowledge for teaching and learning in higher education disciplines as well as frustration about the definition, value, and rewards of SoTL. Members of the movement share many beliefs about the legitimacy and positive value of SoTL. Leadership, finances, legitimacy, recruitment of members, and the development of organizations have been mobilized and strengthened through work at universities, AAHE, the Carnegie Foundation, and disciplinary societies. Some of our outside allies are supportive colleagues and administrators not directly involved in SoTL, and private donors or funding agencies willing to provide financial support for SoTL work.

Past Lessons in the Scholarship of Teaching and Learning

What are some of the key lessons learned during this history of SoTL? First, we have learned, and continue to learn, the importance and value of SoTL to higher education. SoTL contributes to the knowledge base about teaching and learning and is serving as a movement to stimulate networking, research, discussion, and action related to improving teaching and learning.

Second, defining SoTL in a way that makes sense to everyone has been problematic. Many writers have attempted to discuss and refine the SoTL concept (e.g., Baker, 2002; Braxton, Luckey, & Helland, 2002; Cross & Steadman, 1996; Darling, 2003; Glassick, Huber, & Maeroff, 1997; Hutchings &

Shulman, 1999; Kreber, 2001a; Kreber & Cranton, 2000; Paulsen & Feldman, 1995; Rice, 1992; Richlin, 1993, 2001; Schön, 1995; Weimer, 1996).

Definitions tend to focus on activities or processes. For example, Illinois State University, as part of its work with the CASTL program, agreed to conceptualize SoTL as a systematic reflection on teaching and learning made public. In work at the Carnegie Foundation and the American Association of Higher Education, the following definition has sometimes been used: "problem posing about an issue of teaching or learning, study of the problem through methods appropriate to the disciplinary epistemologies, applications of results to practice, communication of results, self-reflection, and peer review" (Cambridge, 2001, p. 8). Kreber and Cranton (2000) view SoTL as "ongoing learning about teaching and the demonstration of such knowledge" (p. 478), while Darling (2003) states that SoTL is "work that encourages an empirical examination of teaching in relation to student learning" (p. 47). Richlin (2001) argues, "The scholarship part of the process involves composing selected portions of the investigation and findings [or integration or reflection] into a manuscript to be submitted to an appropriate journal or conference venue" (p. 61). Martin, Benjamin, Prosser, and Trigwell (1999) argue that the scholarship of teaching is three related activities: engagement with the existing knowledge on teaching and learning, self-reflection on teaching and learning in one's discipline, and public sharing of ideas about teaching and learning within the discipline.

Hutchings (2002a) reminds us that SoTL builds on many past traditions in higher education including classroom and program assessment, K–12 action research, the reflective practice movement, peer review of teaching, traditional educational research, and faculty development efforts to enhance teaching and learning. As Kreber (2001b) and others have pointed out, and as her Delphi study indicates, we lack shared language and meaning in this area. Furthermore, many do not use the term SoTL in the way that Boyer (1990) originally conceptualized the scholarship of teaching. Boyer's scholarship of teaching is closer to what many today refer to as scholarly teaching.

Similar to what others have discussed or implied (e.g., Cross and Steadman, 1996; Healey, 2000; Rice, 1992), I believe Boyer's typology of scholarships conflates two dimensions: type of scholarly *activity* and *topic* or area of scholarship. That is, he delineated four types of scholarship: discovery, integration, application, and teaching. Yet, recent views of the concept of SoTL include *activities* that are discovery, integration, and application where the *topic* is teaching and learning (usually in higher education and often in terms of a specific discipline).

Others have reworked Boyer's types. Baker (2002) outlines four roles (discovery, integration, and two forms of application) within his view of the scholarship of teaching. McKenna, Bickle, and Carroll (2002) argue that discovery, integration, application, and teaching are stages in a scholarly process. They point out that the final stage—the production of a scholarly outcome—is missing and is necessary for any work to "count."

Though Rice (1992) acknowledges this overlap of dimensions and points out that the Boyer scholarship types were to be seen as interdependent, I think this aspect of the typology remains problematic. The conflation of the activity and topic dimensions leads to misunderstanding and confusion, and the questioning of SoTL work as legitimate scholarship.

We have also learned that there are many difficulties with the status and structure of SoTL work. Based on observations of my own campus and discussions with colleagues on other campuses, much SoTL work occurs in isolation, undertaken by one or a small number of faculty members within a department, often working alone. What we know from SoTL work is fragmented and not adequately shared. Many faculty and staff members are unaware of the growing number and range of higher education pedagogical journals, sometimes even of the one(s) in their own discipline. Finally, in many places, SoTL work receives little support, reward, or recognition, or is categorized within reward systems as teaching rather than scholarship.

Current Challenges in the Scholarship of Teaching and Learning

Perhaps not surprisingly, many of these past lessons remain current challenges. First, we still struggle with the meaning of SoTL and related terms. Is there a "best" definition? Do we need consensus on a definition? Is SoTL a "field"? How is SoTL related to traditional educational research or to assessment studies? Is SoTL the process and/or the outcomes? Depending on how we conceptualize SoTL, are we doing more of this work than in the past? Is the work "stronger" than in the past? In my own discipline, Chin (2002) recently published a replication of Baker's (1985) work analyzing articles published in *Teaching Sociology*, in an attempt to categorize those that meet the criteria for scholarship. Chin concludes that there has been modest improvement in the amount and quality of SoTL work in sociology since 1985. The challenge here is to continue the conversation about the nature and meaning of this work, and to find sufficient common ground to allow understanding and collaboration.

Second, a challenge closely related to the first, is to negotiate distinctions between related key terms: distinctions that impact legitimacy, support, evaluation, and rewards. Though there are close connections among them, it is important to distinguish good teaching from scholarly teaching from the scholarship of teaching and learning. My preference is for the following distinctions (see, also, Darling, 2003; Healey, 2000; Hutchings & Schulman, 1999; many of the chapters in Kreber, 2001a). Though *good teaching* has been defined and operationalized in many ways (e.g., student satisfaction ratings, peer observation judgments, self-reflective portfolios), good teaching promotes student learning and other desired student outcomes. Good teaching will support department, college, and institutional missions and objectives. Decades of SoTL and other educational research provide us with a great deal of information on the practices that help promote learning (e.g., Astin, 1993; Chickering & Gamson, 1987; Pascarella & Terenzini, 1991).

Scholarly teaching involves taking a scholarly approach to teaching just as we would take a scholarly approach to other areas of knowledge and practice. Scholarly teaching is a process; scholarly teachers view teaching as a profession and the knowledge base on teaching and learning as a second discipline in which to develop expertise. Thus, scholarly teachers do things such as reflect on their teaching, use classroom assessment techniques, engage in systematic course design, update their courses, discuss teaching issues with colleagues, try new teaching techniques, and read and apply the literature on teaching and learning in their discipline. Scholarly teaching is closely linked to reflective practice (e.g., Brookfield, 1995; Schön, 1983, 1987). This conception of scholarly teaching is related to what Boyer (1990) labeled the scholarship of teaching.

The scholarship of teaching and learning goes beyond scholarly teaching and involves the systematic study of teaching and/or learning and the public sharing and review of such work through presentations or publications. Clearly, there is a focus here on the product or outcome. "Study" is broadly defined given disciplinary differences in epistemology and the need for interdisciplinary SoTL. SoTL, then, shares established criteria of scholarship in general, such as that it is made public, can be reviewed critically by members of the appropriate community, and can be built upon by others to advance the field (Shulman, 2001). Ideally, SoTL also involves application and use.

In this view, it is possible that individuals can teach, though probably not with great effectiveness, and not be scholarly teachers. Individuals can practice scholarly teaching but not actually contribute to the knowledge base by conducting and making public their own SoTL work. In many institutions, good teaching and scholarly teaching would be rewarded under teaching, while the scholarship of teaching and learning would be rewarded under research/scholarship. Recently, some writers have argued that movement through these three types of activities and beliefs—good teaching, scholarly teaching, and SoTL—is a developmental process in a faculty member's career (e.g., Smith, 2001; Weston & McAlpine, 2001).

Third, then, is the challenge to strengthen the legitimacy of quality SoTL work in terms of its status and its applicability. Bass (1999) offers a provocative discussion of the concept of teaching-learning "problems" and their place in the minds of faculty and in SoTL work. Teaching-learning problems are the appropriate topic of ongoing, long-term investigation, not something to be hidden from others or quickly fixed.

Two authors have raised concerns about the current and future status or role of SoTL work. Cross expressed the concern that the scholarship of teaching and learning could become another "tier" in the academic hierarchy—that is, that the perception will be that "those who can't do research in their field, do SoTL, and those that can't do SoTL, teach" (K. P. Cross, personal communication, fall 2002). On the other hand, SoTL might serve as one bridge between our teaching and traditional scholarly roles. SoTL has the potential to increase interest in teaching on the part of those who are primarily traditional researchers, as well as to increase interest in research of those who primarily teach.

In a related vein, Eisenberg (2002), referring specifically to the discipline of sociology, argues that there are two faces in the higher education teaching community. There is the face of the art and practice of teaching and the face of SoTL. Her concern is that there could be a growing gap, or schizophrenia, between these two in terms of collaboration, legitimacy, and support, with a variety of negative consequences. She suggests the need for "educational praxis," "a set of dynamic dialogues and collaborations that serve as the bridge between the practice and art of teaching with the SoTL" (p. 6). I certainly agree that scholarly teachers and those scholarly teachers who also engage in SoTL must collaborate. In an ideal view of SoTL, however, this gap between the two faces would not exist, as SoTL would involve application and practical use. This is related to Braxton, Luckey, and Helland's (2002) notion of the purpose of the scholarship of teaching as "the development and improvement of pedagogical practices" (p.106). As we consider ways to increase the legitimacy and value of SoTL work, appropriate and visible application is one key mechanism.

Another concern has to do with the breadth of the scholarship concept. Are all activities or processes related to our academic lives (teaching, professional service, community service/engagement, research) inherently scholarship? Does such a broad conceptualization undermine the legitimate value of teaching in its own right by implying that teaching has value only if it is labeled scholarly or only if we can define it as scholarship? If we move in the direction of such a broad conception of scholarship, where are the lines between academic activity, scholarly activity, and scholarship? How does this complicate the faculty evaluation process? For example, isn't it possible for a course to be developed in a manner that is not scholarly (e.g., peers are not consulted, curricular literature is not read)? In addition, course development or experimenting with new pedagogies, without characteristics such as reflection, peer review, and public sharing, are clearly worthy of reward but not under the rubric of scholarship.

Braxton, Luckey, and Helland (2002) offer an inventory of the scholarship of teaching that includes both activities/process and outcomes/products, including scholarly activities (e.g., development of a new course, preparation of a syllabus), unpublished scholarly outcomes (e.g., experimenting with a new instructional practice, presenting to colleagues about a new instructional technique), and publications (e.g., classroom research publication, publication of a new pedagogical strategy). They posit that faculty engagement in the scholarship of teaching is visible through the second two categories. Activities in the first would be evaluated/rewarded under teaching. However, though they state that "a distinction between scholarly activities and scholarship undergirds these categories" (p. 141), all three categories are listed under the heading "The Scholarship of Teaching" in their inventory. Perhaps this is just semantics, but semantics matter. This double use of the term the "scholarship of teaching" (as an umbrella concept in the inventory and as specific outcomes that count as research/scholarship) may be confusing to some. The confusion is highlighted when we note that there are no scholarly activities under "The Scholarship of Discovery," only unpublished scholarly outcomes and publications. Why, given the conception of "scholarship of teaching" presented, are not scholarly activities, such as conducting a research study to ascertain new disciplinary knowledge, included under "The Scholarship of Discovery" heading?

Related to these issues is the need to maintain a balance. For most faculty members, SoTL would not and should not replace their traditional disciplinary scholarship, nor does it replace teaching or service. How do all these fit together? What are the priorities? How does someone do work in all these areas? How does this balance vary by institutional or department type or mission? How do we increase the fit between mission and the value of SoTL? We need career models for SoTL at various levels.

Fifth, we also must increase collaboration and sharing of SoTL work, including bringing new players in to the field. For example, we need to target future faculty, new faculty, and staff members involved in student learning. We have the challenge of involving students themselves in our SoTL work, beyond the role of research subject. For example, in a recent SoTL small grant request for proposals at Illinois State University, it was required that each proposal be submitted by a team including, at least, two faculty from the same discipline and one student.

Sixth, we have the challenge of synthesizing what we know, what we don't know, and what we need to know. That is, we have the challenge of setting appropriate SoTL research agendas both within and across disciplinary boundaries. Conversations and sharing at professional meetings (e.g., at AAHE) and special institutes (e.g., the ASA workshop on SoTL), or in journal article reviews and electronically, will be needed to discuss current knowledge and future research needs. There is the related challenge of helping faculty, staff, and students unfamiliar with this work to discover sources of information and learn new sets of literature and additional methodological skills through training, development, and mentoring.

Finally, we face a variety of ethical and methodological challenges in this work, challenges that can impact how the work is accomplished, received, and used. For example, how does SoTL work protect the privacy of, and avoid harm for, our student subjects and colleagues? When is it unethical to do a SoTL quasi-experiment where the control group fails to receive an intervention that is believed to enhance learning? We need to consider federal and local Institutional Review Board guidelines, the ethical codes of our disciplinary societies, the power relationships of faculty and students, and our own personal ethics in answering such questions. (See Hutchings, 2002b for a discussion of ethical issues and SoTL as well as a presentation of several "cases" in this area.)

What is the role of technology as both a topic and a tool in SoTL? In what ways, given practical and ethical limitations, can we improve the quality of the methods of our SoTL work and/or convince others that the work is worth paying attention to despite traditional methodological limitations (e.g., Cross & Steadman, 1996) such as nonrandom samples or the lack of a control group?

Though advice has been offered related to some of these issues (e.g., Braxton, Luckey, & Helland, 2002; Glassick, Huber, & Maeroff, 1997), the use and impact of such advice has been limited. We are challenged to find ways over and around the many barriers to SoTL work, as well as to remove them.

Future Visions for the Scholarship of Teaching and Learning

What might a future vision of SoTL look like? A strong history of SoTL exists on many campuses and in other higher education organizations. Yet, to make significant progress that will impact student learning and development, and faculty lives, we must change the culture. Though this is becoming a worn out phrase, the idea remains true. This change must come on campus from both the grassroots and the upper administrative levels, as well as from various higher education organizations. We must consider factors that will increase the legitimacy of SoTL as work and as a social movement. For example, we can work, in different ways, with innovators and early and middle adopters of this work; be inclusive by recruiting new faculty, senior faculty, staff, and students; utilize highly respected, key faculty leaders; make use of existing governance structures and strategic plans to effect changes in value and reward; and provide adequate and useful faculty development, information, and resources for doing and using SoTL.

This cultural shift must include a change in our views of our roles as faculty and staff who work to enhance student learning. I believe that every instructor (broadly defined) who signs a contract to teach is ethically obligated to become at least a scholarly teacher and some will also choose to engage in SoTL. This is the case whether one teaches ten or 1,000 students, one or eight classes. Just as we do all we can to be scholarly in traditional areas of our disciplines, we must be scholarly about and (for some) practice scholarship in teaching and learning. This is part of what it means to be a professional, and the practice of SoTL is critical to the improvement of teaching and learning. For those involved in doing SoTL, in this vision of the future, reward structures throughout the institution will truly recognize the value of this work.

In this future vision, we need to consider various models of doing, supporting, understanding, and evaluating SoTL work. The models will vary by institutional, disciplinary, or departmental culture and structure. We will need models at multiple levels: individual career, department, discipline, institution, and national. On the one hand, we could continue to work toward common definitions, standards, supports, career models, etc. for SoTL in higher education that cut across contexts and fit more traditional disciplinary scholarship. That is, we could work toward a SoTL that is simply "S." Glassick, Huber, and Maeroff (1997), for example, offer general standards for scholarly work, including clear goals, adequate preparation, appropriate methods, significant results, effective presentation, and reflective critique.

In the 100-page *Scholarship in the Postmodern Era: New Venues, New Values, New Visions* (Zahorski, 2002), the scholarship of teaching and learning is discussed explicitly only once in a brief section and alluded to in only two or three other places. None of the chapters address SoTL as the primary topic. How do we interpret this? Is SoTL still thought of as different or less legitimate and, thus, not worthy of space in this volume? Or, have we made such great progress in the transition from SoTL to "S" that SoTL holds an equal place with other scholarship and is presumed to be a part, implicitly, of the entire discussion in this volume?

On the other hand, it is more likely that SoTL will remain somewhat distinct from traditional disciplinary scholarship. Individuals, departments, and institutions will view this work and organize this work in various ways. For some, SoTL will be their primary line of research; for others it may be a secondary area. SoTL work may be done at only some stages in a faculty member's career cycle. Some might work on SoTL only during a sabbatical; others may integrate it into their ongoing professional life. Some departments may reward SoTL within their existing, traditional reward structures; others may need to create new, special roles or assignments. Huber (2001) illustrates some of these models and paths for doing SoTL work with specific individual case examples. Brief discussions and examples of institutional models and national collaborations have also been offered (Cambridge, 2002). As I finish this chapter, a discussion about the possibility of forming a national organization for SoTL is just beginning. Additional systematic research is needed to assess the nature and outcomes of the models currently used to structure this work at all levels.

A small number of individuals or small teams of faculty members in relative isolation accomplish much of the current SoTL support and work on many campuses. In a vision of the future, we will increase the breadth of involvement in SoTL as well as collaboration on SoTL, both within disciplines and in what Huber and Morreale (2002) call the interdisciplinary trading zones. We will work to broaden the base and increase the diversity of people working together to do and use SoTL work through both research support and development activities. Live and electronic SoTL communities can be created on campuses via brown bags, symposia, lunches, small grants that require teams of investigators, workshops, electronic discussion lists, web pages, etc. We can begin to connect these communities across campuses and disciplines with the help of disciplinary societies, CASTL, and AAHE, for example.

Clearly, a future vision of SoTL includes improvements in development and support for such work. There are many possible strategies (many already in use at a variety of institutions and organizations) for new services and structures to help faculty, staff, and students do this work and do it well (see, also, Kreber, 2001b; Lacey, 1983; Shulman, 1999). Those involved in faculty development should consider managing SoTL small grant programs, designing an institute or course on doing and publishing SoTL work, helping to form and facilitate SoTL writing circles, providing resources (books, journals, web sites) to assist those doing SoTL work, editing draft SoTL grants or articles, finding SoTL mentors, assisting in the identification of SoTL funding sources, and serving as a resource for college and department personnel committees on evaluating and rewarding SoTL work.

Conclusion

The way to a faculty member's heart is through his or her discipline, thus, many, though certainly not all, of these efforts should focus on the department or disciplinary level, making use of the culture (i.e., language, values, informal norms about teaching and scholarship, mechanisms for communication and social change) and the unique characteristics of the discipline (e.g., the ratio of content or skills, outside accreditation body or not, degree or speed of change in knowledge) (Healey, 2000; Jenkins, 1996; Shulman, 1993).

As noted earlier, another vision of the future is that we will routinely use and apply what we find in our SoTL work to pedagogical, curricular, and institutional reform in our institutions. This is the key purpose and benefit of SoTL work. SoTL work can help us implement our missions and strategic plans, reinvigorate faculty members tired of the status quo or the work they have been doing for years, and enhance student outcomes. Those in faculty and organizational development roles should consider doing or supporting work that uses SoTL findings, if they are not already. This could mean serving on strategic planning and related committees, sharing useful studies and results from SoTL work across campus, and working with department personnel to help them see the implications of, and apply, specific SoTL findings. Such work must also be shared outside our institution. Thus, we need to continue the conversation about SoTL that is occurring at the regional and national levels, both discipline-specific and in the broader higher education arena. The soul of SoTL is its public and applied nature.

Finally, assessing the impact of SoTL work is a critical part of any future vision of SoTL. What outcomes would we anticipate from efforts to further encourage, support, reward, and use SoTL? We would expect, for example, increases in reflection and public discussion of teaching and learning on campus, increases in the quantity, quality, and visibility of SoTL work on campus, use of SoTL to assess what we are doing, improved application of SoTL results and their implications to improve teaching and learning in higher education, changes in the reward structure related to SoTL, and increased visibility of faculty and their SoTL work on regional and national levels. If truly successful, perhaps we may see major investments in SoTL, including large grant programs or endowed chairs in SoTL. Finally, and most importantly, attention to the scholarship of teaching and learning will remind us to always ask the key question when making any decision at the university: What is the impact on student learning?

Note and Acknowledgments

This chapter is an elaboration of remarks made at the installation of the Cross Endowed Chair in the Scholarship of Teaching and Learning, Illinois State University, Normal, Illinois, July 2002. I would like to thank Paul Baker, Pat Hutchings, and K. Patricia Cross for their thoughtful comments on earlier versions of this chapter.

References

Astin, A. W. (1993). *What matters in college: Four critical years revisited.* San Francisco, CA: Jossey-Bass.

Baker, P. (1980). Inquiry into the teaching-learning process: Trickery, folklore, or science? *Teaching Sociology, 7*(3), 237–245.

Baker, P. (1985). Does the sociology of teaching inform *Teaching Sociology? Teaching Sociology, 12*(3), 361–375.

Baker, P. (1986). The helter-skelter relationship between teaching and research. *Teaching Sociology, 14*(1), 50–66.

Baker, P. (2002, July). *Teacher-scholars and the scholarship of teaching in the research-intensive university: reflections on a slow revolution.* Paper presented at Mission, Values, and Identity: A National Conference for Carnegie Doctoral/Research Intensive Institutions, Normal, IL.

Bass, R. (1999, February). The scholarship of teaching: What's the problem? *Invention: Creative Thinking about Learning and Teaching, 1*(1), 1–10.

Boyer, E. (1990). *Scholarship reconsidered: Priorities of the professoriate.* San Francisco, CA: Jossey-Bass.

Braxton, J. M., Luckey, W., & Helland, P. (2002). *Institutionalizing a broader view of scholarship through Boyer's four domains* (ASHE-ERIC Higher Education Report, 29 [2]). San Francisco, CA: Jossey-Bass.

Braxton, J. M., & Toombs, W. (1982). Faculty uses of doctoral training: Consideration of a technique for the differentiation of scholarly effort from research activity. *Research in Higher Education, 16*(3), 265–282.

Brookfield, S. D. (1995). *Becoming a critically reflective teacher.* San Francisco, CA: Jossey-Bass.

Cambridge, B. (2001). Fostering the scholarship of teaching and learning: Communities of practice. In D. Lieberman & C. Wehlburg (Eds.), *To improve the academy: Vol. 19. Resources for faculty, instructional, and organizational development* (pp. 3–16). Bolton, MA: Anker.

Cambridge, B. (2002). Linking change initiatives: The Carnegie Academy for the Scholarship of Teaching and Learning in the company of other national projects. In D. Lieberman & C. Wehlburg (Eds.), *To improve the academy: Vol. 20. Resources for faculty, instructional, and organizational development* (pp. 38–48). Bolton, MA: Anker.

Chickering, A. W., & Gamson, Z. F. (1987, June). Seven principles for good practice in undergraduate education. *AAHE Bulletin, 39,* 3–7.

Chin, J. (2002). Is there a scholarship of teaching and learning in *Teaching Sociology? Teaching Sociology, 30*(1), 53–62.

Cross, K. P., & Steadman, M. H. (1996). *Classroom research: Implementing the scholarship of teaching.* San Francisco, CA: Jossey-Bass.

Darling, A. L. (2003). Scholarship of teaching and learning in communication: New connections, new directions, new possibilities. *Communication Education, 52*(1), 47–49.

Eisenberg, A. (2002, August). *Educational praxis: Linking the practice of teaching with the scholarship of teaching and learning.* Paper presented at the American Sociological Association annual meeting, Chicago, IL.

Glassick, C. E., Huber, M. T., & Maeroff, G. I. (1997). *Scholarship assessed: Evaluation of the professoriate.* San Francisco, CA: Jossey-Bass.

Goldsmid, C. A., & Wilson, E. K. (1980). *Passing on sociology: The teaching of a discipline.* Belmont, CA: Wadsworth.

Healey, M. (2000). Developing the scholarship of teaching and learning in higher education: A discipline-based approach. *Higher Education Research and Development, 19*(2), 167–187.

Huber, M. T. (2001). Balancing acts: Designing careers around the scholarship of teaching and learning. *Change, 33*(4), 21–29.

Huber, M. T., & Morreale, S. P. (Eds.). (2002). *Disciplinary styles in the scholarship of teaching and learning: Exploring common ground.* Washington DC: American Association for Higher Education.

Hutchings, P. (2002a, March). *Informal handout and remarks at the SoTL community of practice.* Annual meeting of the American Association for Higher Education, Chicago, IL.

Hutchings, P. (2002b). *Ethics of inquiry: Issues in the scholarship of teaching and learning.* Menlo Park, CA: The Carnegie Foundation for the Advancement of Teaching.

Hutchings, P., & Shulman, L. S. (1999, September/October). The scholarship of teaching: New elaborations, new developments. *Change, 31*(5), 10–15.

Jenkins, A. (1996). Discipline-based educational development. *The International Journal for Academic Development, 1*(1), 50–62.

Kreber, C. (Ed.). (2001a). Scholarship revisited: Perspectives on the scholarship of teaching and learning. *New Directions for Teaching and Learning, No. 86.* San Francisco, CA: Jossey-Bass.

Kreber, C. (2001b). The scholarship of teaching and its implementation in faculty development and graduate education. In C. Kreber (Ed.), *Scholarship revisited: Perspectives on the scholarship of teaching and learning* (pp. 79–88). New Directions for Teaching and Learning, No. 86. San Francisco, CA: Jossey-Bass.

Kreber, C., & Cranton, P. A. (2000). Exploring the scholarship of teaching. *The Journal of Higher Education, 71*(4), 476–495.

Lacey, P. A. (1983). Revitalizing teaching through faculty development. San Francisco, CA: Jossey-Bass.

Martin, E., Benjamin, J., Prosser, M., & Trigwell, K. (1999). Scholarship of teaching: A study of the approaches of academic staff. In C. Rust (Ed.), *Improving student learning: Improving student learning outcomes* (pp. 326–331). Oxford, England: Oxford Brookes University, Oxford Centre for Staff Learning and Development.

Mauksch, H. O., & Howery, C. B. (1986). Social change for teaching: The case of one disciplinary association. *Teaching Sociology, 14*(1), 73–82.

McCarthy, J. D., & Zald, M. N. (1977). Resource mobilization and social movements: A partial theory. *American Journal of Sociology, 82*(6), 1212–1241.

McKenna, J., Bickle, M., & Carroll, J. B. (2002). Using scholarship to integrate teaching and research. *Journal of Family & Consumer Sciences, 94*(3), 39–45.

Pascarella, E. T., & Terenzini, P. (1991). *How college affects students.* San Francisco, CA: Jossey-Bass.

Paulsen, M. B., & Feldman, K. A. (1995). Toward a re-conceptualization of scholarship: A human action system with functional imperatives. *Journal of Higher Education, 66*(6), 615–640.

Pellino, G. R., Blackburn, R. T., & Boberg, A. L. (1984). The dimensions of academic scholarship: Faculty and administrator views. *Research in Higher Education, 20*(1), 103–115.

Rice, R. E. (1992). Toward a broader conception of scholarship: The American context. In T. G. Whiston & R. L. Geiger (Eds.), *Research and higher education in the United Kingdom and the United States* (pp. 117–129). Lancaster, England: Society for Research on Higher Education.

Richlin. L. (Ed.). (1993). Preparing faculty for the new conception of scholarship. *New Directions for Teaching and Learning, No. 54.* San Francisco, CA: Jossey-Bass.

Richlin, L. (2001, Summer). Scholarly teaching and the scholarship of teaching. In C. Kreber (Ed.), *Scholarship revisited: Perspectives on the scholarship of teaching and learning* (pp. 57–68). New Directions for Teaching and Learning, No. 86. San Francisco, CA: Jossey-Bass

Schön, D. A. (1983). *The reflective practitioner: How professionals think in action.* New York, NY: Basic Books.

Schön, D. A. (1987). *Educating the reflective practitioner: Toward a new design for teaching and learning in the professions.* San Francisco, CA: Jossey-Bass.

Schön, D. A. (1995). The new scholarship requires a new epistemology. *Change, 27*(6), 26–34.

Shulman, L. S. (1987). Knowledge and teaching: Foundations of the new reform. *Harvard Educational Review, 36*(1), 1–22.

Shulman, L. S. (1993, November/December). Teaching as community property: Putting an end to pedagogical solitude. *Change, 25*(6), 6–7.

Shulman, L. S. (1999). *Visions of the possible: Models for campus support of the scholarship of teaching and learning.* Retrieved April 28, 2003, from http://www.carnegiefoundation.org/elibrary/docs/Visions.htm

Shulman, L. S. (2001). Remarks at the teaching symposium for the Cross Endowed Chair for the Scholarship of Teaching and Learning, Illinois State University.

Smelser, N. J. (1963). *Theory of collective behavior.* New York, NY: Free Press.

Smith, R. (2001). Expertise and the scholarship of teaching. In C. Kreber (Ed.). *Scholarship revisited: Perspectives on the scholarship of teaching and learning* (pp. 69–78). New Directions for Teaching and Learning, No. 86. San Francisco, CA: Jossey-Bass.

Weimer, M. (1996). Why scholarship is the bedrock of good teaching. In R. J. Menges & M. Weimer (Eds.), *Teaching on solid ground: Using scholarship to improve practice* (pp. 1–12). San Francisco, CA: Jossey-Bass.

Weston, C. B., & McAlpine, L. (2001). Making explicit the development toward the scholarship of teaching. In C. Kreber (Ed.), *Scholarship revisited: Perspectives on the scholarship of teaching and learning* (pp. 89–98). New Directions for Teaching and Learning, No. 86. San Francisco, CA: Jossey-Bass.

Zahorski, K. J. (Ed.). (2002). Scholarship in the postmodern era: New venues, new values, new visions. *New Directions for Teaching and Learning, No. 90.* San Francisco, CA: Jossey-Bass.

Contact:

Kathleen McKinney
Cross Chair in the Scholarship of Teaching and Learning
Professor of Sociology
Box 3990
Illinois State University
Normal, IL 61790–3990
Voice (309) 438-7706
Fax (309) 438-8788
Email kmckinne@ilstu.edu

Kathleen McKinney is Cross Chair in the Scholarship of Teaching and Learning and Professor of Sociology at Illinois State University. She served from 1996 to 2002 as the Director of the Center for the Advancement of Teaching. She directs the CASTL program at Illinois State University and is a 2003–2004 Carnegie Scholar. She serves as a member of the American Sociological Association's Task Force on the Undergraduate Major and the ASA Department Resources Group. Currently, she teaches the Sociology Senior Experience course. She has numerous publications in the areas of sexual harassment in academia, personal relationships, and teaching and learning in sociology.

Section II

Faculty Focus in Faculty Development

2

Triangulating Faculty Needs for the Assessment of Student Learning

D. Lynn Sorenson
Timothy W. Bothell
Brigham Young University

To enhance assessment of student learning, the Brigham Young University (BYU) Faculty Center undertook a needs assessment to guide new initiatives. Researchers reviewed results from the National Survey of Student Engagement and an earlier BYU faculty survey. In addition, they conducted a qualitative study with faculty and administrators. The qualitative study can serve as a model for other faculty developers considering new initiatives. The findings raised thought-provoking issues for faculty development, particularly faculty readiness. As a result of this research, the center bolstered current services and developed new ones to support the assessment of student learning.

Assessment of student learning is a critical part of teaching. Yet, as integral as it is to teaching and learning, it is often ignored in development efforts. In a study at Georgia State University (Commander, Hart, & Singer, 2000), faculty named student performance as the most important indicator of good teaching. However, this study (and others) focuses little on what faculty *need* to effectively assess student performance. How can good teaching and learning be achieved if the needs of faculty for effective assessment are neither known nor met?

Background

Most new faculty developers—and most new faculty development centers—undertake a (faculty) needs assessment as one of their first endeavors. Travis, Hursh, Lankewicz, and Tang (1996) identified "relatively inadequate coverage of this all-important topic [needs assessment] . . . in the available literature . . ." (p. 96). Travis et al. sought to remedy this lack by documenting models and processes for faculty development needs assessment at four institutions: East Texas State University, West Virginia University, University of South Alabama, and The Ohio State University. A 1993 East Texas survey identified constructing effective exams as an area of high interest.

Travis et al. (1996) suggested "to best monitor the pulse of the faculty, needs assessment should be conducted on a continuous, timely basis with variable approaches being used for data collection" (p. 96). They further suggested that "the survey instrument seems to be the weakest link [in needs assessment, favoring instead the] information-rich interview technique" (p. 107).

In the qualitative study documented in this chapter, the researchers at the ten-year-old Brigham Young University (BYU) Faculty Center decided to get more serious about following up on two of the most useful sources for ascertaining the current state of student learning: the *National Survey of Student Engagement—the College Student Report 2000* (NSSE) and a campus-wide survey, the *BYU Faculty Assessment Activity Study, 1999–2000 Academic Year* (FAAS). The NSSE provided a student perspective from which the researchers determined some related faculty development needs. In addition, the FAAS provided a relevant faculty perspective. Shortly after hiring a new faculty center professional—and before he became overwhelmed with new duties—this qualitative study was launched in 2001. It examined faculty needs, perceptions, and issues about the assessment of student learning.

The Status of Assessment

The following is a brief summary of key findings from the NSSE and FAAS.

Frequency of Student Assessment (From NSSE)

Most faculty evaluate student learning at least every two weeks; however, one-fifth do so only once a month at best. The colleges that reported assessing most frequently were:

- Nursing
- Humanities
- Education
- Physical and mathematical sciences

Methods Used to Assess Student Learning (From NSSE)

BYU faculty tend to use more multiple-choice exams with freshmen than faculty at other institutions (see Figure 2.1). A discrepancy exists between the assessment methods faculty reported using most often (e.g., exams, class presentations, quizzes, group projects) and the methods they felt were most effective (e.g., field work, capstone projects, performances).

FIGURE 2.1

NSSE Findings Concerning Types of Exams

In the National Survey of Student Engagement (NSSE), students were asked about the types of exams they take most often.

There were 276 participating four-year colleges and universities with 151,910 student responses (from BYU there were 1,500 students).

Rating Scale: 1 = Mostly Multiple-Choice or Short Answer
7 = Mostly Essay or Open-Ended Problems

MEANS	**BYU** (Research I)	R. I & II NSSE Institutions	Natl. Averages All NSSE Schools
Freshman	**2.88**	3.35	3.79
Seniors	**4.23**	4.29	4.42

Aside from writing assignments, most faculty employed assessment tools they rated as being less effective. These phenomena may occur because faculty select assessment methods based on practical issues (e.g., time required to develop, time required to grade, ease of use by students) rather than basing their choices on (either the perceived or actual) effectiveness of the methods for assessing student learning.

Figure 2.2 shows two graphs which represent the methods faculty used most frequently (in the graph on the left) and their opinions about the effectiveness of each method (in the graph on the right).

FIGURE 2.2
Discrepancy Between Faculty Methods and Faculty Beliefs

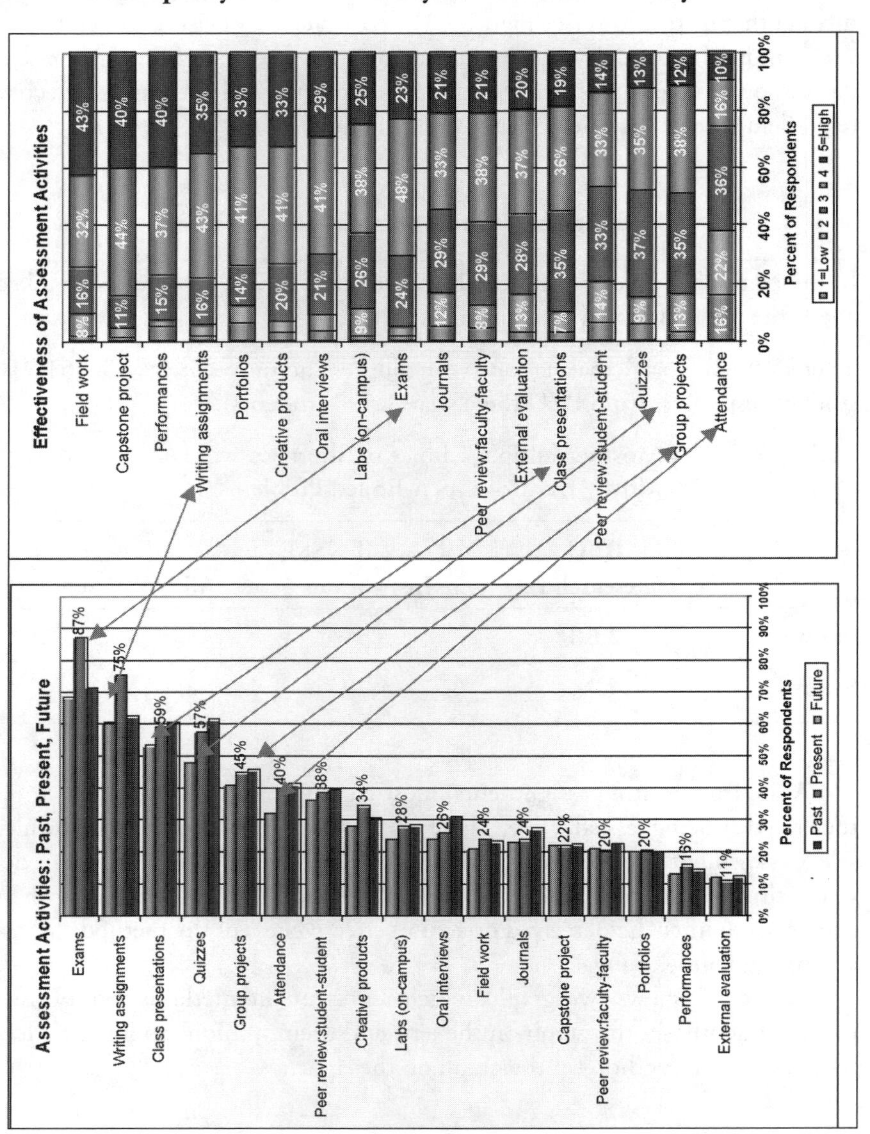

The methods on the left are listed in order of frequency of use with the most frequent at the top. On the right, the faculty perceptions of effectiveness are listed with the methods perceived most effective at the top. The arrows between the two graphs highlight the discrepancy between frequency of use and perceived effectiveness. In other words, the methods of assessment that faculty deem least effective are the methods that they use most.

Development Needs Suggested by National Survey of Student Engagement (NSSE)

The NSSE suggested several areas for consideration: learning to assess and grade student learning, both effectively and efficiently; and the use of mid-course feedback for improvements during a course.

Effectiveness of assessments. According to the NSSE results, BYU faculty often viewed assessment as something they do "to" students rather than something they do "for" students (or for themselves). In addition, faculty viewed the assessment of student learning as a way to confront student understanding, knowledge, and effort. Few faculty viewed assessment of student learning as a tool for determining the effectiveness of the course or the teacher, in contrast with the Georgia State University faculty who saw it as the primary indicator of good teaching.

Again, faculty felt they were effective in assessing student learning, yet they reported that the methods they use most frequently are the methods they feel are *less* effective. Approximately 12% of BYU faculty reported that their current plan for assessing student learning is "ineffective." This could suggest that approximately 200 faculty members and approximately 18,000 students experience ineffective assessment every semester (assuming each faculty member has 30 students per class and three classes per semester).

The colleges that reported the highest percentage of ineffective assessment plans were:

- Religious education
- Engineering and technology
- Biology and agriculture
- Law
- Fine arts and communication
- Family, home, and social science

Grading. Assessment of student learning is inexorably linked to grading. More BYU faculty grade on a fixed standard of performance (criterion-referenced) than on a class curve (norm-referenced). The colleges of nursing, education, religious education, and health and human performance do the most criterion-referenced grading.

Mid-course evaluations. According to the NSSE, more than half of the BYU faculty who administer mid-course evaluations make mid-course adjustments. Colleges that reported the most faculty making mid-course adjustments were:

- Fine arts and communications
- Engineering and technology
- Education

Development Needs Suggested by Faculty Assessment Activity Study (FAAS)

In general, the FAAS suggested that faculty would like more support and resources to improve assessment in their courses. Development needs included assessment of critical thinking, test design issues, classroom assessment techniques, as well as understanding factors that impact student learning.

In choosing from a list of alternatives on the FAAS, respondents most frequently requested support for the assessment of critical thinking, followed by the construction of reliable and valid tests. Curriculum development was the least requested training topic, perhaps because the term was not well understood by most disciplinary faculty. Educationists understand that curriculum development includes not only content issues, but also evaluating and (re)writing objectives, developing more effective learning activities, designing appropriate assessments, and aligning assessment to objectives. However, many noneducationist faculty are unfamiliar with the term "curriculum development." They may believe that it includes *only* content issues (for which they feel no need for help) or they fail to understand the term at all. This may explain why BYU faculty declined asking for help with curriculum development.

Results from the FAAS showed that when given a list of ways to improve the effectiveness of their assessments, faculty selected "TA help" most frequently, followed by "understanding factors that influence student learning." "Technology support" was listed third, and "training" was fourth.

The colleges with the highest number of requests for assessment support were:

- Religious education
- Nursing
- Law
- Humanities
- Health and human performance

With regard to assessing student learning with technology, FAAS revealed that faculty were requesting additional technology support that could be provided by teaching assistants or other technology support staff. Faculty also requested funds for these kinds of endeavors. Half of the faculty would consider having their classroom exams administered online in the testing center and the College of Nursing and the College of Family, Home, and Social Sciences had the most interest in online testing.

Interviewing Faculty to Discern Needs and Priorities

Since 1992, the Brigham Young University Faculty Center has supported faculty with many developmental services and has recently increased its focus in the area of assessment.

This qualitative research was a part of the center's increased emphasis on assessment. To avoid spending time on unnecessary or marginal activities, it was important to hear from faculty themselves about their perceived needs in assessing student learning. The study was not an extensive research project with a large sample size, but rather a small, quick study designed to measure common responses and identify basic themes common to BYU faculty.

The Interview Questions

1) What do faculty need in the area of assessing student learning?
2) What can be done to assist faculty with their needs in assessing student learning?
3) What challenges related to assessing student learning should faculty developers be concerned about?
4) What should be done first (receive highest priority) to assist faculty in the assessment of student learning?

5) Who else on campus should be worked with to improve the assessment of student learning?

6) How should department chairs and deans be involved with improving the assessment of student learning?

The interviews were conducted on campus in faculty members' offices. On average, it took about an hour to complete each interview. Most faculty wanted to hear all six questions before answering any of them. They then spent the majority of the time answering Question 1. In many instances, faculty answered the other five questions while answering the first question. During the interviews, the researcher took notes that were later analyzed and developed into action items.

The Sample

Forty-two faculty were interviewed, five of whom were also serving as administrators at that time. This provided insight from both faculty and administrator perspectives.

Faculty participants were recommended for the interviews by administrators and by faculty developers at the Brigham Young University Faculty Center. During the interviews, some participants suggested additional faculty for the study. In general, the names recommended were faculty members who had reputations as good teachers and/or as effective learning assessors. Table 2.1 illustrates the departments and colleges involved.

2001 Interview Findings

Armed with the results of the NSSE and FAAS, the researchers developed analyses and conclusions from the 42 faculty interviews.

Faculty Needs (Question 1): What Do Faculty Need in the Area of Assessing Student Learning?

The first question that faculty and administrators were asked during the interviews required each individual to think about faculty needs across the entire campus. This approach seemed appropriate since the names provided for the interviews were individuals who had reputations for being effective at assessing student learning. In addition, focusing on the needs of the university as a whole was a strategy designed to help the participants feel less threatened and more comfortable—the interviewees felt no pressure to reveal their own personal needs or weaknesses, but were encouraged instead to think about their colleagues' assessment needs.

TABLE 2.1
Percentage of Sample by Department or Role

Number	Percentage	Department/Role
5	12%	Administration
4	10%	Center for Instructional Design (creates online courses and modules for hybrid courses)
1	2%	Department of Chemistry
1	2%	Department of Communications
1	2%	College of Education
1	2%	College of Engineering
6	14%	BYU Faculty Center
2	5%	College of Fine Arts and Communications
2	5%	General Education and Honors
3	7%	College of Humanities
4	10%	Department of Instructional Psychology and Technology
3	7%	Independent Study
2	5%	School of Music
2	5%	Office of Institutional Assessment and Analysis
4	10%	Religious Education
1	2%	Testing Services

Some responses to this question were different from the findings of the NSSE and FAAS. For example, the FAAS found "TA support" was the most requested assessment need, followed by "understanding factors that influence student learning," and then, "technology support." Yet, faculty interviewed mentioned "training" more frequently than any other need. This may be because the interviews focused on the needs of faculty across the entire university. The FAAS asked faculty about their own personal needs, rather than the needs of generic "faculty." Therefore, the FAAS responses tended to be more specific (e.g., "TA support") than the generic responses of the 2001 interviews (e.g., "training").

The three most frequent responses to this first interview question were:

- Training
- Feedback on exams
- Support to align learning outcomes, instruction, and assessment

In some instances during the interviews, faculty mentioned training and provided specific examples of the topics they suggested for the training. Other times, they would mention training without providing topic ideas. Even after additional probing questions were asked, some faculty could not articulate what type of training was needed.

Even though some faculty see a need for assessment training and support, many lack understanding of what that training might entail. They may have concerns (arising from student evaluations or from peer faculty feedback) that suggest a need for training, but they don't know the assessment issues well enough to state what specific training is necessary.

However, the very few faculty who did provide specific examples tended to brainstorm long lists of ideas for assessment training:

- Practice writing test questions
- Practice choosing appropriate methods
- Support determining outcomes or what they hope students will accomplish
- Make assessment meaningful, "full of heart," and "authentic"
- Align course objectives with assessment
- Create challenging tests
- Decide on a discrimination approach or a mastery approach
- Develop assessments that help students have a learning experience during the exam ("effective assessment enhances a love of learning")
- Help students do self-assessment ("an educated person should be really good at self-assessment")
- Assess students' higher-order thinking skills
- Control grade inflation

- Place more emphasis on formative evaluation to make mid-course changes to improve learning
- Motivate students intrinsically through assessment
- Move assessment to a criterion-referenced system
- Integrate mission of BYU into assessment
- Account for long-term goals of students when planning assessment
- Get students to desire feedback and to take responsibility for their own learning
- Write multiple-choice questions in a way that tests for application
- Test online

It is clear from this list of examples that faculty training needs can be varied in the area of assessing student learning. Since faculty needs are diverse, it may be difficult to narrow the topics for support on assessing student learning (e.g., for workshops). In order to meet diverse needs, assessing student learning may be an area of faculty development that requires more one-on-one consultation than group instruction.

The second most frequent response given to the first interview question was "feedback to improve exams." Many faculty wanted to know if there was a central service or location on campus where exams could be safely left for review and feedback. Most knew where to take their writing projects for review and feedback, and expressed a desire for a similar place to take their exams. They wanted someone to look at their test questions to determine if they were meaningful, clear, valid, reliable, and grammatically correct. Some wanted detailed item analyses to help them decide which items needed revision and which should be removed from their exams.

The third most frequent response to the first interview question on faculty needs was about alignment of course components. Faculty reported a need for support to align learning outcomes, instruction, and assessment. This was an interesting response because the interviewees acknowledged the need for improved alignment but declined help with course design and objectives. When asked what support was needed, faculty frequently reported a campus-wide need for help in the alignment of course components. Yet, when asked directly in follow-up questions about their *own* course objectives or course design, the faculty interviewees declined support and were hesitant to discuss it further.

As noted in the FAAS findings, the researchers hypothesize that many faculty (noneducationists) believe that course design and curriculum development are solely content issues. Most feel secure in their content knowledge and expertise; hence, most did not request support in course design. Nevertheless, assessment *is* an important part of course design and curriculum development. Perhaps faculty fail to understand the integral connection of assessment to course design, instead considering assessment as a component of a course that can be inserted, improved, or removed without relation to other course components. Perhaps they see "alignment" (among objectives, activities, and assessment) as an activity different from course design. This incongruency may present a challenge for faculty developers.

Another interesting finding was that administrators had stronger feelings than faculty about the need for effective course design. Administrators talked about improving the assessment of student learning in terms of redesigning all components of a course and aligning the components to each other. Faculty talked about assessment as if it were disconnected from other components of the course. This was not always the case, but it is interesting to note differences in their perspectives.

Less frequently mentioned responses about faculty needs included:

- Provide more time for teaching in class by assessing out of class
- Provide training to build an effective environment for testing
- Provide training about grading issues (e.g., how to control grade inflation, weighting exams versus assignments, using grading rubrics, training on how to do online submission of grades)
- Support for designing multiple forms of exams
- Support with pre-test assessment to assess student readiness
- Provide handouts, resources, and articles
- Provide training about using work experience, capstone experience, field work as major assessments

Assist Faculty (Question 2): What Can Be Done to Assist Faculty With Their Needs in Assessing Student Learning?

The three most common responses to this interview question were:

- Provide one-on-one consulting support
- Work with department chairs and deans to establish collaborative efforts

- Provide an exam service where faculty can get feedback and suggestions to improve their exams

Obviously, there is some overlap between the most frequent responses provided to interview Question 1 and those provided to interview Question 2. In response to both interview questions, faculty mentioned the need for feedback to improve exams. This was a recurring theme throughout all of the interviews, and underscores a strong need to provide faculty with this feedback.

Faculty also mentioned "training/workshops" in answer to both questions, although for Question 2, training was not in the three most frequent responses. This indicates a perception by faculty that one-on-one consulting may be more useful for their improvement needs than workshops on assessing student learning. This perception may not be shared by all faculty, but the most common response reported was assisting faculty with their assessment needs through "one-on-one consulting."

Almost every administrator emphasized the importance of working with department chairs and deans to establish collaborative efforts. They were more interested in this than were the faculty interviewees. Faculty rarely mentioned the idea of working with colleagues to improve the assessment of student learning. When administrators mentioned collaborative efforts led by department leaders, they spoke about accreditation, research grants, fellowships, large classes, and multiple sections of the same course with several teachers. Administrators may have wanted collaborative work teams because of their perspectives (and pressures) at the department and college level.

Some of the less frequently mentioned responses to Question 2 about assisting faculty included:

- Teach the consequences of ignoring the problem of poor assessment
- Share examples of success
- Connect web resources and announce Brigham Young University Faculty Center offerings on several web pages
- Make faculty aware of misalignment between their course components (objectives, activities, and assessment)
- Find differences among departmental needs
- Designate a testing expert for each college

Challenges (Question 3): What Challenges Related to Assessing Student Learning Should Faculty Developers Be Concerned About?
The most frequent responses to this question included:

- Lack of resources to support faculty with assessment
- Lack of time (faculty are too busy)
- Philosophies and approaches to grading
- Independence (faculty want flexibility and freedom to "do their own thing")

When discussing the issue of resources and time, faculty inevitably brought up their roles at the university—research, teaching, and citizenship. Some discussions about the issue of balancing these roles were typically very passionate and even somewhat disconcerting. Administrators advise faculty to balance scholarship, citizenship, and teaching, and faculty were very conscious of the difficulties in doing that. Many faculty members questioned how they could worry about improving assessment when they had so many demands on their time. Whether it was an issue of busyness, lack of resources (TAs, faculty developers, time with other colleagues), or pursuit of their research interests, the difficulties all seemed to be about competing priorities.

Many faculty members (but not administrators) mentioned grading philosophies as a challenge to improving the assessment of student learning. They stated that some philosophies of grading required challenging, even "tricky," assessment. This type of assessment purposely causes a portion of students to fail. This approach can present obstacles and can be an interesting challenge for the task of improving assessment of student learning.

Other less frequently mentioned responses to Question 3 were:

- Large classes
- TA training
- Complacent faculty
- Grade inflation
- Assessments not authentic
- Lack of feedback to students

Highest Priority (Question 4): What Should Be Done First (Receive Highest Priority) to Assist Faculty in the Assessment of Student Learning?

The most frequent response to this question was simply to educate faculty concerning what resources are available to support them with the assessment of student learning. Faculty were often pleasantly surprised to hear that a faculty developer had been assigned to the task. And they were typically unclear about what other resources were available to assist them.

Some of the less frequently mentioned responses included:

- Develop a stronger voice/advocacy for learning and teaching across campus
- Make workshops practical—hands-on and practice oriented
- Start where the complaints are (as *per* student evaluations)
- Work on courses with high failure rates to improve exams
- Find and work with good practitioners of effective assessment procedures

Working Together (Question 5): Who Else on Campus [besides the BYU Faculty Center] Should Be Worked With to Improve the Assessment of Student Learning?

The most frequent responses given to this question were:

- Center for Instructional Design
- Undergraduate education
- Assessment experts
- Testing services
- Graduate studies
- Independent study

Almost all of these units provide services that assist faculty with instructional design issues.

Administrator Involvement (Question 6): How Should Department Chairs and Deans Be Involved With Improving the Assessment of Student Learning?

The most frequent responses to this question were also the *only* responses to this question:

- Educate them [the administrators]
- Ask them for names of faculty interested in working on assessment
- Provide incentives to faculty (release time, funding for student assistants)

Most of the administrators stated that they had not participated in any of the above three activities.

Summary of 2001 Findings

This study was *not* meant to be an exhaustive research project to discover with irrefutable evidence all of the needs of faculty in the area of assessing student learning. It was meant to be a quick probe into the minds of faculty and administrators concerning the issue. At least five simple conclusions are proffered from this initial study:

1) The methods BYU faculty use most often for assessing student learning are not always those they believe to be most effective.
2) Faculty want training in the area of assessment.
3) Improvement in assessing student learning is sought through one-on-one consulting.
4) Faculty request specific feedback and suggestions on their exams.
5) Faculty needs were varied (e.g., testing through technology, grade inflation, pre-testing, self-assessment). Thus, faculty developers should prepare themselves for a wide range of issues and activities relating to the improvement of assessing student learning.

These findings point to a strong need—and a strong desire—for faculty development in the area of assessing student learning, especially because faculty often do what they feel is less effective. Also, these findings indicate a need for faculty development that cannot be met solely through workshops, but also through one-on-one consulting (which may be preferred). The requests related to one-on-one consulting were diverse and will require assessment expertise.

Thus, faculty development units desirous of increasing their assessment support should increase their own assessment expertise.

Conclusion

As a result of the triangulation of these three studies (NSSE, FAAS, and the 2001 interviews), the Brigham Young University Faculty Center has increased its emphasis on faculty development efforts designed to improve assessment of student learning. To this end, the center initiated the following:

- One-on-one consultations for the improvement of exams (with individual faculty and with administrators)
- Workshops (e.g., assessing more than recall, increasing learning when returning exams, polishing the use of multiple-choice questions, writing effective essay questions, assessing for learning)
- College and department presentations
- Review of items about exams on student evaluations
- Training of student assistants to give exam improvement feedback
- Collaborative, department-specific efforts to improve exams for multisection courses
- Design and development of self-directed guidebooks for improving tests

References

Commander, N. E., Hart, L., & Singer, M. (2000). Preparing tomorrow's faculty: An assessment model to determine institutional needs. *The Journal of Graduate Teaching Assistant Development, 7*(2), 93–111.

Travis, J. E., Hursh, D., Lankewicz, G., & Tang, L. (1996). Monitoring the pulse of the faculty: Needs assessment in faculty development programs. In L. Richlin & D. DeZure (Eds.), *To improve the academy: Vol. 15. Resources for faculty, instructional, and organizational development* (pp. 95–113). Stillwater, OK: New Forums Press.

Contact:

D. Lynn Sorenson
Brigham Young University Faculty Center for Teaching Excellence
4450 WSC
Brigham Young University
Provo, UT 84602
Voice (801) 422-7420
Fax (801) 422-0223
Email lynn_Sorenson@byu.edu

Timothy W. Bothell
Faculty Development Coordinator
Brigham Young University
4450 WSC
Provo, UT 84602
Voice (801) 422-8194
Fax (801) 422-0223
Email tim_bothell@byu.edu

D. Lynn Sorenson, Assistant Director of the Brigham Young University Faculty Center, is serving her second term on the POD Core Committee. She has been involved in faculty development for more than a dozen years, starting at the University of Oklahoma. She holds degrees in English, Education, and Human Relations from (respectively) California State University at San Francisco, University of California at Berkeley, and the University of Oklahoma. She serves on boards of reviewers for Anker Publishing and New Forums Press.

Timothy W. Bothell is the Faculty Development Coordinator for the Assessment of Student Learning at Brigham Young University. He currently conducts workshops and works with faculty one-on-one to improve the assessment of student learning. He also directs the Exam Improvement Center within BYU's Faculty Center. Faculty from all colleges and departments are invited to leave their exams at the center for suggestions and ideas. In addition, as an independent consultant, he advises organizations concerning the return on investment (ROI) of learning.

3

Documenting the Educational Innovations of Faculty: A Win-Win Situation for Faculty and the Faculty Development Center

Phyllis Blumberg
University of the Sciences in Philadelphia

Compiling faculty members' teaching innovations into an annual campus-specific publication allows others to learn about these ideas and adapt them. This chapter will describe 1) the process used to develop such a Document of Innovation, 2) the types of innovation abstracted, and 3) this document's impact on an institution. A dissemination process including individual meetings with campus leaders provides greater visibility for the Teaching and Learning Center and the featured faculty. An analysis of these annual publications yield comprehensive data about the campus' faculty, their innovative teaching trends, and describes the current teaching climate on the campus.

Introduction

Many faculty at the University of the Sciences in Philadelphia (a specialized science and health science university of 2,500 students) have been implementing teaching innovations (such as new ways to get students to engage in the material, or different methods of assessing students), or experimenting with different types of teaching and learning transactions. Many of these innovations could transcend implementation within a specific discipline, yet few people knew what others were doing because this institution lacked a dissemination venue for these ideas. When teaching is often considered a solitary activity (Shulman, 1993), as it is at this university, faculty often have not shared their innovative ideas about teaching with others. Even when faculty talk to each other, it is often only to those within their own department. This has meant that others have been unable to benefit from their colleagues' excellent ideas. The Teaching and Learning Center decided to produce a volume, *Document of Innovations,* containing all these educational innovations so that others may learn about these ideas and adapt them.

This compilation of teaching innovations differs from descriptions of good teaching developed at other universities. Other such documents select faculty to include in the book and often focus on ideas about good teaching or teaching tips. For example, since 1994, the Office of Educational Development at the University of California at Berkeley has asked faculty who have won teaching awards to write an essay about good teaching. Eighty-three of these award winners' essays have been abstracted into a print and an online book, *What Good Teachers Say About Teaching,* that describes the values, beliefs, and practices that have contributed to their success as teachers (Office of Educational Development, University of California at Berkeley, 2002).

In 1990, the Faculty Teaching Excellence Program at the University of Colorado at Boulder published *Compendium of Good Teaching Ideas.* This book, which is for sale and is given to all new faculty, was developed from interviews with faculty who have been recognized for teaching excellence (Faculty Teaching Excellence Program, University of Colorado at Boulder, 1990). In contrast, our *Document of Innovations* includes any instructor who submits an idea and describes specific teaching innovations.

DESCRIPTION OF THE *DOCUMENT OF INNOVATIONS* AND ITS DEVELOPMENT

Each annual edition of the *Document of Innovations* is a compilation of abstracts of teaching and learning innovations submitted by faculty. All submissions are included, with no screening for quality or originality. The center's director and staff edit the abstracts and then compile them into a book for distribution across the campus. The printing costs are about $700.00 per year. The entire document is also featured on the center's web site: http://www.usip.edu/teaching/innovations/index.shtml

The overall goal of the *Document of Innovations* is to improve teaching and learning by promoting teaching as community property and encouraging scholarly teaching (Shulman, 1993). This document fosters teaching as a shared and valued community property and it allows for the public dissemination of ideas on teaching and learning transactions. It also provides faculty recognition for their innovative ideas. Since faculty names and contact information are listed, individuals may talk to their colleagues about how to incorporate these ideas for their own courses. Discourse about teaching among our faculty has started. This is exciting for several reasons. First, it provides a venue for faculty to collaborate on new ideas as faculty adapt other innovations. Second, the presence of this document on campus promotes faculty engagement in scholarly teaching (Hutchings & Shulman, 1999) in that it showcases examples of effective teaching practices. The abstract development process requires that the innovators reflect on what they are doing and share their ideas so that others can evaluate them (Hutchings & Shulman, 1999).

Submission Process

Faculty receive calls for submissions to the *Document of Innovations* and all faculty are invited to participate. In addition, the director of the Teaching and Learning Center individually encourages specific faculty to submit an abstract. Submitters are required to use an abstract submission form (Appendix 3.1) and their abstract is limited to two pages so that the book has a consistent appearance and all entries are treated equally. Faculty innovators from a previous edition are asked to resubmit their abstracts if they continue to implement their innovations. Innovations that appear again are classified as sustained innovations. Innovations do not have to be entirely new ideas; they or other teachers may have used this or a similar idea previously, which encourages greater faculty collaboration. Faculty must submit their innovations electronically to facilitate the production process for the Teaching and Learning Center. The Teaching and Learning Center staff edits the abstracts for style consistency, uniform length, and clarity.

Scope

The *Document of Innovations* annual volumes cover a wide array of educational ideas ranging from different ways to assess students to different types of teaching and learning transactions to working smarter, not harder. The innovations are grouped by category as shown in Table 3.1. The categorization of abstracts is meant to help readers find appropriate innovations that may interest them. Many of the specific types of teaching and learning transactions and assessment ideas are discipline-specific, such as a math lab; others could be implemented across disciplines as they do not relate directly to content. The director places each abstract in one or more categories depending on the type of innovation implemented. For example, an abstract may be listed as active learning, collaborative learning, and student-centered learning philosophy or practice if all three categories reflect the innovation.

TABLE 3.1
Summary of the Featured Categories of Innovations

Categories of Innovations*	2000 Edition	2001 Edition	2002 Edition
Ideas that transcend disciplines	18	27	29
Specific types of teaching-learning transactions:			
• Active learning	20	24	35
• Collaborative learning	8	10	17
• Distance learning	4	5	4
• Service learning	1	1	7
• Simulations	3	5	4
• Student reflection on learning	6	8	15
• Student research		2	2
Assessment/evaluation of students	14	24	29
Other categories:			
• Student-centered learning: philosophy or practice	12	14	13
• Using technology	10	15	11
• Working smarter, not harder	3	7	14

*Abstracts may be counted in more than 1 category.

Seven out of 12 categories experienced at least a one-third increase in the number of innovations described from the first to the third year. Five of these innovation categories reflect the desire to engage in different types of teaching and learning activities beside lecture and the need to evaluate students differently. The two remaining categories that experienced an increase (i.e., ideas that transcend disciplines and working smarter, not harder) reflect a greater understanding of what a teaching innovation can be as a consequence of the publication of the previous volume. With the remaining five categories the number of innovations remained flat. Three of these (distance education, use of simulations and use of technology in general) might indicate that more faculty are not trying technology enhanced teaching methods in spite of the national push and local support to use them.

Currently this center has produced three editions of the document. A profile of the individual documents appears in Table 3.2. Seventy-nine different abstracts were included that featured 51 different faculty. This represents about one-third of the total full-time faculty at this small university. Teams of faculty sometimes work on an innovation together.

TABLE 3.2
A Profile of the Individual Editions of the *Document of Innovations*

Category	2000 Edition	2001 Edition	2002 Edition
Number of individual faculty showcased	21	30	43
Number of abstracts	27	39	42
Number of sustained abstracts	N/A	15	14

Dissemination

All faculty who describe their innovation receive a copy of the book, as do all new faculty. A few copies are given to every department and the library for reference. Some of the innovators are invited to a lunch during new faculty orientation to share their innovative ideas with the recently hired faculty. The director meets individually with all higher levels of academic administration, deans, and chairs, and gives each of them a copy. These meetings allow the director of the Teaching and Learning Center an opportunity to tell chairs and deans about specific faculty members (who may be reluctant to describe their innovations to their supervisors). Such meetings also give greater visibility to the center and provide opportunities to discuss further ways for the center to serve faculty needs. The director also meets with the Offices of Public Relations, Institutional Advancement, and Admissions to give them copies. In the third year, all three of these units wanted more detailed information on the specific innovative projects, each for their own purposes. For example, the public relations staff were looking for stories to tell the media and possible experts on particular topics to be called upon by reporters. The admissions directors want their staff to be able to talk to perspective students and especially their parents about what was going on in the classroom.

DISCUSSION

Impact of the *Document of Innovations*

The *Document of Innovations* has had great impact on this campus. The time involved in the development and the meetings with administration have more than paid off in terms of good visibility for the Teaching and Learning Center and for the featured faculty.

As this was a new idea on campus, faculty had to be convinced that their instructional innovations were worth sharing with others. Some of the faculty who were encouraged to submit were surprised (and flattered) that the director of the Teaching and Learning Center considered their teaching to be innovative or that their ideas should be included in the document. Over time, faculty have begun to think of what they do as worth publishing.

In the three years of compiling these innovations, the status of faculty publishing in this document has grown, as has the perceived value of the book itself. Faculty who are showcased mention their abstracts as documentation of good teaching on their annual reviews and portfolios for promotion and tenure. Chairs have regarded abstracts as part of their faculty's teaching evaluations. There was a 49% increase in the number of faculty who abstracted an innovation from the first edition to the third edition and a 36% increase in the number of abstracts included from the first edition to the third edition. This increase in innovations abstracted and the fact that about one-third of the faculty submit something are good indicators of the increasingly public nature of teaching and the acknowledgement of its importance at this university. It is not known if the true number of innovations on this campus is increasing or just the number of faculty who include their innovation in this document. However, results from the recent Higher Education Research Institute (HERI) faculty surveys (Leibowitz, 2002) indicate that faculty are using a greater variety of instructional and evaluation methods. The instructional and evaluation methods selected in the HERI survey are consistent with those described in the *Document of Innovations.* Both the growth of the abstracts in the *Document of Innovations* and the results of the HERI faculty survey reflect that the culture of this institution is changing to greater value teaching as a community activity.

Demand for the document has increased each year. For example, the chair of the largest department on campus asked that every one of her faculty receive a copy of the second and third editions. The university's president mentioned this document and some of the innovations in his annual address to faculty. All of this contributes to supporting teaching innovations.

While the volumes have increased in size and status, the real growth has been in pedagogy and in a move toward advancing the scholarship of teaching. The *Document of Innovations* publications have contributed to this process in several ways.

The Teaching and Learning Center recognizes innovative teaching through an annual award. Faculty nominate their own innovations for this award. Five faculty described their innovation in an earlier edition of this document and then the next year submitted this idea in a more fully developed form for the award for innovative teaching. With the latest edition, all who applied for this innovative award were included in the *Document of Innovations* as they had to complete the abstract form as part of their award submission. One faculty revised her abstract for a submission for a national teaching award from her professional association.

The experience of writing an abstract for the document motivated some faculty to begin further dissemination of their ideas. Several innovations have been presented as posters or papers at regional or national professional associations. A few are working on an article describing their innovations. Two faculty have conducted formal assessments of their innovations and are doing scholarship of teaching and learning work stemming from their original innovation.

The* Document of Innovations *and the innovations highlighted were used as evidence in the university's self-study report for reaccredidation. The section on innovations in the chapter on Educational Programs and Curriculum in the self-study report begins, "Evidence of curricular innovation can be found in the annual *Document of Innovations.* This document, which is compiled by the Director of the Teaching and Learning Center, is the principal resource of information and curricular innovations" (University of the Sciences in Philadelphia, 2002, p. 10). The accreditation report from the Middle States Commission on Higher Education mentioned the *Document of Innovations* as a strength of the university. Elsewhere in the report the site visit reviewers commended the faculty for trying new ways to teach and for sharing their ideas in the *Document of Innovations.*

The idea of developing annual editions featuring an aspect of faculty work is also now part of the university's culture. It has been suggested that others in the university need to do an annual document of research or civic engagement.

What We Have Learned About Campus Innovators From These Editions?

Truly innovative faculty (in this case, N = 15) are those who innovated every year. Jeanne Narum (2002), director of ICO/PKAL of Project Kaleidoscope, defined bricoleurs as faculty who tinker with their teaching and are successful in finding resources to make changes. The consistently innovative faculty could truly be called bricoleurs. One important characteristic of these faculty is that that they are constantly finding ways to improve their teaching and do not continue to teach as they did. These people might be appropriate to ask to be involved in campus-wide innovation efforts or new pilot projects.

It is also interesting to consider the ways in which the innovations have changed. Over time, more abstracts fit multiple categories, and there are more abstracts that describe more profound innovations where the entire course has been changed as opposed to tinkering with an assignment. The categories of innovations where the largest increase in abstracts has occurred reflect the administration's and the faculty development center's efforts to change teaching.

How long should a new idea still be considered an innovation? A few faculty who described an innovation in the first edition, again in the second as a sustained innovation, and were asked if they wanted to submit it again for the third edition, raised this question. The answer seems to be when the innovation becomes so much a part of the course that it no longer is seen as an innovation but part of the essence of the course. The rate of institutionalization of innovations seems to vary from individual to individual and course to course.

Limitations of the *Document of Innovations*

One major limitation of the version of the *Document of Innovations* described here is that participation is voluntary. No doubt additional faculty are innovating in their teaching, but for various reasons did not submit an abstract. However, given the small size of the faculty (about 145), participation levels are high and seem to be a good indicator of the innovations that are taking place at this university.

Although the submission form asks faculty to reflect on why this innovation is working, most of the abstracts do not show systematic inquiry into why and how this innovation worked. Faculty tend to give impressions or limited data. The *Document of Innovations* is not peer reviewed, nor the abstracts critiqued or evaluated, in contrast to other similar documents that showcase faculty who have won teaching awards. Therefore, this document cannot be seen as scholarship of teaching according to Hutchings and Shulman's (1999) definitions. However, it does serve as a stimulant to begin such scholarship, an important step for faculty who never considered asking systematic questions about the effectiveness of their teaching.

Conclusion

Being innovative and sharing one's innovations in teaching is now a part of the culture at this campus. The faculty's desire to feature their ideas and the acceptance of this document shows the university's commitment to enhancing teaching and the instructional support available to them. Partly due to the *Document of Innovations* and other activities of the Teaching and Learning Center, faculty are very happy to talk about their teaching innovations locally and are becoming more comfortable to do so nationally at professional meetings. These innovations in teaching are becoming common enough that a trend toward more innovative teaching and evaluation was noted as one of the highlights in the summary of the recent HERI study (Leibowitz, 2002) and observed by the recent site visitors for our accreditation review.

Acknowledgments

The author wishes to thank Gabriele Bauer, Peter Frederick, Francis S. Johnson, and the journal reviewers and editors who reviewed a previous version and offered excellent suggestions.

References

Faculty Teaching Excellence Program, University of Colorado at Boulder. (1990). *Compendium of good teaching ideas.* Retrieved March 12, 2003, from www.colorado.edu/ftep/publications

Hutchings, P., & Shulman, L. S. (1999, September/October). The scholarship of teaching: New elaborations, new developments. *Change, 31*(5), 10–15.

Leibowitz, K. (2002). *Higher Education Research Institute Faculty Survey 2001–2002.* Philadelphia, PA: University of the Sciences in Philadelphia.

Narum, J. (2002) *Science for all students.* Paper presented at the American Council on Education conference on Fostering Innovation in Undergraduate Science, Technology, Engineering, and Mathematics for all students, Washington, DC.

Shulman, L. S. (1993, November/December). Teaching as community property: Putting an end to pedagogical solitude. *Change, 25*(6), 6–7.

Office of Educational Development, University of California at Berkeley. (2002). *Compendium of good ideas on teaching and learning.* Retrieved March 12, 2003, from http://teaching.berkeley.edu/goodteachers/index.html

University of the Sciences in Philadelphia. (2002). *The University of the Sciences in Philadelphia: A self-study report.* Submitted to the Commission on Higher Education of the Middle States Association and the American Council on Pharmaceutical Education, Philadelphia, PA.

Contact:

Phyllis Blumberg
Teaching and Learning Center
University of the Sciences in Philadelphia
600 S. 43rd Street
Philadelphia, PA 19104
Voice (215) 895-1167
Fax (215) 895-1112
Email p.blumbe@usip.edu

Phyllis Blumberg is Professor of Social Sciences and Director of the Teaching and Learning Center at the University of the Sciences in Philadelphia. Her main roles include collaboration with faculty to improve their teaching, promoting more learning-centered teaching within the university, and assisting faculty to engage in scholarly teaching. Her research interests include program evaluation, problem-based learning, and self-directed learning.

Appendix 3.1

Document of Innovations Abstract Submission Form

Title of innovation ____

Name of innovator ____

Telephone number ______________ Email address ____________________

Department __________________ Type of students ____________________

Type of course or activity where implemented: required____ elective____
core curriculum_____ professional or advanced______

other, describe ____

Course or activity where implemented ______________________________

Describe rationale or goals of innovative educational activity:

Describe the innovation and its implementation:

Describe outcomes, especially learning outcomes, and impact of the innovation:

Reflect on what's working and why it is working:

Describe student reaction to the innovation:

Will the innovation be sustained within the course? Yes___ No____
If yes, will you do anything differently? Describe:

Will you implement this innovation in other courses? Yes___ No___
Describe:

What advice would you give to other people adapting this innovation?

Other comments

4

Evaluating the Return on Investment of Faculty Development

Timothy W. Bothell
Brigham Young University

Tom Henderson
Washington State University

How can the return on investment of faculty development be determined? One way to do this is through the application of a highly replicated and reported return on investment (ROI) process. This chapter reviews briefly an ROI process used by organizations throughout the world, a process that has been the basis for over 100 published studies and is the most validated and reported ROI process used for determining the monetary impact of learning. The process utilizes a five-level framework and a step-by-step ROI process model. These components are reviewed in this chapter and an example of return on investment based on student retention in a Freshman Seminar Program is explained.

Background on the Return on Investment Process

Return on investment (ROI) evaluation has been conducted by hundreds of organizations to meet the demands of a variety of influential stakeholders. Training departments, consulting teams, executive leaders, and workshop facilitators have been striving to prove the value of their work for several decades. Among all their work, an ROI process has risen to the top as the most commonly used and replicated process for evaluating the return on investment of learning and development. This is the process attributed to the work of Jack Phillips (1997a, 1997b).

The Jack Phillips ROI process is based on nearly 25 years of development. It is a process with many satisfied users; a process defined to meet the demands of many people (e.g., learning coaches, professional developers, consultants, trainers, and educators).

Consultants who have implemented the process report satisfaction with the process and claim it is methodical, systematic, easy to understand, and user-friendly. In addition, executives, managers, and professional evaluators give the process very high marks (Phillips, 2000).

The American Society for Training and Development acquired the Jack Phillips ROI network because the ROI process is the most commonly used procedure for holding training participants accountable and for justifying the costs of development programs (Baron, 2002). All of this points to the strength of the process and to a track record of success in meeting the needs of professional developers striving to determine the ROI of development activities.

Relevance to Faculty Development

Although the Jack Phillips ROI process is widely accepted in many fields, it has not been frequently applied to faculty development. Perhaps the need in faculty development has been small or the field of faculty development vastly differs from other professional development fields. Regardless of the reason for its limited to nonexistent use, the process seems applicable to faculty development. If the process works for training and development units that primarily serve clients through consulting and workshops, why not for faculty development units?

The types of data collected in the ROI process are the types of data that faculty development units need to understand the impact of faculty development activities. Three of the six data types relate to individual changes that can occur within faculty (reactions, learning, and behavior change). The other three data types relate to results that are institutional or important to the bottom line in higher education (institutional results, return on investment, and intangible results). The following is a review of each type of data collected with each step in the ROI process as it relates to faculty development.

Review of the Process

Overview

The ROI process, like many other evaluation processes, involves planning, data collection, data analysis, and reporting. Yet, unlike other evaluation processes, the ROI process is somewhat unique because each part of the process attempts to isolate effects and convert data to monetary values so that benefits of faculty development can be compared to costs. Further, the steps, techniques, assumptions, and calculations in the ROI process follow a conservative approach to build the credibility needed for acceptance of the process. Ultimately, the goal of the ROI process is to obtain data that can be used to calculate ROI.

The formula for the ROI calculation is a simple fraction and easy to calculate. However, collecting the data to put into the calculation can be challenging and must be credible. Figure 4.1 illustrates a simple ROI calculation.

FIGURE 4.1
ROI Calculation

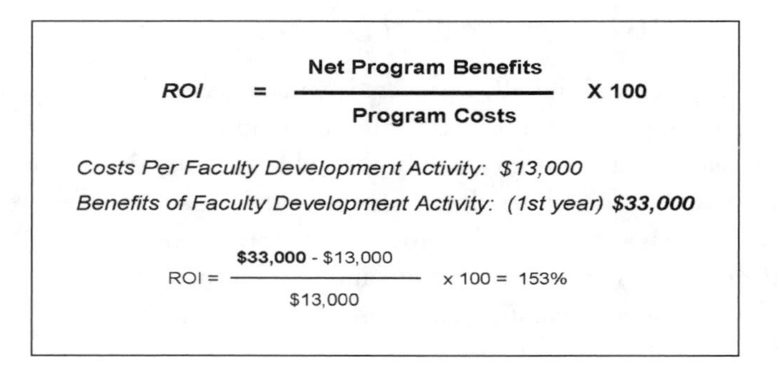

Levels of Evaluation: A Five-Level Framework

The ROI process utilizes a five-level framework, with levels of evaluation that produce six types of data and a step-by-step ROI process model. The five levels of the framework are shown in Table 4.1. Each level represents a type of data collected through application of the ROI process. Thus, five types of data are collected that each corresponds to the levels of evaluation. The sixth type of data comes from data that is not converted to monetary values and therefore is labeled as intangible.

TABLE 4.1
Levels of Evaluation in the ROI Process

Level of Evaluation	Question Answered
Level 1: Reaction	How do participants of faculty development activities react to the faculty development activities?
Level 2: Learning	What do the participants learn from the faculty development activities?
Level 3: Behavior change or application	What specifically do participants of faculty development activities do differently on-the-job and after the faculty development activity?
Level 4: Results (overall institutional results)	How does the entire institution benefit from the improvements individuals made because of the faculty development activities?
Level 5: Return on investment	How do the benefits of the faculty development activity compare to the costs?

The first four levels in the five-level framework were originally conceived by Donald Kirkpatrick (1996) as a model for evaluating training programs. Since their origination, the four levels have been expanded upon by Phillips's work on the ROI process.

Planning

The first step in the ROI process is planning. Purposes of the faculty development activity are explored in this step. If a faculty development activity has an objective related to a bottom-line result for a higher education institution (e.g., student enrollment, graduation rates, alumni giving, increased funding through grants, faculty retention), then the activity is suitable for the ROI process. Thus, the purposes for the faculty development activity are matched up to the purposes for the evaluation. In addition, the timing of data collection procedures is determined for each level of evaluation and instruments and methods are selected.

Another important part of the planning phase of the ROI process includes the collection of baseline data. If data already exist that may be affected by the faculty development activity, then past and current values are collected to serve as baseline measures before the faculty development activity is implemented.

Data Collection

The data collection steps of the ROI process include collecting data during the faculty development activity and again some time after the faculty development activity. Levels 1 and 2 data (reaction and learning) can be collected during the faculty development activity and levels 3 to 5 (behavior change, institutional results, ROI) data can be collected sometime after the activity, as illustrated in Figure 4.2).

FIGURE 4.2
ROI Process Model

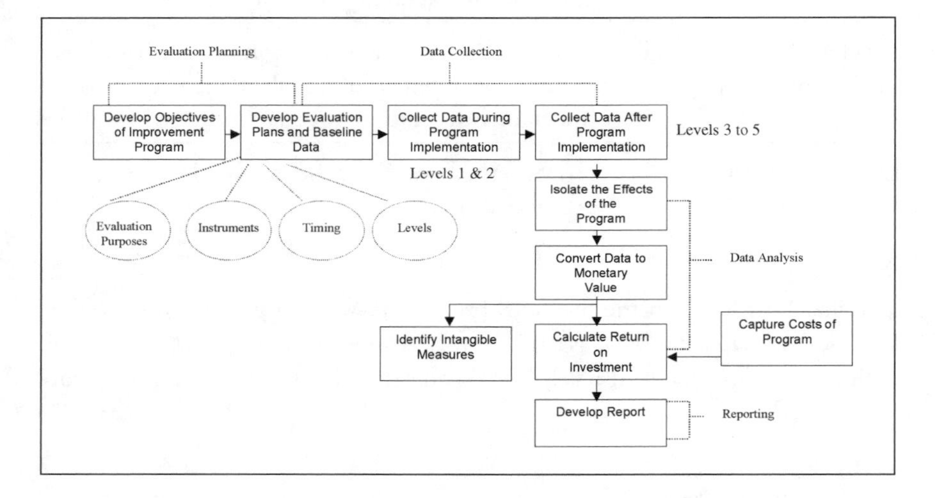

Typically, evaluators use instruments and methods such as questionnaires, interviews, focus groups, assessments, simulations, role plays, and observations to collect data about reaction, learning, and behavior change. The most popular seems to be the questionnaire administered at the end of a faculty development workshop that asks three to five questions about participants' general reactions. Less popular are methods used for determining specifically what faculty do differently after a faculty development activity. Likewise, few studies about faculty development seem to determine influence on institutional results.

Much of the data collected for level 4, institutional results, can be found in the current systems within the institution (e.g., graduation rates, faculty complaints, student complaints, research articles published, research grants funded externally). Some of the data is more amenable to the ROI process, typically labeled "hard data," and some of the data is less amenable to the ROI process, typically labeled "soft data." The challenging part of the ROI process when it comes to level 4 data is converting data to monetary values and isolating the effects of faculty development on the data.

Hard Data Versus Soft Data

Hard data is characterized as objectively based, easy to quantify and measure, relatively easy to assign it monetary values, and credible to institutional leaders. Table 4.2 illustrates the types of hard data that many evaluation professionals use in the ROI process. The data is typically received from organizations in the business of manufacturing, sales, services, etc., but not necessarily for institutions of higher education. Some of the hard data are quality improvements, some are output increases, some of the data refer to time savings, and some are cost savings.

TABLE 4.2

Examples of Hard Data

(not necessarily for academic organizations – but commonly used elsewhere)

OUTPUT	COSTS	TIME	QUALITY
Units Produced	Budget Variances	Equipment Downtime	Scrap
Tons Manufactured	Unit Costs	Overtime	Waste
Items Assembled	Cost By Account	On Time Shipment	Rejects
Money Collected	Variable Costs	Time to Project Completion	Error Rates
Items Sold	Fixed Costs	Processing Time	Rework
Forms Processed	Overhead Cost	Supervisory Time	Shortages
Loans Approved	Operating Costs	Break in Time for New Employees	Product Defects
Inventory Turnover	Number of Cost Reductions	Training Time	Deviation From Standard
Patients Visited	Project Cost Savings	Meeting Schedules	Product Failures
Applications Processed	Accident Costs	Repair Time	Inventory Adjustments
Students Graduated	Program Costs	Efficiency	Time Card Corrections
Tasks Completed	Sales Expense	Work Stoppages	Percent of Tasks Completed Properly
Output Per Hour		Order Response	Number of Accidents
Productivity		Late Reporting	
Work Backlog		Lost Time Days	
Incentive Bonus			
Shipments			
New Accounts Generated			

Soft data is characterized as subjectively based (in many cases), difficult to quantify and measure directly, difficult to assign monetary measurement to its value, and less credible to institutional leaders. Table 4.3 illustrates the types of soft data that many evaluation professionals use in the ROI process.

TABLE 4.3
Examples of Soft Data

(not necessarily for academic organizations – but commonly used elsewhere)

WORK HABITS	CUSTOMER SERVICE	EMPLOYEE DEVELOPMENT/ ADVANCEMENT
Absenteeism	Customer Complaints	Number of Promotions
Tardiness	Customer Satisfaction	Number of Pay Increases
Visits to the Dispensary	Customer Dissatisfaction	Number of Training Programs Attended
First Aid Treatments	Customer Impressions	Requests for Transfer
Violations of Safety Rules	Customer Loyalty	Performance Appraisal Ratings
Number of Communication Break-downs	Customer Retention	Increases in Job Effectiveness
Excessive Breaks	Customer Value	
	Lost Customers	

WORK CLIMATE/SATISFACTION	INITIATIVE/INNOVATION
Number of Grievances	Implementation of New Ideas
Number of Discrimination Charges	Successful Completion of Projects
Employee Complaints	Number of Suggestions Implemented
Job Satisfaction	Setting Goals and Objectives
Employee Turnover	New Products and Services Developed
Litigation	New Patents and Copyrights
Organizational Commitment	
Employee Loyalty	
Increased Confidence	

Whether soft or hard data, level 4 data needs to be isolated to the effects of faculty development and converted to monetary values when possible to prepare for level 5 calculations of ROI. Data not converted to a monetary value is collected and reported as intangible results.

Level 4 Results Influenced by Faculty Development

What are the level 4 results that faculty development influences? Some may be the same as those listed in Tables 4.2 and 4.3, yet most are very different. There is no room for an exhaustive list in this chapter, but Table 4.4 illustrates some of the level 4 results, institutional results, that faculty development can influence. Some of the results are hard data and some are soft data. Discovering and listing these types of results that a particular faculty development activity should influence is a step toward improving efforts to determine the ROI of faculty development.

TABLE 4.4
Institutional Results That Can Be Influenced by Faculty Development

Hard Data	Soft Data
Student Retention	Faculty Job Satisfaction
Student Enrollment	Student Job Placement
Decreased Litigation	Reduced Conflict
Graduation Rates	Improved Teamwork
Time Savings	Reduced Stress
Time Savings Following Up on Complaints	Campus Culture That Values Less Teaching
Increases in Alumni Giving	Leadership Improvement
Faculty Turnover	Improved relationships with National Foundations, Associations and Federal Agencies
Reduced Costs Due to Ineffective Teaching	
Students Repeating Courses (costs to the state or school sponsor)	

Data Analysis

The third phase of the ROI process is data analysis. Steps in this phase include isolating the effects of faculty development, converting data to monetary values, capturing the costs of faculty development, identifying intangible results, and calculating the return on investment. The most difficult steps of the entire ROI process occur in this phase. Isolating the effects of faculty development and converting data to monetary values typically are the most challenging steps in the ROI process regardless of what is being evaluated.

Isolating the effects of faculty development may be the most important step in the ROI process. Without performing this step, the entire process can lose credibility and fail to provide an accurate picture of the return on investment of faculty development.

There are multiple techniques to isolate the effects of faculty development on institutional results, but a detailed discussion of each is beyond the scope of this chapter. Techniques include control group research arrangements, trend-line analysis, forecasting, regression analysis, correlations, and expert estimates.

Likewise, there are multiple techniques for converting data to monetary values, but a discussion of each is not possible here. Converting data to monetary values is a very important step in the ROI process and is absolutely necessary to determine the monetary benefits from faculty development. Although the process is challenging, particularly with soft data, it can be methodically accomplished.

The ROI calculation is based on converting both hard and soft data to monetary values. Then, those values are compared to the costs of faculty development and converted to a percentage. A return of more than 15% to 25% on money spent for faculty development would be more than the typical return expected on other investments made to help institutions operate.

In addition to tangible, monetary benefits used in an ROI calculation, most programs will have intangible, nonmonetary benefits such as increased job satisfaction, increased organizational commitment, improved teamwork, and reduced conflicts. For most institutions, intangible, nonmonetary benefits are extremely valuable, often carrying as much influence as the hard data items.

Reporting the Results of the ROI Evaluation

The final phase of the ROI process is to report the results. Audiences interested in the ROI of faculty development would vary, but certainly some of the people in the audience would include all other faculty developers and university managers responsible for teaching and learning. Yet, regardless of the audience interested in the report of the results, strict adherence to the principles, phases, and steps involved in the ROI process will make the reporting phase more comfortable.

Summary

The ROI process has not been fully applied to faculty development, but it seems to be highly applicable. Further research about what is currently being used to determine the value of faculty development is needed. Many faculty development units are most likely collecting data at levels 1 and 2. Few are likely to be collecting data at level 3, and few if any are collecting data at levels 4 and 5.

Understanding the ROI process could motivate more faculty development units to collect data at higher levels of evaluation and give a common language and framework for accomplishing the challenging task of proving the value of faculty development. One study at Washington State University demonstrates the effects of faculty development-type activities on level 4 results. That study will be discussed in the remainder of this chapter.

The following case study concerning a freshman seminar program attempts to demonstrate the value of faculty development-type activities on institutional results. The study was not a complete application of the ROI process and could be improved upon in several ways related to the ROI process, but the study is a good example of how level 4 higher education results can be influenced by faculty development-type activities.

Case Study: Return on Investment From the Freshman Seminar Program at Washington State University

Overview of the Freshman Seminar Program at Washington State University

Freshman Seminar courses at Washington State University (WSU) are spaces where students gather in learning communities linked to general education courses. The seminars create a space where active, generative learning takes place and where students collaborate to develop a research project from topics in their shared general education course. Experienced and trained undergraduate students serve as leaders in the role of peer facilitator, participating as an academic mentor or as a "hypernaut," an undergraduate multimedia specialist. Graduate students serve as facilitators and assist and mentor the peer facilitators and hypernauts. Faculty in the linked courses also serve as mentors. Freshman Seminar students have created a Flash animation about the program accessible at http://salc.wsu.edu/freshman/details/flash_page.htm.

The Situation That Led to This Study

The Freshman Seminar Program had participated in many assessment studies since its inception but had not completed an ROI analysis. During the spring 2002 term, the Freshman Seminar Program came under review by a subcommittee of the faculty senate. The Center for Teaching, Learning, and Technology at Washington State University was contacted and asked to analyze the benefits and costs of the program in preparation for the subcommittee meeting.

Other Freshman Seminar Assessment Studies

Jean Henscheid, the original coordinator of the Freshman Seminar Program, recognized the important of assessment in analyzing and continually improving the program. Subsequent Freshman Seminar coordinators have maintained that culture of assessment. The assessment findings during the early years of the program are summarized below (Henscheid, 1999):

1) Freshman Seminar students are nearly 5% more likely to be retained to the sophomore year than other freshmen (fall 1996 and fall 1997 cohorts).

2) Freshman Seminar students are, overall, not as well prepared academically as the general university freshman population, yet they achieve better overall grade point averages than like students in their first semester at WSU at all preparedness levels (fall 1997 cohort).

3) Surveys of Freshman Seminar students using the Flashlight Item bank showed:

- Eighty-three percent of students in the seminars say the emphasis on working in groups helps them understand ideas and concepts taught in the course (fall 1998 cohort).
- Eighty-six percent of students in the seminars say they are more comfortable participating in discussions in the Freshman Seminar than in other courses (fall 1998 cohort).
- Compared to media-enhanced lecture classes, students are more likely to feel that they had learned to manage large, complex tasks (fall 1996).
- Compared to media-enhanced lecture classes, students say they are more likely to feel that they have worked through a process to solve complex problems (fall 1996).
- Because the students create projects, 78% say they are better able to communicate their ideas to others (fall 1998 cohort).
- Because the students create these projects, 76% say they are better able to understand ideas and concepts taught in the course, and 79% say they are able to exercise their creativity.
- Seminar students are statistically significantly more likely to read than other students, more apt to be actively engaged in their learning, cooperate with other students, have contact with faculty, and more likely to read basic references and documents (fall 1996 and spring 1997 cohorts).
- The vast majority of seminar students say they would recommend a peer facilitated experience (all cohorts).

The Freshman Seminar has participated in Washington State University's Goals, Activities, and Processes (GAPs) formative assessment survey since its inception during the fall 1999 term. A regression analysis of 2001 GAPs data showed that Freshman Seminar students scored statistically significantly "better" on eight out of nine questions relating to principles of good practice in undergraduate education than other on-campus Washington State University courses using web-based course management systems and that participated in the GAPs (see Table 4.5).

TABLE 4.5

Ordinary Least Squares Linear Regression Coefficients From the Regression Predicting Principles of Good Practice by Freshman Seminar Classes Versus Other WSU On-Campus Courses Using Technology

Dependent variables regressed on categorical variable (0 if Freshman Seminars, 1 if other WSU on-campus course) and age.

The questions stem from the Goals, Activities, and Processes (GAPs) student survey asked: Because of the way your instructor or teaching assistant facilitated electronic communication (such as threaded discussions or streaming media) in this course, how likely were you to:

Possible responses included:
1 = Much less likely; 2 = Somewhat less likely; 3 = About the same;
4 = Somewhat more likely; 5 = Much more likely.
6 = Not applicable (these responses were removed from the analyses)

	Independent Variables						
Dependent Variables (Question Leaves)	Regression Coefficient of Categorical Variable	Standard Error of Categorical Variable Coefficient	Age Coefficient	Standard Error of Age Coefficient	N	Inter-cept	R^2 / Adj. R^2
Ask for clarification	-.518***	(0.097)	-0.072	(0.073)	567	3.89	.062/.059
Discuss course concepts with other students	-.301***	(0.088)	-0.055	(0.066)	563	3.71	.028/.025
Work on assignments with other students	-.869***	(0.094)	-0.037	(0.072)	562	3.86	.153/.150
Ask other students for comments on coursework	-.507***	(0.098)	-0.029	(0.071)	556	3.55	.055/.052
Feel isolated from other students	.555***	(0.108)	0.053	(0.081)	527	2.18	.059/.055
Receive comments from the instructor quickly	-0.159	(0.088)	-0.092	(0.065)	570	3.88	.013/.010
Discuss course concepts with instructor	-.560***	(0.091)	-0.054	(0.067)	561	3.76	.079/.075
Make use of unique abilities to learn	-.418***	(0.09)	-0.107	(0.066)	565	3.85	.055/.052
Challenged to create own understanding	-.210**	(0.089)	-0.078	(0.068)	559	3.81	.017/.014

Family-wise alpha = .005; *p < .05. ** p < .01. ***p < .001 (two-tailed)

Note: Numbers in parentheses are standard errors. The control variable, Age, was not a significant predictor in any of the regression equations.

A qualitative analysis was conducted on Freshman Seminar focus groups. Four questions were asked:

1) What is your (the student's) role in your learning?

2) What is the hypernaut's role in your learning?

3) What is the peer facilitator's role in your learning?

4) What is your definition of critical thinking?

In general, the responses were very positive. An average of all four questions show that 69% of the students in the focus group answered positively, 21% were neutral, and 10% were negative.

ROI Summary (Actual Data Is Not Used to Protect Privacy, but Final Results Are Comparable to the Actual Study)

The focus groups, student Flashlight surveys, GAPs surveys, and analyses of grade point averages all highlighted very positive results from the Freshman Seminar Program but would be classified as soft data because they are difficult to assign monetary value to. However, the increased retention from the Freshman Seminar programs (Henscheid, 2001) provided an opportunity to put a monetary value on at least some of the benefits. A question then immediately presented itself: Would an additional 4% or 5% retention rate pay for the program?

Revenue Assumptions

Using the average increased retention rate of the Freshman Seminar Program, the increased Average Annual Full Time Equivalents (AAFTEs) could be estimated going into the sophomore year. The estimated increase in juniors and seniors was estimated by multiplying the previous year's increase times the retention rate for that year and then truncating the results. For example, the retention rate for sophomores to juniors at Washington State University is approximately 90%. The sophomores retained as a result of the Freshman Seminar program over and above the sophomores not in the seminar program were estimated to be 18.9 students. That estimate was truncated to 18 students.

TABLE 4.6
Estimated Increased AAFTEs From Freshman Seminar at WSU

	Estimated Increase in AAFTEs
From freshman to sophomore	21
From sophomore to junior	18
From junior to senior	16
Total	55

The next question became, would an additional 55 students at WSU (as a result of the Freshman Seminar Program) generate enough revenue to cover the costs of the program and generate a positive ROI? The annual increase in revenue was estimated by multiplying the AAFTEs from the increased retention times the tuition and state support per AAFTE. This estimate is probably conservative; the additional students on campus would generate other revenue via sports passes, recreation center passes, room and board, parking, and participation in other programs.

TABLE 4.7
Estimated Annual Increase in Revenues From the Additional Students Retained by the Freshman Seminar Program

	Estimated Increased AAFTEs	Annual Tuition per AAFTE	Annual State Funds per AAFTE	Total Revenue Increase
Sophomores	21	$3,200	$5,000	$172,200
Juniors	18	$3,200	$5,000	$147,600
Seniors	16	$3,200	$5,000	$131,200
Total Estimated Revenue Increase				$451,000

Estimated Annual Costs

The final questions from this study included: Would $451,000 per year be enough to cover the costs of the Freshman Seminar Program? What kind of an ROI does the program generate? The annual Freshman Seminar budget was $125,000, which included stipends for participating faculty, payment of the graduate student facilitators and undergraduate peer facilitators, and enough to cover supplies and some equipment purchases. However, the salary of the coordinator was not included nor were the costs of direct supervisors, administrative support, or building and equipment cost estimates. Table 4.8 gives an overall summary of the estimated costs of the Freshman Seminar Program. Major direct costs were included in the estimates.

TABLE 4.8
Summary of the Estimated Annual Direct Costs of the Freshman Seminar Program at WSU

1) Annual Freshmen Seminar budget	$125,000
2) Administrative*	57,302
3) Other staff support*	12,192
4) Estimated room depreciation**	7,961
5) Estimated equipment depreciation***	26,750
Total Estimated Annual FS Costs	**$229,205**

*See Table 4.9 for an example of estimating the cost of administration and staff support.

**See Table 4.10 for the estimated cost of depreciation of lab space used by the Freshman Seminars.

***See Table 4.11 for an example of estimating the equipment depreciation for the Freshman Seminar labs.

Questions for all ROI or cost studies focus on "when have the major costs been captured," or "should indirect costs be allocated?" Extra weeks or months could have been spent on this project estimating how to allocate indirect costs. WSU's experience with the Technology Costing Methodology (TCM) reinforced this decision not to estimate all indirect costs to "avoid the effort involved in allocating costs to obtain results that are seldom of managerial utility" (Jones, 2001, p. 16). Tables 4.9, 4.10, and 4.11 show some examples of the detail behind the cost summary and allocation of some major indirect costs.

For many education cost estimates (such as the cost of a class or program) the "people costs" dominate, that is, the cost of salaries, wages, and benefits of the faculty and staff involved with the project. The following estimate includes 100% of the costs (not actual) of the coordinator of the Freshman Seminar Program, plus estimates for the portion of time spent on the Freshman Seminar by

TABLE 4.9
Estimated Administrative Support for Freshman Seminars

	Coordinator 100%	**Associate VP 10%**
Salary per pay period (not actual)	$1,500	$3,800
Number of pay periods	24	24
% allocable to Freshman Seminars	100%	10%
Add benefits	1.27	1.27
Salary and Benefit Costs to FS	**$45,720**	**$11,582**

TABLE 4.10
Estimated Staff Support for Freshman Seminars

Other Staff Support Estimated as:	
Two support personnel earning $24,000 per year each	$48,000
27% benefits	1.27
Estimated time spent on Freshman Seminars	20%
Estimated Staff Support	**$12,192**

the coordinator's direct supervisor, the associate vice president for educational development. The cost of administrative assistance is estimated in Table 4.9.

Freshman Seminars meet in computer laboratories for most of their classes. For this study it was estimated that they used the rooms 75% of the time. Table 4.11 estimates the annual depreciation of equipment; Table 4.12 estimates the annual depreciation of the rooms used for classes/computer laboratories.

Estimated Return on Investment

The estimated return on investment for Freshman Seminars during the last one-year period was ($451,000 – $229,205) / $229,205 or 96.8% which is a very strong ROI. In one academic year, the Freshman Seminar Program at WSU generated almost twice as much revenue as it cost due to the students retained at WSU because of the program.

TABLE 4.11
Estimated Annual Depreciation of Equipment Used in Freshman Seminar Labs

Estimated cost for 40 computers	$ 100,000
Estimated cost for seven scanners and printers	7,000
Total equipment cost	$ 107,000
Assume three-year depreciable life	$ 35,666.67

TABLE 4.12
Estimated Annual Depreciation of Freshman Seminar Labs in the Lighty Student Services Building

1) Original cost of Lighty	$15,872,186
2) Divide by Lighty square feet	94,924
3) Gives cost per square foot	$167.21
4) Depreciation per year / 50 year life / sq. ft.	$3.34
5) Square footage of labs: 260z@1,303 260W@807, & 260F@1,064	3,174
6) Assume 75% use for Freshman Seminar	75%
7) Annual depreciation cost of labs (4x5x6)	$ 7,961

LESSONS LEARNED

Many higher education studies involving cost estimates (as does this ROI analysis) will note that people costs, salaries, wages, and benefits will dominate the costs of a program or unit being studied. Return on investment analysis gives an estimate of added revenues and costs from a program; good estimates if the analyst is careful, but not exact numbers. It is often necessary to explain this to faculty and staff as data is gathered for the analysis. ROI analysis is an effective, well-grounded analysis technique that can be used as a formative assessment tool to show the return of a program and highlight possible areas of improvement. This analysis technique may be a very valuable assessment tool to have as state funding for higher education decreases and as higher education institutions attempt to be more productive.

References

Baron, D. (2002). *ASTD ROI network.* Retrieved November 11, 2002, from http://roi.astd.org/index.aspx

Henscheid, J. M. (1999). *Washington State University freshman seminar program research findings.* Retrieved November 17, 2002, from http://salc.wsu.edu/freshman/details/research_findings.htm

Henscheid, J. M. (2001). Peer facilitators as lead freshman seminar instructors. In J. E. Miller, J. E., Groccia, & M. S. Miller (Eds.). *Student-assisted teaching: A guide to faculty-student team work* (pp. 21–26). Bolton, MA: Anker.

Jones, D. (2001). *Technology costing methodology project.* Retrieved November 19, 2002, from http://www.wcet.info/projects/tcm/TCM_Handbook_Final.pdf

Kirkpatrick, D. L. (1996). *Evaluating training programs: The four levels.* San Francisco, CA: Berrett-Koehler.

Phillips, J. J. (1997a). *Return on investment in training and performance improvement programs.* Woburn, MA: Butterworth-Heinemann.

Phillips, J. J. (1997b). *Handbook of training evaluation and measurement methods.* Houston, TX: Gulf Publishing.

Phillips, J. J. (2000). *The consultant's scorecard: Tracking results and bottom-line impact of consulting projects.* New York, NY: McGraw-Hill.

Contact:

Timothy W. Bothell
Brigham Young University
4432 WSC
Provo, UT 84602
Voice (801) 422-8194
Fax (801) 422-0223
Email tim_bothell@byu.edu

Tom Henderson
Center for TLT
Washington State University
Box 644550
Pullman, WA 99164
Voice (509) 335-6451
Fax (509) 335-1362
Email tom@usu.edu

Timothy W. Bothell is Faculty Development Coordinator for the Assessment of Student Learning at Brigham Young University. He currently conducts workshops and works with faculty one-on-one to improve the assessment of student learning. He also directs the Exam Improvement Center within Brigham Young University's Faculty Center. Faculty from all colleges and departments can leave their exams at the Exam Improvement Center for feedback and suggestions. In addition, as an independent consultant, he consults organizations concerning the return on investment of learning.

Tom Henderson is Assessment Coordinator at the Center for Teaching, Learning, and Technology at Washington State University. He is a co-leader of a WSU team that is adapting the Western Cooperative for Educational Telecommunication's Technology Costing Methodology (TCM) to assess the processes as well as the costs of WSU course development activities and adapt that information to the TCM/mini-Bridge cost simulation model. He has also field-tested the Flashlight Cost Model while analyzing the costs of course management technologies at WSU. He has over 12 years of experience in private sector accounting and financial analysis. He has a PhD in interdisciplinary studies from Washington State University, an MBA in finance from the University of Washington, and a B.S. in accounting from the University of Idaho.

5

Beyond Bean Counting: Making Faculty Development Needs Assessment More Meaningful

Pamela M. Milloy
Corly Brooke
Iowa State University

Faculty development centers face many challenges including shrinking resources while providing an increasing array of programs and services to enhance learning. Needs assessment can be seen as a valuable tool to help centers focus efforts to meet the most salient needs relevant to the institutional mission. This chapter describes a faculty development needs assessment project that was implemented at a large public institution. Data collected was used to focus programming and guide decision-making. Based upon a presentation at the 2002 POD conference, selected needs assessment findings and their programmatic implications for the center are presented.

Teaching and learning centers at large public institutions of higher education face many challenges. One of these is decreasing state appropriations to support programming for faculty development centers. As a result, there is an increasing call for centers to move beyond anecdotal evidence of effectiveness and to provide empirical data that illustrate their impact on teaching and student learning, as well as user characteristics and demand for services.

Another challenge faculty developers face is the emergence of many new and exciting learning-centered initiatives in higher education. Reaching beyond skills and activities, teaching and learning centers are asked to incorporate broad new initiatives such as service learning, learning communities, outcomes assessment, peer review, and electronic portfolio development. Some of these learning innovations are at the heart of the institution's mission and active involvement serves to further weave centers of teaching and learning into the fabric of the institution. With many initiatives worthy of time and attention, it is often difficult to prioritize efforts given restricted resources.

While these are challenging issues, they also represent great opportunities for centers of teaching and learning. These emerging initiatives can greatly improve student learning and can position our centers at the forefront of institutional change. However, to be successful, our centers must be able to identify and address the salient issues.

In both of these situations—budget shortfalls and numerous teaching and learning reform measures—we are challenged to do more with fewer resources. Our services can easily become spread too thin and may become ineffective. How do teaching and learning centers decide which issues are most crucial to their institution's success? How do centers know that their programming is congruent with what will attract and benefit faculty? How can centers further document the need for and success of their services?

One possible answer to these questions is through a comprehensive faculty development needs assessment project. Effective needs assessment provides centers of teaching and learning with the guidance and information to make well-informed and effective decisions about direction, programming, and services. Many faculty developers intuitively know the value of needs assessment, yet lack the resources and information to plan a successful needs assessment project.

This chapter describes the comprehensive faculty development needs assessment project conducted at a large, midwestern, public, land-grant institution in the 2001–2002 academic year. The undergraduate and graduate student enrollment is approximately 27,000 and the faculty size is slightly over 1,800. The faculty development center has been in existence since the fall of 1993. This was the first comprehensive faculty needs assessment project undertaken by the center.

Needs Assessment in the Literature

The literature overwhelmingly stresses the value of faculty development needs assessment, yet, it is a tool greatly underutilized by centers of teaching and learning (Chism & Szabó, 1996; Engleberg, 1991; Harnish & Wild, 1992; Knowlton & Ratliffe, 1992; Travis, Hursh, Lankewicz, & Tang, 1996). Travis et al. (1996) indicated that there is relatively inadequate coverage of the process of needs assessment in the available literature.

Recommendations from research at The Ohio State University in 1996 called for more routine and public reporting of faculty development data

(Chism & Szabó, 1996). Chism and Szabó further claimed that programs should do more needs assessments for goal setting and to inform program planning as "information about who uses faculty development services exists more in the oral tradition than in the literature" (p. 115). "The oral tradition of answers to this question has been established and gone generally unchallenged, reducing the motivation to explore the issue" (p. 125). Chism and Szabó indicated that though some programs collect information on users and outcomes, these data are not routinely communicated to others, allowing the beliefs that are shared orally among faculty developers to continue to flourish. The authors advocated "... more research and responsible reporting concerning the characteristics of those who are served by faculty development programs" (p. 127).

Using needs assessment data as a decision-making tool was the focus of Engleberg's (1991): "Decision-making, not survey results, is the cornerstone of the needs assessment process" (p. 216). This, of course, speaks directly to the value of a needs assessment research project—to inform faculty development staff in making decisions on direction and programming on the basis of research and not subjective impressions and hunches.

Knowlton and Ratliffe (1992) described shrinking state appropriations and suggested that empirical research can help faculty development programs prove their value when budgets are tight. A case study conducted by Harnish and Wild (1992) also addressed the value of assessment in times of limited resources: "Evaluation is an especially important consideration because of its implications for the continued existence (funding) of professional development in the face of budget constrains and dwindling resources" (p. 5). Addressing budgetary as well as credibility issues, Boice (1997) wrote, "Faculty, particularly the considerable numbers who value research and empirical accountability, wonder if their local faculty development centers make a difference that merits the budget they get" (p. 379).

Needs Assessment Methodology

The literature does not reveal a clearly preferred methodology for faculty development needs assessment projects. Numerous authors articulate the benefits of qualitative or quantitative studies, as well as for mixed methodologies. Travis et al. (1996) provided a summary of needs assessment projects at four public institutions, indicating "a multiple data collection method is preferable for obtaining the most complete representation as possible" (p. 98).

Although there is not unanimous sentiment in the literature about the most effective method for needs assessment, an explanatory mixed method design was selected for this study (Creswell, 2002). It was felt this design would provide the center with rich and deep information that would most thoroughly answer the research questions and guide decision-making. Despite the additional requirements of time and financial resources, it was decided that priority would be placed on a cross-sectional survey administered to every member of the faculty to measure their current practices, opinions, and attitudes. From data obtained in the quantitative process, additional questions would emerge and would be explored through a qualitative phase—a series of focus group interviews.

After the decision to use a mixed methods approach was made, the center contracted with the Research Institute for Studies in Education (RISE), located within the university's College of Education. It was felt that utilizing the services of RISE would be beneficial because their staff would:

- Provide expert consultation on the research design and methodology
- Perform sophisticated data analysis beyond the expertise of center staff
- Provide a neutral perspective to administration of the survey
- Increase the professionalism of the survey instrument and focus group protocol
- Decrease the bias that center staff would introduce to the qualitative process
- Help respondents feel more comfortable in their anonymity, therefore increasing the response rate

For these reasons, the decision to contract with RISE for these services was pivotal, leading to an efficient and effective research process and successful conclusion of the needs assessment project.

The Needs Assessment Process

A traditional paper and pencil survey instrument was developed by both RISE and center staff using as a resource the advice and sample surveys received through the POD Listserv (M. Theall, personal communication, August 30, 2001) (Appendix 5.1). RISE advised the center against using an electronic survey format because of poor faculty response rates on previous electronic surveys. Through staff dialogue and planning sessions, ten specific areas were identified for this project, which guided the development of the survey instrument:

1) Familiarity with center's services
2) Level of interest in various aspects of faculty development
3) Perception of the center's effectiveness
4) Type of teaching and learning activities preferred
5) Frequency with which faculty participate in the center's activities
6) Best method of communication with faculty about the center's activities
7) How the institution can best achieve excellence in teaching
8) How the center's services can be improved
9) Why center services are accessed
10) What center services should be provided electronically

Once developed, the survey was pilot tested by 15 faculty and staff members at various levels in the institution and in various colleges and units to remedy unclear points. The center's advisory board was also consulted with regard to the survey design and research questions.

With an in-house developed survey, reliability and validity were concerns. We believed the pilot testing improved the reliability. Center staff also developed an alternative survey form which was administered to about 30 faculty members at a center workshop. Similar results from this survey helped to enhance our confidence in the reliability and construct validity of the instrument.

Center staff felt strongly that the survey design was critical to a successful response rate. Great effort was expended developing succinct survey questions and ensuring that the instrument design was visually appealing and quick and easy to complete and return (i.e., ten to 15 minutes). The survey had 17 questions, including six questions requesting demographic information. Most questions were answered by the respondent using an ordinal scale. Several open-ended questions were also included to allow respondents the opportunity to provide additional suggestions and feedback.

The entire faculty population was surveyed (N = 1,826), including all tenured, tenure-track, and nontenure-track faculty. The survey was sent in campus mail, accompanied by a cover letter on RISE stationery articulating the purpose and sponsorship of the research, encouraging completion, and assuring anonymity and confidentiality of responses. The due date for responses was approximately ten days following the mailing. A second mailing of the survey and revised cover letter was sent to each member of the population not returning the instrument by the due date (n = 1,332). For both mailings, the survey was to be returned to the RISE office, not the center's office, again to reduce any perceived bias or concerns of confidentiality.

The total population was adjusted to account for faculty retirements, resignations, and leaves of absence, and the overall response rate received was 43.8% (n = 781). Statistical tests showed that the response sample provided a 95% level of confidence and that all estimates based on the response sample are within 3% of the population parameters. Based on this conservative estimate of the representative nature of the response, the results are generalizable to our total population with a high degree of confidence.

Demographics of the respondents aligned very closely with the entire faculty population with regard to academic rank, tenure status, college, and department. The exception was gender. A statistically significantly greater proportion of females responded to the survey than expected by chance, $p < .001$.

Once surveys were returned, RISE staff entered the responses into a database, cleaned the data, and performed the statistical analysis. Center staff interpreted, summarized, and reported on the data and decided how well it answered the research questions.

Following the conclusion of the quantitative process, three focus group meetings were held in spring 2002 to allow the center to clarify and expand data obtained in the quantitative phase of the needs assessment project. Center staff, in consultation with RISE staff, developed the focus group protocol. From there, RISE assumed responsibility for the remainder of the qualitative phase of the research to reduce the bias that center staff would inevitably introduce. A random sample of 90 teaching faculty was selected from the survey respondents who indicated that they were "somewhat familiar" and thought the center was "somewhat effective." The center chose this group of faculty because we felt they could provide valuable information to make our programming more effective. Further, we felt our programming changes could most significantly influence and engage those faculty who don't already hold a strong opinion about the center and are not significantly engaged in the center's activities.

Selected findings and programmatic implications from the quantitative and qualitative phases of the needs assessment project are integrated and presented in the following section. The complete report and appendices are accessible through the center's web site provided at the end of this chapter.

Findings and Resulting Programmatic Implications

Familiarity

Sixty-six percent of tenured or tenure-track faculty members who responded to the survey indicated that they are somewhat or very familiar with the center's services. However, 17% of nontenure-track faculty members responded that they are somewhat or very familiar with the center's services. A similar pattern was revealed in participation frequency in the center's events or activities: A statistically significant higher proportion of nontenure-track faculty responded that they never participate in the center's activities, $p < .001$. Alternatively, tenure-track faculty participate in center events with more regularity than one would expect by chance, $p < .001$.

Qualitative data obtained in the focus group sessions also reveal a gap in the center's impact on nontenure-track faculty. Because nontenure-track faculty (lecturers, adjuncts, and clinicians) are increasingly seen to be responsible for a significant portion of undergraduate instruction, the center needs to be more proactive in supporting a culture that values the services of these faculty members. We can do this by expanding and enhancing our programming to meet their unique needs.

Interest in Faculty Development Areas

Respondents were asked to rate their level of interest in various areas of faculty development (Appendix 5.1, question 8), including broad educational initiatives such as service learning and learning communities. In addition, respondents were asked to indicate their level of interest in more specific areas of course planning, student learning activities, and assessment strategies (Appendix 5.1, question 10). In each question, respondents were asked to rate their level of interest by indicating, 1) little or no interest, 2) some interest, or 3) great interest. Alternatively, respondents could indicate "don't know/not applicable."

Table 5.1 shows the level of interest in the broad areas of faculty development. For those respondents who expressed interest, the percent responding, mean, and standard deviation for each are presented. The top three scores in each level of interest are in bold.

Table 5.1
Level of Faculty Interest in Broad Areas of Faculty Development

Area of Interest	**1) Little or no interest**	**2) Some interest**	**3) Great interest**	**Mean**	**SD**	**n**
Scholarship of teaching and learning	27.6%	**45.3%**	**27.1%**	1.99	0.740	713
Principles of student outcomes assessment	25.8%	**51.7%**	**22.5%**	1.97	0.694	721
Developing teaching portfolios	38.6%	40.4%	21.0%	1.82	0.752	710
Developing teaching-centered grant proposals	44.5%	37.2%	18.3%	1.74	0.749	694
Activities designed for new faculty	**53.6%**	32.0%	14.4%	1.61	0.726	631
Integrating service learning into the curriculum	**48.6%**	37.5%	13.9%	1.65	0.711	638
Integrating communication skills across the curriculum	23.7%	**45.7%**	**30.6%**	2.07	0.734	726
Developing learning communities	**45.9%**	42.2%	11.9%	1.66	0.681	687
Large class instruction	39.3%	38.9%	21.8%	1.83	0.763	687
Classroom management	44.2%	41.8%	14.0%	1.70	0.701	694
Intellectual property	43.9%	39.8%	16.2%	1.72	0.725	708

Table 5.2 shows the respondents' level of interest in the more specific areas of faculty development (e.g., developing critical thinking skills, designing effective lectures, etc.). To further clarify levels of interest, faculty were asked to indicate their top three areas of interest (Appendix 5.1, question 11). A weighted frequency calculation shows that the strongest faculty interest is in facilitating effective classroom discussions. Helping students develop critical thinking and problem solving skills and incorporating active learning strategies were the second and third most appealing. Faculty are also highly interested in designing effective lectures and using technology to enhance learning. These data offer a strong indication of areas where the center should focus programming efforts. Furthermore, data from the focus groups revealed that it is the topic of a workshop or forum that motivates

faculty to attend, so the center wants to pay careful attention to offer activities in subject areas where faculty indicate strong interest.

TABLE 5.2
Weighted Frequency as Top Area of Interest in Specific Areas of Faculty Development

Area	Weighted Frequency
Other	13
Accommodating student disabilities/special needs	39
Designing a syllabus	43
Acquiring mid-course student feedback	51
Teaching first-year students	51
Working individually with students	53
Creating course packets	71
Designing service-learning activities	84
Evaluating student progress and assigning grades	84
Creating student learning outcomes	114
Providing feedback on student writing	116
Incorporating field-based/experiential learning	126
Designing assessment strategies	127
Accommodating diverse learning styles	129
Designing effective exams	139
Assessing student learning outcomes	143
Integrating communication skills	152
Developing effective assignments	185
Involving undergraduates in research	187
Optimizing group learning activities	197
Using technology to enhance learning	369
Incorporating active learning strategies	372
Designing effective lectures	388
Developing critical thinking/problem-solving skills	451
Facilitating effective classroom discussions	516

Effectiveness

Respondents were also asked to indicate their perception of the center's effectiveness (Appendix 5.1, question 12), with 15.2% of respondents (n = 119) indicating that our efforts are highly effective as shown in Table 5.3. The percentage of tenure-track and nontenure-track faculty who view the center as highly effective is statistically significantly greater when compared to tenured faculty members, $p \leq .011$. Correspondingly, when faculty rank is examined, assistant professors and instructors view the center as highly effective more frequently than do associate and full professors, $p < .001$.

TABLE 5.3
Center Effectiveness in Addressing Issues Related to Teaching and Learning

Those who marked:	n	Mean Years at Institution	SD	Mode
Not at all Effective	40	17.44	10.669	3, 18*
Somewhat Effective	346	11.91	9.731	1
Highly Effective	119	10.58	9.615	1
Don't Know/ Not Applicable	276	9.10	10.693	1

*Multiple modes

One concern is the 276 respondents (35.3%) who indicated "don't know/not applicable" and therefore do not know about the center's effectiveness or do not feel that the center's programming is applicable. This reveals that a significant number of faculty are not being reached through center services and activities to the point of forming an opinion about the center's effectiveness. The data indicate that the majority of these respondents are nontenure-track faculty. The center has not traditionally directed resources toward the development of nontenure-track faculty and changes are being initiated to address their unique needs.

Gender of the respondent also seems to play a role in the perception of the center's effectiveness. A statistically significantly greater proportion of females view the center as highly effective than do males, $p < .001$.

Further analysis of these data reveal that respondents who describe the center as highly or somewhat effective are in beginning to mid-career, based on mean years of service as shown in Table 5.4. The mean years of service of those who marked "don't know/not applicable" is somewhat lower. Faculty who have been at the institution for a longer period of time perceive the center to be less effective. While the reason for this finding is not known, we know that the faculty members who marked "not at all effective" likely had well-established careers long before the center's inception.

TABLE 5.4
Mean Years of Service at Institution and Center Effectiveness

Those who marked:	n	Mean Years at Institution	SD	Mode
Not at all Effective	40	17.44	10.669	3, 18*
Somewhat Effective	346	11.91	9.731	1
Highly Effective	119	10.58	9.615	1
Don't Know/ Not Applicable	276	9.10	10.693	1

*Multiple modes

Participation
As shown in Table 5.5, over 82% of faculty indicated that they would be somewhat or very likely to participate in workshops as their preferred type of teaching and learning activity (Appendix 5.1, question 13). Workshops are the center's traditional mode of delivery and faculty are accustomed to attending these, which may provide some explanation for the strong response. Other suggested types of faculty development activities may not have been as familiar to faculty and, therefore, received lower scores.

After workshops, respondents were most likely to participate in informal discussions with colleagues about teaching problems, tips, and techniques over coffee or lunch. Focus group participants concurred that they like the opportunity to interact with others whom they see infrequently; therefore, the center will continue to facilitate discussions surrounding teaching issues in informal settings and explore ways to build community through social activities.

Nearly 12% of respondents indicated that they participated in center events often (more than three times per year) and over 45% indicated occasionally (one to two times per year) (Appendix 5.1, question 15). Nearly 43% indicated that they do not participate in center events. The majority of those who indicated that they do not participate are a statistically significantly greater proportion of nontenure-track faculty, $p < .001$. Alternatively, tenure-track faculty participate in center events occasionally (one to two per year) and

Table 5.5
Likelihood for Participation in Types of Faculty Development Activities

Type of Activity	1) Not likely	2) Some-what likely	3) Very likely	Mean	SD	n
Individual consultation with center staff	42.7%	40.5%	16.8%	1.74	0.727	751
Classroom observations with feedback	42.9%	**41.6%**	15.5%	1.73	0.714	741
Small group activities	37.9%	**46.3%**	15.8%	1.78	0.699	736
Workshops	17.6%	41.2%	**41.1%**	2.23	0.730	754
University-wide forums	**46.6%**	38.6%	14.8%	1.68	0.717	741
Institutes/retreats	**66.1%**	26.0%	7.9%	1.42	0.634	734
Faculty development study group (in same discipline)	39.4%	40.5%	**20.2%**	1.81	0.748	749
Interdisciplinary faculty development study group	44.2%	39.0%	16.8%	1.73	0.732	751
Web-based resources and discussion groups	**46.3%**	38.4%	15.3%	1.69	0.722	750
Informal discussions with colleagues about teaching problems, tips, and techniques over coffee or lunch	25.5%	**44.8%**	**29.7%**	2.04	0.742	752
Structured discussions, focused around a reading provided prior to the meeting	45.3%	39.3%	15.4%	1.70	0.72	748

often (three or more per year) more than one would expect by chance, $p < .001$. The data also reveal that women participate in center events/activities more frequently than do men, $p < .005$. Additional analysis reveals that faculty who participate more regularly in center events and activities perceive the center to be more effective.

Communication

Respondents were asked to indicate the best ways for them to be notified of upcoming Center events by placing a checkmark next to the list of communication modes (Appendix 5.1, question 16). More than one box could be checked as a preferred method of contact. Seventy-four percent of respondents indicated that electronic mail is the preferred method of communication. Other methods, which are the center's traditional communication channels, include the center's newsletter (30.4%) and a flyer in the mail (29.8%). Another of the center's traditional modes of communication, notification through the department chairs, was indicated by only 8.8% of respondents. As a result, the center has greatly reduced use of this method when the message is intended for the general faculty population.

Excellence in Teaching

Nearly one-third of all respondents provided comments regarding how the institution can best achieve excellence in teaching (Appendix 5.1, question 17). The following salient themes emerged: 1) teaching should be more highly valued and rewarded at the institution, 2) faculty are severely stretched for time and they have to make time allocation decisions based on what they perceive to be the institution's priorities, and 3) support for the effectiveness of the center's services. One respondent captured the first two themes by writing,

> Our institution can achieve excellence in teaching by valuing and rewarding good teaching. The system is not set up to do so as it is. Research is what really counts; smart faculty know where to put their time and energy. People with a passion for teaching suffer.

While the data gathered from this question confirmed our observations and anecdotal evidence, the general nature of the question did not reveal any new information that informed the center's programming. Rather, these issues need to be addressed at the central administrative level because they necessitate broader cultural change at the institution.

Improving the Center's Services (Focus Group Results)

While responses on the survey highlighted a more general perspective about faculty development, the focus groups provided us with concrete suggestions that have allowed the center to more immediately make improvements in our services. Data obtained in focus group sessions indicated that a faculty member's main reason for participating in center events is that the subject matter topic is of interest to them. Faculty prefer to consult one-on-one with center staff if they are experiencing a teaching problem. There was no indication that faculty attend events because they are required to do so or that they attend to validate the quality of their teaching.

Another research question answered through the focus group process concerned how the center's services can be improved. One suggestion for improvement was that the center market its services better. The sentiment was the center is effective and provides valuable services, but more faculty should know about the variety of assistance provided. An email reminder of events was mentioned as a marketing tool. As a result of these comments, the center has developed a weekly e-newsletter. Over 600 faculty members voluntarily subscribed to receive the weekly "News & Tips" and have responded very favorably. Not only are faculty reminded of events via this communication method, but the center is able to promote the variety and range of its services. Each weekly tip includes a specific suggestion for a strategy to enhance learning with a web link to provide extended information.

Although the email notification appealed to faculty, the focus group participants did not favor a change to web-based faculty development to replace workshops and other events. They mentioned that interacting and learning from one another is what makes center events valuable and this would be lost through computer-based programming.

Another focus group suggestion, which the center has implemented, is the adoption of theme tracks. Focus group participants felt that a university-wide theme might unite all teaching training sessions for a given period of time and that an integrated curriculum, with sessions that build upon each other, might be offered for designated faculty members. As a result of these comments and survey findings, the center chose critical thinking as the theme for the 2002–2003 academic year. A workshop with a critical thinking topic has been held and the first fall newsletter announced the theme and provided a list of critical thinking resources for faculty. The center has continued to incorporate the critical thinking theme throughout its programming.

The center has expanded its services to include advisers and teaching assistants. While recognizing that these employees are not our primary audience, the center can provide services to support their teaching efforts. As one example, the center offered a teaching and learning circle in spring 2002 regarding the overlap of advising and teaching.

A gap in the center's impact on nontenure-track faculty was illuminated in this study. As background information, the university recently changed its classification system for adjunct and other nontenure-track faculty. In the past, nontenure-track faculty were seen as temporary hires; in fact, the center was discouraged from directing resources toward their professional development. However, beginning July 1, 2002, there was a change in classification titles for these faculty members, who are now called lecturers and clinicians. It is now generally recognized and accepted that these faculty members are hired to teach, and in many cases are the first faculty that our freshman students encounter. The center recognizes that, since our goal is to enhance student learning, we need to direct resources and programming for the benefit of non-tenure-track faculty.

The center has begun addressing the needs of this population by altering the fall orientation to be more inclusive so all faculty participate in similar programming. In addition, these faculty are now invited to apply for institutional grants and participate in all of the center's programming.

Other suggestions to improve the center included taking services directly to departments to make programming more discipline-specific. One respondent, in support of departmental-level training, stated that, "when it applies to elementary education it has absolutely nothing to do with engineering." Furthermore, "going to their house" was suggested as a solution for lack of faculty time to participate in center's activities. To encourage teaching development at the departmental level, the center initiated a small grants program (up to $1,000) for departmental activities related to teaching and learning. Sixteen applications were received and funding was awarded to 11 departments. Examples of how departments have used these funds included bringing in an outside expert to lead conversations about teaching issues, organizing a retreat for teaching faculty to develop a year-long series of teaching seminars, and developing a comprehensive learning outcomes assessment plan. The center will assist departments with funded projects based upon their specific needs and interests.

Another suggestion from the focus groups was that faculty who participate in center events should receive recognition. The center is considering sending a letter to the faculty member (with a copy to the department chair) acknowledging his or her participation. Some felt that this outcome would strengthen the value of center events.

An online registration system for center workshops and forums was another suggestion to help the center more easily and effectively manage user data while achieving greater client responsiveness. A personal follow-up letter would be more easily generated with an electronic download list of attendees.

Finally, the center has joined with the Office of the Provost to greatly enhance the orientation program for new tenure-track faculty. For the first time in fall 2002, a full day of programming was offered to address new faculty development and teaching needs. Programming was planned throughout the year for new faculty and a web site was developed to address their specific needs. The orientation event was well attended and program evaluations revealed that the attendees found it very valuable. Plans are underway for additional enhancements in the program for fall 2003.

Lessons Learned

Several lessons were learned with regard to the development and administration of both the quantitative and qualitative phases of the needs assessment project. Quantitative analysis of the data revealed several changes that would improve the usefulness of the survey. For instance, on four questions the respondents had a choice of "Don't know/Not applicable" (Appendix 5.1, questions 8, 9, 10, and 12). Data analysis indicates that it would have been preferable to separate these into two responses. For example, if a faculty member marked "Don't know/Not applicable" about service learning, we could not ascertain whether he or she did not know the definition of service learning, or whether it does not apply to his or her professional responsibilities.

The question in which respondents were asked to indicate which type of teaching and learning activities they would most likely attend was too narrow (Appendix 5.1, question 13). More specific options should have been provided regarding the types of activities that the center could facilitate, for example, a workshop series or peer review groups, and the preferred length of time that faculty would be willing to spend at these activities.

The question in which respondents were asked the frequency of participation in center events was also too narrow (Appendix 5.1, question 15). In retrospect, it would have been better to write the question to measure overall contact with center services (individual consultations, visits to the center library, etc.) and not just events and activities. In addition, the question was not time specific. Some respondents may have participated in three activities in one particular year and none in the next and therefore would not have been able to identify an appropriate response.

The specific research question to ascertain why faculty access center services should have been asked on the survey and not gathered from the focus group interviews. Different center services are accessed for different reasons, and we believe this would have been better measured on the quantitative portion of the project in a forced choice question.

The timing of the qualitative phase of the project could have been improved. The focus group sessions were held too late in the spring semester and recruiting faculty to participate proved to be difficult. Additional faculty participants could have increased the richness of the information obtained.

Conclusion

This faculty development needs assessment project has provided the center with high-quality data upon which to base programming decisions. It has energized the center's staff. It is rewarding to know that where we place our efforts and emphases aligns with faculty interest. It was affirming to learn that the faculty who use our services find our programming to be effective. Furthermore, due to the results, we have been able to focus our programming and our delivery strategies. We have also become more inclusive by more actively promoting our services to new faculty and to nontenure-track instructors. Planning the center's programming based upon faculty needs as expressed in the needs assessment project has resulted in increased participation and interest in center events.

Equipped with the breadth and depth of the information provided in this research project, the center's administration feel better prepared to meet the challenges that our center, and many others like us, face in today's uncertain environment. Budgets fluctuate and administrators come and go, but we feel that we are well positioned to move forward in a positive way—to help our institution, our faculty, and our students be successful in advancing learning.

References

Boice, R. (1997). What discourages research-practitioners in faculty development? *Higher Education: Handbook of Theory and Research, 12*, 371–435.

Chism, N. V. N., & Szabó, B, (1996). Who uses faculty development services? In L. Richlin & D. DeZure (Eds.), *To improve the academy: Vol. 15. Resources for faculty, instructional, and organizational development* (pp. 115–128). Stillwater, OK: New Forums Press.

Creswell, J. W. (2002). *Educational research: Planning, conducting, and evaluating quantitative and qualitative research.* Upper Saddle River, NJ: Merrill/Prentice Hall.

Engleberg, I. N. (1991). Needs assessment: The first step in staff development. *Journal of Staff, Program, and Organizational Development, 9*(4), 215–222.

Harnish, D., & Wild, L. A. (1992). Faculty speak: A way to assess the impact of professional development on instruction. *Journal of Staff, Program, and Organizational Development, 10*(1), 5–12.

Knowlton, L. M., & Ratliffe, S. A. (1992). Statewide staff development survey reveals trends and outcomes in California. *Journal of Staff, Program and Organizational Development, 10*(2), 111–116.

Travis, J. E., Hursh, D., Lankewicz, G., & Tang, L. (1996). Monitoring the pulse of the faculty: Needs assessment in faculty development programs. In L. Richlin & D. DeZure (Eds.), *To improve the academy: Vol. 15. Resources for faculty, instructional, and organizational development* (pp. 95–113). Stillwater, OK: New Forums Press.

Note and Acknowledgments

The full report of the needs assessment project and all appendices are available at http://www.cte.iastate.edu. The authors wish to thank the center's staff and RISE for their valuable contributions to this project.

Contact:

Pamela M. Milloy
Program Coordinator
Iowa State University
Center for Teaching Excellence
104 Lab of Mechanics
Ames, IA 50011
Voice (515) 294-4512
Fax (515) 294-8627
Email Pamela@iastate.edu

Corly Brooke
Director, Center for Teaching Excellence
Iowa State University
104 Lab of Mechanics
Ames, IA 50011
Voice (515) 294-2402
Fax (515) 294-8627
Email cbrooke@iastate.edu

Pamela M. Milloy recently completed her M.S. in higher education at Iowa State University and is a Program Coordinator at the Center for Teaching Excellence and the Office of the Vice Provost for Undergraduate Programs. Her scholarship includes topics such as faculty development needs assessment and service learning.

Corly Brooke is Director of the Center for Teaching Excellence and Associate Vice Provost for Undergraduate Programs at Iowa State University (ISU), as well as holding the academic rank of Professor of Human Development and Family Studies. She is Co-director of Learning Communities at ISU, and her scholarly work focuses on effective strategies for enhancement of learning in large classes and effective classroom management.

Appendix 5.1

The Center for Teaching Excellence (CTE) Needs Assessment Survey, Iowa State University

Please clearly mark or check the appropriate boxes below. Thank you!

1. Please indicate your academic rank.

   ☐ Full Professor ☐ Associate Professor ☐ Assistant Professor ☐ Instructor

2. Please indicate your tenure status.

   ☐ Tenured ☐ Tenure track ☐ Continuing Adjunct ☐ Nontenure track
   (e.g., adjunct, affiliate, temporary, or visiting)

3. Please indicate your gender.

   ☐ Female ☐ Male

4. Typically, how many credit hours do you teach at Iowa State University in an academic year (fall, spring, summer)? ________

5. How many years have you been teaching at the college level? ________

6. How many years have you been teaching at Iowa State? ________

7. How familiar are you with the services available through ISU's Center for Teaching Excellence (CTE)?

Very familiar	Somewhat familiar	Not at all familiar
☐	☐	☐

8. The CTE would like to provide various opportunities for faculty development. Which of the areas below would be of interest to you? Please mark the box that most closely matches your level of interest.

	Great interest	Some interest	Little or no interest	Don't know/ Not applicable
a. Scholarship of teaching and learning	☐	☐	☐	☐
b. Principles of student outcomes assessment	☐	☐	☐	☐
c. Developing teaching portfolios	☐	☐	☐	☐
d. Developing teaching-centered grant proposals	☐	☐	☐	☐
e. Activities designed for new faculty	☐	☐	☐	☐
f. Integrating service learning into the curriculum	☐	☐	☐	☐

g. Integrating communication skills across the curriculum (i.e., auditory, oral, visual, written)	☐	☐	☐	☐
h. Developing learning communities	☐	☐	☐	☐
i. Large class instruction	☐	☐	☐	☐
j. Classroom management	☐	☐	☐	☐
k. Intellectual property (e.g., copyright, plagiarism, Internet use)	☐	☐	☐	☐
l. Other ______________ (please specify)	☐	☐	☐	☐

Overall, how effective do you think the CTE has been in addressing issues of faculty development at ISU?

Highly effective	Somewhat effective	Not at all effective	Don't know/Not applicable
☐	☐	☐	☐

10. The CTE would like to assist faculty in various areas of course planning, student learning activities, and assessment strategies. Which of the areas below would be of interest to you? Please mark the box that most closely matches your interest.

Course Planning	Great interest	Some interest	Little or no interest	Don't know/ Not applicable
a. Designing a syllabus	☐	☐	☐	☐
b. Creating student learning outcomes	☐	☐	☐	☐
c. Creating course packets	☐	☐	☐	☐
d. Accommodating diverse learning styles	☐	☐	☐	☐
e. Accommodating student disabilities/ special needs	☐	☐	☐	☐
f. Developing effective assignments	☐	☐	☐	☐
Student Learning Activities				
g. Facilitating effective classroom discussions	☐	☐	☐	☐
h. Designing effective lectures	☐	☐	☐	☐
i. Incorporating active learning strategies	☐	☐	☐	☐
j. Incorporating field-based/experiential learning	☐	☐	☐	☐
k. Designing service-learning activities	☐	☐	☐	☐
l. Optimizing group learning activities	☐	☐	☐	☐
m. Integrating communication skills	☐	☐	☐	☐
n. Providing feedback on student writing	☐	☐	☐	☐

o. Using technology to enhance learning	☐	☐	☐	☐
p. Designing effective exams	☐	☐	☐	☐
q. Teaching first-year students	☐	☐	☐	☐
r. Involving undergraduates in research	☐	☐	☐	☐
s. Working individually with students	☐	☐	☐	☐
t. Developing critical thinking/ problem-solving skills	☐	☐	☐	☐
Assessment Strategies				
u. Designing assessment strategies	☐	☐	☐	☐
v. Assessing student learning outcomes	☐	☐	☐	☐
w. Acquiring mid-course student feedback	☐	☐	☐	☐
x. Evaluating student progress & assigning grades	☐	☐	☐	☐
y. Other ______________________ (please specify)	☐	☐	☐	☐

11. Of the items in question #10, please rank order the letters that represent your top three areas of interest:

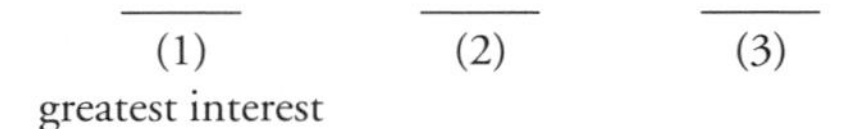
_____ (1) greatest interest   _____ (2)   _____ (3)

12. Overall, how effective do you think the CTE has been in addressing issues of teaching and learning on campus?

Highly effective	Somewhat effective	Not at all effective	Don't know/Not applicable
☐	☐	☐	☐

13. In which of the following types of teaching and learning activities would you be most likely to participate? Please mark the appropriate box.

	Very likely	Somewhat	Not likely
a. Individual consultation with CTE staff	☐	☐	☐
b. Classroom observations with feedback	☐	☐	☐
c. Small group activities	☐	☐	☐
d. Workshops (one meeting focused on a technique or strategy)	☐	☐	☐
e. University-wide forums	☐	☐	☐
f. Institutes/retreats (2–3 days)	☐	☐	☐

g. Faculty development study group (i.e., three or more faculty in the same discipline who meet regularly to discuss teaching issues) ☐ ☐ ☐

h. Interdisciplinary faculty development study group (i.e., three or more faculty in different disciplines who meet regularly to discuss teaching issues) ☐ ☐ ☐

i. Web-based resources and discussion groups (e.g., listserv/chat rooms) ☐ ☐ ☐

j. Informal discussions with colleagues about teaching problems, tips, and techniques over coffee or lunch ☐ ☐ ☐

k. Structured discussions, focused around a reading provided prior to the meeting (e.g., a teaching and learning circle) ☐ ☐ ☐

l. Other ____________________ (please specify) ☐ ☐ ☐

14. Of the items in question #13, please rank order the letters that represent your top three areas of interest:

____	____	____
(1) greatest interest	(2)	(3)

15. How often have you participated in CTE events or activities?

Often (3 or more/year)	Occasionally (1–2/year)	Not at all
☐	☐	☐

16. What is the best way for CTE to notify you of upcoming events? (Please check all that apply.)

☐ Newsletter ☐ Notified through DEO
☐ Email ☐ *Today's News* on the ISU home page
☐ Flyer in the mail ☐ CTE web site (http://www.cte.iastate.edu)
☐ Other ______________________________ (please specify)

17. General comments. Please let us know your opinions about how Iowa State University can best achieve excellence in teaching.

Thank you for participating in this survey! [Fold in half, staple, and mail.]

RISE
E005 Lagomarcino Hall

Section III

Curriculum Design and Evaluation

6

Color-Coded Course Design: Educating and Engaging Faculty to Educate and Engage Students

Marlene M. Preston
Virginia Polytechnic Institute and State University

In a weeklong seminar, "Course Design to Foster Student Engagement and Learning," faculty created course charts to reflect their various plans for an upcoming semester. With colorful Post-it Notes, they applied theoretical principles of course design. Participating in the kind of active environment they might want to create for students, faculty constructed their charts, rearranged the components to achieve balance across the semester, and discussed the plans with their colleagues. This case study includes the rationale for and description of "Color-Coded Course Design," a process that allows faculty to recognize and experience the power of an active classroom.

Many faculty have a tried-and-true approach to course design. They may use a straightforward, teacher-centered process of receiving a teaching assignment, choosing a book, creating assignments for the semester, and sprinkling in some tests for "good" measure! They move on to develop their lecture materials, pull together a syllabus, and march off to the first day of the semester. While curriculum designers may cringe, many faculty are comfortable with this approach, and they may be looking only for some superficial tweaking to spark their courses. In an attempt to find a tool that would create fundamental change in their design process, I developed a color-coded design process that challenges faculty to consider a wide range of interdependent course components. The following case study examines the goals, strategies, and outcomes for a faculty development activity designed to engage faculty in the same way that they should be engaging their students in the classroom.

The Goals of the Design Workshop

The context for this case study is the annual week-long workshop offered by the University Writing Program under the auspices of Virginia Tech's Center for Excellence in Undergraduate Teaching. This faculty development activity has been in place for ten years and has recently evolved from a set of activities devoted primarily to supporting faculty who are implementing writing intensive courses to a more comprehensive focus on course design. The logic of this change is that faculty members need to understand how a more holistic design framework could enhance student communication skills, promote student engagement, and foster intellectual development. The revised workshop would feature integration of student writing and speaking as part of the course plan—informal writing and speaking for processing new ideas, and formal writing and speaking for demonstration of mastery.

As I structured a week-long workshop, "Course Design to Foster Student Engagement and Learning," I considered many of the same components I would advocate to faculty for their consideration in course design: needs, goals, learners, content, environment, instructional strategies for delivery and processing, pacing, and assessment/demonstration of mastery.

In their applications for the workshop, faculty described their areas of interest. Most expressed a need to heighten student involvement in their classes. Some had recognized a gap between their current practice and the kind of student engagement they had either read about or heard about. In broader terms, I identified two gaps: 1) between their current practice and contemporary learning theory, and 2) between their personal experience as students and the experience they desired for their own students. Not only were they unfamiliar with the learning theory, but they also had not experienced active classrooms when they themselves were undergraduates. Especially at a research institution, some felt little incentive to risk stepping out of familiar teacher-centered design patterns.

As experts in the theory of their own disciplines, faculty would not necessarily be interested in studying the complexities of learning theory. My training in curriculum and instruction was important to them, and they would trust me to pass along the highlights; most were more interested in application. To capture their interest and meet that need, I had to develop a plan that would embed the theory and would produce concrete strategies for future course design.

To heighten interest in effective course design and student engagement, a learning environment was designed to make faculty feel safe enough to take risks, to experiment with their course designs, and to participate fully in the activities designed to promote learning and application of new strategies. The promotion of the workshop included the following information:

"We'll start with your course materials and consider the following as we meet each day:

1) Ways to organize those materials for maximum student attention and benefit

2) Approaches to classroom implementation that include student writing and speaking

3) Choices for efficient and meaningful assessment

By the end of our week together, you'll have a solid framework for your fall class."

The language was chosen to frame the workshop in a way that seemed familiar to faculty—promising to build on their existing materials and avoiding any mention of group activities or playfulness! Faculty would have to attend the workshop and build some trust before being asked to bond in base groups, share concerns and even mistakes, and work within the kind of climate they might eventually want to see in their classrooms—safe, but appropriately challenging.

Color-Coded Course Design Tool

The Color-Coded Course Design Tool became a vehicle to examine course planning at deep levels. The use of course-design charts with poster-sized graph paper and Post-it Notes created a colorful work environment, allowed faculty to rearrange course components, and fostered problem solving with peers. This approach to design extended what is offered in design texts and templates by providing a hands-on, collaborative environment that removed much of the abstractness inherent in design theory. Additionally, it was rooted in a faculty member's current design approach, rather than beginning with the curriculum designer's gap analysis based on the evaluation of multiple facets.

The Color-Coded Course Design Tool evolved from a simple chart I had developed earlier to discuss pacing for the semester. I had created this chart as a graphic to support my discussions with faculty about the differences between semesters with a mid-semester break and those with a late semester break. My colleague, Margaret Hable, a consultant with our Center for Excellence in Undergraduate Teaching, suggested that we transfer my chart to poster-board for each participant with exhibits of these boards around the room. After considerations of portability and costs, I searched for chart-sized graph paper that we could easily hang on the walls. With Post-it-style graph paper secured, an undergraduate student set to work creating a chart for each participant to reflect either fall or spring semester. She marked the dates of the semester along the horizontal axis at the top, including breaks and exams (see Table 6.1). She did *not* fill in the topics that faculty would eventually consider in the left column. Faculty added those topics as we moved from one concept to the next during the workshop.

TABLE 6.1

Partial Course Design Template for Fall Semester

Course Components	**8/26 Week 1**	**9/2 Week 2**	**9/9 Week 3**	**9/16 Week 4**	**9/23, etc.**
1) Content—pink					
2) Delivery—turquoise					
3) Assignments—blue					
4) Tests and quizzes—red					
5) Environment and motivation—green					
6) Processing—yellow					
7) Mastery—purple					
8) Skills—orange					
9) Other?					

DESIGN OF THE WORKSHOP

The week's design included attention to content, collegiality, and comfort for faculty as they would be urged to shift from a teacher-centered design process to a more learner-centered design process. We planned to provide brief presentations about learning theory and assignment design, much time for faculty conversation with colleagues and attention to their own course designs, and a pleasant setting. Rather than trying to teach all the concepts related to course design, we wanted faculty to be aware of concepts, feel the power of the activities, identify useful strategies for their own courses, and find resources for further investigation. Any presentation about learning theory or course design principles was brief and followed by some individual or group activity.

We used a large dining room with round tables, sufficient wall space for the wall charts, and flexible work and eating space. Our caterer decided on ethnic foods from various countries—a theme for each day—and we planned reminders for faculty to think about the diversity in their classrooms as we "visited" a different country each day. Overall, we planned for an experience that would be friendly and productive.

Faculty were assigned to base groups comprised of faculty in similar disciplines. These groups were used as a starting point each day although other configurations were also made—groups of faculty teaching the same age students or teaching in the same types of classrooms (lab, large lecture, seminar). Faculty moved into these groups to gain multiple perspectives as various topics arose.

At each table, faculty found their personal materials and "table copies" of various resources. Each participant received gifts: a journal (a classic composition book with the marbled black-and-white cover) for reflection writing, a copy of John Bean's *Engaging Ideas* (1996), and a folder in which to collect handouts or notes. Over the course of the week, faculty were asked to do informal writing in their composition books, to read specific sections in the main text, and to review table copies of other texts. These texts included numerous books related to student writing and college teaching:

*The Craft of Scientific Writing (*Alley, 1996)

A WAC Casebook (Anson, 2002)

Knowing and Reasoning in College (Baxter-Magolda, 1992)

Making Their Own Way (Baxter-Magolda, 2001)

New Paradigms for College Teaching (Campbell & Smith, 1997)

Teaching Within the Rhythms of the Semester (Duffy & Jones, 1995)

The Course Syllabus (Grunert, 1997)

The Transition to College Writing (Hjortshoj, 2001)

Active Learning (Johnson, Johnson, & Smith, 1998)

How Writing Shapes Thinking (Langer & Applebee, 1987)

Writing to Learn (Sorcinelli & Elbow, 1997)

Grading Students' Classroom Writing (Speck, 2000)

Helping Students Write Well (Walvoord, 1986)

*Thinking and Writing in College (*Walvoord & McCarthy, 1990)

The texts not only supported the week's work, but also gave faculty a glimpse of the resources available for their use in our teaching center and writing program. Faculty reviews were written on index cards, discussed in base groups, and compiled by the end of the week for everyone's use.

Beginning With the Known: Teacher-Centered Design Decisions

To begin work with the Color-Coded Course Design Tool, each participant received a poster-sized chart already marked with the weeks of the semester and a multicolored collection of Post-it Notes. Faculty labeled the charts with their names and courses and then proceeded to label and complete the first four rows of the chart, reflecting an existing plan for the semester. Thus, the activity opened in a faculty comfort zone—a teacher-centered starting point—but one that affirmed prior knowledge and acknowledged faculty as experts, people who would be contributing their expertise to the workshop along with the presenters. This also served as somewhat of a diagnostic activity because it revealed any determination to cover material even if the time was inadequate for student activity and processing. Attention to prior knowledge and expectations would also be the first consideration we would want faculty to make concerning their own students.

Row 1: Course content. To start with material the faculty knew well, our first topic of discussion was content. Faculty were asked to bring six to eight main topics/concepts/ideas to the first day's meeting. They were also asked to review the course description (which some faculty admitted they had never read before), and to bring any course goals they had established or prior syllabi. On one color of Post-it, they listed one topic on each note and then arranged the topics on the chart as they might be taught across the semester. We acknowledged their expertise in this area and didn't presume to suggest any rearrangement of topics, nor did we limit the number of topics, even though some faculty couldn't reduce the number to eight.

Row 2: Delivery of information. Again, as a point of familiarity, faculty listed their delivery strategies on a second color of Post-its, and positioned these notes across the row. Many notes listed "lecture" in every block across the row. A few included notes about individual student or group presentations designed to teach course content to the class.

Row 3: Assignments. Reflecting an existing course or a typical plan, faculty used a third color note for any reading assignments, graded homework, and writing or speaking assignments. They effortlessly sprinkled these assignments across the row with some kind of formula, such as homework every week, writing every three weeks, and maybe an oral presentation at the end of the semester.

Row 4: Tests and quizzes. Still building on their typical plans, faculty then used a fourth color Post-it to depict a pattern of quizzes and tests to coincide with the topics and assignments.

When they had finished rows one through four of their charts, faculty posted their charts around the room and seemed confident that they had already mastered the art of course design. Some probably figured the course planning had been accomplished, and we should move on to writing a syllabus.

Learner-Centered Instructional Considerations

However, we then moved on to strategies that enhance motivation, engagement, and long-term learning. Beginning at this point in the workshop, faculty were encouraged to reexamine their assumptions about course design.

Row 5: Environment and motivation. We began to discuss various aspects of motivation and classroom/campus climate, including prior knowledge, individual differences, student goals, predictable distractions, and student energy. Focusing on the need for individuals to feel connected and safe, we discussed ways to build community, to create an atmosphere in which students are not afraid to experiment and take risks. Based on the work of Duffy and Jones (1995), we talked with faculty about the predictable cycles of the semester that should be considered as part of course planning:

- Early Semester: Set context. Assess skills, expectations, and prior knowledge. Build community.
- Mid-Semester: Maintain interest. Balance the routine and the surprise. Build skills and content mastery. Alternate presenters of course content. Weeks two through 12 most useful for presentation, processing, application of new material.
- Late Semester: Wind down. Summarize. Articulate connections of course material to other courses. Encourage student reflection.

We assigned a fifth color for these considerations, and faculty added notes to their course charts. They were encouraged to plan time during the first weeks of class to capitalize on student interest and energy, to identify prior knowledge, and to help students set goals. They were reminded that even in our workshop, we had immediately established base groups to help participants connect with colleagues. We considered the placement of semester breaks, weather, mid-week football games, seniors who are interviewing, and freshmen who are homesick. While we may not appreciate the fact that a football game or fraternity rush distracts our students, we suggested that faculty at least consider their impact on the learning environment. Faculty were also urged to plan time for reflection at the end of the semester.

As faculty acknowledged the "dead" times during the semester and the futility of addressing content when students are exhausted, they broke into groups based on the level of students in their classes. Without regard for discipline, they shared observations and solutions related to their freshmen, sophomores, juniors, or seniors. They discussed ways to engage their students and protect themselves during times when students were not likely to be responsive.

When they approached their charts with the fifth row of notes, they were forced to rearrange some earlier notes. If the first week of the class would be used for community building and consideration of students' prior knowledge, that first topic in the Row 1 (content) had to move to week two. If the semester had only a late break, such as a fall break at Thanksgiving, faculty had to reconsider the amount of content they could present to fatigued students during the week before Thanksgiving and in the week between Thanksgiving and exams.

While this row became somewhat of a catch-all, these discussions seemed to create the most fundamental change in the ways faculty thought about student learning and course pacing. By this point in the workshop, faculty were beginning to experience the power of their work in teams and the advantages of consulting with one another.

Row 6: Processing. How do students learn? How do they move from the lecture to the exam to the long-term acquisition of information? Faculty discussed their own strategies for learning and ways to help students understand new concepts and make meaning for themselves. We also discussed students' ways of knowing, based on the work of Marcia Baxter-Magolda (1992 & 2001) and the developmental levels at which students are ready to undertake various levels of complexity and uncertainty. Faculty were somewhat familiar with the literature on learning styles, and this discussion of processing helped them consider ways to provide multiple types of experiences of students. We began to consider the ways in which faculty can support students as they process new material, connect it to concepts they already know, recognize its value, and consider its useful application.

Faculty reviewed the homework assignments (Row 3), and considered alternatives to straight-recall questions about the content of a chapter. We challenged faculty to incorporate opportunities for cooperative learning so that students could learn the value of interdependence and enriched problem solving.

We considered the literature related to informal writing and speaking, and asked faculty to build in opportunities for reflection writing, journals, impromptu speeches, group discussion—any activity that would allow students to communicate their understandings and questions to others. Bean's (1996) text was especially useful in the consideration of groups and informal writing. On a sixth color of Post-it Notes, faculty planned these activities across the semester.

Row 7: Demonstrating mastery. Once students have processed new ideas, of course, they should have the opportunity to demonstrate their mastery of those ideas. Faculty were asked to review assignments in Row 3 and the tests and quizzes listed in Row 4 and to consider alternate ways for students to demonstrate mastery. For example, a group presentation could replace a test and a week of lecture on a topic. At this point in the workshop, we discussed assignment development and formal writing and speaking. As coordinator of the University Writing Program, I had the sense that faculty had previously heard enough from me about the power of writing in their courses, so we invited a guest presenter to discuss the development, implementation, and assessment of formal writing assignments. Faculty found the sections in *Engaging Ideas* (Bean, 1996) to be particularly helpful regarding feedback on student papers and managing the paper load. On a seventh color of Post-it Notes, faculty added notes about formal assignments, including attention to the timeframe for outlines and drafts.

In terms of more traditional tests, we reminded faculty about the need for valid assessments that matched the course goals. We provided other campus resources to address specific assessment questions.

We also reminded faculty to plan time for thorough evaluation of student work so that students were not asked to turn in subsequent papers before previous papers or essay exams had been graded. Again, faculty adjusted Post-it Notes on various rows of their course charts to allow for better feedback to students. (Later a faculty member noted that she needed to line up the course charts for each of her courses so that she didn't set herself up to grade major assignments from different courses at the same time.)

Row 8: Skill-building. Once the course components seemed set, faculty were asked to consider student skills. Did students have the skills to write a research paper, present a group discussion, use Blackboard or PowerPoint? We reminded faculty to consider student preparation for these assignments. Had students received formal instruction on the use of the library or the processes for group problem solving? Faculty needed to plan time to ascertain student skills and/or teach some of these processes before they could expect students to perform well.

As faculty added the eighth color of Post-It Note for lessons in information literacy, writing process, or oral presentations, they found themselves shifting other Post-its to create time for these "extra" lessons.

Reconsideration of Course Components

As faculty completed the rows of their course charts, the room was festooned with colorful displays of their work. They were invited to explore the designs colleagues were working on, and there was much discussion as faculty problem solved with partners about the fit of certain course components. Over the course of the week, we had invited guest faculty to join us for lunch and to discuss their successes with course design and student writing. Conversations with other participants and with faculty "experts" who visited the workshop had sparked some new ideas about content and strategies.

Now that they had a concrete picture of the semester, faculty struggled to fit everything in, shifting Post-it Notes on various rows. Some reviewed their content delivery plans and sought to reduce the lecture time. Some asked for more information about case studies as they considered incorporating group work on cases. Others were planning to use student oral or written presentations to deliver content.

Other participants added further rows for considerations unique to their own courses. Some created a row of color to show time necessary for feedback and processing of student work so that they could better balance these demands with other components. Others created a row for group processes and products so that they could see the timeline for the development of a group project, including instruction about groups and group meeting time in class so that faculty could monitor progress.

Syllabus Design

Although some faculty had wanted to move to syllabus design early in the week, we cautioned them not to lock into a syllabus until they felt sure they had considered all of the facets of their courses. Finally, we reviewed syllabi components, shared various models, and attempted to see what students see when they read a syllabus. On each table was a copy of *The Course Syllabus: A Learning-Centered Approach* (Grunert, 1997), which we had referred to during the week and which most faculty had at least perused by the end of the week. The creation of a syllabus, however, would be completed once faculty left the workshop.

Faculty Response

Faculty offered positive feedback about the workshop, but some of them had to be won over as the workshop progressed. Some faculty seemed to hold onto the notion that learning can't be fun. They seemed suspicious of activities that created movement in the room, group conversation, or even laughter. Clearly they were used to and most comfortable with a lecture format. However, most began to come around to the warmth of the environment, greeting base groups as they would old friends, offering to mentor others, and even dressing for the country represented by the lunch of the day! Many hallmarks of learning communities emerged—shared work in a shared space, interdependence, inside jokes, and course design charts as artifacts. Faculty also began bringing their own favorite resources to share with groups, such as web sites for case studies and lists of grammar reminders.

Participants returned again and again to the rows on their charts, rearranging and often deleting as they examined the match of the content with course goals and student needs for long-term learning. They came to trust their colleagues and solicit their advice when they were struggling with competing course components.

Of course, there was one exception who repeatedly claimed that the concepts did not apply in his course. His body language and side comments to those at his table nearly undermined the work of that group. He even finished the week with a harangue to the presenters and fellow participants about the "touchy-feely" nature of the activities. Of course, he had declined to participate in most of them, so certainly he experienced no transformation. Amazingly, once the workshop was over, he contacted another participant (in a different discipline from his own) and asked for assistance with his course. The workshop setting was apparently too public for him, but he did attend each day and then finally created his own support system to work on course design and instructional strategies.

As the workshop drew to a close, faculty were already considering applications for the design tool. One person asked about using the Color-Coded Course Design Tool with graduate students to give them a "picture" of the semester; others were considering office walls upon which to hang the charts while they continued to experiment with the arrangement of the Post-it Notes. Others were squirreling away pockets full of Post-it Notes so that they could use them later when they worked on their course charts. Many faculty borrowed books from our center's library so that they could further explore some of the concepts we had introduced.

At the end of the workshop, faculty feedback was positive. One faculty member asked permission to do a mini-workshop to share the strategy with her colleagues in career services. Participants immediately used the tool after the workshop. One found application in her study-abroad course in Australia:

> Here I am "down under" with the students studying information technology, and we are having a ball. I used the ideas from the workshop to design the writing assignment we are using—the workshop was just wonderful. I will be using all the ideas as I continue work on the new course I am teaching this fall, but I did want you to know that the workshop had an immediate impact on me for the Study Abroad.

Other comments included the following:

> My charts are on the wall of my office and I'm referring to them religiously. I feel completely inspired for the fall; this was the best thing that ever happened to me as a teacher.

> My colleagues are so impressed by the accounts I give and the stunning Post-it plan that they've asked me to summarize the workshop for them at a faculty development meeting in a couple of weeks. I benefited from reviewing the main ideas again, and several of the other teachers expressed interest in attending the next workshop!

> I believe it shows that you can teach an old dog new tricks, as I learned several things I intend to try out in the fall.

> My class prep is going wonderfully. Yours is the best workshop I have ever been to . . . in terms of applying knowledge to real-life stuff.

> I am continuing to work on my Post-it plan. It has been extremely helpful for me. I am a visual learner, so this was a great way for me to see how it will come together for the semester.

After the May workshop, faculty were invited to a reunion during fall semester so that they could share successes and problems—especially any new complexities that arose because of a course-design decision. Although the reunion meeting was held in October, one participant came in his beach T-shirt and sandals, wanting to recall the warm days of May when we worked together on course design. (Yes, he's the one who dressed in ethnic costume for the meals, too.) Faculty discussed their use of the plan, their need for more wall space in their offices, and the "mistakes." For example, one faculty member scheduled a test the morning after a mid-week football game. Although he admitted that he wouldn't have considered this previously, he ended up moving the test because he realized that he could have avoided the problem had he checked that calendar to begin with. Another had planned a final week of the semester for reflection and review so that students could put her course into perspective.

Application

The Color-Coded Course Design Tool could work for any course across a broad range of disciplines. Titles of rows, colors of Post-its, activities, and resource materials might easily be shifted to match the goals of various audiences.

While it was used in this workshop with experienced faculty, it could also be useful with beginning teachers or graduate students, those who have not yet developed a "picture" of the entire semester based on their own experience. One faculty member suggested that she might ask her graduate students to map out their learning plans for the semester in the same way she was mapping out her teaching plan.

Once the group experience has been accomplished, an individual could certainly shift the chart into a spreadsheet and could move course components electronically. More sophisticated technology could also build on the basics as determined in the initial design. As we prepare for the next iteration of this workshop, we have identified an instructional technology consultant who will work with the participants on individual plans.

Conclusion

The Color-Coded Course Design Tool allowed faculty to graphically represent the various course activities across a semester, identify activities competing for student or faculty time, experiment as they rearranged components, and experience the energy of an active classroom as they interacted with each other to develop and polish their products. As faculty were led into a realm of design they may not have previously considered—the learner-centered design considerations—they were essentially forced to review their previous teacher-centered design decisions. One participant wrote for our center's newsletter:

> When I first learned of this workshop, the title appealed to me because I was looking for a way to restructure the design of some of my courses. So, when I signed up, I was focusing on the "Course Design" aspect, and regarding "Student Engagement" as a sort of subplot. However, the weeklong workshop demonstrated that without sufficient student engagement, even the most efficient course design is rather a waste of time. Student engagement both in and out of the classroom is now the core goal for all my classes, and the jumping-off point for my course design, rather than an after-thought (Carroll, 2002).

The exact building blocks and colors of the chart as explained here are not as important as faculty's growing recognition that effective course design is a complex puzzle, demanding attention to student engagement in the learning process.

References

Alley, M. (1996). *The craft of scientific writing.* New York, NY: Springer-Verlag.

Anson, C. (2002). *A WAC casebook: Scenes for faculty reflection and program development.* New York, NY: Oxford University Press.

Baxter-Magolda, M. (1992). *Knowing and reasoning in college.* San Francisco, CA: Jossey-Bass.

Baxter-Magolda, M. (2001). *Making their own way: Narratives for transforming higher education to promote self-development.* Sterling, VA: Stylus.

Bean, J. (1996). *Engaging ideas: The professor's guide to integrating writing, critical thinking and active learning in the classroom.* San Francisco, CA: Jossey-Bass.

Campbell, W. E., & Smith, K. A. (1997). *New paradigms for college teaching.* Edina, MN: Interaction.

Carroll, K. (2002, Fall). Faculty design courses to engage students—University Writing Program Annual Workshop. *Virginia Tech Center for Excellence in Undergraduate Teaching Newsletter,* 6.

Duffy, K., & Jones, J. (1995). *Teaching within the rhythms of the semester.* San Francisco, CA: Jossey-Bass.

Grunert, J. (1997). *The course syllabus: A learning-centered approach.* Bolton, MA: Anker.

Hjortshoj, K. (2001). *The transition to college writing.* Boston, MA: Bedford-St. Martin's.

Johnson, D. W., Johnson, R. T., & Smith, K. A. (1998). *Active learning: Cooperation in the college classroom.* Edina, MN: Interaction.

Langer, J. A., & Applebee, A. N. (1987). *How writing shapes thinking.* Urbana, IL: National Council of Teachers of English.

Sorcinelli, M. D., & Elbow, P. (Eds.). (1997). Writing to learn: Strategies for assigning and responding to writing across the disciplines. *New Directions for Teaching and Learning, No. 69.* San Francisco, CA: Jossey-Bass.

Speck, B. W. (2000). Grading students' classroom writing: Issues and strategies (ASHE-ERIC Higher Education Report, 27[3]). Washington, DC: George Washington University, Graduate School of Education and Human Development.

Walvoord, B. E. (1986). *Helping students write well: A guide for teachers in all disciplines.* New York, NY: The Modern Language Association.

Walvoord, B. E., & McCarthy, L. P. (1990). *Thinking and writing in college: A naturalistic study of students in four disciplines.* Urbana, IL: National Council of Teachers of English.

Contact:

Marlene M. Preston
Coordinator, University Writing Program
Assistant Director, Center for Excellence in Undergraduate Teaching
105 Hillcrest
Virginia Tech
Blacksburg, VA 24060
Voice (540) 231-9832
Email mpreston@vt.edu

Marlene M. Preston is Coordinator of the University Writing Program at Virginia Tech. She also serves as Assistant Director of the Center for Excellence in Undergraduate Teaching and offers faculty development workshops related to curriculum design and the development of student discourse. As a faculty member in the Department of Communication, she serves as Course Director for Communication Skills I and II, a freshman sequence that she designed to foster student writing and speaking skills. She helped to establish a campus speaking center for students, CommLab, and participates in the university's Learning Communities Initiative.

7

From SGID and GIFT to BBQ: Streamlining Midterm Student Evaluations to Improve Teaching and Learning

Margaret K. Snooks
Sue E. Neeley
Kathleen M. Williamson
University of Houston-Clear Lake

Faculty members want feedback about ways to improve learning. Midterm assessments are more useful than end-of-term student evaluations. Not all institutions provide faculty development consultants. This chapter presents an innovative process appropriate for institutions currently without teaching enhancement centers. The Bare Bones Questions (BBQ) process consists of empathic trained colleagues facilitating students' evaluative discussions. Students and faculty members are overwhelmingly positive about the process piloted for the past three years. Students' suggestions can include simple changes in classroom environment or enhanced sensitivity to cultural diversity. BBQ may build intra-institutional collegiality by reducing the isolation of teaching.

Not all institutions support faculty development centers, but their faculty want to improve student learning. This chapter presents an innovative, collegial-based approach to midterm student evaluations that can be available to faculty members without access to trained development specialists. Our innovation, Bare Bones Questions, or BBQ, was developed specifically from faculty development research including the venerable Small Group Instructional Diagnosis (SGID) (Redmond & Clark, 1982) technique of the 1980s and the Group Instructional Feedback Technique (GIFT) (Angelo & Cross, 1993) of the 1990s. The Bare Bones Questions process has been piloted and modified for six long semesters. Making this collegial process viable at an institution may reduce the isolation of college teaching and encourage administrators to fund faculty development centers.

The Value of Midterm Consultation and Student Feedback

Faculty development literature provides valuable insight into ways of improving teaching and learning. Models include classroom observations with feedback from trained consultants. Teaching, evaluated for the purpose of enhancement, is dramatically improved as evidenced by scores on student ratings (Brinko & Menges, 1997). Instructional consultation often involves four basic components: the initial contact, a pre-visit conference, information collection in a classroom, and a feedback session when problems are diagnosed and solutions explored. Teachers report faculty development consultation is beneficial for many years.

But what exists for faculty members without access to faculty development experts? Most institutions offer structured end-of-semester student evaluations, but their usefulness for improving teaching and learning is questionable. Many standardized questionnaires purport to measure teaching but apply only a few dimensions using Likert-scale responses. "Teachers have every right to be demoralized by such a simplistic approach—the nuances of teaching cannot possibly be captured this way" (Palmer, 1998, p. 143). A study of student satisfaction with end-of-course-student-ratings (ECSR) discovered student dislike of ECSR forms because responses cannot be explained and questions are repetitive (Wulff, Staton-Spicer, Hess, & Nyquist, 1985). Students did not believe ECSR comments were taken seriously or were used to improve teaching. Students were most satisfied with methods that resulted in instructors using their feedback to make changes during a semester, so they could benefit promptly from suggestions. Students also preferred expressing their opinions orally during group interaction. The authors concluded that the most useful data reflects the unique complexity and context of each individual classroom. Other faculty development experts recognize that end-of-term evaluations offer few solutions for instructors and may be denigrated by students since a course is basically finished by the time students do their evaluations.

Small Group Instructional Diagnosis

Small Group Instructional Diagnosis was developed by D. Joseph Clark at the University of Washington as an alternative to both end-of-semester student evaluations and expensive, elaborate, and more time-consuming faculty consultation procedures (Redmond & Clark, 1982). The SGID process consists of five steps. First is an initial conference with a consultant where instructors explain their teaching style and interests. Next comes the classroom visit. The instructor introduces the consultant and leaves. Singly or in small groups, students answer three questions: 1) What do you like about the course? 2) What do you think needs improvement? 3) What suggestions do you have for bringing about these improvements? After about ten minutes, the consultant brings the whole class together and requests the most important answers. These are written and given to the instructor. At their next conference, instructor and consultant discuss alternative approaches to the class and what the instructor might say to students at the next class meeting. In step four, the instructor uses about ten minutes to clarify student opinion, respond to student feedback, and summarize intended changes. The final step is a follow-up conference with the consultant later in the semester to discuss the success of the changes. The authors suggest the main advantages of SGID are effectiveness, it takes only 30 minutes of class time, and both instructors and students react positively to the experience.

Coordinators, faculty members, and students rated SGID superior to end-of-semester evaluation questionnaires. SGID students showed a significantly higher level of motivation. "These results . . . indicate that students who had the opportunity to voice their concerns at midterm were more favorably disposed to the instructor's efforts, with a resulting change in their motivational output toward the end of the course" (Redmond & Clark, 1982, p. 10). SGID was endorsed as the principal method of formative classroom assessment even for mature, tenured faculty (Bennett, 1987). It was used for fine-tuning teaching, assessing textbook and instructional changes, investigating problems, and improving classroom climate. The instructor's return session with students is a unique teaching opportunity for now very receptive students. Students, accustomed to receiving rather than contributing, report that ". . . their appreciation is profound when dialogue places them in an active role" (Bennett, 1987, p. 103).

Consultants at the University of Michigan's Center for Research on Learning and Teaching (CRLT) added "collecting small-group feedback from students" to their existing consulting process (Black, 1998). Elaborate training sessions for consultant-facilitators include reading, practicing data recording and giving feedback, videotaping, and role-playing. SGID is used for consulting with teaching assistants, new faculty members, experienced faculty who are developing new courses or encountering a difficult group of students, departmental development programs, and any faculty members who want to improve teaching. According to Black, a disadvantage is SGID takes a lot of time, at least four hours, for both consultant and instructor, but all who use SGID learn an incredible amount about teaching.

Group Instructional Feedback

In higher education literature, an SGID-like process, titled Group Instructional Feedback Technique, appears as one of 50 classroom assessment techniques (Angelo & Cross, 1993). GIFT is referenced in a section on "Techniques for Assessing Learner Reactions to Instruction." Teacher evaluations are used for reappointments and tenure and promotion, but few help faculty improve their teaching. GIFT was designed to "capitalize on the ability of groups to give more comprehensive and useful feedback than individuals" (Angelo & Cross, 1993, p. 321). Student feedback is a GIFT in two senses of the word: Instructors get organized data filtered through a detached but sympathetic information gatherer. GIFT differs only slightly from SGID. A visiting assessor asks previously agreed-upon precisely worded questions. Students take three to four minutes to write answers alone and another three to four minutes to compare answers with others. Common responses are put on the board and students are asked to raise hands to indicate percentage agreement. When comparing GIFT in terms of cost in time and energy, the authors rank it "medium" for faculty preparation and student response, and "medium to high" for faculty analysis of collected data. Modified questions are:

> What aspects of the course assist you in learning? What aspects of the course environment hinder your learning? Give some suggestions to improve the learning environment of the course. Has this course been what you expected when you signed up for it? Explain. (Santanello & Eder, 2001, p. 6)

The authors emphasize a pre-classroom visit so a colleague will know as much as possible about a course in advance, including items the "host professor" wants investigated and what areas they do not want discussed. The feedback session is "a sharing of pedagogical techniques and experiences to be followed by a thoughtful and scholarly written report to the host professor" (Santanello & Eder, 2001, p. 7).

DEVELOPMENT AND PILOTING OF BBQ

Our interest in midterm student evaluations came from a faculty-initiated discussion group called Learning Innovators. BBQ is both faculty directed and administered. Our provost recently began funding formation of a Teaching-Learning Enhancement Center. His support is partially due to faculty members' persevering efforts to improve teaching and learning. BBQ was developed because we were interested in improving teaching but lacked access to consultants. Our first innovation was making the process collegial; we had to rely on each other rather than on faculty development experts. Our work somewhat resembles peer partner programs (Morrison, 1997).

After reviewing faculty development research, we drew the most salient parts of SGID and GIFT and shaped them to fit our faculty and institution. Our primary model, SGID, was developed to shorten the time consultants spent arriving at solutions for faculty members (Redmond & Clark, 1982). Time is an issue for all faculty members, as well as for consultants. BBQ is designed to provide maximum amounts of valid and useful information for faculty at the least possible cost in time, since most who teach feel overwhelmed by expectations for preparing and teaching classes, attending meetings, performing service, conducting research, writing, and publishing.

A second innovation involved streamlining the process. The first fall we followed a traditional SGID model, including the pre-visit conference focusing on "host" faculty members' concerns. This took at least 30 minutes. We arrived at the beginning of a three-hour class, and were introduced as a fellow teacher observing class who would then facilitate a group evaluation at the end. We observed and wrote down observations until 30 minutes remained in the class period. The instructor left the room and SGID began. Students were divided into small groups of three to four, and each group given a sheet of paper with three questions and about three inches of space for answers below each question. Each group answered the following questions: What does this instructor do in this class that helps you learn? What hinders your learning in this class? What are one or two specific suggestions of ways to improve your learning in this class? After about 15 minutes, when the conversational buzz was almost gone, we took the entire class through all three questions again, asking each group to report what was most important. Group answers were written on the blackboard, class consensus confirmed on each statement. A student copied answers off the board as discussion was facilitated. Students were thanked for their input, groups' written answers were gathered up, and class dismissed. The typing of observations and student feedback took at least four hours. Additionally, there was the time for the follow-up visit with colleagues to relate students' answers. The host-instructor was always delighted with very useful student input, but the process took facilitating colleagues at least eight hours or the equivalent of one full day of work. Clearly, this process was too time-consuming for even the most accommodating and empathic colleague to take on in addition to existing teaching duties.

To save time, the following spring we eliminated the pre-visit conference between instructor and colleague-facilitator and asked the same three questions in every class. We shortened classroom observation and scripting to an hour, but the process was still too costly in time. In the next iteration, classroom observation was eliminated and we simply facilitated student discussions in the last 30 minutes of class after instructors left the room. This was doable from a busy faculty member's perspective and still produced rich, useful data. Students continued to be overwhelmingly positive about the process and even asked us to come into other classes. We explained we only come at the invitation of faculty members. Students are awed by the fact that their instructors are interested in student suggestions. We named the process BBQ for Bare Bones Questions. It is too attenuated to be a true SGID but more organized and collegial than GIFT. We demonstrated our innovation at two teaching conferences that summer and fall.

Demand for BBQ services soon outstripped time available since we all carry full-time teaching loads. This led to yet another innovation we call "collegial training." Training consists of three parts: 1) A faculty member observes the BBQ process facilitated in a colleague's classroom with permission of the colleague, 2) BBQ is carried out in the new colleague's class by an experienced facilitator, and 3) the "new" colleague then facilitates BBQ in another colleague's classroom. In one and one-half hours, instructors learn about the process through observation, by receiving information about their own classes, and by facilitating BBQ for a colleague. A new BBQ facilitator colleague can now be added to the list. The second fall we accomplished 13 BBQs, including both graduate and undergraduate classes. We covered all teaching time slots—morning, afternoon, and night. Each semester more faculty members become involved. BBQ is truly a bare bones question process since we have pared down the time faculty spend, but they can still discover what students believe will improve their learning. Information comes in time for faculty members to make course changes in response to student suggestions. We are not trained faculty development consultants; we are colleagues trying to help each other improve student learning. Our recommendations for implementing BBQ can benefit faculty members at institutions lacking faculty development centers.

RECOMMENDATIONS FOR IMPLEMENTATION OF BBQ

The Bare Bones Question process, or BBQ, is most useful when it takes place about midterm, while there is still time to make changes in a course. BBQ should take place after a major grade is given to students, for example, about two weeks after a major test. If colleagues hear about BBQ, but are not sure about having it done, we encourage them to observe the process in a colleague's class with that colleague's permission. Coordination between "host instructor" and "colleague facilitator" is accomplished quickly by phone or email. There is no preliminary consultation since all classes are asked the same three questions. We usually facilitate BBQ the last 30 minutes of a class period. An exception is night classes held from 7:00 to 9:50. It is too much to ask a colleague to come at 9:20 but we found starting at the beginning of class meant delays due to the late arrival of some students. Our current night class solution is to facilitate BBQ the last 30 minutes of the first half of class before the break. In three-hour classes that break comes about halfway through a class period. We agree with Tiberius (1997) that teachers should not perform evaluations in their own classes, although Angelo and Cross (1993) propose this as a last resort. An alternative suggestion is having it done by a committee of students. For us, the idea of doing it ourselves or using student committees raises red flags about the validity of what students will say.

We recommend instructors tell students at the beginning of class that a colleague is coming to discover their ideas about ways to improve learning. When facilitating colleagues appear, they are introduced and the instructor leaves. To encourage student comfort we tell a little about ourselves, such as courses we teach, about Learning Innovators, and our own interest in improving learning. We acknowledge that students are accustomed to end-of-semester evaluations, but the purpose of BBQ is to identify improvements while the class is ongoing. We praise the instructor for wanting their students' opinions. We read the three questions and explain they will be discussed first in small groups and then as a whole class. We assure students that 1) this is being done because their instructor cares about students and wants to improve their learning, 2) what students say is confidential, will be summarized for their instructor, and no student will be identified, 3) their instructor is the only person who will see student comments, and 4) student information will be aggregated and presented to the instructor as coming from the entire class and this is why agreement is so important. We find putting group answers on transparencies is more useful than blackboards or flip charts. Back in our offices we type students' opinions right off of the transparencies. Students watch to see that we print exactly what they say. If a group reports something another group has already said then we put check marks next to that answer. In our report to instructors, we might make a note of the fact "five groups mentioned this helps."

Some experts argue in favor of facilitation by colleagues in the same discipline to better understand what students say, but we disagree for the sake of validity. To ensure truthful student answers we believe colleague pairings should be across disciplines or schools. Central to validity is anonymity for students who may be suspicious of facilitating faculty members who know them from other classes. Some students are afraid a facilitator may remember who said what and tell an instructor. In BBQ, a colleague-facilitator is only required to be an intelligent and honest transmitter of information. We have tried it both ways and believe validity issues outweigh other concerns.

In the literature, a 24-hour turnaround is suggested, but we recommend feedback be given to instructors at least before the next class meeting. This gives instructors time to organize their response to student suggestions and think about possible changes. In the literature, opinions vary as to the form feedback should take. We suggest it be typed and handed to an instructor at a face-to-face meeting. Interacting face-to-face allows the receiving colleague an opportunity to ask questions to about the report. We tried saving time by eliminating this conference and using email or campus mail, but were dissatisfied. We find student responses always generate questions from faculty and clarification is best done face-to-face. Our current approach is for facilitating colleagues to make appointments with instructors, go to their offices, and explain they are empathic colleagues and NOT trained faculty development consultants. Instructors then read students' feedback. The facilitating colleague may inquire if students' comments ring true or make sense. Instructors can ask for clarification on items. This feedback session gives both instructors and facilitating colleagues a sense of accomplishment and closure. At their next class meeting instructors thank students for their input, summarize it, ensure accuracy, and discuss possible course changes for the remainder of a semester. This, in turn, also gives students a sense of acknowledgement and closure.

Decorum and Ethics in Collegial Feedback

Based on experience, we believe strongly that BBQ colleagues should act as empathic peers in the truest sense. Within a collegial pair neither person is the "expert." A facilitating colleague is not a consultant but a conduit of student statements. If expertise is assumed to reside in a facilitator colleague then a receiving colleague may perceive student dissatisfactions as valid if accompanied by advice from a facilitating colleague. Palmer (1998) proposes respecting each other's vulnerability, although it is difficult to resist the temptation to make suggestions. Norms in academia lead us to believe "...we were put on earth to advise, fix and save each other, and whenever an opportunity to do so presents itself, we should seize it!" (Palmer, 1998, p. 151). Our BBQ volunteer and paired colleagues report being reassured by sharing student comments because results dramatically demonstrate commonalities in student suggestions regardless of discipline.

A major emphasis is that instructors read and understand exactly what their students said. Students' ideas accurately conveyed enhance the richness and value of the data. By following this method of operation for several semesters neither resentment nor hostility has been generated among cooperating colleagues since we are equals or peers helping each other. Lenze (1997) believes a meaningful, nonthreatening feedback session is crucial because the receiving instructor is vulnerable; her experience is that most instructors react favorably because SGID is "...a concrete, confirming, constructive and thoughtful" (p. 146) experience. After answering any questions about students' remarks, an appropriate closing statement is, "Thanks for inviting me to your class, I enjoyed working with you. If you have any questions or comments about the feedback feel free to let me know" (Border, 1997, p. 24).

Ethics in consulting should be applied in this peer-based process (POD Network, 2001). Trust is an essential component between colleagues who pair up for BBQ. The instructor must feel safe and be assured that what students say will be held in confidence by the facilitating colleague. As is true for consultants, BBQ results should not be discussed with any person other than the teaching colleague. "No information should be given to a teacher's supervisors, to other teachers, nor should it be used in any written correspondence about a teacher" (Border, 1997, p. 19).

A related issue is that instructors should be able to trust that feedback relayed by a colleague is truthfully what students said. Wilbee (1997) suggests that only helpful feedback should be given about things that a teacher can actually change, and Lenze (1997) suggests altering the feedback report if students' comments are more critical than positive in nature. We disagree with the idea of filtering negative student comments. We recommend all feedback, representing class consensus, be included. Receiving colleagues must believe facilitators are honest in their reports, neither exaggerating nor enhancing student comments with their own "spin."

We also agree that the most useful feedback is based on teacher behaviors, reflects students' needs, and suggests ways to improve learning. Student input about teaching behavior is central for instructional improvement. For example, a common complaint is teachers not leaving slides up long enough for students to copy what they think is important. Useful feedback is, "It would help learning if a copy of transparencies or slides could be put on reserve in the library or posted on the web." Many changes are fairly simple. For example, it could be assumed that providing detailed outlines of each class lecture/discussion is helpful. However, some students are accustomed to lectures based solely on textbooks and may wonder how the numbered outlines relate to the textbook chapter numbers. Implementing BBQ can bring this confusion to light and result in a change in the course, such as typing corresponding chapter numbers at the top of lecture/discussion outlines or writing "This is NOT in the textbook" or "Some of this material is found at the beginning of Chapter 5." After BBQ, one computer engineering instructor eliminated the last three required class projects, saying he agreed with students it was too much work for one semester. Another faculty member did not realize how distracting hallway noise was to students since her back was to the doorway. Thanks to BBQ, this situation was brought to her attention and now she closes the door when she begins teaching.

BBQ Benefits All Stakeholders

When learning is improved, there is a win-win-win situation. Faculty members, students, and institutions all reap the rewards. Personal benefits for faculty members occur when our own classes are visited but we also learn by hearing from colleagues' students. Through round-robin collegial training, more and more faculty members are drawn into the practice of listening to students and improving courses accordingly. Faculty members actually have a minimum of two opportunities to hear from peers' students about what is helpful and what hinders. After these two experiences, faculty members understand the validity of data generated in their own classrooms. Observation in other teachers' classrooms also takes much of the "sting" or "pain" from what could be an ego-bruising experience. Both experienced and fledgling teachers report being enlightened by students' comments. There is no other way faculty can get this information. Faculty members worried about colleagues hearing student comments that might reflect badly on their teaching are relieved of this concern after hearing from students in colleagues' classes.

When midterm evaluations are peer facilitated another benefit occurs for faculty. One challenge to postsecondary teaching is what Palmer (1998) refers to as the isolation of teaching.

> Academic culture builds barriers between colleagues even higher and wider than those between us and our students. These barriers come partly from the competition that keeps us fragmented by fear. But they also come from the fact that teaching is perhaps the most privatized of all the public professions. (p.142)

Palmer writes that although there are no formulas for good teaching it may help to talk to fellow teachers in a community of pedagogical discourse. BBQ faculty members, as colleagues, feel less isolated. Since it is voluntary, BBQ may also ameliorate faculty fears about both peer review and student evaluations. By increasing collegiality and improving student learning and attitudes, BBQ resolves several potentially negative situations facing faculty members.

Midterm assessments benefit students in several ways. Angelo and Cross (1993) believe GIFT helps students develop an ability to draw inferences, evaluate teaching methods and materials, work productively with others, and cultivate a commitment to honesty. When students think about their own learning processes learning improves. Tiberius (1997) describes SGID as "... a combination of a leaderless small group discussion followed by an unstructured, whole class interview ..." (p.60). Since student groupings are leaderless there is less inhibition to speaking frankly. Students are flattered by teachers' interest in their opinions, especially if teachers take some of their suggestions. With BBQ, teachers find out how students believe learning could be improved. Truthfulness is improved by having students speak after a faculty member has left a classroom. Black (1998) cautions that if an instructor ignores students' suggestions then class atmosphere could be harmed and negative comments could snowball as students share frustrations. As an alternative, she suggests individual responses followed by a time-consuming analysis of patterns by consultants. We have not found this to be a problem. Our students are very vocal. We always emphasize the importance of whole class consensus and assure students they do *not have to find something wrong* with a class. We do ask for each group's most important responses and we complete the first question before moving on to the next. We also alternate the order in which groups speak. Our students are comfortable about saying "We disagree!" when other groups make their statements. In a few classes the students appear to be evenly divided on what would help. In such cases, we put on our report that there was disagreement.

Conclusion

BBQ is truly a bare bones process, paring down time spent by faculty interested in knowing what their students think at midterm. We began using the traditional five-step SGID, including observation and scripting of colleagues' three-hour classes followed by students' discussions. The process, including preparing the report, took about eight hours. This was too much to ask of even our most empathic colleagues. We streamlined BBQ over several semesters. While time is saved, neither informational quality nor validity is lost. BBQ offers many of the benefits of SGID with the exception of advice from faculty development experts. By using teaching peers, BBQ saves time and money. It eliminates the pre-classroom conference and shortens the post-classroom session. It simplifies midterm student evaluations by making them a colleague-to-colleague service. By interacting with students from colleagues' classrooms, faculty members gain a new competency, as well as a different perspective. Students benefit by hearing whether or not their opinions are similar to or different from other's opinions. In this way students "... begin to understand what sort of a challenge confronts an instructor trying to provide worthwhile learning experiences for students who have different learning needs and expectations" (Weimer, 1990, p. 107). Students also learn to express constructive criticism of teaching and better understand their experiences in other classrooms. BBQ is a valid way to discover what students believe will improve their learning and may even be an option for faculty development experts overwhelmed with demands for their services. For thousands of institutions without consultants, BBQ is a viable alternative with significant benefits for all participants.

Note

BBQ was first presented at 2001 Texas Lilly Conference on College and University Teaching at Southwest Texas State University in San Marcos. Based on new research findings, a revised format and an interactive session was presented at the 9th Annual Meeting of the Southwestern Business Administration Teaching Conference at Texas Southern University later that same year.

References

Angelo, T. A., & Cross, K. P. (1993). *Classroom assessment techniques.* San Francisco, CA: Jossey-Bass.

Bennett, W. E. (1987). Small group instructional diagnosis: A dialogic approach to instructional improvement for tenured faculty. *The Journal of Staff, Program, and Organization Development, 5,* 100–104.

Black, B. (1998). Using the SGID method for a variety of purposes. In M. Kaplan & D. Lieberman (Eds.), *To improve the academy: Vol. 17. Resources for faculty, instructional, and organizational development* (pp. 245–262). Stillwater, OK: New Forums Press.

Border, L. L. B. (1997). The creative art of effective consultation. In K. T. Brinko & R. J. Menges (Eds.), *Practically speaking: A sourcebook for instructional consultants in higher education* (pp. 17–24). Stillwater, OK: New Forums Press.

Brinko, K. T., & Menges, R. J. (1997). *Practically speaking: A sourcebook for instructional consultants in higher education.* Stillwater, OK: New Forums Press.

Lenze, L. F. (1997). Small group instructional diagnosis (SGID). In K. T. Brinko & R. J. Menges (Eds.), *Practically speaking: A sourcebook for instructional consultants in higher education* (pp. 143–146). Stillwater, OK: New Forums Press.

Morrison, D. E. (1997). Overview of instructional consultation in North America. In K. T. Brinko & R. J. Menges (Eds.), *Practically speaking: A sourcebook for instructional consultants in higher education* (pp. 121–129). Stillwater, OK: New Forums Press.

Palmer, P. J. (1998). *The courage to teach.* San Francisco, CA: Jossey-Bass.

POD Network. (2001). Ethical guidelines for educational developers. In D. Lieberman & C. Wehlburg (Eds.), *To improve the academy: Vol. 19. Resources for faculty, instructional, and organizational development* (pp. xvii–xxiii). Bolton, MA: Anker.

Redmond, M. V., & Clark, D. J. (1982). Student group instructional diagnosis: A practical approach to improving teaching. *AAHE Bulletin, 34,* 8–10.

Santanello, C., & Eder, D. (2001). Classroom assessment techniques. *Thriving in academe, 19,* 5–8.

Tiberius, R. (1997). Small group methods for collecting information from students. In K. T. Brinko & R. J. Menges (Eds.), *Practically speaking: A sourcebook for instructional consultants in higher education* (pp. 53–63). Stillwater, OK: New Forums Press.

Weimer, M. (1990). *Improving college teaching: Strategies for developing instructional effectiveness.* San Francisco, CA: Jossey-Bass.

Wilbee, J. (1997). Instructional skills workshop program: A peer-based model for the improvement of teaching and learning. In K. T. Brinko & R. J. Menges (Eds.), *Practically speaking: A sourcebook for instructional consultants in higher education* (pp. 147–156). Stillwater, OK: New Forums Press.

Wulff, D. H., Staton-Spicer, A. Q., Hess, C. W., & Nyquist, J. D. (1985). The student perspective on evaluating teaching effectiveness. *Association for Communication Administration Bulletin, 53,* 39–47.

Contact:

Margaret K. Snooks
School of Human Sciences and Humanities
University of Houston-Clear Lake
Houston, TX 77058-1098
Voice (281) 283-3381
Fax (281) 283-3408
Email Snooks@cl.uh.edu

Sue E. Neeley
School of Business and Professional Administration
University of Houston-Clear Lake
Houston, TX 77058-1098
Voice (281) 283-3219
Fax (281) 283-3951
Email Neeley@cl.uh.edu

Kathleen M. Williamson
School of Business and Professional Administration
University of Houston-Clear Lake
Houston, TX 77058-1098
Voice (281) 283-3192
Fax (281) 226-7317
Email Williamson@cl.uh.edu

Margaret K. Snooks has been a faculty member in the School of Human Sciences and Humanities at the University of Houston-Clear Lake (UHCL) since 1991. She was recently appointed co-convener of the developing UHCL Teaching Learning Enhancement Center. Her research interests include ways to improve teaching and learning at the postsecondary levels of education. She teaches undergraduate and graduate courses in the Program of Fitness and Human Performance, including courses in health psychology and women's health. In 2002 she published in *Health Care for Women International* and in *Women in Higher Education: Empowering Change.*

Sue E. Neeley is an Associate Professor and Coordinator of the Marketing Program at the University of Houston-Clear Lake. Her research interests include marketing strategy (particularly the relationship between market share and profitability), business-to-business customer relationship management, and the scholarship of the enhancement of teaching and learning. She has conducted numerous workshops on innovative methods of using mid-semester student feedback to improve learning and student involvement in the learning process. Her research has been published in the *Journal of Business Research, Journal of Services Marketing, Mid-Atlantic Journal of Business, Journal of Business Education,* and *The Handbook of Business Strategy,* as well as the proceedings of professional conferences.

Kathleen M. Williamson has been a faculty member in the Marketing Department of the School of Business and Public Administration at the University of Houston-Clear Lake since 1998. She teaches Principles of Marketing, Marketing Information, Integrated Marketing Communications, and E-Marketing Management to undergraduate and graduate students. Her research interests include Internet marketing, customer relationship management, and the scholarship of teaching and learning.

8

A Versatile Interactive Focus Group Protocol for Qualitative Assessments

Barbara J. Millis
U. S. Air Force Academy

A highly flexible focus group protocol captures efficiently and economically useful data for immediate and longitudinal course and program assessment. Special features include an index card activity that deals with satisfactions levels and a Roundtable/Ranking activity that allows participant-generated judgments about the most positive and the most negative features of a course or program. These latter activities, with data displayed in an Excel histogram and in a colored-coded Word table, can be used for what is called a "Quick Course Diagnosis" (QCD).

Assessment is becoming increasingly important on most campuses: The U.S. Air Force Academy (USAFA) is no exception. In fact, since its highly successful North Central Association accreditation review and the appointment of a full-time director for academic assessment, USAFA has been increasingly recognized as a leader in the assessment field. For the past several years, the Center for Educational Excellence (CEE) has been increasingly involved in helping departments gather and interpret both quantitative and qualitative data.

To meet the need for qualitative data, we have developed a unique process—highly structured interactive focus groups—to get information and insights from those most directly affected by curriculum and pedagogical transformations: the students. The use of focus groups in academia is not a new practice. Wright and Hendershott (1992), for example, find focus groups to be an invaluable means of tapping student perceptions within a university setting. They feel that interactions among students, particularly when the facilitators are able to probe responses, yield rich data that cannot be obtained from traditional surveys.

However, the focus group protocol developed and refined at USAFA is unique because of its highly structured approaches to data collection and because of the power of the resulting reports. These focus groups employ a variety of techniques to maximize data collection from as many students as possible. We use a survey (optional); an index card activity; a cooperative, group-based activity called Roundtable/Ranking; and a series of open-ended questions. Faculty members interested in personal information about their individual courses have welcomed this focus group protocol. Focus groups have also been widely used for curriculum review and reform at the department level by course directors responsible for preparing the syllabus, ordering texts, and coordinating courses taught by more than one instructor. They have also been used to assess the impact and value of a major and to compare experimental courses with those traditionally taught. Additionally, they have been used to evaluate special programs such as a new one-week summer engineering course for high school students. To simplify terminology, we will refer to the contact persons, whether faculty members, course directors, or department assessment representatives, as "clients."

The focus group protocol is typically used with student volunteers who come to a neutral location to share ideas and experiences about their courses or about their programs of study. To encourage representative samples, instructors teaching each section of a course will draw the names of two students and ask them to represent the class at a focus group scheduled (usually) in the early evening. It is difficult for them to say no, unless they have a genuine conflict. But, in some key cases, the same focus group protocol has worked effectively with a complete population sample that includes all students enrolled in a given course (up to 18). To assess, for example, the effectiveness of a new core law course, all students enrolled in the three pilot sections were interviewed by a CEE representative and a member of the law department who knew the course content, but who was not teaching this course at the time.

These focused student interviews seek to gather as much data as possible within a 50-minute time limit and to gather it systematically so that long-term comparisons are possible as courses or programs are modified.

The Client Interactions

All focus groups begin with a client-centered discussion to explore the following: 1) the objectives for the focus group, 2) questions and activities that will likely yield valuable data, and 3) the "logistics" involved, including selection of the students, the room layout, and any refreshments (pizza works well). The CEE uses a paired approach with one staff member responsible for conducting the actual session (the facilitator) and another staff member responsible for logistics, including the audiotaping arrangements and the preparation of the final reports. Typically, the facilitator conducts the client interview, and based on the identified needs, prepares a survey instrument, if desired, and PowerPoint slides with the course-specific open-ended questions. During the actual session, the facilitator takes the more active role, but the logistics person, who is introduced as an equal partner, is also free to ask probing questions as the discussion unfolds. Likewise, when the third step occurs—a feedback interview with the client(s)—both CEE parties contribute ideas and impressions. A fourth step is highly desirable, but not always possible, depending on the timing of the focus group: a feedback session between the client and the actual students interviewed or the students they represented.

The Student Survey

A short student survey is an optional way to gather additional information without increased time involvement because it is usually completed by early arrivals before the start of the actual focus group session. The students, after being welcomed, receive the survey as they arrive for the focus group. This practice reinforces the seriousness of the project and helps students feel at ease when they are given an initial task to perform. The questions on the survey (Appendix 8.1) are often idiosyncratic, such as asking students how much time they devote to the course.

Instructions for Students

After the expected students arrive, the facilitator explains the nature of the session, including the ground rules for discussion. Students also understand the confidentiality of the responses and the use to be made of them. The purpose of the focus group session is to gather information for constructive changes; the facilitator informs students that they will receive feedback from the instructor if the logistics allow for it. They also learn that, to provide a complete record of their comments, the session will be audiotaped. Only a community-based transcriber will hear the tape with their voices. To further ensure confidentiality, students use a number they acquire through a count-off as identification, rather than their names. They preface all remarks with their assigned number. Students quickly adopt the practice of saying things such as, "This is Student Number Six: I disagree somewhat with Number

Five's comment because his experience is so limited, but I think that Number Four and Number 17 really clarified the issues."

The Initial Focus Group Activity Using Index Cards

After the students complete the survey, if one is included, and hear the opening information, they are handed an index card. Working independently, they jot down on the card a word or phrase to describe the course or program and a number from one to five to indicate their satisfaction level. Usually the facilitator has the students indicate, round-robin fashion, their responses. These range from numbers and comments such as, "I gave it a five and an 'Awesome'" to "I gave it a number one. My comment [for a geography course] was 'As dry as eating saltines in the Sahara.'" This pubic disclosure serves a number of functions: 1) It enables students to feel comfortable with their peers because everyone has been up-front about their overall feelings; 2) facilitators also learn quickly whether they are faced with happy or unhappy campers, knowledge that can help frame probing questions; and 3) an atmosphere of trust and open disclosure is established up-front before any of the open-ended questions—often more sensitive—are asked.

The Open-Ended Questions

Two types of general questions then follow, some that everyone responds to (round-robin) and some where anyone may answer. The facilitator and the client discuss beforehand which questions all students should answer and which ones are suitable for random responses. Given the time constraints, no more than two questions should be round-robin style. These open-ended questions (Appendix 8.2) typically target issues of particular concern to clients. For example, an English professor wanted to understand the impact of one-on-one grading conferences that replaced traditionally marked papers. A political scientist was concerned about low course critique ratings and wanted feedback from students that could help her strengthen her teaching methods. The law department was interested in the value of a new textbook in a core course. The management department was concerned about the quality of advising that their majors received. The physics and math departments wanted to know the value of preflights, a series of web-based questions that students complete prior to each lesson. A course director in the computer science department wanted to assess the impact on learning and attitude of students programming Lego robots: multiple focus groups targeted the Lego courses (experimental) and traditionally taught courses (control).

A Structured Group Activity: Roundtable/Ranking

A group-based assessment activity called Roundtable/Ranking allows students to identify and clarify their own issues. Unlike the volunteer open-ended questions where some students may remain silent, this highly structured activity ensures equitable contributions from all participants. The facilitator places the students into small groups, and gives each group a handout (Appendix 8.3) with specific instructions to brainstorm all the strengths of the course or program and then to brainstorm all the things about the course that could be improved. These two activities follow rapidly, one after the other, so the students don't get into an analytical mode. The paper circulates rapidly from one student to another as each adds an idea, saying it aloud. Then, each group rank-orders the strengths of the course and then the weaknesses. The rank-ordering activity is critical because it enables students to reach consensus on their priorities and to eliminate any idiosyncratic responses. The brainstorming and ranking parts of Roundtable/Ranking together take only ten minutes out of the 50 minutes available.

The focus group session typically concludes with more open-ended questions. Depending on their complexity, we usually offer eight to ten questions for open discussion. Before leaving, the two CEE staff members make a point of thanking students for their contributions.

The Client Reports

All clients receive a neat, comb-bound summary report with colorful graphics. If we conducted focus groups for multiple sections of a course or program, often a single report captures combined data. Any survey results are assembled and displayed appropriately. The index card data are presented through a colorful Excel histogram (Appendix 8.4). Each column's height corresponds to the number of students selecting that rating. For example, if ten students indicated a satisfaction level of "four" for a course, that column would be twice as high as the one representing the five students who gave it a "two." Listed within each column are the descriptive words or phrases (e.g., "Stimulating," "Awesome," "A Real Challenge"). The histogram provides an easily interpreted overview of students' satisfaction levels. As improvements occur over time, clients can expect to see the heights of the "four" and "five" columns rise accordingly, thus providing longitudinal assessment data. In fact, CEE also prepares special reports summarizing longitudinal data, especially in anticipation of accreditation visits.

The responses to the open-ended questions are word-processed by a medical transcription service. This service, which charges about $75 per transcription, emails the final results within 24 hours so that CEE staff members can review and possibly edit them. Editing usually involves correcting the spelling of unfamiliar Air Force terms or locations ("TDY" or "Misawa Air Force Base"). The transcripts identify each student by their number and provide an in-depth record of all comments. A typical entry might look like this: "Student Seven: Unlike Student Two, I felt the evaluation methods were extremely fair because the essays gave us a chance to demonstrate what we actually knew. I found myself integrating ideas in ways I hadn't thought of before." After several years of stressed-out secretaries and untimely reports, we now budget yearly for these invaluable professional transcription services.

The Roundtable/Ranking data are displayed in a color-coded Word table (Appendix 8.5). All the strengths and weakness appear under each team number. A CEE assessment expert identifies trends through a quick cluster analysis and color-codes them systematically. For example, all the strengths and weaknesses listed by any team that relate to teaching methods might be coded in yellow. Evaluation items might be coded in green. Because these colors remain consistent, the tables, like the histograms, make interpretations and changes over time easy to spot.

The Client/CEE Feedback Session

Rather than simply hand off a report for each focus group, CEE staff members prefer to meet with an individual client or sets of clients, such as all those teaching a core course. That way we can be certain that the data are understood and properly interpreted. We also like to explore ways of strengthening a course, program, or major. The data provided in these three reports—the Excel histogram reflecting the index card information, the transcript of the open-ended question responses, and the Word table reflecting trends evident during the Roundtable/Ranking activity—provide a solid basis for informed, research-based decision-making.

Quick Course Diagnosis

Because these focus groups proved so valuable to departments and individual faculty members, the demand for them skyrocketed. With a limited staff, this demand was difficult to meet. Thus, we began offering an abbreviated version of the focus group protocol, known as a Quick Course Diagnosis (QCD). This innovative practice received recognition at the 2001 POD conference as a "Bright Idea." For a QCD, one, rather than two, facilitators comes to a class and administers only the index card activity and the Roundtable/Ranking activity. We eliminate the round-robin sharing of the index card data typically done during the focus group protocol. Time is saved also because students do not need assigned numbers to assure their anonymity because there are no open-ended questions to audiotape. Thus, the entire process can be completed in 15 minutes. To augment this data, we now spend another five minutes reaching a whole-class consensus on the top three strengths of the course and the top three "weaknesses" (things to improve). The consensus is reached quickly because each Roundtable/Ranking team indicates their top strength and their top weakness, which the facilitator records rapidly on the chalkboard. If there are duplications, the reporting team adds its second choice. Depending on the number of teams, there will be approximately five items in each category. Each student then votes on their top choice for a strength and a top choice for a weakness. Ties are quickly broken by additional votes so that the top three strengths and the top three weaknesses are clearly identified. A student copies everything from the board while the votes are tallied, thus giving CEE a permanent record.

As with the focus groups, a faculty development assessment specialist prepares client reports. Clients requesting a QCD receive: 1) an Excel histogram with the index card information indicating the satisfaction level with the course/program/major and the words or phrases describing it; 2) a Word table reflecting the data generated by each team, color-coded to reflect trends; and 3) a second Word table based on the whole-class consensus, similarly color-coded to emphasize trends. These reports can be generated very rapidly—five to 15 minutes each—because we use templates and because we do so many focus groups and QCDs (typically over 30 a semester) that the assessment specialist becomes adept at preparing them. Although QCDs are not as rich in data as the focus groups because of the omission of open-ended questions, the three reports prove extremely valuable. This trade-off results in less class time, fewer facilitators, and decreased costs because there is no need for the transcription service.

Differences Between a QCD and an SGID

Many faculty developers are familiar with a widely used assessment tool called Small Group Instructional Diagnosis (SGID). It is based on research conducted by Joseph Clark (Clark & Redmond, 1982) when he served as a FIPSE (Fund for the Improvement of Postsecondary Education) project director at the University of Washington, Seattle. Practitioners such as Diamond (2002) and Wulff (1996) agree on the basic steps involved.

The SGID session is framed by a pre- and post-client interview. During the 30-minute in-class interview with students—usually conducted at the midterm point—the facilitator introduces himself or herself, explains the SGID process, and asks students to form groups of six to eight and select a recorder. The students then discuss the questions on the SGID feedback form with the student recorder writing down the points on which they reach consensus. The form prompts them to identify the strengths of the course backed up by concrete examples and the "weaknesses" of the course, backed up by specific suggestions for constructive changes. After this process, which typically takes only eight to 12 minutes, the facilitator records—or asks a student to record—the comments of each group on a central chalkboard. Another student recorder copies everything from the board for later analysis. Facilitators have several key tasks. They ask students for clarification or amplification on ambiguous points, and they seek to determine whether there is whole-class consensus on the issues raised. This can be accomplished by asking for a show of hands indicating agreement or disagreement with particular comments.

To prepare the client report, the SGID facilitator analyses and organizes the material to make it meaningful to the instructor. The comments can be arranged, for example, in order of frequency under the central headings of "Things to Continue," "Things to Consider Changing," and "Suggestions." The facilitator tries to "chunk" data under common themes to be shared with the instructor through a carefully crafted letter. Not all comments are included verbatim, particularly those with potentially hurtful phrasing. But representative comments can give the flavor of the SGID experience.

Both QCDs and SGIDs provide useful options to offer faculty clients. As should be evident, the QCD protocol is indebted to the inventors and practitioners of the SGID. However, there are some significant differences that faculty developers should weigh before recommending a specific approach. The QCD has four distinct advantages over the SGID. First, the index card activity with its resulting histogram is a unique and highly effective assessment activity, allowing longitudinal comparisons to track improvements. Second, because of its highly structured nature, the QCD requires far less in-class time to administer than an SGID. Even with the discussions that arise during the whole-class consensus period, virtually any experienced facilitator can be in and out the door in 20 minutes. Although the SGID protocol presumably takes no more than 30 minutes to complete, in practice, many faculty developers find that it takes far longer because of the need for amplification and clarification. Third, probably the most important advantage of the QCD over the SGID lies in the ease with which valuable reports are generated. With an SGID, the facilitator must prepare a formal letter to the client summarizing the data, making judgments about what to include and what to omit, and offering recommendations. Such a report can take hours to prepare because it involves not only cluster analysis to identify trends but also requires the careful selection of representative comments and careful attention to the tone of the letter. The QCD reports, on the other hand, can be prepared by a third party, usually an assessment expert, who becomes skilled at "pouring" the acquired data into templates. Thus, often overworked teaching center staffs are able to produce valuable assessment data within a fraction of the time required for the SGID analysis. Fourth, the Excel histograms and color-coded Word tables provide impressive evidence of assessment efforts. Accrediting bodies—including the Higher Learning Commission, the Association to Advance Collegiate Schools of Business (AACSB), and Accreditation Board for Engineering and Technology (ABET)—have all reacted with high praise to the reports generated by the QCDs and focus groups. These reports, unlike the highly personalized SGID letters, allow systematic longitudinal analysis. The histograms, for example, reveal highly visible changes in satisfaction levels. It is easy to build charts comparing semester-by-semester or year-by-year responses. The color-code Word tables, placed side by side, quickly reveal whether or not deliberate changes have had the desired effect. If, for example, students one semester identified a poorly written textbook as a course weakness and the textbook was changed, then the color identified with textbook issues would, during follow-up QCDs or focus groups the next semester, ideally drop off the "weakness" chart.

SGIDs, perhaps because they are more labor intensive, do offer some advantages over QCDs. For example, they yield examples and suggestions for changes that might not emerge in the QCD protocol. Because of the extended discussion where the team reports are recorded on the board, the facilitator has more opportunities to engage the students in thoughtful reflection. Most SGID facilitators, for instance, challenge students to refine phrasing so that it is as constructive as possible, a valuable learning experience.

Savvy faculty developers will keep both options in their toolboxes, offering clients with limited time the choice between either a QCD or an SGID. Clients wanting more in-depth feedback and who are willing to invest 50 minutes, will benefit from the full-blown focus group with a transcript of students' responses to open-ended questions.

Conclusion

The focus group protocol is highly versatile. We have used it, for example, to assess several regional and national conferences, including the American Association for Higher Education assessment conference. Our sessions in the last time slots enabled us to model the focus group process while collecting genuine data from conference attendees. Additionally, three faculty focus groups formed the heart of an off-campus consultation to determine faculty perceptions of their professional development opportunities at a small liberal arts university. In this case, faculty "scribes" captured the gist of the open-ended comments, thus eliminating the need for an audiotape and later transcription. Not surprisingly, we learned that focus groups produce rich data from faculty members as well as from students. This versatile protocol can be used with virtually any type of constituency.

The most valuable application of focus groups remains our own use of them for course and program assessment. Because the popularity of this assessment tool has grown incrementally, many clients include focus groups in their course syllabi. Many cooperative focus groups conclude with the following open-ended question: "Please comment on the value of this focus group session." This request invariably draws positive responses from cadets who have been asked to complete numerous assessment instruments, tests, and activities since they first set foot on the Air Force Academy. Without exception, all student focus groups have indicated that they like the purpose and format of these structured interviews. They enjoy the informal interactions far more than paper-and-pencil surveys or bubble sheets. They are flattered that their opinions matter.

CEE can genuinely assure cadets that their opinions matter. Many positive course changes have resulted from the student input gathered through these cooperative focus groups. For example, as a result of focus groups, the law department made significant changes in their course structure and content, in their textbook, and in their methods of evaluation. A core course melding geography and meteorology adopted new texts and activities that fostered integration. As a result of focus group feedback, faculty are also working to incorporate active learning and cooperative learning approaches into this core course. An experimental first-year course in problem-based engineering added more "scaffolding" for students over a three-year period. A pilot "First-Year Experience" course will undergo major changes in its next iteration, due, in part, to data captured through focus groups with students. The management department made key changes in their core course and in their major ("closing the loop") prior to their highly successful accreditation review by the AACSB. The list could continue almost indefinitely.

CEE staff members are delighted with the positive results of focus groups and the spin-off QCDs, even though our workload has increased as a result. For more information, including sample reports, please go to www.usafa.af.mil/dfe/.

Note

Special thanks go to Lt. Col. (Ret.) Marie Revak, former Director of Academic Assessment, and to Mr. Curtis Hughes, Deputy Director, Academic Assessment, U.S. Air Force Academy, who developed the Excel histogram and Word table formats. Mr. Hughes also provided editorial insights for this chapter.

References

Clark, D., & Redmond, M. (1982). *Small group instructional diagnosis: Final report.* Washington, DC: Fund for the Improvement of Postsecondary Education. (ERIC Document Reproduction Service No. ED217954)

Diamond, N. A. (2002). Small group instructional diagnosis: Tapping student perceptions of teaching. In K. H. Gillespie (Ed.), *A guide to faculty development: Practical advice, examples, and resources* (pp. 82–91). Bolton, MA: Anker.

Wright, S. P., & Hendershott, A. (1992). In D. H. Wulff, & J. D. Nyquist (Eds.), *To improve the academy: Vol. 11. Resources for Faculty, Instructional, and Organizational Development* (pp. 87–104). Stillwater, OK: New Forums Press.

Wulff, D. H. (1996, Fall). *Small group instructional diagnosis (SGID).* Training workshops conducted at the U. S. Air Force Academy.

Contact:

Barbara J. Millis
Director of Faculty Development
HQ USAFA/DFE
2354 Fairchild Drive, Suite 4K25
USAF Academy, CO 80840-6220
Voice (719) 333-2549
Fax (719) 333-4255
Email Barbara.millis@usafa.af.mil

Barbara J. Millis, Director of Faculty Development at the U. S. Air Force Academy, frequently offers workshops at professional conferences (American Association of Higher Education [AAHE], Lilly Teaching Conferences, Association of American Colleges and Universities [AAC&U], etc.) and for various colleges and universities. She publishes articles on a range of faculty development topics, and co-authored with Philip Cottell *Cooperative Learning for Higher Education Faculty* (Oryx Press [now Greenwood]) and with John Hertel *Using Simulations to Promote Learning in Higher Education* (Stylus Press). Appearing shortly from Stylus Press will be *Using Academic Games to Enhance Learning in Higher Education.* Her interests include cooperative learning (see *Enhancing Learning—and More!—Through Cooperative Learning:* http://www.idea.ksu.edu/papers/Idea_Paper_38.pdf), peer review, academic games, classroom observations, microteaching, classroom assessment/research, critical thinking, how students learn, and writing for learning. After the Association of American Colleges and Universities selected the U. S. Air Force Academy as a Leadership Institution in Undergraduate Education, she began serving as the liaison to the AAC&U's Greater Expectations Consortium on Quality Education.

Appendix 8.1

Some Open Questions: Physics Focus Group

Assigned Number:

Please Indicate your section number:

1) Why do you think your instructor assigns preflights?

2) How are the preflights used during class time?

3) Do you think that doing the preflights is a good use of your study/preparation time? Please explain.

4) Compared to your other activities, what is your estimate (hours spent or percentage of your time) of time spent with physics?

5) On a scale of 1 to 5 (1 = lowest and 5 = highest) rate your amount of effort in the course:

Compared to other students in your section?	1	2	3	4	5
Compared to your other courses?	1	2	3	4	5
Compared to the amount of effort you might have extended?	1	2	3	4	5

Comments:

6) Do computer network problems impact your work in this course? If so, what percent of the time?
   0%–10% 11%–20% 21%–30% 31%–40%
   41%–50% More?

   Comments:

7) On a scale of 1 to 5 (1 = lowest and 5 = highest) how would you rate the effectiveness of the evaluation methods (quizzes, papers, exams, etc.) used in the course? Please add explanatory comments.

   1 2 3 4 5

   Comments:

Appendix 8.2

Sample Focus Group Questions for MGT 210
(The Core Management Class Required of all Students)

- What were your expectations for Mgt 210? Were they met?
- What management skills are important to you? Has Mgt 210 helped you with them?
- Are there topics presently covered in Mgt 210 that should be omitted? Please elaborate.
- How do the evaluation methods used in Mgt 210 allow you to demonstrate your level of mastery of course material? Please explain.
- What changes in the evaluation methods would you recommend? Please explain.
- How did the teaching methods used in Mgt 210 help you learn?
- In what ways did your instructor contribute to your experience in Mgt 210?
- What is the most important thing you've learned from Mgt 210?
- What do teachers in other courses do that significantly enhance your learning?

Appendix 8.3

Roundtable Activity # 1

Index card numbers (top right corner): ____ ____ ____ ____ ____

Passing this sheet of paper rapidly from one person to another, please jot down all of the relevant strengths of the course, saying them aloud as you write.

Working as a team, rank order the strengths you identified, with the most important ones at the top of your list. Rank at least three by writing the numbers "1," "2," and "3" next to the strengths you identified.

Roundtable Activity # 2

Passing this sheet of paper rapidly from one person to another, please jot down all of the "negatives" of the course—the things you would change—saying them aloud as you write.

Working as a team, rank order the weaknesses you identified, with the most significant ones at the top of your list. Rank at least three by writing the numbers "1," "2," and "3" next to the weaknesses you identified.

Appendix 8.4

Index Card Data

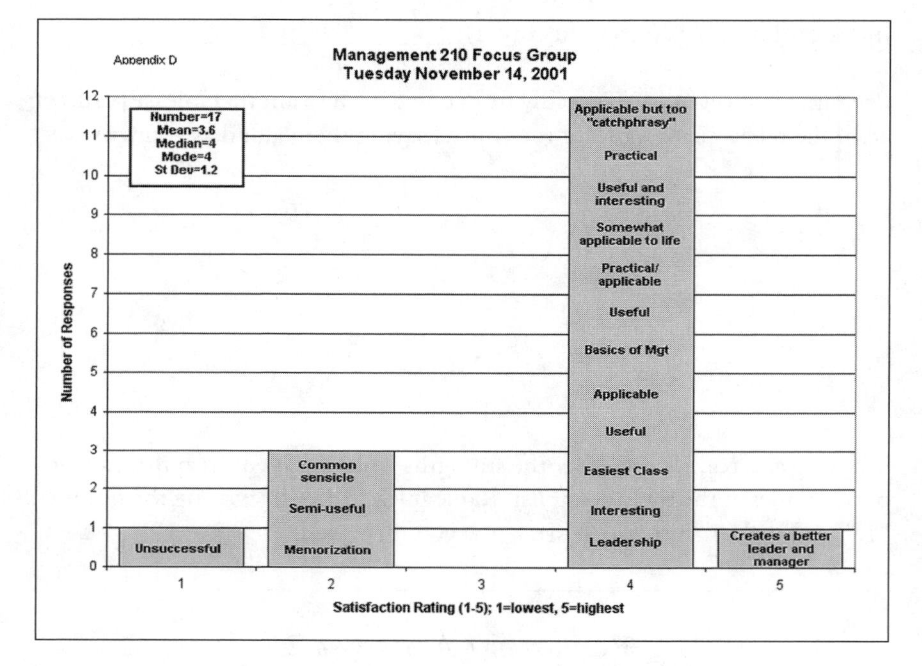

Appendix 8.5

Mgt 210, Focus Group
November 14, 2001

Rank-Ordering of Course Strengths

Team One	Team Two	Team Three	Team Four
Applicable to AF and real life	Teachers	Applicable	Personal finance
Experienced and enthusiastic instructors	Relevance	Leadership	Goal setting
Financing block	Organization	Financing	Motivation and leadership
		All-encompasing	

Thread	Color Code	Number of Occurrences
Applicable		3
Personal finance		3
Leadership		2
Instructors		2

Rank-Ordering of Course Weaknesses

Team One	Team Two	Team Three	Team Four
Memorization of terms	GR	More conceptual	Remove CPM
"Wordy"	Terms	More group interaction	Reduce memorization
CPM	Lack of current events	More on investing	Lack of application

Thread	Color Code	Number of Occurrences
Memorization of terms		4
CPM		2
More application		2

Section IV

Faculty Development Tools

9

A Transformative Model for Designing Professional Development Activities

David Langley
Indiana State University

Terence W. O'Connor
The College of New Jersey

Michele M. Welkener
Indiana State University

A new model for professional and organizational development is presented based on concepts derived from Wilber (2000) and Astin (2001). The model consists of an individual/public dimension and a reflection/performance dimension. Four quadrants that result from connecting these dimensions are formed: 1) individual reflection, 2) public reflection, 3) individual performance, and 4) public performance. We believe this model offers faculty developers a framework for designing thoughtful programs to aid faculty in meeting the wide range of internal and external demands that confront higher education institutions.

The purpose of this chapter is to present a comprehensive model for professional development based on concepts underlying transformational change for institutions of higher education (Astin, 2001; Wilber, 2000). We view the model as one vehicle to resolve the tensions created when faculty attempt to align their beliefs and skills with changing institutional expectations. In particular, the model provides a framework for the ongoing development of professional skills to help the faculty member adapt to these expectations.

The chapter is divided into five sections. First, we briefly outline our perspective on the nature of professional development for faculty. Next, the model is presented and connected to our emerging perspective. The third section lists the guiding assumptions or principles that have informed our development of the model. In the fourth section, we describe the opportunities and challenges that arise for faculty developers who wish to frame their programs based on the model. Finally, we conclude by providing a defensible warrant for exploring the model as scaffolding for professional and organizational development.

Perspective on Professional Development

The driving forces affecting today's universities are pressuring institutions to make fundamental changes in the traditional assumptions that guide faculty in their workday. For example, new faculty are assumed to be (or rapidly become) competent in the use of information technologies in their teaching (Farquhar, 2001). A more diverse group of students entering college (Swail, 2002) and an increased emphasis on globalization in undergraduate education (Green, 2002) have stretched faculty to adopt appropriate pedagogies to meet these demands. The market-oriented system of higher education, a growing list of for-profit higher education companies (Newman & Couturier, 2001), and the ever-present fiscal pressures on higher education institutions (Lovett, 2002) eventually find their way into the academic lives of faculty. As a consequence of these forces, institutions have stressed the necessity of ongoing faculty renewal to cope with these changes (Farquhar, 2001)—a process that Cranton (1996) has termed transformative professional development.

We believe that the role of professional development involves guiding individuals as they negotiate the challenges described above. Because the relationship between a faculty member and an institution is complex and dynamic, the role of professional development in mediating this relationship cannot be simplistically designed. For example, faculty bring many personal elements to their work at the institution—expectations, motivations, assumptions, and knowledge. If these elements were precisely aligned with the demands of the institution, then professional development would be unnecessary. In the changing environment of higher education, however, these institutional demands require flexible, adaptable faculty who are capable of revising their expectations and assumptions—that is, faculty who are willing to engage in transformative learning (Cranton, 1994, 1996; Mezirow, 1991, 2000).

From an organizational development perspective, a university that acknowledges and supports the continuous renewal of faculty recognizes that this transformative learning is the basis for becoming a learning organization (Senge, 1990). Rather than a provider or transmitter of information, a professional development program in a learning organization is defined by its ability to help individuals respond effectively to the ongoing changes of the institution. This approach must go well beyond occasional workshops and reflection activities. What follows is a framework that outlines the key requirements of a systemic approach to professional development.

The Four Quadrant Model for Professional Development

Our model for professional development is designed to accommodate not only inevitable institutional changes but faculty adaptations to those changes. Table 9.1 outlines the essence of the model being proposed.

Table 9.1
The Four Quadrant Model for Professional Development

	Reflection	**Performance**
Individual	Critical examination of professional issues based on a personal perspective. Examples: • Reading professional literature on portfolio development • Reading about the steps to successful grant writing • Reflecting on alternative classroom pedagogies	Observable professional or technical skills necessary for achieving scholarly outcomes. Examples: • Learning how to use Microsoft Office • Acquiring competence in multivariate statistical analysis • Developing more advanced skills in creative arts performances (music, theater, art)
Public	Critical examination of professional issues based on collaborative input. Examples: • Participating as a team member in revising curricula • Having a dossier reviewed by colleagues prior to submission • Discussing the merits of a new teaching approach with a colleague	Scholarly outcomes observable to the professional community. Examples: • Presenting a paper at a conference • Presenting a creative work at an exhibition • Publishing an article in a refereed journal

We propose that professional development activities can be classified into two dimensions: individual/public and reflection/performance. Four quadrants that result from connecting these dimensions are formed: 1) individual reflection, 2) public reflection, 3) individual performance, and 4) public performance. The dimensions and related quadrants flow from similar constructs identified by Wilber (2000) and Astin (2001). Wilber's terms (individual/collective and interior/exterior) are the genesis for our adaptations to his model for the professional development setting.

Our primary thesis is that these four quadrants represent components that need to be examined and addressed to support the growth of faculty. Each quadrant contributes to the overall capabilities of faculty in their work. In addition, the model challenges program directors to consider how both dimensions could be addressed in a comprehensive approach to enhance the professional capabilities of all faculty.

The Individual/Public Dimension

A professional development program that facilitates the relationship between a faculty member's personal orientation and the changing demands of the institution must acknowledge the individual/public dimension. The *individual* component is comprised of those feelings and beliefs that articulate a faculty member's identity, sense of accomplishment, and satisfaction; it is the source of commitment and morale. This component also comprises the array of knowledge and skills that every faculty member brings to any performance demand.

The *public* component is one in which roles, duties, shared agreements, and standards are created and observed. Most notably, it defines the terms of institutional engagement that produce required outcomes, leading to the organization's success. The first demand of professional development, therefore, is to assist faculty members as they understand the changing individual/public tension and negotiate an acceptable fit within this dynamic relationship.

The Reflection/Performance Dimension

Institutional driving forces often present deep challenges to a faculty member's vision and commitment. These challenges implicate the need for *reflection/performance,* the second important dimension for professional developers to consider.

Reflection requires an individual to examine personal assumptions and is vital to the re-construction of prior beliefs. In addition, dialogue is a public form of reflection that allows dependable public agreements to emerge. Reflections must be balanced, however, by observable *performance.* Individuals must possess knowledge and skills that allow them to accomplish professional goals. In addition, higher education institutions have implicit and explicit standards to gauge faculty productivity. Public, summative assessments of performance are, in fact, the primary focus of review for evaluating faculty performance, while reflection tends to be viewed as a process that lies outside of traditional evaluation approaches.

To reprise, the relationship between faculty members and institutions appears to be reconstructed along four components: *individual reflection, public reflection, individual performance,* and *public performance.* The manner in which professional activities are woven together into a program should be based on a needs analysis that specifically identifies issues in each of these four components. What individual assumptions, left unchanged, will hinder this project? What public reflections must be shared and agreed upon through dialogue with the university community? What individual performance skills and knowledge are required for success? What performance outcomes and evaluations will be used to publicly validate that success? From our perspective, these questions highlight the major issues that must be addressed in selecting appropriate activities for faculty renewal.

A traditional program might focus on the public performance quadrant and limit professional development activities to providing information regarding technical aspects of work responsibilities. We assert that a comprehensive program for professional development can be designed around activities that deliberately address all four areas of professional competence. Conversely, failure to develop effective programs may be linked to a lack of addressing one or more of these areas.

Guiding Assumptions of the Model

Guiding assumptions underlying the model simplify and redirect the work of philosopher Ken Wilber (2000) toward a professional development setting. Wilber generated the model after an exhaustive search of common elements in hierarchical organizational structures found in a variety of disciplines. The "four corners of the universe" (p. 139) emerged as a product of categorizing these hierarchies. Adaptations of Wilber's model have been used as organizational frameworks in school curriculum design, political science, business management, nutrition education, and prison education (Wilber, 2000).

Four assumptions emerge from our integrative approach:

1) It follows that professional development activities are more comprehensively addressed—and may be more successful—when each quadrant exerts an appropriate impact on those activities.

2) While each quadrant can be viewed as an outcome (e.g., gaining personal insight into an issue could be a *product* in the individual reflection quadrant), the most valued outcome for many universities is likely to be the public performance quadrant. From a political perspective, professional developers may present the remaining three quadrants (individual reflection, individual performance, public reflection) as *processes* by which a super-ordinate goal can be achieved in the public performance quadrant.

3) Faculty may approach any professional development activity by more deeply exploring the relationship between the activity and each quadrant. For example, learning online course technology may involve increasing individual performance skills to use a software program in meeting the larger goal of developing an online course. At the same time, improving personal capacities for critical examination (individual reflection) is necessary to help the faculty member design a more appropriate course based on learning-centered principles.

4) The model can be applied to any of the traditional spheres of professional development, including teaching, research/creative activity, service/outreach, and professional and technical competencies.

Applying the Model in a Professional Development Program: Opportunities and Challenges

The model suggests a set of expected outcomes for faculty as they travel down a career path. Using language consistent with the model, we suggest that a faculty member who is functioning at a high level 1) demonstrates an ongoing capability to critically examine actions and beliefs (*individual reflection*), 2) actively engages in collegial discourse to meet professional obligations in the university and external community (*public reflection*), 3) has developed appropriate professional and technical skills to meet responsibilities in teaching, research, and service (*individual performance*), and 4) produces a valued set of scholarly outcomes that are observable to the university community (*public performance*). This vision for a more complete scholar should drive the design of a program to accommodate faculty growth across any career stage. What opportunities are present in a professional development program to exploit the characteristics of the model?

Opportunities

Two applications of the model are listed below. These examples illustrate how the model can be used as a faculty development tool on an individual and program level.

1) *Individual consultations* with faculty regarding the resolution of particular teaching concerns can profit from the model's approach. Consider a faculty member who is interested in developing an appropriate pedagogical approach for an upcoming course with a large enrollment. To successfully achieve this goal, four questions compatible with the model can be posed during a consultation: 1) What kinds of materials will you need to read or what issues do you need to consider in preparing to work on your task (*individual reflection*)? 2) What conversations will you need to have (and with whom) in order to get another perspective or feedback on your task (*public reflection*)? 3) What professional or technical skills do you need to have or develop to successfully complete the task (*individual performance*)? 4) What should be the expected outcome (product) and what timeline is necessary to be successful (*public performance*)?

2) *Workshops* that focus on developing faculty competencies in specific curricular tasks can benefit from framing the task within the model. For example, faculty who are learning how to develop a course syllabus can be expected to 1) critically reflect on the type of student learning desired in the course (*individual reflection*), 2) gain and use feedback from workshop participants about the proposed syllabus (*public reflection*), 3) assemble a set of materials and produce/format the written text (*individual performance*), and 4) produce the completed syllabus and defend its development on the first day of class to students (*public performance*).

Challenges

We continue to reexamine our assumptions about the model and how it may best serve the field of faculty development. We have been challenged by a host of issues that require resolution and outline three of these issues below.

1) It is apparent that the faculty designer may emphasize certain quadrants based on the nature of the task. For example, imagine a new faculty member who has a professional development plan that focuses on learning to enhance quantitative statistical competencies in data analysis. This

goal primarily emphasizes *individual performance* skills and could be viewed as a necessary means to achieve a more efficient method of analyzing research data to increase publication productivity (*public performance*). The role of reflection may not be as strong in this task, although it is unlikely that it could be eliminated. This example does not invalidate the model but reminds faculty developers to avoid the assumption of equal emphasis (time, effort, focus) for every quadrant.

2) The order of addressing each of the quadrants in completing a professional development activity is not straightforward. Given a situation in which public performance is considered the end product, it seems likely that individual differences will arise regarding preferences for sequencing the remaining three processes. Should a faculty member initiate efforts on completing the task through individual reflection, or should collaborative input (*public reflection*) take precedence? Are there individual performance skills that need to be shored up prior to the reflective process? Are there tasks for which "preferred pathways" or sequences exist for every faculty member? These empirical questions require the weight of systematic data collection for resolution.

3) Wilber's (2000) model described developmental steps for each quadrant in such a way that each succeeding step transcends but includes its predecessors. Connections across equivalent levels in the quadrants were also labeled. A logical extension of Wilber's model for our purposes would suggest that faculty will experience phases in their growth in each quadrant. A clear description of these phases would enhance our understanding of adult development. This level of sophistication exceeds our current use of the model in a professional development setting but challenges us to examine how we may gain from more deeply exploring the approach adopted by Wilber.

Conclusion

We have recently tested the model in a university-wide curriculum seminar at Indiana State University and have emerged with a growing respect for the magnitude of faculty development issues that can be accommodated by the model. The model's apparent simplicity—two dimensions that define four quadrants—belies the complexity of development found in Wilber's (2000) approach with similar constructs. Nevertheless, testing the limits and benefits of the model seems warranted because the model takes into account both the formative nature of development (reflective processes) and the necessary products or summative demands desired by the university (performance). In addition, the two dimensions (individual/public and reflection/performance) define the boundaries of professional development for university faculty in the three areas of scholarship as well as other professional competencies.

We believe this model offers faculty developers a framework for designing thoughtful practice to aid faculty in meeting the wide range of internal and external demands that confront higher education institutions. Awareness of the four quadrants and a need to attend to each in a deliberate fashion holds promise for making our professional development efforts more effective, long lasting, and meaningful. If professional developers desire programs that facilitate transformation, it seems necessary to do so with more sophisticated and powerful models of personal and social change. The proposed model recognizes the dialectic between individual and public within an organization; it acknowledges the dynamic between reflection and performance that is crucial to real learning.

The flexibility of this model empowers developers to consider the philosophical perspective they bring to its use, the needs of audience members, and the emphases appropriate for designing experiences that promote holistic growth given specific learning goals. Although further exploration is needed to empirically ground our proposed model, we hope this framework contributes to an important and expanding discourse on transformative learning experiences for faculty. We invite readers to join us in examining this model for its applicability in various contexts—from the small-scale process of one-on-one faculty consultation to the large-scale process of shaping and implementing a systematic, connected series of programs.

References

Astin, A. W., & Colleagues. (2001, July). *Toward a theory of institutional transformation in higher education.* Paper presented at the annual meeting of the AAC&U Institute on Campus Leadership for Sustainable Innovation, Leesburg, VA.

Cranton, P. (1994). *Understanding and promoting transformative learning: A guide for educators of adults.* San Francisco, CA: Jossey-Bass.

Cranton, P. (1996). *Professional development as transformative learning: New perspectives for teachers of adults.* San Francisco, CA: Jossey-Bass.

Farquhar, R. (2001). Faculty renewal and institutional revitalization in Canadian universities. *Change, 33*(4), 12–20.

Green, M. (2002). Joining the world: The challenge to internationalizing undergraduate education. *Change, 34*(3), 12–21.

Lovett, C. (2002). Cracks in the bedrock: Can U. S. higher education remain number one? *Change, 34*(2), 10–15.

Mezirow, J. (1991). *Transformative dimensions of adult learning.* San Francisco, CA: Jossey-Bass.

Mezirow, J. (2000). Learning to think like an adult: Core concepts of transformation theory. In J. Mezirow & Associates (Eds.), *Learning as transformation: Critical perspectives on a theory in progress* (pp. 3–33). San Francisco, CA: Jossey-Bass

Newman, F., & Couturier, L. (2001). The new competitive arena: Market forces invade the academy. *Change, 33*(5), 10–17.

Senge, P. (1990). *The fifth discipline: The art and practice of a learning organization.* New York, NY: Doubleday.

Swail, W. (2002). Higher education and the new demographics: Questions for policy. *Change, 34*(4), 14–23.

Wilber, K. (2000). The four corners of the known universe. In K. Wilber (Ed.), *The collected works of Ken Wilber* (Vol. 8, pp. 135–148). Boston, MA: Shambhala.

Contact:

David J. Langley
Center for Teaching and Learning
Indiana State University
127 Dreiser Hall
Terre Haute, IN 47809
Voice (812) 237-4452
Fax (812) 237-3053
Email dlangley@indstate.edu

Terence W. O'Connor
School of Education
The College of New Jersey
2000 Pennington Road
Ewing, NJ 08628
Voice (609) 771-2100
Email oconnor@tcnj.edu

Michele M. Welkener
Center for Teaching and Learning
Indiana State University
127 Dreiser Hall
Terre Haute, IN 47809
Voice (812) 237-3057
Fax (812) 237-3053
Email mwelkener@indstate.edu

David J. Langley is Interim Director of the Center for Teaching and Learning and Associate Professor in the Department of Physical Education at Indiana State University. His work at the center focuses on generating and implementing various campus-wide initiatives on faculty development. His scholarly interests in higher education involve transformative learning, models for professional development, and assessment practices.

Terence W. O'Connor is Dean of the School of Education and Professor in the Department of Educational Administration and Secondary Education at The College of New Jersey. He was awarded a three-year FIPSE grant in 2000 on promoting strategic teaching to enhance the academic competencies of students in transition courses. He has been a frequent presenter at numerous conferences in higher education and is currently completing a book on patterns and routines underlying successful teaching.

Michele M. Welkener serves as the Assistant Director of the Center for Teaching and Learning at Indiana State University, where she designs and implements professional development programming for teaching assistants and faculty. Creativity and college student development are at the center of her interdisciplinary scholarship.

10

A Systematic, Hands-On, Reflective, and Effective (SHORE) Approach to Faculty Development for New and Seasoned Faculty

Scott E. Hampton
Craig D. Morrow
Ashleah Bechtel
Marjorie H. Carroll
United States Military Academy

The purpose of the faculty development program for teaching Introduction to Psychology in this study is to further develop skills for new and seasoned faculty to enable them to teach and inspire students more effectively. This Systematic, Hands-On, Reflective, and Effective (SHORE) approach provides a forum to practice teaching skills, gain familiarity with course material, incorporate classroom management techniques, evaluate teaching effectiveness, and build a cohesive teaching team. Evaluative feedback indicates the approach positively affects both the faculty and 1,100 students annually. Implications for faculty development programs and research are also discussed.

There are many approaches to developing faculty in higher education. However, when many colleges make attempts to incorporate faculty development programs, Murray (1995) noted that they "tend to rely on a smorgasbord of [ad-hoc] activities rather than a unified plan with clear and coherent strategies based on articulated objectives" (p. 559). Weimer (1997) reviewed the impact of the most common instructional interventions to improve teaching in higher education and found the following to be most effective, in order of effectiveness: personal consultation, teaching workshops/

seminars, research grants, peers, and teaching resource materials. Additionally, Mintz (1999) added that faculty development should be more holistic in nature than just "how to teach" workshops. The developmental process should foster social interaction among colleagues, and encompass the values of the institution. As such, a systematic approach to faculty development would strive to integrate pedagogical instruction with hands-on teaching opportunities within the social context of the university and/or department setting.

Another important aspect of faculty development involves reflection on teaching experiences. Allen's (1991) view of a reflective thinking or practitioner program involves information on teaching, guided practice, teaching experience with guided reflection, peer visitations and consultations, consultations with faculty and supervisor, and self-reflection. Ideally, then, this valuable reflective component should also be systematically integrated into a faculty development program.

In addition to the holistic, hands-on, and reflection components, reviews of faculty development literature (Ingram 2001; Murray, 1999) highlighted other effective faculty development components, including a climate that fosters development, a formalized and structured program linked to the institution's mission, linking faculty development to the reward structure, faculty ownership in designing and delivering faculty development, collegial support for good teaching, and a culture of good teaching that is valued by administrators. Thus, effective faculty development is far from a smorgasbord of activities to allow faculty to sample. Instead, it should involve a systematic process to maximize faculty development, teaching practice, and reflection within a context that matches the needs and goals of the faculty and institution.

Faculty at West Point typically experience a 30% turnover of instructors each year, which necessitates a systematic and integrative approach that ensures new instructors are prepared to teach. Like teaching assistants and inexperienced faculty for many other universities, the new instructors at West Point typically assume responsibilities for teaching the introductory undergraduate courses. The current program focuses on the General Psychology Program in the Department of Behavioral Sciences and Leadership at West Point, which developed and implemented an intensive faculty development program for both its new and seasoned faculty. The objective of the program is to produce effective educators through a developmental process that allows participants to practice teaching skills, gain familiarity with course material, incorporate classroom management techniques, evaluate teaching effectiveness, and build a cohesive teaching team. The purpose of this chapter is to discuss the Systematic, Hands-On, Reflective, and Effective (SHORE) nature of this faculty development program.

Systematic Approach

The faculty development program is conducted primarily during the summer, but continues throughout the year in a four-phase process. Although minor modifications to the program are made annually, the basic structure of the workshop has been found to be an effective means of preparing junior faculty and enhancing the skills of more seasoned faculty. For example, the current program involved four new faculty members who joined eight seasoned faculty members in the General Psychology Program. Through a sponsorship program, seasoned faculty begin a dialogue with the new instructors before they arrive at West Point to familiarize the new instructors with the course, the faculty development process, and the expectations. Additionally, the sponsor will facilitate their transition into the new community. This sponsor will also typically serve as the new instructor's mentor as they go through the first year of professional development in the department, which provides the type of personal consultation common to many of the most effective instructional interventions (Weimer, 1997).

Four Phases

The program is divided into four distinct phases. The first two phases occur during the new faculty members' first two months at the academy, prior to the start of the fall academic term. The third phase is conducted throughout the fall semester, while the fourth phase is conducted during the spring semester. Each phase has a distinct purpose with respect to faculty development and course curriculum.

Phase I (summer). The first phase is designed to prepare new faculty members for their first teaching assignment in the General Psychology course, or as a refresher for those faculty members who have been away from teaching for a number of years. First, however, the department chair and program managers provide an overview of the department's mission and vision, which illustrate the commitment and value placed on teaching at the academy. Additionally, several activities in the socialization process of new faculty include a walking tour of the campus, recreational softball games, and numerous luncheons among the faculty. Families also participate in several social activities such as boat rides and picnics.

After the department overview, faculty are instructed in course and lesson design and development using the systematic design of instruction (SDI)

(Dick, Carey, & Carey, 2001). This provides faculty members with the tools necessary to develop their own courses and lesson plans and a basic knowledge of how students learn and how to motivate students in the classroom according to Keller's ARCS model of motivation (Keller, 1987a, 1987b). Subsequent activities in the workshop are often linked to this theoretical framework to enhance student learning and motivation in the classroom. Again, new faculty and their sponsors work alongside each other to review and practice the fundamentals of designing instruction.

The remainder of Phase I focuses on course content and practice teaching. Before the new faculty practice teach, however, they review the assessments for each content area, which models the SDI process. The seasoned faculty then model the lessons for the first half of the General Psychology course to the new faculty. Both new and seasoned faculty serve as students for the modeled classes, replicating an actual classroom setting. After the first content area of the course is modeled, the new instructors each practice teach one of the lessons to their peers and the seasoned faculty who serve as their students.

During these lesson models, which are also videotaped, the seasoned faculty also try to model student behaviors in order to practice classroom management techniques. For example, one instructor may try to answer all the questions and another may try to get the instructor to address an irrelevant topic. The goal is to provide the new instructors with opportunities to experience numerous classroom situations in a safe and supportive environment to enhance their confidence and ability to handle such situations as they arise with their students. By the end of Phase I, the new instructors have taught three lessons and seen the lessons and assessments for the first half of the course.

Phase II (summer). The second phase provides faculty time to prepare their lesson plans for the first half of the course before the fall term begins and continue their orientation to the academy's history, goals, and numerous programs. During this phase, new faculty attend orientations and sometimes literally see many of the activities and events outside of their department that contribute to the academy's mission. For example, they can visit field training of cadets or take a more detailed historical tour of the installation. Spouses are also invited to many of these orientations to facilitate their transition to, and understanding of, the academy. Seasoned faculty and mentors are also available to assist with questions in lesson design and development. In addition to teaching new faculty, the faculty development program fosters collegiality among the new and seasoned faculty and enculturates the new faculty to the mission and values of the institution.

Phase III (fall). During the fall term, new faculty continue to meet with the seasoned faculty during weekly seminars to share lesson strategies about the second half of the course. These informal discussions provide a forum to discuss various strategies, lessons learned, and teaching practices. Additionally, new faculty can view modeled lessons from a video library, if desired. The course supervisor also visits classes to provide teaching consultations to both new and seasoned faculty.

Again, reinforcing the SDI process, the new faculty review and calibrate the assessments for each content area before they discuss and teach lesson strategies for that area. Because the General Psychology course uses the same exams for all sections, which focus on application of psychology concepts to leadership scenarios through multiple choice and short essay questions, faculty practice grading student exams to calibrate their grading scheme.

Finally, students provide all faculty with midterm and end-of-course ratings to provide feedback to individual instructors. These confidential student ratings are only seen by the instructor, which fosters self-assessment and personal teaching development.

Phase IV (spring). By the start of the spring term, all new faculty have taught for an entire semester and the program focus shifts from teaching to course curriculum. Lessons learned and teaching tips are still shared among the faculty in the weekly meetings. Faculty also continue to calibrate assessments before they teach each content area, as well as gathering student feedback. However, curriculum content now becomes the primary focus. Both new and seasoned faculty review the curriculum of the course to ensure integration of the latest research findings in the field. The course director continues to provide teaching consultations to instructors who also provide peer consultation to each other. Additionally, new and seasoned faculty are videotaped in a teaching lab to continue their self-assessment and to provide videotaped lesson models for future faculty. Thus, this systematic four-phase structure of faculty development in the department is a continuous process that extends throughout the entire year for both new and seasoned faculty. By the end of the spring term, the new faculty have joined the ranks of the seasoned faculty; they then help develop the new faculty when they arrive the following summer. The systematic process continues the cycle of developing a new group of faculty, while at the same time, continuing the development of the seasoned faculty.

HANDS-ON APPROACH

The hands-on approach to faculty development reinforces the principle of learning by doing by allowing new faculty to practice teach in authentic classroom situations. Faculty are given time to design lessons to teach and then provided opportunities to practice these lessons in the summer before the fall term begins. An integral and critical aspect of the practice teaching sessions is the practice at providing feedback on teaching practices. During Phase I, seasoned faculty provide feedback to new faculty on their practice teaching lessons. Additionally, the new faculty provide feedback to the seasoned faculty on their modeled lessons. This dual-direction feedback system fosters collegiality among all faculty. Even the most senior faculty are open to candid feedback from new faculty because of their commitment to teaching excellence. This feedback approach continues throughout the academic year as the course director provides feedback to new and seasoned faculty and peers provide feedback to each other.

Another hands-on aspect that illustrates the faculty ownership component (Ingram, 2001; Murrray, 1999) is that faculty members within the General Psychology Program in the department conduct the entire faculty development process discussed thus far. The course director solicits input from all faculty when developing the annual development plan and then all available faculty participate in the development plan. Both new and seasoned faculty engage in a systematic and hands-on participatory approach to faculty development.

REFLECTION

Learning by doing is enhanced through reflection throughout this faculty development program. The hallmark of the faculty development experience in this program is the continuous feedback surrounding the process, which facilitates reflection. As part of the faculty development experience, and in keeping with reflective thinking researchers, the program provides opportunities for faculty to practice teaching and to reflect on strengths, areas of improvement, and instructional strategy, and to share these reflections with other faculty. As described earlier, this faculty development program incorporates all components of Allen's (1991) view of a reflective thinking or practitioner program: 1) information on teaching; 2) guided practice; 3) teaching experience with guided reflection; 4) peer visitations and consultations; 5) consultations with faculty and supervisor; and 6) self-reflection. After each modeled or practice teaching lesson in Phase I, faculty reflect on the effectiveness of their strategy with their peers and mentor, using a printed checklist as a guide (see

Appendix 10.1). Both peers and mentors enable all faculty to reflect-in-action and reflect-on-action (Schön, 1987) during the program to enhance the overall effectiveness, learning, and development of new and seasoned faculty. One supervisor of the program often emphasized that the seasoned faculty would actually benefit more from this modeling and feedback process of the workshop than the new faculty (Beach, 1993). Because of the seasoned faculty modeling and openness to feedback, new faculty members are quickly assimilated into the culture of the department and readily accept feedback from other faculty members when they begin to provide instruction.

In addition to allowing new faculty members to exercise the instructional style before a nonjudgmental audience, the practice teaching sessions also serve to enhance new faculty members' self-awareness of their own strengths as well as those areas most likely to profit from further attention. To maximize the utility of these sessions, each period of practice teaching is videotaped for the instructors' own critical review. Because many new faculty members choose to practice teach lessons closely related to their particular area of expertise, the entire faculty receives a de facto workshop on recent developments in a variety of content areas. All participants gain from the innovative strategies and references to the latest research in the field. The day following the practice teaching, the new faculty member will sit down with his or her mentor and reflect upon the feedback received and how to improve the lesson strategy based on that feedback.

Research on effective faculty development interventions note that "[the] ideal type of consultant is a colleague in one's own department who is an up-to-date specialist in the specific discipline and who also can serve as a model in instructional methods" (Maxwell & Kazlauskas, 1992, p. 356). The mentor in this faculty development program fulfills this ideal type of role.

Instructors also reflect on feedback from mid- and end-of-course student surveys. Reviews of student ratings literature reveal that midterm student ratings feedback can have positive impacts on teaching practices, ratings of teaching effectiveness, and student motivation (Cohen, 1980; L' Hommedieu, Menges, & Brinko, 1990). Receiving such feedback throughout the year facilitates instructor awareness of strengths and weaknesses in their teaching strategies and practices. Most instructors reported that they modified aspects of their classroom strategies as a result of cadet mid-semester feedback. The focus on self-awareness during faculty development is instrumental in allowing faculty to read and act on this feedback without feeling threatened.

Effectiveness

In addition to integrating the six components of effective faculty development programs highlighted in the literature and illustrated throughout this chapter, results from faculty and student surveys point to the success of the department's faculty development program according to pre- and post-tests. The objective of the program is to develop the pedagogical skills of the instructors in general and prepare them to teach General Psychology more effectively during the academic year in particular. The five major goals for Phase I of the program include becoming an effective teacher, being comfortable with course content, incorporating classroom management, evaluating appropriateness and effectiveness of instruction, and working as and feeling like a member of the course faculty team.

Faculty survey results and instructor comments immediately following Phase I illustrate the positive impact of Phase I on preparing new faculty to teach the course. The results summarized below and in Table 10.1 illustrate the new instructors' confidence in their level of preparation and ability to accomplish the workshop objectives. Table 10.1 also illustrates the gain in new faculty confidence from pre- to post-workshop assessment in several objectives.

Goal 1: Become an Effective Teacher

This goal includes a focus on instructors who are student-centered, influential, value learning, able to provide efficient instruction, and who believe in their ability as well as that of their students. This outcome was measured through the statements "design an instructional strategy," and "implement an instructional strategy," because instructors had to show the aforementioned attributes during their practice teaching or lesson modeling. New faculty rated their feeling of preparedness much higher after Phase I of the program in the summer than they did before they began the program. New instructor written feedback supported this rating:

> [The most worthwhile events were] the practice teaching and evaluation. It was immensely important and helpful to see myself on tape and to hear feedback on my class.
>
> The modeled lessons were excellent and the feedback and experience of the practice teach sessions were critical.
>
> I'm 100 times better [at teaching] than 3 weeks ago.

TABLE 10.1
New Faculty Survey Questions Before and After Phase I of the Faculty Development Program

New Faculty Survey Questions (n = 4)	Pre-test	Post-test
How prepared are you to accomplish the following goals? (1 = Not prepared 3 = Prepared 5 = Well prepared)		
1. Become an effective teacher	2.67	4.75
a. Design an instructional strategy, given a lesson analysis, the test & list of available materials		
b. Implement an instructional strategy		
2. Be comfortable with course content	N/A*	4.75
a. Understand partial and full models of course lessons		
b, Practice teach course lessons		
3. Incorporate classroom management	N/A*	4.75
Incorporate the following into the classroom:		
a. Films/TV clips in classes		
b. Conferences/discussions		
c. Role-playing exercises		
d. Practical exercises		
e. Practice integrating exercises		
f. Classroom administrative procedures		
4. Evaluate appropriateness and effectiveness of instruction	2.67	4.5
a. Administer tests		
b. Grade tests		
5. Work and feel as a member of the course faculty team	4.33	5
Rate each activity according to how well it prepared you to accomplish the following goals	N/A*	
(1 = Unsatisfactory 3 = Average 5 = Outstanding)		
1. Department welcome orientation		4.75
2. Course orientation		4.75
3. Systematic Design of Instruction (SDI)		4.75
4. Teaching strategies		4.75
5. Administrative policies and procedures		4.75
6. Content area overviews		4.75
7. Partial class models and feedback		4.75
8. Full class models and feedback		4.75
9. Practice teaching and feedback		4.75
10. Exam review before covering the content area		5
11. Exam calibration		5

* N/A because pretest administered before exposure to modeled classes and practice teaching.

Goal 2: Be Comfortable With Course Content

This goal involves instructors becoming subject matter experts by utilizing returning faculty or outside sources as resources, as well as practice teaching and giving feedback to returning faculty. This outcome was measured with ratings of the instructor's understanding of material covered in class models and practice teaching. New faculty rated their level of preparedness to teach the course as high.

Goal 3: Incorporate Classroom Management

Instructors must plan their classes, be prepared, have organized instructional activities, and most importantly, stay on time and on task. This outcome was measured through ratings in the following areas: classroom administration procedures, incorporation of films, role-playing exercises, practical exercises, and integrated performance objectives. Again, new faculty rated their level of preparedness in this area as high.

Goal 4: Evaluate the Appropriateness and Effectiveness of Instruction

Instructors are able to evaluate individual strengths and weaknesses in teaching throughout the year. The survey question, "Evaluate the appropriateness and effectiveness of instruction," assessed this objective. New faculty rated their level of preparedness as quite low before Phase I and much higher after Phase I. Written feedback supported this rating. One new instructor wrote:

> I now have an understanding of how active learning is incorporated into our lesson. These activities also allowed me to identify what will be difficult for the cadets, possible trouble spots I may encounter and various strategies that seem to work well.

Goal 5: Work and Feel Like a Member of the Course Faculty Team

Instructors feel like part of the team and have pride in the department. The survey question, "Work and feel as a member of the PL100 committee team," assessed this objective, which received a perfect "5" rating from the new faculty. Again, written feedback also supported this rating. For example, one new instructor wrote: "The mentor program was the most enjoyable part of the program. It enabled me to thoroughly study and observe the lesson development process." Evidence of the collegiality of the new and seasoned faculty is summarized by two new instructors' comments about what they liked most about the workshop:

I felt welcome and that the previous years' instructors really want us here.

The feeling of safety. It was OK to make mistakes and I was offered opportunities to correct mistakes or come up with alternate strategies.

Thus, survey results and new instructor comments seem to indicate that the program was very effective for preparing the new faculty to teach and also integrating them into the department faculty team. When specifically asked to rate each activity from Phase I of the program according to how well it prepared you to accomplish the program goals, the average rating for all activities was 4.75 on a 5-point Likert scale with 5 representing "outstanding" (see Table 10.1).

To assess the effectiveness of the faculty development program, we also looked toward the students and their performance and attitudes toward their instructors and the General Psychology course. Ideally, effective teachers should have a positive impact on student learning and student attitudes (Reiser & Dick, 1996). Seldin (1999) claims that student ratings are the most prevalent source of evaluating teaching effectiveness in higher education and McKeachie (1997) adds, "Student ratings are the single most valid source of data on teaching effectiveness" (p. 1219). Additionally, reviews of the literature reveal that student ratings of particular outcomes are positively related to learning outcomes. Thus, we examined the impact of the faculty development program on student attitudes through student ratings (Cohen, 1980; Feldman, 1989).

One way to measure student learning is the successful completion of the course. In a typical year, less than ten students in 1,100 will fail the course, which is an overall pass rating of over 99%. The class average for the General Psychology course, which requires cadets to demonstrate content knowledge and application of that content, is typically near 83%, a "B" average.

Additionally, one of the academic goals for the academy is understanding of human behavior (USMA Academic Board and Office of the Dean, 1998). On an end-of-course student survey, the majority of students responded "agree" or "strongly agree" to the statements "It was important for me to learn and master all that I could from this course" and "I think I can apply concepts I learned in the course later in life and career." Overall, students felt they gained an understanding of human behavior and how to apply it in their future roles.

End-of-course student ratings also reveal that instructors who participated in this workshop were rated higher than the academy average in many areas, such as instructor encouragement, enthusiasm and motivation, stimulation of critical thinking skills, class preparedness, concern with student learning, and mastery of subject material. Four of these rating dimensions were significantly different ($p < .01$). What makes this difference interesting, however, is the institutional requirement at West Point that all academic departments have new instructor faculty development programs before the academic year begins. Higher ratings in the Department of General Psychology may be due to the combined effects of the systematic approach, practical hands-on experiences, feedback, and reflection upon those experiences throughout the academic year. On the other hand, it could also be due to the nature of the interesting and relevant content taught to freshman in introductory psychology. Incidentally, one rating on fellow students' contributions to learning was significantly lower than the academy mean. This could be due to the individual learning emphasis in such an introductory course as compared to many other upper class courses that tend to have more collaborative projects.

Table 10.2 also illustrates extremely favorable student responses to departmental questions on instructor enthusiasm, communication, and lesson structure. The modeling of lessons by seasoned faculty seems to have a positive influence on new instructor lesson planning and delivery as evident by the extremely high student rating of 4.91 to the question "My instructor had a structure or plan for every lesson's learning activities." A sample of additional student comments to the question "What comments or suggestions would you like to leave with your instructor?" includes:

> I really enjoyed your class. It was my favorite Academic course of my plebe [freshman] year and I learned a great deal about myself, others, and how I can apply this knowledge as a learner in the Army. Thanks.
>
> Your enthusiasm helped remind me why I'm at this school and showed me the type of leader I want to become.

The faculty development program, then, seems to produce confident and competent faculty that students notice and positively regard.

Recommendations

Although it may not be feasible for every university to operate a faculty development program to the degree that this program has at West Point, it is possible for faculty members to take pieces of this exemplar and fit it to meet their institutional needs. If new instructors do not arrive until just before the semester, seasoned faculty members could coach and mentor them into the

TABLE 10.2

A Comparison of Student Survey Responses Between USMA Courses and Psychology Course[1]

USMA Questions[2]	**USMA**		**Psychology**		
	M	SD	M	SD	T
1) This instructor encouraged students to be responsible for their own learning.	4.48	.64	4.52	.57	1.68
2) This instructor used effective techniques for learning, both in class and for out-of-class assignments.	4.22	.9	4.61	.57	*16.36
3) My instructor cared about my learning in this course.	4.45	.75	4.72	.51	*12.66
4) My instructor demonstrated respect for cadets as individuals.	4.57	.68	4.8	.46	*11.96
5) My fellow students contributed to my learning in this course.	3.99	.94	3.87	.85	*-3.38
6) My motivation to learn and to continue learning has increased because of this course.	3.92	1.05	4.02	.87	1.13
7) This instructor stimulated my thinking.	4.22	.86	4.47	.64	*9.34
8) In this course, my critical thinking ability increased.	4.01	.94	4.06	.81	1.48
Program Only Questions			M	SD	
9) My instructor communicated effectively (e.g., appropriate level, spoke clearly, inflections, etc.).			4.76	.51	
10) My instructor was enthusiastic and energetic when presenting course material.			4.75	.57	
11) My instructor had a structure or plan for every lesson's learning activities.			4.91	.3	
12) My instructor was concerned with my learning (e.g., encouraged questions and discussion, encouraged AI when appropriate, seemed approachable for help).			4.79	.46	
13) My instructor showed me ways in which the course was of practical significance and applicable in my future (e.g., military applications, future course applications, or common applications).			4.66	.53	
14) My instructor helped motivate me to do my best work and gain maximum benefit from the course.			4.41	.72	

1 Represent Mean scores for 12 instructors
2 Scale range: 1 = Strongly disagree to 5 = Strongly Agree
*p<.001

department. These new instructors could then shadow seasoned faculty to observe them teaching classes. Likewise, the seasoned faculty members could observe new instructors teaching or review videotapes of their classes to provide valuable and supportive feedback and reflection opportunities.

Researching the specific aspects of faculty development is a worthwhile endeavor. The program described in this chapter has evolved into its current state over many years. Soliciting feedback from faculty and students and analyzing such feedback and student performance continually helps improve the efficiency and effectiveness of the faculty development process. A critical and efficient aspect of this program is that it is entirely resourced by the academic department, with the institutional support and priority given to faculty development by the academy dean and department head.

Disclaimer

The views presented in this chapter are those of the authors and do not necessarily represent the views of the Department of Defense or its components.

References

Allen, R. R. (1991). Encouraging reflection in teaching assistants. In J. D. Nyquist, R. D. Abbott, D. H. Wulff, J. & Sprague (Eds.), *Preparing the professorate for tomorrow to teach: Selected readings in TA training* (pp. 323–317). Dubuques, IA: Kendall/Hunt.

Beach, J. (1993, Summer). *Address to faculty.* Department of Behavioral Sciences and Leadership, West Point, NY.

Cohen, P. A. (1980). Effectiveness of student-rating feedback for improving college instruction: A meta-analysis of findings. *Research in Higher Education, 13,* 321–341.

Dick, W., Carey, L., & Carey, J. (2001). *The systematic design of instruction* (5th ed.). Boston, MA: Addison, Wesley, & Longman.

Feldman, K. A. (1989). The association between student ratings of specific instructional dimensions and student achievement: Refining and extending the syntheses of data from multisection validity studies. *Research in Higher Education, 30*(6), 583–645.

Ingram, K. (2001). The effects of reflective thinking training on TAs' reflective thinking, use of instructional activities, instructional effectiveness, motivation to teach and their students' attitudes toward instruction. (Doctoral Dissertation, Florida State University, 2001). *Dissertation Abstracts International, 62*(2), 486.

Keller, J. M. (1987a). Strategies for stimulating the motivation to learn. *Performance & Instruction, 26*, 1–7.

Keller, J. M. (1987b). The systematic process of motivational design. *Performance & Instruction, 26*, 1–8.

L' Hommedieu, R., Menges, R., & Brinko, K. (1990). Methodological explanations for the modest effects of feedback. *Journal of Educational Psychology, 82*, 232–241.

Maxwell, W. E., & Kazlauskas, E. J. (1992). Which faculty development methods really work in community colleges? A review of research. *Community Junior College Quarterly, 16*, 351–360.

McKeachie, W. J. (1997). Student ratings: The validity of use. *American Psychologist, 52*, 1218–1225.

Mintz, J. M. (1999, Spring). Faculty development and teaching: A holistic approach. *Liberal Education, 85*(2), 32–37.

Murray, J. P. (1995). Faculty (mis)development in Ohio two-year colleges. *Community College Journal of Research and Practice, 19*, 549–563.

Murray, J. P. (1999). Faculty development in a national sample of community colleges. *Community College Review, 27*(3), 47–64.

Reiser, R., & Dick, W. (1996). *Instructional planning: A guide for teachers* (2nd ed.). Boston, MA: Allyn and Bacon.

Schön, D. A. (1987). *Educating the reflective practitioner: Toward a new design for teaching and learning in the professions.* San Francisco, CA: Jossey-Bass.

Seldin, P. (1999). Current practices—good and bad—nationally. In P. Seldin & Associates, *Changing practices in evaluating teaching: A practical guide to improved faculty performance and promotion/tenure decisions* (pp. 1–24). Bolton, MA: Anker.

USMA Academic Board and Office of the Dean. (1998). *Educating army leaders for the 21st century.* West Point, NY: United States Military Academy.

Weimer, M. (1997). Exploring the implications: From research to practice. In R. P. Perry & J. C. Smart (Eds.), *Effective teaching in higher education: Research and practice* (pp. 411–435). New York, NY: Agathon.

Contact:

LTC Scott E. Hampton
Department of Behavioral Sciences and Leadership
United States Military Academy
West Point, NY 10996
Voice (845) 938-5637
Email LS0425@usma.edu

Major Craig D. Morrow
Department of Behavioral Sciences and Leadership
United States Military Academy
West Point, NY 10996
Voice (845) 938-4806
Email LC4122@usma.edu

Major Ashleah Bechtel
Chief, Specialized Training Management Branch
Total Army Personnel Command
Alexandria, VA 22314
Email Ashleah.Bechtel@hoffman.army.mil

Marjorie H. Carroll
Department of Behavioral Sciences and Leadership
United States Military Academy
West Point, NY 10996
Voice (845) 938-5642
Email LM5467@usma.edu

LTC Scott E. Hampton, PhD, is a career officer in the United States Army. He currently serves as an Assistant Professor at the United States Military Academy and is responsible for teaching cadets and officers on topics related to psychology, teaching, training, and leadership. His research interests include student ratings feedback, instructional consultation, faculty development, and teaching. His doctorate is in instructional systems from Florida State University.

Major Craig D. Morrow is a career officer in the United States Army. Currently assigned as an Assistant Professor at the United States Military Academy, he teaches Developmental Psychology and General Psychology. He earned his graduate degree in developmental psychology from the Pennsylvania State University.

Major Ashleah Bechtel entered the United States Army in 1991 as an Adjutant General Corps officer. She is currently responsible for managing all specialized training for enlisted soldiers to include the noncommissioned officer education system.

While assigned to the United States Military Academy she taught psychology and counseling. Her research interests include eating disorders, military families and stress, and faculty development. She received her master's in counselor education from the University of North Carolina at Greensboro.

Marjorie H. Carroll is Assistant Professor of Psychology at the United States Military Academy. She is responsible for teaching introduction to psychology, research methods and statistics, theories of personality, and abnormal psychology. Her research interests are in the areas of memory and attributions of responsibility in rape scripts. She received her doctorate in clinical psychology from St. John's University.

11

Foucault and the Practice of Educational Development: Power and Surveillance in Individual Consultations

Peter Felten
Deandra Little
Allison Pingree
Vanderbilt University

A common goal of educational development is to create a neutral, "safe" place for clients in individual consultations. Such an approach, while well intentioned, obscures the multifaceted web of power threading through and around our work. Using Michel Foucault's theories of sovereign and disciplinary power, we trace the forms that power can take in specific types of consultations (small group instructional diagnosis, course evaluations, and videotape). While power is always "dangerous," it is less likely to be damaging if we are conscious of its presence and impact—and of our own participation in its complexity.

In "Teaching Through Discussion as the Exercise of Disciplinary Power," Stephen Brookfield (2001) draws on French philosopher and social theorist Michel Foucault to analyze the circular and complex flow of power and surveillance that emerges in any pedagogical context. Brookfield shows that, paradoxically, even benign or democratically oriented teaching techniques can reiterate the very power structures they are designed to dismantle; seating people in a circle for discussion, for example, can unintentionally alienate those who choose not to participate. As a result, then, teachers can "often end up with an incomplete and naïve understanding of how power manifests itself in college classrooms" (p. 262).

Brookfield's analysis extends beyond instructors to educational developers. His advice seems particularly striking, given that such development work is so often framed as nonhierarchical, neutral, and safe (POD Network, 2002). In POD's guide for new faculty developers, Jenson (2002) explains that the consultant's role is "not to torture, but to nurture; not to disparage, but to encourage; not to command, but to coach; not to correct, but to suggest; not to clone but to hone" (p. 98). Brookfield (2001) concurs: "empowering teachers to be creative risk-takers is what we're about as faculty developers" (p. 261). However, Brookfield also suggests that developers should "recognize the presence of power in our daily practices, particularly the false face of apparently beneficent power exercised to help teachers or learners realize their full potential" (p. 262).

The purpose of this chapter is to look through a Foucauldian lens at possible false faces of apparently beneficent power in the context of individual consultations. By examining common types of consultations conducted by educational developers (small group instructional diagnosis, teaching evaluations, and videotape), we explore how power and surveillance shape individual work with clients. Our intention is not to offer definitive formulas or strategies for eliminating power in consultations. Instead, we contend that educational developers will become more reflective and capable practitioners when they have a clearer sense of what Brookfield (2001) calls the "unanticipated consequences of our supposedly empowering practices" (p. 262)—particularly as these emerge in our individual consultation work.

Michel Foucault, French Social Theorist

In *Discipline and Punish: The Birth of the Prison* (1995), Foucault examines mechanisms of power at work in social and state institutions, particularly as these shifted from sovereign power exercised by kings over their kingdoms to disciplinary power exercised over and between subjects within the social body of city-states. Foucault's definitions of sovereign and disciplinary power are pertinent for our examination of power and surveillance in individual consultations because they explain the relationship between power and the production of knowledge as reciprocal—even within a seemingly democratic or safe environment like educational consulting. As Foucault (1980a) insists,"[t]he exercise of power perpetually creates knowledge and conversely, knowledge constantly induces effects of power" (p. 52).

Foucault defines sovereign power as power that operates unidirectionally and hierarchically. In a system of sovereign power, the source of power is visible and acts intermittently to punish, reward, or respond to a specific set of circumstances, as in times of war or crisis. This type of power emanates from particular, identifiable individuals (e.g., the king or sovereign) or is administered by visible agents acting on behalf of these individuals. Within the classroom, instructors hold some degree of sovereign power; they are visible and identifiable representatives of power for their students and exercise power intermittently over students' lives through assignments and grading.

Although sovereign power is often exercised in visible, rigid, and established patterns in traditional university hierarchies, disciplinary power is at work as well. Unlike sovereign power, disciplinary power is not centralized in a perceivable source; there is no one person establishing and enforcing the rules that govern and socialize. Instead, this power is all-pervasive and embedded within the everyday lives and actions of individuals. "Employed and exercised through a net-like organization" (Foucault, 1980b, p. 98), disciplinary power operates as a web of power relations threaded between and among individuals and groups. As exercised through this multidirectional net, disciplinary power becomes an essentially corrective force fostering normalization and conformity. It operates through, and in turn constitutes, the processes by which we discipline ourselves to conform to an imagined ideal or norm.

The primary purpose of disciplinary power is to train subjects to fit the norms of a specific discipline. Through disciplinary modes such as surveillance and the examination, Foucault suggests that certain qualities, skills, and social behaviors are measured against the norm, leading to censure or reward. We contend that the assessment and consultation models employed in educational development are examples of such norming processes. In effect, these rituals, as examinations, produce "a normalizing gaze, a surveillance that makes it possible to qualify, to classify and to punish [and that] establishes over individuals a visibility through which one differentiates them and judges them" (Foucault, 1995, p. 184).

Disciplinary power, then, is exercised invisibly through instruments of surveillance over subjects who are aware they are being surveyed. As Foucault (1995) insists, "It is the fact of being constantly seen, of being able always to be seen, that maintains the disciplined individual in his subjection" (p. 187). Or, as Brookfield (2001) further explains,

> in a society subject to disciplinary power, we discipline ourselves by watching others and ourselves . . . we watch ourselves because we sense that our attempt to stay close to the norm is itself being watched by another, all-seeing, presence. We carry within us the sense that "out there," in some hidden undiscoverable location, "they" are constantly observing us. (p. 268)

Being a subject within a disciplinary society such as the university means having a heightened awareness of being observed, assessed, and judged by others; indeed, a well-defined relation of surveillance is, for Foucault (1995), "inscribed at the heart of the practice of teaching" (p. 176).

To what extent might surveillance be "inscribed," as well, at the "heart of the practice" of teaching the teachers—at the heart of educational development? That is, how do both sovereign and disciplinary power affect not only classroom instructors but also the developers who consult with them? Are there "false faces of apparently beneficent power" involved in educational consultations—and if so, what do they look like? Do they differ depending on the nature of the teaching data (videotape, student course evaluations, etc.) that underlies the consultation?

Such questions might be uncomfortable for us as developers, since we often try to work as counterpoints to the barriers that sovereign power creates in our institutions. But in swerving away from such questions, we may fail to recognize how and where we nonetheless operate within, and even perpetuate, a web of disciplinary power—and in that blindness, potentially exacerbate the very power dynamics we work to mitigate.

In order to clarify how such "false faces" of beneficence and "unanticipated consequences" of power might emerge, and how awareness of them can increase (instead of inhibit) developers' capabilities, we will now consider how both sovereign and disciplinary power circulate through the creation of common forms of teaching data, and through the individual consultations emerging from them: consultations on small group instructional diagnoses (SGIDs), on student course evaluations, and on videotapes.

Small Group Instructional Diagnosis Consultations

Typically facilitated around midterm, the SGID provides feedback within a given semester, thus promoting dialogue and the clarification of student and instructor expectations and allowing for timely corrective action in the classroom. As explained by Clark and Redmond (1982), the SGID was purposefully designed to elicit feedback, not evaluation: "the very word 'evaluation' connotes a judgment of goodness or badness. We learned not to call SGID evaluation but rather to label it a feedback process" (p. 4). Because the SGID is intended to function as a formative rather than a summative or evaluative instrument, it has become a multi-purpose tool at some institutions, where it is used to provide feedback to individual faculty, to inform coordinators of multisectioned courses or of TA training on the effectiveness of their overall course or program, and to assess the efficacy of classroom or curriculum design (Black, 1998).

The SGID, though designed for assessment purposes, does reveal an evaluative overlay when we consider the way that disciplinary power works through it. Inherent in the SGID is the idea that comparing student feedback with instructor goals will help diagnose problem areas in classroom instruction, allowing the instructor to enhance his or her teaching, to clarify the purpose of the course, and to assist student learning. In other words, educational developers (and teachers requesting an SGID) often hold the assumption that an SGID will give an instructor useful information that may potentially improve his or her teaching. Foucauldian analysis, however, raises the question of whether the SGID process produces "better" teaching or simply "more normal" teaching.

Even granting that the SGID process reinforces positive behaviors and can potentially correct ineffective behaviors, it also allows students to discipline or compel instructors to fit the assumed norms of good teaching. Although student remarks have the power to shape the course only as the instructor permits, their remarks still function as form of social control. For the instructors, the SGID serves as an examination—a test Foucault (1995) describes as "a normalizing gaze" (p. 184) through which they are made aware of being watched and judged by their students. Moreover, the feedback process confirms that the instructors, in their attempts to meet the norm, are aware of "being watched by another, all-seeing, presence" (Brookfield, 2001, p. 268).

The open-ended questions used in the SGID process mean that this examination introduces less explicit norms than teaching evaluations do, thus requiring students to bring their own norms into the process. The SGID surfaces individualized assumptions about teaching because it permits, and even encourages, students to scrutinize their instructors with a "normalizing judgment" by measuring them against their own unspoken understandings of how a "professor" or "teaching assistant" should and does behave. The diagnosis emphasizes the importance of watching and reporting on how well or poorly the class, and by extension, the instructor, fit the norms of instruction that students have internalized. Concerns about standards of normalization or judgment are often apparent in students' remarks on the efficacy of the curriculum, pedagogical methods, or fairness of grading standards. Even such commonplace student comments as "she assigns too much reading" and "his tests are too hard" imply a norm. In effect, the SGID functions as one of the processes by which professors and teaching assistants discipline themselves to conform to an imagined ideal, a norm acknowledged (if not clearly defined) by students, faculty, and administration alike.

Given the cloak of anonymity and the voice of consensus through the structure of the SGID, students are able to evaluate the instructors and the course without fear of punishment or anticipation of individual rewards. Because it grants the students an outlet for expression, the SGID disrupts the hierarchical power structure of a traditional classroom. If couched in terms of sovereign power, the SGID allows a measure of resistance; it gives the "common people" a voice and encourages them to speak in favor of or against the "ruler." The common SGID technique of gathering a wide range of student perspectives, rather than insisting on a consensus of opinion—which Clark and Redmond originally conceived as "a critical part of the SGID process" (Diamond, 2002, p. 85)—creates a more democratic environment and allows for more student voices to be heard and acknowledged. Yet this instrument, however inclusive, heightens both the students' and instructors' awareness of being surveyed or being coerced through evaluative observation. In this way, the SGID reinforces the implicit understanding that disciplinary power is exercised through surveillance.

At first glance, educational developers seem separate from the power dynamic operating in the SGID. As outside observers, they simply record and report the students' comments. However, even if they act according to common practices for consultations, taking "non-judgmental, objective observational notes [or giving] feedback in a non-threatening, non-directive manner" (Black, 1998, p. 246), consultants are still enmeshed within a web of disciplinary power. Accordingly, reexamining the SGID process from the Foucauldian perspective forces us to face a separate but related set of norms—those involved in gathering the data for and presenting it during the individual consultation. Although developers do not judge instructors per se, through the SGID process, they do survey and examine them. The developers are responsible for administering the instrument—the means by which "normal" and effective teaching is measured and defined—for gathering the data, and for recording and interpreting it for the instructor. Whether or not developers invoke their own knowledge of teaching as authoritative during the consultation, that is, whether or not their individual approaches to consultation are collaborative, confrontational, or prescriptive—to name but a few models of client-developer interaction (Brinko, 1997)—they are the assumed experts and thus wield disciplinary power during the consultation, both because they represent the students' voices through the feedback process and because they represent a larger ideal of best practices for teaching excellence.

The educational developer's voice in this process is often overlooked, but it is crucial to recognize that this voice shapes how information is gathered and recorded and how it wields disciplinary power through the SGID. Through this instrument, the consultant brings his or her own teaching norms to bear in a number of ways, from deciding which points to clarify in the student discussion to selecting which comments to include or emphasize in the report, and even to choosing whether or not to share research on established norms for effective teaching during the follow up consultation. Although naming this power does not make it disappear from SGID consultations, as we might hope, recognizing it does allow us to respond to it consciously and reflectively. The alternative—failing to acknowledge this subtle but dangerous web of power—means compromising the core values educational developers hold dear.

Student Course Evaluation Consultations

The SGID typically occurs only at the instructor's request. Student ratings, on the other hand, have become a nearly universal requirement for faculty and teaching assistants. Student course evaluations remain the primary, often the only, systematic source of data used to evaluate teaching at many colleges and universities in the United States (Cashin, 1999). Even when students and institutions use course evaluations responsibly, faculty may experience the process as intrusive, frustrating, and frightening (Ory, 2001). Course evaluations in many ways replicate Foucault's concept of a "panoptic prison" where, as McDonough (1993) describes it, inmates "are constantly aware that their behavior is subject to surveillance and observation. However, they are also unaware of when and how this surveillance occurs" (¶ 7). Faculty know *that* and *when* students will fill out the evaluations, but not *when* or *how* students will form their judgments. Faculty likewise do not often know when and how their evaluations will be interpreted by the sovereign powers at the university (i.e., department chairs, deans, tenure and promotion committees, and so on).

Course evaluations thus offer an institutionally sanctioned way for students to exert disciplinary power over faculty by judging faculty against both the rating's explicit and the student's implicit norms of good teaching. Like the SGID, the evaluation process typically provides students with anonymity, permitting them to report without consequence on their surveillance and judgments of faculty. The power students exert is complicated by the ambiguity common in student feedback. Narrative comments often contradict each other and can include deeply personal praise or criticism of a teacher. Since faculty (and others reading the evaluations) cannot probe for clarification from the students, the written comments can be difficult to understand

(Lewis, 2001). Quantitative scores may be no better, despite the precise numbers in the data. Franklin (2001) highlights a mistaken "tendency to view numbers as more objective and possibly less subject to dispute than more qualitative approaches" (p. 88).

Just as the disciplinary power inherent in course evaluations is ambiguous, so too is the sovereign power exerted through the institutional use of evaluations. Student ratings are connected to the institution's sovereign power to appoint or deny reappointment to faculty and teaching assistants. Even if explicit policies exist about when and how evaluations are to be used in personnel decisions, the contradictions and uncertainty inherent in student ratings create difficultly for decision-makers. Seldin (1999) notes a "growing chorus of complaints from those who serve on tenure and promotion committees that they are given little solid information about classroom teaching performance" (p. 22). This contributes to what Theall and Franklin (2001) call "major problems in day-to-day practice" of making sense of even technically rigorous evaluations: "student ratings are often misinterpreted, misused, and not accompanied by other information that allows users to make sound decisions" (p. 46).

Faced with so much uncertainty, some faculty and TAs turn to consultants at their university's teaching center (Knapper & Piccinin, 1999). Many such centers emphasize their separation from their school's formal system of judging and evaluating faculty—and in so doing, place themselves outside the visible hierarchy of sovereign power. However, such centers are not outside the ring of disciplinary power, even if they have strict confidentiality policies, since such policies only separate educational developers from sovereign power. Disciplinary power, by contrast, is impossible to avoid. Indeed, a client's motivation for meeting a consultant may stem from the client's perceptions of the consultant's disciplinary power—power rooted in the consultant's expertise in interpreting student ratings and understanding of campus policies and practices about course evaluations.

These perceptions empower the consultant, even if he or she does not recognize it. As with an SGID consultation, the developer's choices about whether and how to respond to a client's situation represent, in effect, an exercise of disciplinary power. In a consultation with a tenure-track faculty member concerned about her teaching evaluations, for example, one developer might recommend safe but limited techniques in an effort to bump up the scores of a traditional lecturer, thus privileging the client's need to build a solid tenure file over the students' need for an optimal learning environment; another developer in that same consultation might suggest more radical changes to promote active learning, thereby enhancing student learning despite the likely short-term decline in student ratings (Franklin, 2001). The developer, by necessity, makes choices during a consultation, and those choices are an exercise of disciplinary power over the client. A consultant may strive to create a safe and nurturing environment for the conversations about student course evaluations, but disciplinary power cannot be removed from the room.

Videotape Consultations

Of all the modes of educational development consultation, the videotape presents conditions that could seem most Foucauldian of all: The omnipresent eye of the camera monitors the teacher's every move. Surveillance—the fact of being constantly seen—is rendered utterly explicit. Part of the power of this medium in educational development is that, unlike SGIDs or student evaluations, teachers constantly encounter the medium itself in their everyday lives: It is nearly impossible to avoid video-based representations of human experience at all levels of culture, from television to home videos to security cameras monitoring shoppers. Because filmic representations are so culturally pervasive, then, videotapes of teaching have a particularly strong weight attached to them, even before the consultation begins.

How a videotape of teaching is made is freighted with acts of interpretation and thus disciplinary power as well. Decisions about when and how to focus on students or the teacher, when and how to zoom in or out, or what camera angles to use are just a few examples of ways the creation of a videotape can shape the disciplinary power dynamics in the data itself. An additional layer, in a higher education setting, is the use that sovereign powers make of teaching videotapes. That is, videos are created and analyzed not only for formative purposes, but also increasingly for summative purposes in tenure, promotion, or review portfolios. As such, the data in a videotape can incite some of the same power dynamics and high stakes as those connected with student course evaluations.

An educational videotape consultation, then, can present a highly overdetermined power disequilibrium between consultant and client. Indeed, given clients' familiarity with and reliance on videotape in popular cultural experience, the videotape may seem to offer a more straightforward or objective transcription of one's teaching (versus having to "interpret" written text) and thereby more easily capture what is "really" going on in the classroom. Such confidence in the truth and importance of visual data may lead a client to certain assumptions about the consultant's role—for example, that the consultant can see the "reality" of a classroom situation most clearly and tell the client what to do to "fix" it, or that the consultant might watch the videotape as a mode of examination in order to "grade" the teaching. In these modes, clients imbue consultants with both disciplinary and sovereign forms of power.

Educational developers have created a variety of ways to navigate within this highly charged medium of teaching data. Taylor-Way (1988) suggests a structured and reflective approach for videotape consultations. Often, videotape consultations are framed as a shared conversation between teachers, with the remote control in the hands of the client and with the implied message of "this is your consultation, not mine." Lewis (2002) recommends being aware of, and know how to distinguish among, the many hats that consultants (in general) can wear: data collector, data manager, facilitator, support system, counselor, information source.

Whatever the consultational framework, though, educational consultants typically try to disavow positions of power, steering away from the notions of telling clients what to do—and videotape consultations are no exception. For example, Knapper and Piccinin (1999) conclude that many developers believe in a "value-free approach to consultation, perhaps equivalent to client-centered therapy, in which the teacher's goals are preeminent, instructional problems are defined by the person seeking advice, and strategies are selected accordingly, even if the consultant has private doubts about them" (p. 5). Hicks (1999) reiterates this point, claiming that "the literature on instructional consultation almost always assumes that the power to set the agenda will lie with the academic seeking advice and assistance" (p. 14).

In our attempts to let the client shape the consultation agenda, however, developers can sometimes pursue an illusion: that such a transaction is value-free, neutral, unimpeded, or not substantially shaped by power dynamics. By contrast, important gains can come from consultants being more explicit and conscious about our own power positions, and about our own assumptions about other factors shaping the consultation, such as the nature of authority, knowledge, and expertise.

In other words, even as we often move to establish a horizontal equilibrium of shared power, consultants paradoxically may push power further out of equilibrium. This is because in assuming a power- and value-free environment, consultants may instead unknowingly insert their own assumptions about what should be the nature, focus, and purpose of the consultation—all without taking the time to be explicit about their views or to understand their clients' perspectives on those same issues. As Knapper and Piccinin (1999) assert, educational developers need to "spell out the conceptual basis for their work, dealing both with the consulting strategies they use to identify problems and effect change and with the conceptions of teaching that underpin the advice they offer" (pp. 5–6). As Jenson (2002) recommends, "know the limits of your position," "prepare to work with each client and each situation individually," and "be aware of the client's expectations in conferring with you" (pp. 92–94).

Power and Danger in Consultations

As is evident in all of these analyses, danger and risk emerge in educational consultations in a variety of ways. Evaluative teaching data can threaten faculty and teaching assistants' careers. Consultants can potentially wield considerable power over clients' perceptions of their student ratings and feedback and of themselves as teachers—this power can also extend to clients' careers. Consultations are also dangerous for developers. Our credibility as colleagues with useful expertise and resources is at stake, and in times of budget cuts and scarce resources, such credibility may seem particularly important to uphold.

The danger involved in power relations extends to those outside the consultation room, too. The students (current and future) of clients who voice their views are vicariously present during consultations and stand to be affected by them. Similarly, clients' attitudes toward their institutions potentially are at stake, endangering the university's sovereign powers. Department chairs and others exercising sovereign power at the university are not in jeopardy of losing their institutional power, but their disciplinary power may be reduced (or expanded) depending on clients' reaction to the consultation experience. In short, the nature of disciplinary power makes individual consultations a dangerous encounter for all involved.

Possible Responses for Educational Developers

Given this complex and dangerous web of power layers—the many ways in which what we intend as democratic moves may in fact reiterate the power structures we are trying to counteract—educational developers may wonder what kinds of responses, if any, may be useful to themselves and their clients. Foucault (1983) urges us to face such dangers squarely: "If everything is dangerous, then we always have something to do" (p. 231). In the presence of such danger, then, what should educational developers do? More specifically, in what ways can an awareness of the "unanticipated consequences of our supposedly empowering practices" actually lead to more effective practice? What are possible roles for the consultant in noticing, reinforcing, reflecting on, and resisting power (and the norms that underlie it)? The following are some approaches that may begin to answer these questions.

Power Is Dangerous, but Not Necessarily Bad

The presence of power is not necessarily bad. Indeed, as Foucault (1983) insists: "My point is not that everything is bad, but that everything is dangerous, which is not exactly the same as bad" (pp. 231–232). Thus, to recognize the ways in which various assessment instruments function as examinations or as instruments by which teaching is normalized is not to label them as necessarily problematic. It does, however, acknowledge not only the layers of power involved in the data itself, but also our own positions of power in collecting the data and bringing our expertise into consultations. It also recognizes that we, as educational developers, have a voice in this process, not only as student comments are gathered and reported back to the instructor but also as we choose to frame problems and recommend pedagogical changes to clients.

Educational Developers Can Use Their Powers to Reflect and Reinforce

As educational developers, we can use the kinds of power we have: power in our roles as expert resources on teaching assessment processes; power in our awareness of how sovereign and disciplinary power may be operating at our institutions; and power as the facilitators of communication in potentially charged consultations where language and tone have important consequences, and where safety and confidentiality can be used either as positive forces or as causes of shame and isolation.

Educational Development as Resistance

Ultimately, such practices and awareness can form a kind of resistance, leading to what Foucault calls an ethic of care. As McDonough (1993) asserts, "Caring relations for Foucault... must constantly be open to critical scrutiny... in order to criticize something effectively, we must care deeply about something else" (¶ 11). Because we care deeply about teaching and learning, educational developers are compelled to act. The dangers presented by power and surveillance should not limit us. Instead, as philosopher and cultural critic Susan Bordo (1997) insists, since "[c]ertain and conclusive knowledge of the effectiveness of our actions... is not available to us, [we should assess] the chief dangers or needs of a situation—the practices that require demystification, criticism, transformation—and we act" (p. 191). It is our responsibility and opportunity to resist the many forms that power can take: to identify and discuss the disciplinary power of client perceptions about evaluations; to educate sovereign decision-makers about best practices in using ratings; to help students think explicitly about the norming power of their assessments of instructors; and to reflect together as educational developers about how power is at the core of our work, despite our attempts to avoid it.

In the end, even though elements of surveillance and power permeate our work as consultants, an awareness of these dynamics—and of the "unanticipated consequences" that stem from them—can lead to deeper reflection and thus to a form of resistance that offers some amount of hope and care. As Foucault (1983) asserts, "my position leads not to apathy but to a hyper- and pessimistic activism" (p. 232). McDonough (1993) adds that "the incitement to care has the panoptic effect of creating individuals who are increasingly willing, even eager, to make themselves visible, open to scrutiny" (¶ 10). By modeling such processes of self-scrutiny, we as educational developers may begin to recognize the forms of unacknowledged power we exert, beneficent though they seem. Making our own power visible is the first step in actively resisting it, as we, as well as our clients, navigate the compelling and intense power relations that comprise institutions of higher education.

Note

If you are interested in thinking more concretely about these issues, please visit our web site for case studies and reflection questions on power in SGID, teaching evaluation, and videotape consultations: http://www.vanderbilt.edu/cft/resources/gleanings/casestudies.htm

References

Black, B. (1998). Using the SGID method for a variety of purposes. In M. Kaplan & D. Lieberman (Eds.), *To improve the academy: Vol. 17. Resources for faculty, instructional, and organizational development* (pp. 245–262). Stillwater, OK: New Forums Press.

Bordo, S. (1997). *Twilight zones: The hidden life of cultural images from Plato to O.J.* Berkeley, CA: California University Press.

Brinko, K. (1997). The interactions of teaching improvement. In K. T. Brinko & R. J. Menges (Eds.), *Practically speaking: A sourcebook for instructional consultants in higher education* (pp. 3–8). Stillwater, OK: New Forums Press.

Brookfield, S. D. (2001). Teaching through discussion as the exercise of disciplinary power. In D. Lieberman & C. Wehlburg (Eds.), *To improve the academy: Vol. 20. Resources for faculty, instructional, and organizational development* (pp. 260–273). Bolton, MA: Anker.

Cashin, W. E. (1999). Student ratings of teaching: Uses and misuses. In P. Seldin & Associates, *Changing practices in evaluating teaching: A practical guide to improved faculty performance and promotion/tenure decisions* (pp. 25–44). Bolton, MA: Anker.

Clark, D., & Redmond, M. (1982). *Small group instructional diagnosis: Final report.* Washington, DC: Fund for the Improvement of Postsecondary Education. (ERIC Document Reproduction Service No. ED217954)

Diamond, N. A. (2002). Small group instructional diagnosis: Tapping student perceptions of teaching. In K. H. Gillespie (Ed.), *A guide to faculty development: Practical advice, examples, and resources* (pp. 82–91). Bolton, MA: Anker.

Foucault, M. (1980a). Prison talk. In C. Gordon (Ed. & Trans.), *Power/knowledge: Selected interviews and other writings, 1972–1977* (pp. 37–54). New York, NY: Bentham.

Foucault, M. (1980b). Two lectures. In C. Gordon (Ed. & Trans.), *Power/knowledge: Selected interviews and other writings, 1972–1977* (pp. 78–108). New York, NY: Bentham.

Foucault, M. (1983). On the genealogy of ethics. In H. L Dreyfus & P. Rabinow (Eds.), *Michel Foucault: Beyond structuralism and hermeneutics* (pp. 231–232). Chicago, IL: The University of Chicago Press.

Foucault, M. (1995). *Discipline and punish: The birth of the prison* (A. Sheridan, Trans.). New York, NY: Vintage Books. (Original work published 1977).

Franklin, J. (2001). Interpreting the numbers: Using a narrative to help others read student evaluations of your teaching accurately. In K. G. Lewis (Ed.), *Techniques and strategies for interpreting student evaluations* (pp. 85–100). New Directions for Teaching and Learning, No. 87. San Francisco, CA: Jossey-Bass.

Hicks, O. (1999). A conceptual framework for instructional consultation. In C. Knapper & S. Piccinin (Eds.), *Using consultants to improve teaching* (pp. 9-18). New Directions for Teaching and Learning. No. 79. San Francisco, CA: Jossey-Bass.

Jenson, J. D. (2002). If I knew then what I know now: A first-year faculty consultant's top ten list. In K. H. Gillespie (Ed.), *A guide to faculty development: Practical advice, examples, and resources* (pp. 92–98). Bolton, MA: Anker.

Knapper, C., & Piccinin, S. (1999). Consulting about teaching: An overview. In C. Knapper & S. Piccinin (Eds.), *Using consultants to improve teaching* (pp. 3–7). New Directions for Teaching and Learning, No. 79. San Francisco, CA: Jossey-Bass.

Lewis, K. G. (2001). Making sense of student written comments. In K. G. Lewis (Ed.), *Techniques and strategies for interpreting student evaluations* (pp. 25–32). New Directions for Teaching and Learning, No. 87. San Francisco, CA: Jossey-Bass.

Lewis, K. G. (2002). The process of individual consultation. In K. H. Gillespie (Ed.), *A guide to faculty development: Practical advice, examples, and resources* (pp. 59–73). Bolton, MA: Anker.

McDonough, K. (1993). *Overcoming ambivalence about Foucault's relevance for education.* Retrieved March 23, 2003, from http://www.ed.uiuc.edu/eps/pes-yearbook/93_docs/mcdonoug.htm

Ory, J. C. (2001). Faculty thoughts and concerns about student ratings. In K. G. Lewis (Ed.), *Techniques and strategies for interpreting student evaluations* (pp. 3–15). New Directions for Teaching and Learning, No. 87. San Francisco, CA: Jossey-Bass.

POD Network. (2002). *Ethical guidelines for educational developers.* Retrieved March 23, 2003, from http://www.podnetwork.org/development/ethicalguidelines.htm

Seldin, P. (1999). Current practices—good and bad—nationally. In P. Seldin & Associates, *Changing practices in evaluating teaching: A practical guide to improved faculty performance and promotion/tenure decisions* (pp. 1–24). Bolton, MA: Anker.

Taylor-Way, D. (1988). Consultation with video: Memory management through stimulated recall. In K. G. Lewis (Ed.), *Face to face: A sourcebook of individual consultation techniques for faculty/instructional developers* (pp. 159–191). Stillwater, OK: New Forums Press.

Theall, M., & Franklin, J. (2001). Looking for bias in all the wrong places: A search for truth or a witch hunt in student ratings of instruction? In M. Theall, P. C. Abrami, & L. A. Mets (Eds.), *The student ratings debate: Are they valid? How can we best use them?* (pp. 45–56). New Directions for Institutional Research, No. 109. San Francisco, CA: Jossey-Bass.

Contact:

Peter Felten
Vanderbilt University
Center for Teaching
Box 351537
Nashville, TN 37235
Voice (615) 322-7290
Fax (615) 343-8111
Email peter.felten@vanderbilt.edu

Deandra Little
Vanderbilt University
English Department
Box 351654
Nashville, TN 37235
Voice (615) 322-2541
Fax (615) 343-8028
Email deandra.j.little@vanderbilt.edu

Allison Pingree
Vanderbilt University
Center for Teaching
Box 351537
Nashville, TN 37235
Phone (615) 322-7290
Fax (615) 343-8111
Email Allison.pingree@vanderbilt.edu

Peter Felten is Assistant Director of the Vanderbilt University Center for Teaching, and he teaches courses in history and American and southern studies. His current research explores how emotion shapes learning in service-learning courses, and how teaching and learning in history are changed by the use of visual in addition to textual sources.

Deandra Little is a full-time lecturer in the English Department at Vanderbilt University and teaches courses in English and women's studies. Her current research interests include the ethics and efficacy of reimagining the classroom as a site for community-building, both within courses using social software and as a bridging between course and the larger community through service learning.

Allison Pingree is Director of the Vanderbilt University Center for Teaching, and teaches courses in English, American and southern studies, and women's studies. Her current research interests include emotion in the classroom, one-on-one teaching and mentoring, and leadership and organizational change.

12

Approaching Faculty Development Support From the Grassroots: Establishment of an Innovative, Formal, Untenured Faculty Organization

Ellen N. Junn
Ellen Kottler
Jacqueline K. Coffman
Pamella H. Oliver
Fred Ramirez
California State University, Fullerton

This chapter describes an innovative faculty support program designed for untenured faculty and full-time lecturers. Working closely with members of the administration, untenured faculty and full-time lecturers established and created a voluntary, formal, cross-departmental faculty organization called the ULO (Untenured Faculty and Full-Time Lecturer Organization). The ULO has formal bylaws, elected officers, and a mission that initiated activities all designed to support junior faculty and full-time lecturers within the college. Even within its initial year, this organization offered a significant variety of meaningful support activities with positive outcomes. The activities include formation of a Research Writing Workgroup, workshops on the tenure and promotion process, teaching brown bags, greater opportunities for leadership development and service, reduced sense of faculty isolation (Fullan, 1993) and stress, and enhanced collegial social opportunities. Discussed here are activities, current accomplishments, strengths, challenges, caveats, and recommendations.

In recent years, many faculty development programs have added programs specifically designed to support and assist new, untenured faculty (e.g., Boice & Turner, 1989; Menges, 1996; Noonan, 1980; Pierce, 2001). Indeed, Nelsen (1980) cited research from the Association of American Colleges Project on Faculty Development showing that faculty themselves were expressing a growing interest and need for programmatic support for junior faculty beginning in the 1980s. Similarly, Stanley and Chism (1991) and Sorcinelli (1988) both provided data on the needs, concerns, and characteristics of new faculty and the implications these have for the development of meaningful faculty development programs.

However, in most instances when campuses have implemented programs of support for junior faculty, these programs are developed and constructed by administrators and faculty developers, often without the direct participation and involvement of the junior faculty themselves. Whereas programs of this nature can still benefit junior faculty enormously, a more grassroots approach is not as common. There are several reasons this might not occur. First, new junior faculty are assumed not to be as knowledgeable of the kinds of support they might need. Second, junior faculty have such limited time due to the pressures of preparing new classes and engaging in scholarship and service activities, that they might not have adequate time to devote to faculty development planning. Another reason might be that faculty development programs are often developed prior to the arrival of new faculty and hence obviate their participation.

This chapter describes the formation of an innovative, volunteer, grassroots, and formalized approach to faculty development that includes the active and full participation of junior tenure-track faculty and full-time lecturers within a college setting. These faculty work very closely with the dean's office to identify, develop, plan, and implement a variety of support programs for junior faculty. In brief, a formal, inclusive, cross-departmental junior faculty organization called the Untenured Faculty and Full-Time Lecturer Organization (ULO), complete with bylaws, elected officers, and a clear mission, was established to plan and implement activities and mobilize resources for junior faculty within the college.

There are multiple benefits to this type of formal organization.

- The ULO has greater faculty buy in, as it is perceived to be a faculty driven, grassroots organization that can communicate directly with the dean's office regarding faculty needs.

- Because it is an open faculty organization, as opposed to a college committee, it has the advantage of being much more inclusive of all junior faculty, since committees appointed by the dean traditionally have a much smaller, representative membership drawn from all departments.
- The activities of the ULO are kept independent of the tenure and promotion process (and its often attendant stressors), although happily, participation in the organization may also be recognized as service to the college.
- Because it is a faculty organization with active faculty officers and members, attendance and enthusiasm for activities and events sponsored by the organization is greater, and possible fears of intimidation involving the dean's office or senior faculty are removed.
- Engaging junior faculty in the formalities of calling and conducting meetings, writing agendas and bylaws, running elections, and implementing various activities and events provides them with very valuable professional and leadership development opportunities in a relatively risk-free context.
- This model is an especially useful vehicle for socializing junior faculty particularly, in where there is a significant ratio of junior faculty to senior faculty, as experienced in our college.
- Formation of an inclusive junior faculty organization provides multiple opportunities throughout the year to develop and deepen community-building support networks among faculty.

Background Information and Establishment of the ULO

California State University, Fullerton, has a successful and comprehensive Faculty Development Center (FDC). Because the center serves almost 2,000 faculty (i.e., untenured tenure-track, mid-career, senior, part-time faculty, and full-time lecturers), many of the programs provide support to faculty at a more general level and thus do not always address the ongoing, more specialized needs of junior faculty within smaller, disciplinary-specific college contexts.

For example, the previous FDC director did revitalize a campus-wide faculty organization fondly referred to as the UFO (Untenured Faculty Organization). Although this interdisciplinary group of UFO faculty met occasionally and provided ideas for workshops and brown bag seminars that the FDC director hosted for the group, the overall turnout at events remained small and the organization soon dissipated as interest in more general topics (e.g., housing issues) waned. In the end, the UFO served as more of a social gathering—with at least one family-invited potluck evening each year, hosted at one of the junior faculty homes. Although building cross campus community is a vital activity, at that time it was more difficult to rally junior faculty to make the commitment to dedicate their time and energy to leading a campus-wide faculty organization, as many of these faculty wondered if devoting their time would be advisable, given their need to pursue their scholarly and service agendas within their own departments and colleges.

Thus, the college-based ULO began when the dean asked the associate dean to convene a luncheon for all the junior untenured faculty and full-time lecturers in the college to welcome them to the new academic year and assess their needs. During this luncheon, as the faculty broke into smaller focus groups, it became clear that junior faculty were interested in a number of crucial issues including support for research, teaching issues, negotiating tenure and promotion, and developing increased collegiality and social support.

As a result of the discussion, the associate dean and the junior faculty discussed the possibility of forming a formal, college-specific, untenured faculty organization that would provide direct and timely support to junior faculty in their scholarship, professional development, and service activities. Establishing a formal, college-based, untenured faculty and full-time lecturer organization with direct communication, credibility, and visibility with the dean's office was extremely appealing to the junior faculty. It was received with much enthusiasm and promised to serve as an excellent grassroots vehicle for identifying, developing, and implementing specific programs and activities to support faculty needs.

The ULO Organization

The organization of the ULO is defined in formal bylaws, written and approved by the general membership (the bylaws are posted on the ULO web site: http://hdcs.fullerton.edu/ULO/). The ULO was established as a college-based organization dedicated to providing voice and support to the college's untenured faculty and full-time lecturers that pledged to work collaboratively with the dean's office in order to achieve the following goals:

- To effectively represent and promote a college-wide climate that is sensitive, representative, and fair to all untenured faculty and full-time lecturers.

- To build a strong voice with regular, effective, formal communication and programmatic input to the dean and other relevant college committees.
- To develop and implement a variety of faculty support activities and programs for untenured faculty and full-time lecturers in collaboration with the dean's office.
- To provide support and input in the fair recruitment, hiring, retention, or promotion of untenured faculty and full-time lecturers and administrators on campus.
- To build strong, effective linkages with the university administration and with the surrounding community.
- To encourage and empower individuals in the organization to become more actively involved in important university, community, professional, and political service with the purpose of creating a more harmonious and diverse community.
- To create a social support network to build partnerships and personal friendships among the members of the organization.

The organizational and meeting structure reflects the group's philosophy of striving to maximize faculty time and efficiency. The ULO consists of three overlapping groups: general members, executive board members, and special interest group (SIG) members. General membership is open to all untenured faculty and full-time lecturers in the college. Although the group has an open enrollment policy, at the beginning of the school year, a specific invitation to join is issued to all eligible members. Currently, 39 out of 81 eligible tenure-track and full-time lecturer faculty have officially joined as ULO members. Consistent with the goal of having no extraneous meetings, there is one general membership meeting per semester. The executive board met on a monthly basis during the first-year formation of the organization and subsequently will be meeting two times a semester. Special interest groups may meet more or less frequently, depending on their needs. The associate dean attends ULO meetings as a show of support and as a resource to assist with plans or activities, and provides the group with access to student or clerical assistance as needed.

The executive committee consists of the following officers: president, vice president, secretary, historian reporter, public relations chair, election committee chair, and all chairs of special interest groups. The duties and responsibilities of these officers are outlined in the formal bylaws. All members, tenure track or full-time lecturers, are eligible for serving in any position for a term of one-year term with a maximum of two years. The elections are held in the spring using a nomination slate created by consensus. The board keeps in regular contact with the associate dean and with each other through informal meetings and email.

The final area of membership consists of the special interest groups. The seven SIG chairs include: research support, teaching support, service and professional activities, tenure and promotion issues, multicultural issues, student-related issues, and new faculty orientation. These SIGs are formed on the basis of member interest and operate somewhat autonomously but still under the direction of the ULO board. Each of the seven special interest groups is free to identify and develop its own meeting schedule and host a variety of events. These meetings or seminars are open to all ULO members as well as to other interested faculty in the college. Electronic announcements and notification of ULO events and activities come directly from the ULO president or may be referred to the associate dean who sends the email out through the college's email distribution listing of faculty. Additionally, information is posted on the ULO web site hosted by the college.

ULO Activities and Successes

The ULO has been successful in achieving at least six major positive accomplishments in the following areas:

- Improving greater interdisciplinary engagement in research and writing through the implementation of a Research Writing Group;.
- Clarifying the retention, tenure and promotion process.
- Providing a forum for collegial discussions regarding teaching issues.
- Promoting leadership development.
- Enhancing community-building and social support networks.
- Using technology for more effective communication.

Each of these accomplishments will be discussed below.

Research Writing Group

Boice (1987, 1989) and others (e.g., Gray & Birch, 2001) have written about the importance of assisting faculty with their scholarly productivity. Indeed, publication in peer-reviewed journals has become the coin of the realm for many institutions in making faculty tenure and promotion decisions (Bellas & Toutkoushian, 1999). Not surprisingly, producing scholarly, peer-reviewed publications was a top priority for the ULO, and one of its first activities was to establish a Research Writing SIG under the leadership of its chair. The ULO Research Writing Group was a forum in which untenured faculty regularly shared their research interests and manuscript drafts for peer feedback in a safe, constructive, and timely manner. The group met once a month, and sometimes twice a month according to the participants' needs and requests. Meetings were set so that each participant took turns sharing rough drafts of articles, conference presentation proposals, or various scholarly items for others in the group to review. In most cases, two colleagues would serve as peer editors for each manuscript. These peer editors provided feedback and commentary on each piece of work within a specified timely frame.

An important incentive created by the Research Writing Group was that once a faculty member committed to having his or her work reviewed, if a faculty member failed to have the work ready for review by the deadline, he or she would have to buy lunch for all the members that day, or submit a monetary "donation" to each member of the group. The Research Writing Group found that this small, but simple rule acted as a powerful incentive for keeping faculty accountable to themselves and to each other in completing their work on schedule. One comment on the forced deadlines was as follows: "The research group has really helped me this year. Primarily, the forced deadlines kept me on pace. I would never have completed as much work without the support of this group of peers." These deadlines helped to emphasize the importance of consistently carving out regular time for research and writing, especially when faced with the often more immediate demands of a heavy teaching load and service activities (Boice, 1989).

Another comment included, "This group provided me with constant support and encouragement, and valuable 'tips' regarding research for me to use or modify to suit my needs. Above all, it provided me with the accountability that I needed and prefer." Another success story comes from a faculty member who said,

> As a result of my involvement, an article I co-authored was presented for review to the Research Writing Group for very helpful feedback before it was submitted for publication consideration to a national journal. In addition, I used the group for feedback when I responded to a call for presenters for a national organization. The proposal was later accepted!

The forced deadlines proved very successful for faculty productivity. There were 12 active members within the Research Writing SIG from various disciplines, and over 20 articles have been accepted for publication to date. In addition to increased productivity, the collegiality and cross-disciplinary dialogue also benefited faculty members in terms of expanding their own thinking about their research. Finally, although the group does focus primarily on research and obtaining tenure and promotion, the overarching philosophy of the group is to assist and support one another on and off campus, and, consequently the group has formed closer, collegial relationships as another positive outcome.

The Research Writing SIG has also been helpful in identifying needed resources and requesting the dean's office to purchase resource materials and reference books that multiple faculty in the college could share in furthering their scholarship. For example, the dean's office recently secured copies of the most recent editions of Caball's Education Directories that have now been added to the dean's library for use by the faculty.

Retention, Tenure, and Promotion Issues

For new faculty, learning about the formal, structured elements of achieving tenure can be overwhelming, intimidating, and stressful. A variety of complex university and college documents, policies, and processes govern how untenured faculty must meet and demonstrate progress toward, and attainment of, established performance criteria while developing themselves as educators, researchers, and community members both inside and outside the university. The importance of these issues is heightened as individuals prepare the critical, detailed, and sometimes highly prescriptive documentation that will be reviewed during the tenure process. Indeed, because the retention, tenure, and promotion process is multifaceted, information on the process sometimes varies between colleges on campus. Therefore, holding meetings specific to a college helps to minimize any ambiguities that might occur during discussions with colleagues in other colleges across campus.

In order to maximize clarity and alleviate some of these concerns, the ULO co-hosted with the dean's office a hands-on workshop on the tenure process specifically for faculty in the college. The Office of Faculty Affairs and Records personnel are actively involved in this process provided guidance and detailed information about required documentation, the process, related procedures, and helpful hints for the grateful and highly attentive faculty attending the workshop. In fact, one workshop participant commented,

> My experience in our last meeting was very positive and I found the meeting we had regarding RTP to be very helpful. Also, being in the presence of other faculty who are going through the same struggle helps validate and normalize our anxieties and insecurities. Thanks for all the hard work you put into this. I hope I can be more actively involved next year!

In addition to supporting faculty through the required documentation process, the ULO has publicized other related campus workshops and events that contribute to the building of teaching, research, and service activities for tenure review. For instance, the ULO highlighted and alerted faculty in the college to a variety of workshops and training sessions conducted by the campus's Faculty Development Center (e.g., research grant opportunities, microteaching seminars, web site development workshops, technical training for statistics).

Teaching Issues

Similarly, the ULO Teaching Issues SIG alerts members to other related campus workshops on teaching issues and hosts separate workshops based on topics that college faculty have expressed an interest in discussing further. As an example, the ULO invited the assistant dean of student affairs to facilitate a brown bag discussion regarding campus policies on student attendance and plagiarism and various strategies for dealing with both situations. This informal lunch was well attended and faculty dialogue was both rich and informative. Faculty appreciated the opportunity to reflect on their teaching (Schön, 1983).

Leadership Development

Junior faculty generally have limited opportunities and time to engage in sustained and meaningful leadership activities, and yet successful faculty are expected to show professional growth and development in this area as they progress in their careers. Indeed, sometimes department chairs intentionally shy away from nominating their junior faculty for leadership roles in the college for fear that these roles carry potential risks, or because of political reasons and/or extensive time commitments that would otherwise go toward successful teaching and publication of research scholarship. Fortunately, this model offers junior faculty a beneficial, yet relatively risk-free context within which to exercise their leadership skills.

More specifically, this model affords junior faculty with a number of important leadership building skills. For example, ULO faculty carrying out the roles, responsibilities, and duties associated with establishing and running an effective organization will enhance their leadership and administrative skills (e.g., calling and running meetings, writing agendas, working collaboratively with others, securing resources, hosting events). Second, ULO members also have the opportunity to interact formally with the dean's office and with other department chairs, thus enhancing interpersonal skills and expanding their networks. Third, active membership in ULO governance provides faculty with the opportunity to see various levels of leadership skills modeled and to test and hone their skills in a relatively risk-free and nonthreatening context. For example, as one executive member stated,

> The ULO provided me with the opportunity to develop personal relationships with people in the college and to develop professional relationships as well. First of all, it offered a leadership position in the college. After assuming a position on the board, I began to interact with people from across the college through the board meetings and programs sponsored by the organization.

Enhancing Community-Building and Social Support Networks

Formation of the ULO stimulated significantly more regular and sustained interaction among the new faculty, providing for enhanced personal and professional growth. Among the myriad of larger university programs, the ULO served first to provide small group opportunities for new faculty to meet and build personal relationships. Many of the faculty had just moved to the area and were interested in meeting people, networking, and making friends. They were searching for references and information to help them settle in new communities as well as in their new faculty positions. For example, one new faculty member said, "Because of the ULO, when I walked into the elevator, I looked around and realized I could greet five of the six people there by name and even identify their departments. What a comforting feeling!" Similarly, another faculty member had the following to say:

> The ULO has met my professional and personal needs on several levels: First, being new to the campus, it has been a great venue for meeting faculty within the college. It has also been enlightening to share teaching and portfolio experiences and tips informally. The sessions on student affairs and portfolio development have been educational. In fact, positive comments on ULO involvement were made by my portfolio reviewers (shows our group is valued by the college!).

Thus, an often repeated refrain from ULO members is that the organization has made a meaningful difference in making the transition to the college and with fellow colleagues easier, much more friendly, and enjoyable.

Using Technology for More Effective Communication

In order to facilitate communication, the college hosts the ULO web site: http://hdcs.fullerton.edu/ulo/default.htm. The bylaws, meeting agendas, a list of officers, a list of current members, photo gallery, and calendar of events can be accessed on this web site. Also archived are the "ULO Updates," an electronic newsletter sent by email to the members. A final tool is "Useful Links" which connects faculty to resources and information from the library, FDC, academic affairs, and faculty affairs. The ULO president serves as the primary contact person and she posts information on a regular basis for members. This site is particularly useful for new faculty as a place to find a variety of important and timely information.

Future Plans and Directions

The ULO plans at least five activities for 2004. First, the ULO will continue to recruit new, active members with greater publicity. Second, the ULO will continue to support and build on the activities of the already successful SIGs. For example, in fall 2003, the Teaching SIG will sponsor a facilitated workshop on how women and minority faculty can cope effectively with difficult or challenging students. Third, the ULO has secured approval and funds from the dean's office to host the first joint ULO and dean's office welcome luncheon for all new tenure track and full-time lecturers this fall. Fourth, the ULO will host a meeting, much like the initial focus group, with current and new ULO members to identify new areas of interests and strengthen continuing activities. Fifth, the ULO will work collaboratively with the dean's office on the various social, community-building events that were hosted last year (e.g., faculty potluck dinners, faculty hiking trip, Monday brown bags). Enthusiasm for the organization is high and faculty continue to be actively engaged in the establishment of this organization.

Challenges and Caveats

Since junior faculty and full-time lecturers are very busy with teaching, research, and service activities, there were several challenges. For example, the greatest difficulty was in scheduling meetings and events. Due to varied faculty schedules, it became necessary to alternate the days and times when meetings were held. This enabled interested members to attend some, if not all, of the activities. It was extremely important to plan at least a month ahead and publicize early as well.

A second difficulty involved a slight turnover rate for some of the SIG chairs. Whereas the first slate of officer positions filled easily, as the semester progressed, a few SIG chairs voluntarily resigned when their teaching or research activities prohibited them from carrying out SIG activities effectively. However, when these few vacancies became available, the ULO president emailed an announcement to the members that the positions were now available, and, as a result, new faculty quickly became involved in these leadership positions within the organization.

Interestingly, an unforeseen difficulty came from a few department chairs who voiced some minor concerns that their faculty might turn their attention away from department service and committees to the ULO, or that permitting this group of junior faculty to organize might ferment increased distance between junior and senior faculty. Finally, some chairs wondered exactly what formal relationship the ULO had with the dean's office. To address these concerns, the associate dean invited ULO officers to present at one of the dean's council of chairs' regular meetings. At the meeting, the dean and associate dean provided a brief history and rationale for the group. Then the ULO executive board members presented the ULO mission, bylaws, an overview of events and activities, and the web site. As a result of the meeting, the chairs felt reassured and agreed that it was inspiring to see and hear from a clearly enthusiastic and well-organized group of junior faculty working together. Not only were they appreciative to learn of the organization's work, but they now support the ULO and its activities, and they easily saw how these activities would continue to strengthen the leadership potential of junior faculty.

Finally, an obvious determinant of the success of this model assumes a strong and committed leadership on the part of the faculty elected as executive board members and a mutually trusting relationship between faculty and the dean's office. In our case, we were fortunate to have a highly dedicated, well-organized, collaborative group of executive board faculty with excellent leadership skills. However, a more novice group can be mentored and supported by strong leadership on the part of an associate dean, some other high level administrator in the dean's office, or a senior tenured faculty member.

Conclusions and Suggestions

In the course of one school year, the ULO organization was formally established with a wide-ranging calendar of meetings, activities, and events for all junior faculty and full-time lecturers within a college setting. A series of programs was on a variety of topics, such as retention and promotion, teaching issues, and support for faculty research and writing. Executive board faculty were actively involved, and faculty participation and attendance at the events was strong and well received, with highly complimentary and appreciative feedback from members.

The benefits of this innovative, grassroots model of faculty development for junior faculty are many. First, it does not require significant organizational or administrative time or effort and is cost effective. Second, the programs developed are well attended and well received since the junior faculty themselves are intimately involved in identifying their needs and implementing activities. Third, this model is flexible in that it can provide support for the faculty's multiple needs, ranging from research to teaching and more. Fourth, as Romer (1980) points out, college committees can be useful in managing faculty development, provided they are very carefully selected and charged. Expanding on this notion, our model of establishing a formal faculty organization with an infrastructure composed of an executive board, SIG members, and members at large provides even greater faculty outreach, participation, and inclusiveness. Similarly, Siegel (1980) describes empirical findings regarding faculty development programs showing that programs that are more flexible and solicit wider faculty engagement are more effective. Fifth, the ULO offers the additional benefits of enhanced leadership development and collegial networking for faculty. Sixth, it provides a safe forum for junior faculty to register formal judgments as a group regarding significant college-based issues without jeopardizing or singling out a specific faculty member (e.g., selection on a new dean or other politically loaded decisions). Seventh, programs such as these are evaluated favorably by accrediting bodies, since many accreditation bodies now specifically look for institutionalized faculty development support programs.

College deans wishing to institute a similar model of faculty development are advised to first ascertain if their junior faculty are interested in participating actively in this collaborative model. Importantly, to make this joint effort more manageable for junior faculty, the dean must ensure that another key senior level administrator, such as an associate dean, will assume primary responsibility for working closely with the group and for furnishing access to necessary clerical staff, serving in a central dissemination and communication role, offering politically astute advice where needed, identifying resources, and advocating for funding for desired activities. Finally, deans implementing this model would be wise to work closely with department chairs to keep them informed, comfortable, and supportive of the new faculty organization from its inception.

In sum, this grassroots approach to supporting junior faculty represents a rich, flexible, highly productive, and mutually beneficial approach to meeting the ever-changing needs of junior faculty, making their transition to the university a rich, successful, and rewarding one as highly valued members of the institution.

References

Bellas, M. L., & Toutkoushian, R. K. (1999). Faculty time allocations and research productivity: Gender, race, and family effects. *The Review of Higher Education, 22(4)*, 367–390.

Boice, R. (1987). Is released time an effective component of faculty development programs? *Research in Higher Education, 26(3)*, 311–326.

Boice, R. (1989). Procrastination, busyness, and bingeing. *Behavior Research Therapy, 27(6)*, 605–611.

Boice, R., & Turner, J. L. (1989). The FIPSE-CSULB mentoring project for new faculty. In S. Kahn (Ed.), *To improve the academy: Vol. 8. Resources for faculty, instructional, and organizational development* (pp. 117–141). Stillwater, OK: New Forums Press.

Fullan, M. (1993). *Change forces: Probing the depths of educational reform.* Bristol, PA: Farmer Press.

Gray, T., & Birch, J. (2001). Publish, don't perish: A program to help scholars flourish. In D. Lieberman & C. Wehlburg (Eds.), *To improve the academy: Vol. 19. Resources for faculty, instructional, and organization development* (pp. 268–284). Bolton, MA: Anker.

Menges, R. J. (1996). Experiences of newly hired faculty. In L. Richlin & D. DeZure (Eds.), *To improve the academy: Vol. 15. Resources for faculty, instructional, and organizational development* (pp. 169–183). Bolton, MA: Anker.

Nelsen, W. C. (1980). Faculty development: Perceived needs of the 1980's. In W. C. Nelsen & M. E. Siegel (Eds.), *Effective approaches to faculty development* (pp. 145–149). Washington, DC: Association of American Colleges.

Noonan, J. F. (1980). An institute on teaching and learning for new faculty. In W. C. Nelsen & M. E. Siegel (Eds.), *Effective approaches to faculty development* (pp. 49–70). Washington, DC: Association of American Colleges.

Pierce, G. (2001). Developing new faculty: An evolving program. In D. Lieberman & C. Wehlburg (Eds.), *To improve the academy: Vol. 19. Resources for faculty, instructional, and organizational development* (pp. 253–267). Bolton, MA: Anker.

Romer, A. (1980). The role of a faculty committee in facilitating faculty development. In W. C. Nelsen & M. E. Siegel (Eds.), *Effective approaches to faculty development* (pp. 77–83). Washington, DC: Association of American Colleges.

Schön, D. A. (1983). *The reflective practitioner: How professionals think in action.* New York, NY: Basic Books.

Siegel, M. E. (1980). Empirical findings on faculty development programs. In W. C. Nelsen & M. E. Siegel (Eds.), *Effective approaches to faculty development* (pp. 131–144). Washington, DC: Association of American Colleges.

Sorcinelli, M. D. (1988). Satisfactions and concerns of new university teachers. In J. G. Kurfiss (Ed.), *To improve the academy: Vol. 7. Resources for faculty, instructional, and organizational development* (pp. 121–131). Stillwater, OK: New Forums Press.

Stanley, C. A., & Chism, N. V. N. (1991). Selected characteristics of new faculty: Implications for faculty development. In K. J. Zahorski (Ed.), *To improve the academy: Vol. 10. Resources for faculty, instructional, and organizational development* (pp. 55–63). Stillwater, OK: New Forums Press.

Contact:

Ellen N. Junn
College of Human Development and Community Service
Dean's Office, EC-324
California State University, Fullerton
800 N. State College Boulevard
Fullerton, CA 92834-6868
Voice (714) 278-4365
Fax (714) 278-3314
Email ejunn@fullerton.edu

Ellen Kottler
School of Education, EC-190
California State University, Fullerton
800 N. State College Boulevard
Fullerton, CA 92834-6868
Voice (714) 278-5193
Email ekottler@fullerton.edu

Jacqueline K. Coffman
Department of Child and Adolescent Studies, EC-105
California State University, Fullerton
800 N. State College Boulevard
Fullerton, CA 92834-6868
Voice (714) 278-3740
Email jcoffman@fullerton.edu

Pamella H. Oliver
Department of Child and Adolescent Studies, EC-105
California State University, Fullerton
800 N. State College Boulevard
Fullerton, CA 92834-6868
Voice (714) 278-2896
Email poliver@fullerton.edu

Fred Ramirez
School of Education, EC-190
California State University, Fullerton
800 N. State College Boulevard
Fullerton, CA 92834-6868
Voice (714) 278-7643
Email framirez@fullerton.edu

Ellen N. Junn is Professor of Child and Adolescent Studies and Associate Dean in the College of Human Development and Community Service at California State University, Fullerton. She received her B.S. in experimental psychology from the University of Michigan and her M.A. and PhD in cognitive and developmental psychology from Princeton University. Her research, publications, and presentations focus on college teaching effectiveness, faculty development issues, educational equity, public policy issues involving children and families, and children's cognition regarding social relationships. Prior to becoming Associate Dean of the college, she was the founding Director of the Faculty Development Center for the university.

Ellen Kottler is a Lecturer in the Department of Secondary Education. She received her B.A. in psychology from the University of Michigan, M.A. in curriculum and instruction from Eastern Michigan University, and an Ed.S. in instruction and curriculum from the University of Nevada, Las Vegas. A former teacher and curriculum specialist in the area of secondary social studies, she has presented at numerous conferences in social studies education and teacher education. Her areas of research interest include beginning teacher support, teacher preparation, social studies education, and children with limited English.

Jacqueline K. Coffman is Assistant Professor of Child and Adolescent Studies at California State University, Fullerton (CSUF). She received her B.A. and M.A. from CSUF in psychology and her PhD from Claremont Graduate University in developmental psychology. Her research, presentations, and publications focus on home environment, culture, cognitive development, achievement motivation, and birth order. Departmental activities have included creation of a new course on assessing and observing development and participation in a community-based pregnant minors program and collaboration with public schools.

Pamella H. Oliver received her PhD in clinical psychology from the University of Southern California in 2001. Her research focuses on the influence of families on child development, with a particular emphasis on the effects of family conflict and parenting on children. She is currently an Assistant Professor in the Department of Child and Adolescent Studies at California State University, Fullerton.

Fred Ramirez is Assistant Professor of Secondary Education in the School of Education at California State University, Fullerton. He received his B.A. from San Diego State University, M.A. from Loyola Marymount, and PhD from Indiana University in curriculum studies. He currently oversees one of the professional development districts, and is chair of the multicultural education courses for his department. His research interests include P–12 parental involvement, rethinking multicultural education, school reform (K–16), and public policy. He has presented and published in national and international conferences and journals, and in his spare time volunteers in community efforts and works with a nonprofit organization on parents and technology within urban environments.

13

Fostering Diversity in a Faculty Development Organization

Mathew L. Ouellett
University of Massachusetts, Amherst

Christine A. Stanley
Texas A&M University

Since 1994, the Professional and Organizational Development Network in Higher Education (POD) has articulated a goal of becoming a more multicultural organization. In support of this goal, POD sponsors two key initiatives: travel and internship grants. This chapter offers an historical overview of the first nine years of these programs, selected perspectives from participants on the individual and organizational benefits of these initiatives, and a context within which to explore how POD is evolving as a multicultural organization and how it may benefit from increased attention to diversity related issues in the future.

The research literature on multicultural organizational development is consistent with the view that an organization's efforts at fostering diversity necessitate a systemic perspective. These efforts include a critical look at every aspect of the organization, such as mission, resources, processes, product, and people as components of growth in an effort to create diversity and social justice (Jackson & Hardiman, 1994; Jackson & Holvino, 1988; Katz, 1978). The Professional and Organizational Development Network in Higher Education (POD) is one such example. Established in 1975, when a small group of faculty developers first met at Airlie House in Virginia, the organization now supports a network of over 1,200 members comprised of faculty and teaching assistant (TA) developers, administrators, faculty, educational consultants, and others who support the value of teaching and learning in higher education. POD spans the United States, Australia, Canada, Hong Kong, Ireland, Israel, Korea, Puerto Rico, Scotland, South Africa, the United Kingdom, and the West Indies.

POD is a unique organization, with several strengths for positioning itself to become a multicultural organization. It has a legacy of commitment to professional and organization development; an organizational emphasis on community, collegiality, and networking; and a leadership role in the improvement of teaching and learning in higher education (Stanley & Ouellett, 2000). In addition, the wealth of publications and resources that document the linkages made between diversity and teaching development efforts have produced rich and ongoing dialogues in the field of professional development on models and best practices in multicultural teaching and learning (Border & Chism, 1992; Collett & Serrano, 1992; Cook & Sorcinelli, 1999; Ferren & Geller, 1993; Kardia, 1998; Ouellett & Sorcinelli, 1995, 1998; Schmitz, Paul, & Greenberg, 1992; Stanley & Ouellett, 2000).

In 1993, POD took a bold step and created a committee called the Diversity Commission. One of 15 committees in POD that serve to enhance the work and governance of the organization, the Diversity Commission is the largest committee with nearly 20 members. It is the only committee with dedicated, annual funds of nearly $10,000, which are used primarily for creating and sustaining internship opportunities in faculty development and disseminating travel grants to underrepresented institutions. It is clear that diversity is important to the organization and its members. "The process of achieving a multicultural organization is evolutionary and occurs in stages" (Stanley & Ouellett, 2000, p. 40). We would like to take a historical look at these initiatives and share perspectives from a select group of the membership who have been beneficiaries of the organization's efforts at diversity to examine how POD is developing as a multicultural organization.

History of the Diversity Commission

In 1992, at the POD annual conference at the Saddlebrook Resort in Tampa, Florida, 24 members came together to form a Diversity Interest Group. Their first action was to write a letter to the Core Executive Committee (i.e., the POD Board of Directors—the current president, immediate past president, president elect, the executive directors, and the chair of the finance and audit committee) to suggest ways in which POD could encourage a more diverse membership base for the organization. At the heart of the conversations was a realization that POD needed to attract a broader membership in order to become a more multicultural organization. In 1993, under the presidential leadership of Don Wulff, a volunteer group began to explore organizational models for diversity. After looking at efforts within other, related higher education organizations (e.g., American Association for Higher Education), they developed and presented a proposal to the Core Executive Committee. This proposal focused on ways to make "... diversity a priority within POD and articulated the necessity of making diversity an explicit goal in membership outreach to underrepresented groups and institutions" (Stanley & Ouellett, 2000, p. 41).

In 1994, the Core Committee accepted this proposal. Members of the Diversity Interest Group then became the Diversity Committee, which was later renamed the Diversity Commission. The Diversity Commission's efforts were first focused on outreach to institutions and groups that had been historically underrepresented in the organization. Although the Diversity Commission was established with a recruitment goal in mind, it was increasingly consulted about organizational efforts toward diversity, such as conference planning, conference site selection, publications, and the like. One way to address retention as well as recruitment was to award travel grants to underrepresented institutions and to develop internship grant opportunities for future faculty developers of color who are interested in faculty development. What began as a general recruitment initiative became a conceptual springboard for broader organizational assessment and changes. Recruitment is synergistically tied to retention, and it was determined that POD not continue to recruit individuals from underrepresented groups and institutions without also paying attention to what their experiences were like once they arrived in the organization. These "efforts toward valuing diversity may begin with recruitment, but not changing the nature of the organization to provide for ongoing retention of our new members is counterproductive" (Stanley & Ouellett, 2000, pp. 41–42).

To enhance the entrée of travel grant recipients to the organization more broadly, POD also instituted an array of related initiatives. These efforts included an annual reception hosted by the Diversity Commission; greater emphasis on individual contact with travel grant recipients before, during, and after annual conferences; encouraging co-presentations with long-term members; and supporting local and regional networking for access to resource materials and support.

Creating a More Multicultural Organization: Travel Grants and Internship Grants

The Diversity Commission began to network with Historically Black Colleges and Universities (HBCUs), Native American Tribal Colleges (Tribal Colleges), and Hispanic-Serving Institutions (HSIs). Between 1994 and 2002, the Diversity Commission successfully recruited 40 underrepresented institutions to the annual conference through the dissemination of travel grants. Travel grants are designated to help awardees help underwrite expenses related to conference travel, accommodations, and registration fees. In the early years of the travel grant program, faculty and administrators of HBCUs, Tribal Colleges, and HSIs were specifically sought out. More recently, travel grants have also been awarded to people of color at predominantly white institutions (PWIs), and Historically Disadvantaged Institutions (HDIs) in South Africa. See Appendix 13.1 for a complete list of the participating institutions.

In 1995, the Diversity Commission began to explore ways in which the organization could nurture the growth of diverse professionals in the field. The commission looked at "pipeline" issues, or the way in which new members choose and are socialized into the field of faculty development. Specifically, the goal was to create opportunities for graduate students and faculty members of color to learn about and gain experience in faculty and instructional development.

A survey of 1,117 faculty development professionals in 1995 revealed that only about 5% were people of color: African American, Asian, Hispanic American, and Native American. The demographic profile of faculty developers also revealed that 19% were between the ages of 56–65, 51% between the ages of 46–55, 25% between the ages of 35–45, and 5% under 35 years of age (Graf & Wheeler, 1996). Clearly, the small number of faculty development professionals of color does not reflect the diversity of the faculty, academic staff, or students in higher education in general.

In response to this need, an internship opportunity, the POD Faculty/Instructional Development Training Grant program, was developed. The explicit purpose of this program is to provide a POD member institution with funding to support the development of an internship opportunity for a person of color who wishes to explore professional opportunities in faculty and/or TA development. Awards are based on a competitive funding process in which institutions are asked to submit a detailed outline of their immediate and long-term goals for sustaining these efforts. Additionally, successful institutions are expected to match the award and to demonstrate a plan for how they will sustain this opportunity over time. Initially, the program offered up to $1,000 (1995) but based upon feedback from early recipients, the award was first raised to $2,000 (1997) and is now $4,000 (2000–current). From 1995–2002, six POD member institutions received internship grants. Most recently, the University of Michigan's Center for Research on Learning and Teaching (CRLT) received a second internship grant award in the fall of 2002.

2002 Survey of POD Travel and Internship Grant Recipients

To date, Diversity Commission and Core Committee members have relied primarily upon informal communication and individual networks to gather feedback on the experiences of grant participants and to monitor the usefulness and the benefits of the internship and travel grant programs over the ensuing years. Generally positive, the informal consensus held that these were useful programs that offered benefits for both award recipients and POD. Due to the all-volunteer nature of most initiatives in POD, the gathering of systematic assessment and evaluation data was not attempted before this effort. Below we describe the design of the survey and the results of this assessment effort.

Survey Design

In the fall of 2002, rosters of the names and contact information of all past travel and internship grant recipients were collected and updated. Since 1994, a total of 47 travel grants have been awarded and 45 were used. Of these original 45 awardees, 14 participants have since left their original institution and we were unable to locate current contact information for them. Therefore, 31 past travel grant recipients were left as potential survey participants. The internship program, launched in 1995, had a much smaller cohort of six institutional participants sponsoring a total of eight interns. We were able to contact and interview one key contact person at each of the six institutions and a total of six of the eight interns. Below we describe our findings. Themes are identified from the perspectives of travel grant recipients and then from the perspectives of internship grant recipients.

POD Diversity Commission Travel Grant

Methods

We sought to collect feedback from all 47 past grant recipients about their experiences in the POD travel grant program. Current email and surface mail addresses were verified through Internet searches and calls to colleges and universities of record. If an individual had left an institution, attempts were made to locate that person, both through inquiries at his or her former college or university, and through an Internet name search. Fourteen awardees had subsequently left their institution, with no available forwarding information.

We were able to find current contact information for 31 participants, and an electronic survey was sent via email in October 2002. Those who did not respond were contacted by phone (either in person or via a message) if a phone number was available. A second email was sent in late November 2002 to those who had not responded to the first email.

Response Rate

Surveys were completed by 19 of the 31 possible respondents. Twelve respondents for whom we had contact information did not complete the survey; however, three of these were recipients who provided verbal feedback at the 2002 annual POD conference. The overall response rate to the survey was 61% of grant recipients for whom we had contact information (see Table 13.1).

TABLE 13.1
Travel Grant Survey Responses

Total Travel Grants Awarded	Current Contact Information	No Response	Response
47	31	12	19

The feedback below is based upon responses from the 19 travel grant recipients who received the grant in years ranging from 1994 to 2002. Respondents who received the travel grant quite a few years ago predictably had lower participation rates and, when available, less vivid recollections (and less detailed feedback) than more recent recipients.

Highlights

In all, survey respondents were positive about their experiences and encouraging of the continuation and growth of the travel grant program. They cited the importance of this support as allowing them to attend the conference, the positive personal contact with POD members, and the high quality of the conference itself as three of the grant program's particular strengths.

> The communication with [the coordinator of the travel grant program], a member of the diversity commission, has been outstanding. She keeps me well-informed about what is going on with POD.

> The chance to get to know the organization through the conference was quite valuable.

What worked well? The majority of respondents said that they would *not* have attended the POD conference if they had not received the grant, almost unanimously because of financial reasons. Thus, the grant provided needed access to the conference. They also cited as important benefits the ease of the application process and the positive relationships built with POD members and with the POD organization as a whole.

What did participants gain? In the short term, participants reported that they gained a great deal of intellectual stimulation and information from the conference itself, and developed new professional relationships. For some, it provided an eye-opening introduction to the field of faculty and instructional development, especially for graduate students and those new to this work. One of the important organizational development goals of this program is to bring more people of color into the field and, to that end, these grants appear effective.

> The conference gave [me] perspective on faculty development and heightened [my] interest in the field.

The content of the conference stimulated ideas that many grant recipients followed up on in their home institutions. Respondents also noted that whether or not they had continued their involvement with POD, they had maintained a network of colleagues whom they met at the conference. The importance of developing ongoing relationships with awardees is also evident in the interest shown by recipients who applied for and received travel grants to continue attending the annual POD conferences over several years.

Respondents were pleased with what they perceived to be an application process with fewer than usual hurdles. Many awardees cited the importance of keeping the program easily accessible. For example, several remarked on how much they appreciated the opportunity to submit letters of application electronically and the regular contact with one designated person representing the Diversity Commission and POD.

What did not work well about the travel grant program? The majority of respondents answered that everything went well with the grant program. Three grant recipients noted challenges covering their travel and conference costs prior to receiving reimbursement. Also, one respondent suggested that the program could be improved by having clearer outcome goals and greater post-conference follow-up with awardees.

Suggestions to improve the travel grant program. A number of respondents suggested that travel grant opportunities could be even better publicized. Other recipients suggested immediate follow-up with grant recipients to better incorporate them into POD, perhaps through a mentorship network. Finally, a few members suggested increased flexibility in reimbursement procedures.

POD Diversity Commission Internship Grant

The POD Diversity Commission has supported the Internship Grant Program since 1995. Internship grants have been awarded to six institutions in support of eight individual interns. Recipients include the University of Michigan's Center for Research on Learning and Teaching (CRLT) (1995); the University of Southern Colorado's Faculty Center for Professional Development (1995); the University of Massachusetts Amherst's Center for Teaching (CFT) (1997); Indiana University–Purdue University Indianapolis's (IUPUI) Center for Teaching and Learning (2000); the University of Connecticut's Institute for Teaching and Learning (2000); and Arizona State University's Center for Learning and Teaching Excellence (CLTE) (2001). Two institutions sponsored two interns with their grants: University of Southern Colorado (1995) and Arizona State University (2001).

Procedure

Feedback was solicited from a total of 14 people (six teaching center directors and eight interns) about their experiences in the POD internship grant program. We received 11 responses. Various data collection methods included an electronic survey, review of final reports submitted to POD from participating institutions, phone interviews, and a focus group at the annual POD conference in Atlanta, Georgia, in October 2002. Some data were collected through interns' written summaries of their experiences, and, in one case, a director's final report. Not all recipients directly answered all questions.

Response Rate

The feedback below is based upon responses from 11 individuals, including five people designated as the institutional contact person, and six interns of five institutions that received the grant (see Table 13.2).

TABLE 13.2
Internship Grant Survey Responses

Internship Grants Awarded	Potential Pool	No Response	Response
Institutional Contact Person	6	1	5
Interns	8	2	6

Highlights

What worked well? It should be noted that because of the nature of this initiative, far fewer institutions and individual awardees have participated in the Internship than in the Travel Grant Program. However, some themes were so consistent that they appear to have resonance beyond specific institutional needs or idiosyncrasies. For example, interns noted consistently that the Internship Grant helped them to develop mentoring and other relationships with professionals working in the field of faculty development. The interns who seemed most enthusiastic about their experiences worked with highly involved mentors who were also strong advocates for the program and their success. Interns also found the conference to be useful and inspiring.

> I was . . . fortunate to be the protégé of a professional who is well known and respected in her field. I was especially conscious of her interest in my success and the uniqueness in her mentorship that made my internship a success.

Internship projects/outcomes. Grant recipients worked on a wide range of projects, and interns' experiences varied from institution to institution. The most common types of projects included diversity workshop and seminar facilitation, development of diversity-related materials such as websites and resource guides, presentations at professional conferences, teaching-related activities, and attendance at POD conferences.

What was gained from the internship experience? Foremost, interns cited the positive mentoring and network of collegial relationships they developed as the most important (and rewarding) aspect of the internship.

> The knowledge I gained from this internship was not an exercise in acquiring best practices as end products. It was actually an opportunity to foster and fuse ideas with colleagues who intellectually believed in my ideas.

Consistently, interns reported that the opportunity to work closely with directors, faculty, and staff in the host centers for teaching contributed importantly to the success of the internship experience. As may be expected, the mentoring experiences of interns varied somewhat across years and institutional settings. Also, interns represent a wide range of profiles related to stages of career. At the time of their internship, five were doctoral-level graduate students and three were full-time tenure track-faculty members. The eight past interns were split equally between those specifically interested in a career in faculty and instructional development and those who viewed their internship experiences as contributing to different career goals in higher education (e.g., tenure-track faculty lines). At the time of this study, one past intern now serves as chair of her college's faculty development committee, one intern was hired by her center as a permanent instructional development consultant, and one intern has a full-time position in student affairs with significant responsibilities related to faculty and instructor development.

Over the duration of the program, the Internship Grant application and selection process has strengthened the planning, goal setting, and assessment processes for internships. Interns also appreciated the ability to forge connections with other colleagues (and role models) at the national conference.

> I was able to speak with many of the people who had authored articles and books that I had used in my comprehensive exams and other research papers like Nancy Chism and Bill McKeachie.

Interns also gained familiarity with the field of faculty development and perspectives on multiculturalism and diversity, organizational development in the context of higher education, and institutional dynamics.

Directors reported that institutions gained high quality materials produced by the interns, new relationships with different faculty members, and ties with future staff and faculty members.

> [The intern] has been instrumental in the achievements of the Diversity Inquiry Group, which is a group of faculty and staff devoted to multicultural teaching. She has done several workshops for the Office for Professional Development and has been very instrumental in working with our own staff on diversity issues, offering workshops and helping to design other activities.

What suggestions were offered to strengthen the program? Very few suggestions for improving the Internship Grant program were offered by the interns or center directors. Several respondents did offer that more proactive follow-up measures be taken with interns after their internship concludes, in order to maintain their interest in the field and to encourage and foster future careers in faculty development. One idea for implementing such an effort was to formalize and extend the mentoring program for travel and internship grant recipients to further strengthen their ties to POD. Other ideas included a listserv for current and past interns and posting the names of interns on the POD listserv to encourage communication about potential positions in the field.

Directors of centers for teaching were most positive about the flexibility provided by the Internship Grant. This flexibility allowed them to tailor internship experiences to the skills and interests of the intern, as well as to support projects suitable to the needs of their program, faculty, and institution. All directors perceived the contributions of their intern(s) to be of significant value to their centers (e.g., developing a multicultural resource directory, forging improved relationships with faculty members, offering workshops and individual consultations on issues related to teaching inclusively).

In sum, the interns and directors were largely satisfied with their Internship Grant experiences and enthusiastic about the continuation of the program. Importantly, receipt of this Internship Grant does appear to serve as a catalyst for engaging interns further in faculty and instructional development careers.

Discussion

POD, under the auspices of its Diversity Commission, has sponsored travel and internship grant programs for nine years as one organizational intervention to support becoming a more multicultural organization and to foster a more representatively diverse field of faculty and instructional developers.

These two programs are different in terms of the level of investment required of individual participants, the roles played by their home institutions, and the level of formal support offered by POD. Consequently, each program appeals to quite different participants. The travel grants are dedicated almost exclusively to the interest of supporting the participation of people of color at the annual POD conference. Very often, this support makes the crucial difference in a participant's ability to attend a faculty development conference. Internship grants require a commitment of the participating center for teaching to structure a meaningful experience for their intern(s). Often, the actual nature of the internship is tailored to the strengths and interests of the intern, but across the board, mentoring is perceived to be a critical outcome.

POD has steadily increased the budget allocations for each of these programs and supported the integration of concomitant diversity-related initiatives that act to broadly institutionalize these priorities and goals. It seems clear from participation rates, and the increasingly competitive nature of the travel and internship grants, that these programs provide important services.

The Diversity Commission: A Model for Mentoring and Creating Organizational Change

The Diversity Commission is serving as a model for mentoring and creating organizational change. Stanley and Ouellett (2000) examined POD's path to becoming a multicultural organization. Based on the adaptation of the developmental stages of multicultural organizations by Jackson and Hardiman (1988), they outlined six stages in POD's growth as a diverse organization (see Figure 13.1):

- Stage One: Exclusionary Organization
- Stage Two: Club
- Stage Three: Compliance Organization
- Stage Four: Affirmative Action Organization
- Stage Five: Redefining Organization
- Stage Six: Multicultural Organization

We propose that POD operates often in the context of a Stage Five organization. We are "actively engaging in envisioning, planning, and problem-solving to find ways to ensure the full inclusion of all" (Stanley & Ouellett, 2000, p. 45). While an organization is rarely completely defined by any one stage of the multicultural organization model offered below, through the Internship and Travel Grant programs it is clear that POD is actively defining and manifesting itself as such an organization.

FIGURE 13.1
Stages in the Development of a Multicultural Organization

Stage	Type	Descriptors
One	Exclusionary Organization	Mission and membership criteria openly discriminate.
Two	Club	Mission, policies, norms, and procedures allow for a few "selected," "right" representatives.
Three	Compliance Organization	Provides some access without departing from mission, structure, culture. Maintains status quo.
Four	Affirmative Action Organization	Recruits and promotes members of social groups other than the "majority." Training provided.
Five	Redefining Organization	Actively engages in envisioning, planning, and problem solving to find ways to ensure the full inclusion of all.
Six	Multicultural Organization	Reflects contributions of diverse cultural and social groups; acts on commitment to eradicate social oppression in all forms; all members are full participants; follows through on external social responsibilities.

(Jackson & Holvino, 1988)

Centers for teaching and faculty and instructional developers are now regularly called upon to help faculty members, departments, and colleges address teaching and learning issues related to diversity and inclusion. POD has a unique role to play in preparing and supporting its members to better meet these challenges. We suggest that one important way to do this is by sustaining within POD a multicultural organization development initiative that is reflective, self-critical, and transparent.

FUTURE DIRECTIONS: FEEDBACK FROM BENEFICIARIES OF TRAVEL AND INTERNSHIP GRANTS

The nature of the success of these two diversity-related initiatives, the internship and travel grant programs, reflect some of the same strengths that make

POD a generally successful organization. This is perhaps best expressed by a travel grant recipient who wrote:

> Personally, I was overwhelmed by the warmth, love, and support expressed by the members of the diversity committee and the POD group as a whole.

Conclusion

In light of recent organization-wide strategic planning and assessment efforts, and as an aide to future planning efforts of the Diversity Commission, in 2002, the authors initiated this first comprehensive assessment and evaluation of the travel and internship programs. It is also hoped that this effort will become part of an ongoing stream of such assessment efforts and will contribute to educating POD members (and potential future members) about the internal and external benefits of these programs.

The Travel Grant program has contributed significantly to the diversification and expansion POD's ties to a number of HBCUs, HSIs, Tribal Colleges, and HDIs. In recent years these ties have also extended to people of color working in the context of predominantly white institutions. While some travel grant recipients do move on to other goals quickly, in reviewing the distribution of travel grants over time, we noted that some of the earliest awardees continue to this day to have regular and important roles within POD. Selected examples of this include travel grant recipients who have gone on to serve POD as elected members of Core and the Core executive committee, chair of a standing committee, conference plenary and keynote presenters, and as current liaisons with HBCUs, HSIs, Tribal Colleges, and HDIs, as well as other institutions and the organizations that serve them (i.e., the HBCU Faculty Development Network). Additionally, travel grant awardees have presented programs that made important contributions to the scope of activities, plenary sessions, and programs at POD annual conferences, and they have provided important insight into and understandings of the experiences of faculty and academic administrators of color across all types of institutions.

FIGURE 13.2
Travel Grants to Individuals by Type of Institution 1994–2002

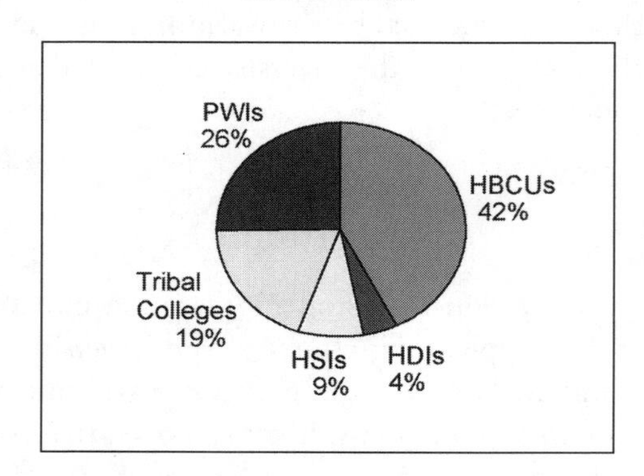

To date, the internship program has primarily provided an opportunity for centers for teaching at public universities to sponsor a person of color as an intern. Such efforts have clear benefits for institutions as well as interns. Of the eight past interns, at least three have moved into positions with duties related to faculty and instructional development.

Based upon this study, the Internship and Travel Grant programs appear to contribute importantly to POD becoming an inclusive, multicultural organization. It is important to note that the strength and vitality of the Travel and Internship Grant programs rest on the values, beliefs, and norms intrinsic to the organization broadly. POD members have a well-earned reputation for being welcoming of and generous to each other. One of the great strengths of POD is its emphasis on collegiality. Participants, therefore, quite rightly perceive such behaviors as genuine attributes of organizational norms and expectations.

> I perceived the [Diversity Commission] committee was genuinely interested in both my attendance and my involvement at the Atlanta conference. The grant opportunity did not feel like a "token" effort. This speaks to the sincerity and awareness of POD leaders.

Much can be learned from the organizational processes of reshaping POD as a model 21st-century organization so that its members may better meet the demands of their own faculty members and institutions. The membership of POD appears to be increasingly diverse and international. In a similar light, many of its institutions are sensitive to the need to sustain and support increasingly diverse populations of undergraduate and graduate students and faculty members. As a truly inclusive organization, POD and its membership will become increasingly skilled in multicultural competencies, multiculturally appropriate teaching and learning development consultation, and the development of inclusive faculty and instructional development programs within the context of home institutions.

As POD continues to build the multicultural organization it aspires to be, we suggest that there would be great benefit to replicating the membership survey conducted in 1995 (e.g., demographic profiles, job descriptions, members' priorities, length of membership in POD). It would be beneficial to be better able to track changes over time in the demographic profile of POD's membership. These data, if collected regularly, would provide us with one index by which to mark our progress toward becoming a multicultural organization. We also suggest that more structured mentoring programs be offered for all new POD members, with special care given to travel and internship grant award recipients (e.g., encouraging communication links between past and current interns and between host institutions). While current practices result in many worthy accomplishments, significant progress would result from additional, ongoing efforts to collect from traditionally underrepresented groups in POD their perceptions and feedback. Such efforts as these clearly benefit all POD individual and institutional members.

Acknowledgments

The authors wish to acknowledge the research assistance and contributions of Heather Bourne, University of Massachusetts Amherst.

References

Border, L. L. B., & Chism, N. V. N. (1992). The future is now: A call for action and a list of resources. In L. L. B. Border & N. V. N. Chism (Eds.), *Teaching for diversity* (pp. 103–115). New Directions for Teaching and Learning, No. 49. San Francisco, CA: Jossey-Bass.

Collett, J., & Serrano, B. (1992). Stirring it up: The inclusive classroom. In L. L. B. Border & N. V. N. Chism (Eds.), *Teaching for diversity* (pp. 35–48). New Directions for Teaching and Learning, No. 49. San Francisco, CA: Jossey-Bass.

Cook, C. E., & Sorcinelli, M. D. (1999). Building multiculturalism into teaching development programs. *AAHE Bulletin, 51*(7), 3–6.

Ferren, A., & Geller, W. (1993). Faculty development's role in promoting an inclusive community: Addressing sexual orientation. In D. L. Wright & J. P. Lunde (Eds.), *To improve the academy: Vol. 12. Resources for faculty, instructional, and organizational development* (pp. 97–108). Stillwater, OK: New Forums Press.

Graf, D. L., & Wheeler, D. (1996). *Defining the field: The POD membership survey.* Ames, IA: The POD Network.

Jackson, B., & Hardiman, R. (1994). Multicultural organizational development. In E. Cross, H. Katz, F. Miller, & E. Seashore (Eds.), *The promise of diversity* (pp. 231–239). Chicago, IL: Irwin Professional Publishing.

Jackson, B., & Holvino, E. (1988). Developing multicultural organizations. Creative change. *The Journal of Religion and the Applied Behavioral Sciences, 9(2),* 14–19.

Kardia, D. (1998). Becoming a multicultural faculty developer. In M. Kaplan & D. Lieberman (Eds.), *To improve the academy: Vol. 17. Resources for faculty, instructional, and organizational development* (pp. 15–33). Stillwater, OK: New Forums Press.

Katz, J. (1978). *White awareness: Handbook of anti-racism training.* Norman, OK: University of Oklahoma Press.

Ouellett, M. L., & Sorcinelli, M. D. (1995). Teaching and learning in the diverse classroom: A faculty and TA partnership program. In E. Neal & L. Richlin (Eds.), *To improve the academy: Vol. 14. Resources for faculty, instructional, and organizational development* (pp. 205–217). Stillwater, OK: New Forums Press.

Ouellett, M. L., & Sorcinelli, M. D. (1998). TA training: Strategies for responding to diversity in the classroom. In M. Marincovich, J. Prostko, & F. Stout (Eds.), *The professional development of graduate teaching assistants* (pp. 105–120). Bolton, MA: Anker.

Schmitz, B., Paul, S., & Greenberg, J. (1992). Creating multicultural classrooms: An experience-derived faculty development program. In L. L. B. Border & N. V. N. Chism (Eds.), *Teaching for diversity* (pp. 75–87). New Directions for Teaching and Learning, No. 49. San Francisco, CA: Jossey-Bass.

Stanley, C. A. (2001). A review of the pipeline: The value of diversity in staffing teaching and learning centers in the new millennium. *The Journal of Faculty Development, 18*(2), 75–85.

Stanley, C. A., & Ouellett, M. L. (2000). On the path: POD as multicultural organization. In M. Kaplan & D. Lieberman (Eds.), *To improve the academy: Vol. 18. Resources for faculty, instructional, and organizational development* (pp. 38–54). Bolton, MA: Anker.

Contact:

Mathew L. Ouellett
Center for Teaching
301 Goodell
University of Massachusetts Amherst
140 Hicks Way
Amherst, MA 01003–9272
Voice (413) 545-1225
Fax (413) 545-3829
Email mlo@acad.umass.edu

Christine Stanley
Associate Director, Center for Teaching Excellence
Texas A&M University
232 Blocker MS 4246
College Station, TX 77843
Voice (979) 862-2718
Fax (979) 845-9242
Email cstanley@coe.tamu.edu

Mathew L. Ouellett is Associate Director of the Center for Teaching at the University of Massachusetts Amherst, where he works with faculty and teaching assistants on developing skills for teaching and learning in the diverse classroom. He also serves as an adjunct faculty member in the School of Education where he teaches in the higher education and social justice programs. For the past ten years he has also taught graduate courses at the Smith College School for Social Work. He has consulted with hundreds of individual instructors and many departments and colleges on teaching development and diversity initiatives. Most recently, he is author of the chapter, "Teaching for Inclusion" in *Engaging Large Classes: Strategies and Techniques for College Faculty*, edited by C. A. Stanley & M. E. Porter (2002).

Christine A. Stanley is Associate Professor of Higher Education Administration and Associate Director of the Center for Teaching Excellence at Texas A&M University. She teaches courses on college teaching, professional development in higher education, and diversity and social justice in higher education. She is a consultant to many colleges and universities in the area of diversity, faculty development, and teaching large classes. She is co-editor of a recent book, *Engaging Large Classes: Strategies and Techniques for College Faculty* (2002). She is past president of the POD Network in Higher Education (2000–2001) and past chair of the Diversity Commission (1994–1998). She serves as Senior Editor for the New Forums Press series on faculty development.

Appendix 13.1

Institutions Participating in the Travel Grant Program

Historically Black Colleges and Universities (HBCUs)

Bowie State University
Clark Atlanta University
Dillard University
Florida A&M University
Howard University
Jackson State University
Johnson C. Smith University
Morehouse College
Oakwood College
Prairie View A&M University
St. Augustine's College
Spelman College
Stillman College
Texas Southern University
Tougaloo College
Xavier University of Louisiana

Tribal Colleges and Universities

Fort Peck Community College
Lac Courte Oreilles Ojibwa Community College
Little Big Horn College
Navajo Community College (now Diné College)
Nebraska Indian Community College
Oglala Lakota College
Salish Kootenai College
Sinte Gleska University
Standing Rock College (now Sitting Bull College)

Hispanic Serving Institutions (HSIs)

Heritage College
Pima Community College
San Antonio College
The National Hispanic University

Historically Disadvantaged Institutions (HDIs)
University of the Witwatersrand, South Africa

Predominantly White Institutions (PWIs)
Arizona State University
Louisiana State University
Molloy College
New York University
Portland State University
Quinebaug Valley Community College, CT
Santa Fe Community College, FL
Syracuse University
University of Colorado at Boulder
University of Northern Iowa
University of Texas El Paso

Institutions Participating in the Internship Grant Program
Arizona State University
Indiana University–Purdue University Indianapolis
University of Massachusetts Amherst
University of Michigan, Ann Arbor
University of Southern Colorado
University of Connecticut

14

Playing Well With Others: Academic Development as a Team Sport

Nancy Van Note Chism
Indiana University–Purdue University Indianapolis

An important first step to attacking significant institutional problems is working across the organizational silos that encompass campus units. This chapter draws upon an experience in collaboration through which an academic development center chose to partner with a variety of campus units to address a vexing problem facing many campuses: unacceptable rates of first-year student retention. The chapter then goes beyond the case to identify the kinds of collaborations that can be created to treat other pressing academic issues and highlight characteristics of successful collaborations that academic development centers can initiate or join.

Once upon a time, there was a teaching center that really was not very valued. Requests for consultation were few, workshop attendance was low, and major institutional decisions were always made without the help of the center. Then a change came upon the land, and the center was deluged with requests: Can you do service learning? What about outcome-based assessment? Know anything about "smart classrooms"? The center's teaching consultants went from being able to catch up on reading on a slow Friday afternoon to looking longingly at unread piles of new books and journal articles on their desks, reminiscing about the good old quiet days when there was time to think and read.

* * * * *

This tale describes a general pattern increasingly noted by academic development centers—the change from being a marginalized unit on campus to being the all-purpose teaching and learning support center. While there are indeed positive aspects to this state of affairs, centers are struggling to define priorities, obtain resources, and respond effectively to a wide range of needs. This chapter describes one strategy for operating in this environment of demand: forming partnerships with other units to address complex institutional needs. It begins with one story, the Gateway Program at Indiana University–Purdue University Indianapolis (IUPUI), and goes on to articulate issues and implications for the work of academic development in general.

The Gateway Initiative

For years, IUPUI had been concerned with its very low first-year student retention rates. Themes found in faculty experience and the literature (Braxton, Bray, & Berger, 2000; Cubeta, Travers, & Sheckley, 2001; Furr & Elling, 2002; Hu & St. John, 2001; Johnson, 1997; Lang, 2001; Tharp, 1998) had described the many challenges the institution faced in retaining students: demographic characteristics of the IUPUI student were among the most frequently cited. As an urban institution, IUPUI enrolls a primarily commuter student body. Student employment is high (an average of 19.5 hours per week for full-time freshmen). First-year students also have many family obligations (an average of six hours per week). Together, these obligations are primary to the lives of many students—attention to school ranks a distant third. Over 60% of IUPUI students lack the core high school coursework needed for college success. Their standardized test scores (an average 957 combined SAT) and high school grade point averages are low. A state-supported institution, IUPUI gets only limited subsidy and is not well financed. Its subsidy and tuition are lower than most other public institutions. Yet, even in periodic comparisons with other urban schools with similar conditions, the first-year student dropout rate has been unacceptably high.

In the face of intense pressure from the trustees and state legislators, the IUPUI administration decided to dramatically step up efforts to improve the retention rate. The dean of University College (UCOL), home of undeclared undergraduates and student academic support services, was asked to collaborate with the director of the Center for Teaching and Learning (CTL) to mount a new initiative. The wisdom of uniting the administrators charged with learning and teaching enhanced the collaborative possibilities of this endeavor from the start.

One of the first steps in the process was to convene a town meeting to hear faculty, students, and administrators define the nature of the problem and suggest solutions. From this initial meeting, a group of key leaders was identified and invited to be part of a ten-person team at a summer academy hosted by the American Association for Higher Education. The team was composed of an associate dean for instruction, a department chair, four teaching faculty from the first-year courses, a librarian, a student, and the two convening administrators from University College and the Center for Teaching and Learning. The team termed the first-year courses targeted for their efforts as "Gateway" courses and began to call itself "the Gateway group."

The group proposed several central activities: a regular series of forums at which faculty teaching the courses would share dilemmas and successes; regular meetings with key deans, department chairs, and faculty involved in the Gateway courses to discuss progress and needed resources; a grants program to encourage inquiry, development, and dissemination of promising practices; and enhanced support from University College and the Center for Teaching and Learning for the students and faculty in these courses. The summer team members agreed to serve as a continuing steering group for these activities, but invited several others, including the director of institutional research and the associate dean from the other major school offering Gateway courses, to join the effort.

Throughout the retention initiative, which continues to the present, the collaboration of multiple units on campus has been engaged.

The Office of Information Management and Institutional Research (IMIR)
This unit was essential for providing good data on the original nature of the problem and emerging patterns of progress. Faculty were extremely attentive to the demographic information. Using numerous charts, the very talented and articulate director of this unit was able to dispel incorrect ideas about the comparative performance of IUPUI with respect to peer institutions and was able to provide facts to support or challenge the suspicions that faculty had about the many ways in which the situations of IUPUI students were like or unlike their own student experiences. The use of data throughout the forums and meetings with schools and departments offering Gateway courses was invaluable. Charts showing rates of withdrawals and grades of "D" or "F" in these courses, coupled with enrollment numbers, were used to identify a core group of troubled Gateway courses for special attention. Sorting the data by sections and departments pointed to the special instructional issues that had to be engaged, enlarging the conception of the attrition problem beyond blaming it on student characteristics and habits. As interventions were attempted or grant projects proposed, IMIR continued to advise on data collection or to supply information useful for planning or tracking progress.

Administrators in Academic Units

Issues that were raised at the initial town meeting, such as the teaching reward system within units and the allocation of resources to courses, pointed to administrative decisions that students and faculty identified as detrimental to the Gateway courses. Through the involvement of key administrators in both the guiding of the Gateway initiatives and the examination of courses in their own units, the organizational development dimensions of the issues surfaced. Administrators who had previously invested most of their attention on courses in the major or graduate years were now stimulated to look at the "service" courses as they prepared for the Gateway meetings. The preparation involved dialogue with the faculty who taught these courses and identification of ways in which the dean or chair could better support this work. At the meetings, UCOL and CTL were able to offer services at very critical junctures, increasing the likelihood of use of these services. For example, opportunities to link courses with special critical thinking or tutoring initiatives in UCOL were articulated and arrangements forged. Issues of curriculum design or orientations to teaching for part-time faculty led to collaborations between CTL and the units. The conversations created the "reachable moment" that the service units needed. At the same time, insights from the schools and departments concerning how the service units might better support them were also articulated, leading to program development.

Research and Sponsored Programs (RSP)

As the Gateway group sought to mount a grants program, staff from RSP were tapped as consultants to shape the requests for proposals and help run the grants process. RSP staff were also enlisted to help identify external sources of funding for first-year retention activities, as well as to consult with faculty preparing funding proposals to these entities.

Student Life and Diversity (SLD)

It became apparent that out-of-classroom issues were quite important in the retention puzzle. Creating involvement and a sense of community were identified as key areas for improvement. Members of the SLD administrative team were added to the Gateway group and enlisted as partners in activities as concrete as buying outdoor furniture to encourage student interaction and creating a rich calendar of activities, leadership courses, and diversity study groups.

Office of Human Resources

Because many students complained of interactions with staff of administrative personnel, the Office of Human Resources became a partner to the Gateway group in working with staff in such areas as customer service and appreciation for diversity. Having friendly student support services in such areas as financial aid, enrollment, registration, and fee payment emerged as a crucial aspect of retention that needed attention.

Staff from the two major organizing units, UCOL and CTL, also made major contributions to the retention effort, shifting services to areas that needed them most and taking on new projects identified in conversations with academic units or in forums. Administrators from these units pursued institutional arrangements (such as drop-add processes and attendance requirements) that emerged as problematic in the conversations about retention.

These collaborations are resulting in dramatic retention rate increases of more than 3% each year, as well as in a new sense of community. Faculty teaching first-year courses now know their colleagues in other courses. Administrators know their first-year faculty better. Students and faculty realize that they are facing challenges similar to those of their peers in other units and are trying many different solutions. A rich body of practice-based knowledge is being generated and shared. The Gateway effort was recognized with a Certificate of Excellence in the annual Hesburgh Award competition in 2002, and IUPUI was identified as a model program in the Greater Expectations Program of the Association of American Colleges and Universities.

The Art of Collaboration

The results of the Gateway initiative are strikingly different from what might have occurred had the IUPUI academic development center approached the issue simply by instituting more workshops on teaching first-year courses or offering consultation services to instructors in these courses. The beauty of collaboration is joint ownership, multifaceted problem definition, and awareness and use of common resources. Occasions for situating the services available from CTL arose from conversations, rather than explicit marketing strategies. Ways to shape the services to meet needs emerged from the forums and meetings and grant proposals. The process of doing the work of academic development became much more organic and nested within the common work of the organization. Finally, the expertise, authority, and resources of other academic or support units were brought to bear on the central issue, an issue so large that it could have totally consumed the CTL, had it been working alone.

At the same time, some cautions need to be mentioned. Efforts such as Gateway have to be tied to an issue that is central to the work of the institution, an issue that crosses unit boundaries and represents an institutional priority. Second, extra coordination is needed any time multiple units are involved in common work. This appears to slow down the process and make it much more cumbersome. As Brown (1990) points out, "Collaboration may, of course, result in more efficient use of time and money, but few are likely to make that assumption in advance" (p. 246). There is also the possibility of domination and conflict. The loose configuration of the Gateway group (which still resists being called a "committee") was important to the effort described earlier, since it depended on a nonhierarchical, grassroots image. Other cases may call for tighter control, but collaborative groups are likely to grapple with disagreements about decisions and domination of one unit or one voice.

Not every issue that comes to the academic development office requires partnership, but the most important ones do. Questions that involve the central teaching mission of the institution are likely candidates for collaboration. These include such issues such as reforming general education requirements, planning for assessment of student performance or programs, examining an evaluation of teaching system, implementing service learning, using instructional technology wisely, and making the classroom and campus climate more welcoming of diversity. Although members of campus communities are most accustomed to doing their work in parallel play fashion, major efforts such as those described earlier cross unit lines and can best be approached in coordinated fashion.

Formation of a Consortium

Units with any responsibility for the issue can meet to discuss the nature of the problem or opportunity. They can share information, exchange perspectives, and map out the work that needs to be done. Each unit can agree to take responsibility for accomplishing a piece of the plan. A lead unit or a leadership team of people from two or more units can be designated to coordinate the process, or the units can come together at periodic intervals to review progress. The Gateway program is an example of this, as is the IUPUI Online initiative, which concerns the establishment of a new approach to developing and offering distance education courses.

Contribution of Talent to Lead Unit

A lead unit can be designated and other units can contribute staff time to the accomplishment of goals that are important to all. This approach can involve formal release time or special assignment arrangements. When heads of the respective units involved are committed to the project and responsibilities and credit for the work are shared, this strategy makes sense. The CTL at IUPUI has been assigned special staff lines from the campus technology service unit to foster the development of faculty in using the campus online course management system and in learning about effective use of learning technologies. The technology unit understands that these initiatives must be led by those who have learning expertise and a mission to support teaching, rather than those with expertise in infrastructure issues. Both units realize that this collaboration is necessary for their common goals.

Creation of Special Project Team

Several units can contribute resources to the creation of a new task group or coordinating body formed to approach a project. The new group, which might involve additional staff recruited and hired especially for the project, will usually be situated within one unit, but can also involve joint appointments, special temporary appointments, or consultants. For example, the CTL transferred a staff member to the unit charged with campus assessment to prepare for the visit of the Commission on Higher Education. This person acted in a leadership capacity, involving units throughout campus in contributing information necessary for the self-study.

Whatever format is used, there are several important characteristics of good collaborations that can be described. First, the issue at the heart of the collaboration must be important to all. While it may be more central to the work of one or more units, the problem or opportunity must be thought of as congruent with the mission and values of the unit as well as the institution. In reviewing a variety of successful collaborative efforts, Schroeder (1998) observed that "... most of the collaborative partnerships resulted from a 'triggering' opportunity which represented a particular felt need within the college or community" (¶ 18). It is tremendously helpful if the charge behind the issue comes from central administration, but in cases where this is not so, strong agreement on the importance of the work across units is critical.

Next, those who will be partners in the collaboration should be involved in defining the scope of the issue and the work. While ideas on others who should be involved often arise during the course of the collaboration, it is beneficial at the start of a project for the first collaborators to be intentional in identifying the names of others who should be invited to help. As quickly as possible, these units should be engaged in conversations about their interest and possible contributions. Much has been written about the various ways that different units on campus think, particularly the contrast between academic affairs and student affairs units (Brown, 1990; Engstrom & Tinto, 2000; Fried, 1995; Kuh, 1993; Schroeder, 1998). These differences involve norms, routine ways of acting, status, and values that are deeply entrenched in the positions that various people hold within a campus community. Early involvement of multiple units has the advantage of enabling the problem definition to be expanded.

The work group should also attempt to avoid status distinctions and operate in team fashion. This recognition of mutual interdependence and respect for the expertise of others is essential to the collaboration. Fried (1995) talks about border crossings in the context of student and academic affairs collaborations, but her points are applicable to a broader array of collaborations. She says that actors in border-crossing partnerships:

> Don't speak each other's language, aren't familiar with the protocol in each territory and are generally uncomfortable in each other's neighborhoods. Getting to know each other professionally can be considered a cross-cultural experience for each.... When newcomers and established residents develop trusting relationships in which each other makes an effort to understand the worldview of the other, newcomers can be accommodated into the existing structures with a minimum of conflict. (p. 179)

Such respect for multiple points of view is more likely when an additional characteristic, a spirit of inquiry, drives the collaboration. Wenger, McDermott, and Snyder's (2002) "community of practice" notion describes a promising model for such activities (Chism, Lees, & Evenbeck, 2002; Wenger, 1999). The collection of information, especially institutional data or findings from the scholarship of teaching and learning or other practice-based inquiry on campus, is particularly helpful in moving collaborations forward. As the members of the group analyze this information and derive implications for practice, they arrive at praxis that enables them to move forward together.

The tendency of work groups is to divide tasks and reassemble when pieces of the work are completed. However, Engstrom and Tinto (2000) point out that "... this type of experience has not typically made individuals aware of the underlying assumptions and values that guide actions" (p. 434). For example, when the task might ordinarily be thought of as a student affairs responsibility, engaging a partner from another unit to work with the student affairs partner can create new ideas on approaches to the task as well as new understandings on the part of the partner concerning the complexity and challenge of student affairs work. In the Gateway efforts, UCOL usually identifies the need to support students through tutoring as a way of addressing courses with high failure rates, while CTL tends to look at supporting the faculty member through helping with course redesign or new teaching approaches. Thus, establishing cross-group partnerships for the accomplishment of certain tasks can be very beneficial.

Successful collaborations also involve equitable commitment of resources from the participating units. Although some units are more invested and more resourced than others, each needs to contribute in proportion to its capacity. Inevitably, when one unit takes on substantially more leadership responsibility, it is thought of as dominating the collaboration. The situation can also lead to decline in involvement of other units, who may think that the work of the dominating partner will excuse them from further effort. Balancing contributions takes continued vigilance: It is easy for one unit's enthusiasm or energy to take over.

Sustaining the collaboration involves continued work. Regular communications and the creation of special occasions, such as retreats at a state park or dinners celebrating a milestone, are important support mechanisms. Outside recognition of the importance of the partnership by key leaders at the campus or external groups who make awards or celebrate special projects can do much to maintain the motivation of the individuals who are part of the collaboration. Cultivating group humor through creating insider language or rituals can be enormously helpful as well.

Finally, mechanisms for continued assessment of progress are essential for the maintenance of collaboration. Periodic checks on plan accomplishment, on the impact that the work of the group is having, and on the health of the collaboration itself keep the group focused and committed.

Conclusion

While not the only solution to the heavy demands made of academic development centers recently, collaboration with campus units is a key strategy. It rightly recognizes that major issues involve many units on campus and can only be addressed well by the formation of partnerships among these groups. Academic development is indeed a team sport.

References

Braxton, J. M., Bray, N. J., & Berger, J. B. (2000). Faculty teaching skills and their influence on the college student departure process. *Journal of College Student Development, 41,* 215–227.

Brown, S. (1990). Strengthening ties to academic affairs. In M. J. Barr, M. L. Upcraft, & Associates, *New futures for student affairs* (pp. 239–269). San Francisco, CA: Jossey-Bass.

Chism, N. V. N., Lees, N. D., & Evenbeck, S. (2002). Faculty development for teaching innovation through communities of practice. *Liberal Education, 88*(3), 34–41.

Cubeta, J. F., Travers, N. L., & Sheckley, B. G. (2001). Predicting the academic success of adults from diverse populations. *Journal of College Student Retention, 2,* 295–311.

Engstrom, C. M., & Tinto, V. (2000). Developing partnerships with academic affairs to enhance student learning. In M. J. Barr, M. K. Desler, & Associates (Eds.), *The handbook of student affairs administration* (2nd ed., pp. 425–452). San Francisco, CA: Jossey-Bass.

Fried, J. (1995). Border crossings in higher education: Faculty/student affairs collaboration. In J. Fried & Associates, *Shifting paradigms in student affairs: Culture, context, teaching and learning* (pp. 171–188). Washington, DC: American College Personnel Association.

Furr, S. R., & Elling, T. W. (2002). African-American students in a predominantly White university: Factors associated with retention. *College Student Journal, 36,* 188–199.

Hu, S., & St. John, E. P. (2001). Student persistence in a public education system: Understanding racial and ethnic differences. *The Journal of Higher Education, 72,* 265–286.

Johnson, J. L. (1997). Commuter college students: What factors determine who will persist and who will drop out? *College Student Journal, 31,* 323–333.

Kuh, G. D. (1993). *Cultural perspectives in student affairs work.* Lanham, MD: University Press of America.

Lang, M. (2001). Student retention in higher education: Some conceptual and programmatic perspectives. *Journal of College Student Retention, 3,* 217–229.

Schroeder, C. C. (1998). *Collaboration and partnerships.* Retrieved April 6, 2002, from http://www.acpa.nche.edu/seniorscholars/trends/trends7.htm

Tharp, J. (1998). Predicting persistence of urban commuter campus students utilizing student background characteristics from enrollment data. *Community College Journal of Research and Practice, 22,* 279–294.

Wenger, E. (1999). *Communities of practice: Learning, meaning, and identity.* Cambridge, England: Cambridge University Press.

Wenger, E., McDermott, R., & Snyder, W. M. (2002). *Cultivating communities of practice: A guide to managing knowledge.* Cambridge, MA: Harvard Business School Press.

Contact:

Nancy Van Note Chism
IUPUI Office of Professional Development
Associate Vice Chancellor for Professional Development
755 W. Michigan St.
Indianapolis, IN 46202
Voice (317) 274-8889
Fax (317) 278-3602
Email nchism@iupui.edu

Nancy Van Note Chism is Associate Vice Chancellor for Professional Development and Associate Dean of the Faculties at Indiana University–Purdue University Indianapolis and Associate Professor of Educational Leadership and Policy Studies at Indiana University. She has worked in academic development since 1985 and has served as president of the Professional and Organizational Development Network in Higher Education.

Section V

Student Learning and Faculty Development

15

Problem-Based Service-Learning: Rewards and Challenges With Undergraduates

Kenneth France
Shippensburg University

Students in three Abnormal Psychology sections participated in problem-based service learning (PBSL). Desired learning outcomes included humanizing persons diagnosed with mental health disorders and more fully appreciating challenges experienced by such individuals. Students completing the PBSL projects evidenced decreased negative feelings and increased positive feelings toward consumers of mental health services. According to the community partners, students made valuable contributions to both the organizations and the mental health consumers served by those organizations. Students saw the activity as being challenging and rewarding.

Academic service learning involves effort to enhance the quality of life through collaborative endeavors among the professor, students, community organizations, and the targeted beneficiaries. It also enriches classroom-focused learning by providing real-life opportunities for students to use and think about academic content (Howard, 2001). Problem-based learning has students think through relevant issues, clarify aspects of the problem, locate and use relevant resources, investigate crucial principles, and incorporate appropriate concepts into their solutions (Duch, Groh, & Allen, 2001). A melding of academic service learning and problem-based learning occurs in problem-based service learning (PBSL; Gordon, 2000). In addition to the characteristics of the two parent approaches, PBSL employs five fundamental components: specification of desired learning outcomes, collaboration with a community partner (typically a nonprofit organization) whose mission is directly related to the course content, implementation of real solutions to a broad problem posed by the community partner, enhancement of students' knowledge and skills, and frequent reflection and feedback among all involved parties.

Kezar (2002) asserted that professors should think holistically about learning outcomes and not limit students to narrowly defined cognitive development. Eyler and Giles (1999) discovered that some of the largest effects of service learning were associated with increased tolerance and enhanced citizenship skills. This study focuses on the development of such attributes, and apparently provides the first experimental evidence of PBSL-related change based on pre- and post-measures compared to a randomly assigned control group.

In my Abnormal Psychology sections, one of the goals is for students to humanize individuals who experience mental disorders. By that I mean seeing such persons as fellow human beings rather than as fearing-invoking, one-dimensional representations of mental illness. Another goal is for students to more fully appreciate the numerous challenges experienced by those who have serious mental disorders. The possibility of making greater progress toward these goals led me to try PBSL. I was intrigued by its potential to engage students and community members in joint efforts to solve real problems.

During the 2001–2002 academic year, for the first time in my teaching, I employed PBSL with one of my two Abnormal Psychology sections in the fall and with both sections in the spring. I did not provide advance notification to the fall students that PBSL would be part of one course so that the traditional section could serve as a control group. None of the sections were listed as a PBSL course. Each section met at a midday time on Mondays, Wednesdays, and Fridays for 50 minutes.

Method

Participants

There were three PBSL sections and one non-PBSL section. At the end of the term, the final enrollments for the four sections were fall section A, 30; fall section B, 27 (non-PBSL); spring section C, 30; and spring section D, 29. The withdrawals by students who attended at least one class were, respectively 1, 1, 5, and 1. The numbers of students who provided pre- and post-measures of feelings were 30, 26, 25, and 29, respectively.

Procedure

Prior to the start of the semesters, I sought a community partner for each PBSL class. That process took up to three months. The partner I used both semesters (sections A and D) was a mental health association serving three counties. The organization's mission includes promoting mental health, advocating for mental health consumers and their families, encouraging understanding and acceptance among the general public with regard to challenges experienced by individuals with mental illness, spurring social action in support of adequate mental health services, and eliminating the stigma associated with mental illness. The partner for section C was a nonprofit corporation operating in two counties. That program serves adults with serious and persistent mental disorders by providing group homes, supervised apartments, and a drop-in center.

Eventually, a representative of the nonprofit organization wrote a letter (based on a draft I provided) inviting participation by the class in addressing a perceived problem. For the partner used both semesters, the letter stated that the problem was to "develop ways for [mental health] consumers to be more active advocates." For the spring-only partner, the problem was to create "strategies for our consumers to improve their ability to live and function in the community, which includes developing and using natural support systems." The letter included a timeline that noted when the representative would visit the class early in the semester (week three) and dates for the following: deadline for proposals (week five), date for return of the proposals with her feedback (week six), deadline for final reports (week 12), and date for feedback from her on the completed projects and final reports (last week of class).

During both the implementation and proposal development phases, I required students to meet face-to-face with consumers. Activities included socializing, seeking input, and requesting feedback. The proposal developed with consumers had to include the following elements: identification of a specific problem and provision of relevant background information, goals and detailed plans that were realistic, clear explanations of how consumers and group members were going to interact, and a concrete description of how the project was going to have an impact on the problem identified by the community partner.

The course syllabus described desired learning outcomes associated with the PBSL sections. Two of the goals were humanizing persons who have mental health diagnoses and more fully appreciating challenges facing such individuals. Students addressed those issues in their final reports. Pre- and post-measures of the students' feelings toward persons with serious mental disorders provided additional data relevant to the learning goals.

On the morning of the first class day for the two sections of the course in the fall, I flipped a coin to determine which section would participate in PBSL. During the first class period in all four sections and prior to passing out the syllabus, I gave each student a form with the following instructions.

> Imagine that in a few minutes from now you are going to have one-to-one conversations with some individuals who have serious mental disorders. How would you feel about interacting with individuals who have serious mental disorders? Check all that apply: hesitant, confident, scared, eager, apprehensive, composed, nervous, enthusiastic, anxious, comfortable, doubtful, interested, reluctant, willing.

There were seven positive feeling words and seven negative feeling words. I used the number of adjectives checked to generate positive and negative score-based descriptors, with a maximum score of 7 and a minimum score of 0.

On the first day of class, I provided each PBSL student with the community partner's letter and a syllabus that described the goals and activities of their community project learning experience. On the second day of the traditional class, I formed out-of-class groups (created according to when students said they were free to meet) of about four students each in which team members would work to produce two case studies; took pictures of the groups, which helps me to learn the students' names and, by putting a large label on the back of each photo, provides a space to record the groups' out-of-class meetings with me); and participated in "interview the professor," in which small groups generated and asked questions relating to the course, the discipline, and me. The PBSL sections engaged in the same activities (their out-of-class groups would produce projects rather than case studies) along with some additional tasks. The teams developed ideas about what effective collaboration looks like and sounds like. I compiled the information and provided it to them in a handout at the next class meeting. On the third day of class, the PBSL groups developed quality criteria for the form, content, process, and impact of the proposal, implementation, and final report. I added my thoughts and developed a composite quality criteria handout for the entire class to use, which I distributed at the next class meeting. (Examples of quality criteria handouts are available upon request from the author.)

In week three, the community partner liaisons visited class for about 20 minutes, had the students sign confidentiality statements, and responded to questions. Both the community liaisons and I strongly encouraged the students to begin visiting consumers. I stated that I would not accept any proposal that was based solely on student ideas without consumer input.

Students working in small groups accomplished all of the PBSL components. There were no individual PBSL requirements in addition to the group project, which counted as one of four equally weighted components of the course (the others being two exams, and the average of 11 quizzes).

Seaman (2000) noted that one sure way to sink a PBSL effort is to pile on a project requirement to a course that is already full. Compared to the traditional version of the course, I made the following additional adjustments. During the tenth and 11th weeks of the course, the class did not meet for five 50-minute periods in order for students to have additional time to implement their projects, and we covered 11 rather than 13 chapters in the text.

Students produced a variety of projects (see Table 15.1 for a sample). The first three projects in the table addressed the goal of helping consumers become more effective advocates. The focus was on providing ways for consumers to communicate their message to encourage understanding and acceptance of challenges faced by persons with mental disorders and to decrease the stigma associated with mental illness. The last two projects in the table sought to help consumers live and function in the community.

TABLE 15.1
Student Projects

Title	**Description**
Informing the public about mood disorders	Wrote an article for the campus newspaper; produced a campus symposium
Educating children about mental disorders	Prepared information about mental disorders and presented it to a second-grade class
Addressing the communication gap between mental health patients and police officers	Published a brochure and distributed it to law enforcement and mental health organizations
Educating consumers on financial skills	Produced a notebook with chapters on establishing good credit, balancing a checkbook, maintaining a budget, buying/renting a house, and buying a car
Promoting responsibility and sense of worth	Gave plants to consumers and helped them learn plant-care skills

Team members sought consumer input regarding needs, thoughts about how to meet those needs, opinions of possibilities the students might pursue, contributions and reactions to specific student endeavors, and opinions of completed projects. Some students continued working with consumers after the semester was over. Students spent from two to more than ten hours with consumers, working with one to more than ten individuals. Typically, students spent 15 to 25 hours on the project. Most of the groups contacted the community partner representatives during both the proposal development phase, that involved the creation of a project plan, and the implementation phase, in which the students carried out the plan. (One-third of the project grade was based on the proposal and two-thirds on the implementation and final report.)

On the day in which the PBSL classes turned in their final reports, students completed the same survey form they had completed on the first day of class. For the spring sections, I also asked the students to rate how they actually felt during their first meeting with consumers.

RESULTS

Feelings Toward Consumers

I conducted a MANOVA on the feeling words scores from the survey, with Positive and Negative as the two dependent variables; Time was a within subjects factor, and Section was a between subjects factor. This analysis, in which I used the Wilks' Lambda statistic, showed Time to be significant, $F(2, 105) = 31.64$, $p < .001$ and also indicated a marginal interaction between Time and Section, $F(6, 212) = 2.14$, $p = .05$. I also conducted mixed 2 X 4 ANOVAs on the positive feeling words scores and on the negative feeling words scores, again with Time as a within subjects factor and Section as a between subjects factor. The results revealed a significant Time by Section interaction for the positive descriptors, $F(3, 106) = 3.28$, $p = .024$, but not for the negative descriptors. I followed that analysis with several univariate tests for each of the two types of scores. The means and standard deviations are shown in Table 15.2. There were no significant differences among the pre-test frequencies for the positive and negative feeling words or among post-test frequencies for the negative feeling words. There were, however, significant differences between the post-test frequencies for the positive descriptors. Because, in post hoc tests, there were no significant differences among the three PBSL sections on the positive descriptors, I combined these sections and contrasted them with the control section. The linear contrast between the control section ($M = 3.42$, $SD = 1.94$) and the three PBSL sections combined ($M = 4.49$, $SD = 1.59$) was significant, $F(1, 106) = 7.03$, $p < .01$. I also conducted mixed 2 X 4 ANOVAs on the positive feeling words scores and on the negative feeling words scores, again with Time as a within subjects factor and Section as a between subjects factor. The results revealed a significant Time by Section interaction for the positive descriptors, $F(3, 106) = 3.28$, $p = .024$, but not for the negative descriptors. Paired samples tests on the combined PBSL sections showed significantly more positive feeling words at the end of the semester ($M = 4.49$, $SD = 1.59$) than at the start of the term ($M = 3.00$, $SD = 1.71$), $t(83) = -8.32$, $p < .001$. A similar comparison of positive feeling words from students in the non-PBSL section did not reveal a significant difference between the pre-test positive feeling words ($M = 3.00$, $SD = 1.85$) and the post-test positive feeling words ($M = 3.42$, $SD = 1.94$), $t(25) = -1.34$, $p > .05$.

TABLE 15.2

Means and Standard Deviations of Positive and Negative Feeling Words Reported by Non-PBSL and PBSL Students at the Beginning and End of the Semester

	Positive Feeling Words				**Negative Feeling Words**			
	Non-PBSL		**PBSL**		**Non-PBSL**		**PBSL**	
	M	**SD**	**M**	**SD**	**M**	**SD**	**M**	**SD**
Pre-test	3.00	1.85	3.00	1.71	1.69	1.59	1.62	1.38
Post-test	3.42	1.94	4.49	1.59	1.46	1.42	1.00	1.14

For the next set of comparisons, I set the significance level at .01 to adjust for multiple tests. Because there were no significant differences between two spring PBSL sections' score-based positive descriptors or between their score-based negative descriptors, I combined the positive feelings scores for the two sections, as well as the negative feelings scores. The means and standard deviations are shown in Table 15.3. For the positive feeling words, paired samples tests showed nonsignificantly fewer positive feeling words for the actual first meeting ($M = 2.43$, SD = 1.73) than for the pre-test ($M = 3.04$, $SD = 1.80$), $t(53) = 2.20$, $p = .03$, and significantly more positive feeling words for the post-test ($M = 4.67$, $SD = 1.48$) than for the actual first meeting ($M = 2.43$, $SD = 1.73$), $t(53) = -8.61$, $p < .001$. For the negative feeling words, paired samples tests showed significantly more negative feeling words for the actual first meeting ($M = 2.76$, $SD = 1.48$) than for the pre-test ($M = 1.74$, $SD = 1.38$), $t(53) = -4.80$, $p < .001$, and significantly fewer negative feeling words for the post-test ($M = .96$, $SD = 1.16$), than for the actual first meeting ($M = 2.76$, $SD = 1.48$), $t(53) = 7.31$, $p < .001$.

TABLE 15.3

Means and Standard Deviations of Positive and Negative Feeling Words Reported by Spring PBSL Students at the Beginning of the Semester, for Their First Visit With Consumers, and at the End of the Semester

	Positive Feeling Words		Negative Feeling Words	
	M	SD	M	SD
Pre-test	3.04	1.80	1.74	1.38
First Meeting	2.43	1.73	2.76	1.48
Post-test	4.67	1.48	.96	1.16

The data showed that at the end of the course, students in the PBSL sections endorsed significantly more positive feeling words than did members of the control section. The PBSL students also reported significantly more positive feelings toward consumers than at the beginning of the semester, whereas the non-PBSL students did not show a significant increase. Another finding was that at the beginning of the spring semester the PBSL students underestimated their negative feelings. (They eventually chose more negative feelings to describe their actual first meeting with consumers.) Of greatest importance, though, is that at the end of the semester the reported negative feelings toward consumers (.96) were 65% lower than for the actual first meeting (2.76), and the reported positive feelings toward consumers (4.67) were 92% higher than for the actual first meeting (2.43).

Student Ratings of the Courses

For student ratings of the courses, the number of students who completed evaluations (ratings and anonymous comments) for sections A, B, C, and D were: 28, 22 (non-PBSL), 27, and 26. On a 6-point scale ranging from strongly disagree (1) to strongly agree (6), the student ratings for judging the professor to be effective in teaching the course were 5.8 for the control group (section B), 5.4 for the fall PBSL students (section A), 5.6 for section C in the spring, and 5.7 for section D in the spring.

Students' Use of Office Hours

For several years I have been employing out-of-class writing groups in which students collaborate on projects, such as case studies, and write group papers. I strongly encourage the groups to meet with me several times so I can give them feedback on their efforts prior to the date the final version is due. In the fall semester, the control class groups met with me an average of meeting with me 5.4 times to discuss their case studies. The PBSL groups met with me an average of 6.9 times (2.7 times to discuss the proposal, 1.7 times during implementation, and 2.5 times to discuss the final report).

Student Comments on Two Learning Goals

In their final reports, students addressed the learning goal of humanizing persons who have mental health diagnoses and evidenced in their writing that they more fully appreciated challenges faced by such individuals. The following comments are typical of what students wrote.

> We learned that people who have disabilities are truly unique individuals who want the same things in life that most of us take for granted, such as maintaining a job, meeting responsibilities, and feeling proud of one's work. . . . Through doing something positive to improve the opportunities of the mentally handicapped individuals of our community, we understood that we could become involved in our society and evoke change.

Anonymous Student Remarks About the Course

At the end of the semester students anonymously responded to open-ended probes about the course. Of the 81 PBSL students (91% of those registered) present for those evaluations, 56 (69%) of them had PBSL-related comments that I interpreted to be positive, such as these two.

> The most positive aspect was our problem-based project because we had to deal with relevant issues and we got to work with real people. It was the most beneficial experience I have had in college so far.

> I am glad we had the opportunity to do the outreach program. If I had been given a choice about doing it, I probably would not have chosen to do it, but I'm glad I did it. It was one of the best learning opportunities I had in college. I had a good time doing it and I learned a lot. The most frustrating part was coming up with an idea, but in real life you will also be faced with frustrating circumstances.

Two students (2%) complained that the project took too much time, which I interpreted as being negative comments. Seven students (9%) made comments in the vein of the following remark, "The beginning is too vague and, having never done anything like it before, made it difficult to get started. I liked the project once it got started and thought it was a good idea."

Comments by Representatives of the Community Partners

Representatives of the community partners expressed their appreciation for being involved in the classes. Both community partners expressed the opinion that consumers had been helped by the projects and asked to continue their association with the course during the next semester.

Discussion

Non-PBSL students did not significantly change their reported positive or negative feelings toward persons diagnosed as having serious mental disorders. Compared to the non-PBSL students, the PBSL participants reported significantly more positive feelings at the end of the semester. When compared to reports of how they felt during their actual first meetings with consumers, at the end of the semester the spring PBSL students listed significantly more positive feelings and significantly fewer negative feelings. The PBSL students also helped consumers, gave needed assistance to the community partners, and provided beneficial information to a variety of other groups.

Students in the three sections experienced all of the previously identified characteristics of PBSL. The students, community organizations, consumers, and professor engaged in collaborative efforts intended to enhance consumers' quality of life. Students applied academic content (e.g., their course-based knowledge regarding challenges associated with various mental disorders) to real-life situations. Team members considered relevant issues (e.g., what content knowledge to apply), clarified aspects of the problem (e.g., what was a realistic issue for them to address), then identified and used appropriate resources (e.g., the knowledge and talents of the consumers themselves) and concepts (e.g., diagnostic and treatment information). The syllabus described learning outcomes (including humanizing consumers and more fully appreciating challenges they face) in which students demonstrated progress through their comments and reported feelings. The community partners engaged in activities directly relevant to the course (one was a mental health association and the other was a nonprofit corporation serving persons diagnosed with serious mental disorders). The partners posed broadly defined problems. Students learned information (e.g., the effects of medications) that they then saw as being relevant in their problem-solving projects. Throughout the course, the students, consumers, community partners, and professor freely exchanged feedback.

As noted earlier, about one student in ten thought they should have been told more specifically what to do. As I discussed with the classes several times, though, one of the crucial aspects of PBSL is to provide a problem that is purposely broad in order to allow for creativity on the part of the students. Specifically telling students what to do would deprive them of a valuable learning opportunity.

The two most common difficulties mentioned by students were time management and the vagaries of working with real programs and real people in the community. Both were challenges that all of the groups eventually confronted and resolved in productive ways.

When teaching the course during the 2002–2003 academic year, I moved the community partner visit to the second day of class, so that students would have more time to interact with consumers during the proposal development phase. Another adjustment came from an idea described by Weimer (2002). I had each group select one or two group liaisons whom I hosted for lunch every other Friday. (One Friday I met with representatives from the first section and the next Friday I met with representatives from the second section.) While enjoying a pizza and some soda, we discussed how the groups were functioning, progress they were making, and challenges they were facing. In addition to being interested in information from other groups, the representatives said they appreciated feedback from students and me on their group's efforts.

In each PBSL section, I had one or two groups complain to me about the lack of effort by some members. The group's agreed-upon descriptions of effective collaboration provided an excellent resource for reaffirming the performance standards expected within the group. The grade assigned for the project was a maximum grade. If the team members agreed that everyone had done what was expected of them, then the team decided that everyone should receive the maximum grade. Some groups decided that not everyone had fulfilled their responsibilities, and those persons received lower grades as agreed upon in consultation between the group and me.

PBSL presents certain challenges for all involved. Although recognizing there may be some struggle along the way, the consensus opinion among the students, community partners, participating consumers, and myself is that the resulting learning and service are well worth the effort.

Acknowledgments

The author wishes to thank Adrian Tomer, Diane Clark, and Angela Bartoli for their consultation during preparation of the manuscript.

References

Duch, B. J., Groh, S. E., & Allen, D. E. (2001). Why problem-based learning? A case study of institutional change in undergraduate education. In B. J. Duch, S. E. Groh, & D. E. Allen (Eds.), *The power of problem-based learning* (pp. 3–11). Sterling, VA: Stylus.

Eyler, J., & Giles, D. E., Jr. (1999). *Where's the learning in service-learning?* San Francisco, CA: Jossey-Bass.

Gordon, R. (2000). Problem based service learning: The power of learning through service. In R. Gordon (Ed.), *Problem based service learning: A fieldguide for making a difference in higher education* (2nd ed., pp. 1–13). Keene, NH: Education by Design.

Howard, J. (2001). *Michigan Journal of Community Service Learning: Service-learning course design workbook.* Ann Arbor, MI: OCSL Press, The University of Michigan.

Kezar, A. (2002). Assessing community service learning: Are we identifying the right outcomes? *About Campus, 7,* 14–20.

Seaman, R. (2000). Project design. In R. Gordon (Ed.), *Problem based service learning: A fieldguide for making a difference in higher education* (2nd ed., pp. 15–23). Keene, NH: Education by Design.

Weimer, M. (2002). *Learner-centered teaching: Five key changes to practice.* San Francisco, CA: Jossey-Bass.

Contact:

Kenneth France
Department of Psychology
Shippensburg University
Shippensburg, PA 17257
Voice (717) 477-1108
Fax (717) 241-2534
Email franceassoc@earthlink.net

Kenneth France is Professor of Psychology at Shippensburg University and is the Coordinator of the Summer Academy for the Advancement of College Teaching, as well as the Annual Conference for the Advancement of College Teaching and Learning (both sponsored by the Pennsylvania State System of Higher Education). He serves as Editor of the *Psi High Newsletter,* a publication for high school psychology teachers in Pennsylvania, and he is the lead trainer for a network of suicide prevention trainers in Pennsylvania. He practices clinical psychology at Franco Psychological Associates in Carlisle, Pennsylvania, and he is the lead mentor for New Hope Online, an Internet-based crisis intervention service.

16

Effective Peer Evaluation in Learning Teams

Debbie Williams
Doug Foster
Bo Green
Paul Lakey
Raye Lakey
Foy Mills
Carol Williams
Abilene Christian University

Evaluating student performance in learning teams is challenging. This chapter reviews the student learning team and peer evaluation literature. The authors share the results of their experience using four rubrics for peer evaluation in student learning teams. Student learning teams involve forming students into teams for the semester to enhance their active learning. A portion of the course grade is dedicated to team quizzes, activities, and projects. The authors conclude that peer evaluation data should be used both formatively and summatively to enhance team cohesion and accountability and provide their preferred rubric for the peer evaluation process. Usage of forced differentiation in peer evaluation is discussed. A mathematical formula for calculating the impact of peer evaluations in learning teams on course or team project grades is presented.

In an effort to increase students' level of active learning, faculty often use learning teams. Evaluating student performance in student learning teams is particularly problematic, and both students and professors may have differing perceptions that spark questions:

- To what degree can the professor truly determine the functionality of the team?

- To what degree have all the students in each team earned the team grade?
- How reliable is student feedback without requiring students to differentiate among team members' performance?
- How reliable is student feedback about team members' performance without self-evaluation?
- How should the professor use student feedback to determine the percentage of a team grade to award individual team members?

Students' major criticism of "working in groups" is a lack of mutual accountability and fairness. They detest a perceived lack of peers' participation—the "free rider" syndrome (Clary, 1997)—and are suspicious of the instructor's assigning of grades, which may or may not accurately reflect their performance (Woods, 1994, 1997). Further, many are unwilling to differentiate between performances of peers in their teams and some are reluctant to assign low evaluation scores to their peers. Instructors who teach using learning teams recognize that we must solicit student feedback, but how do we obtain student feedback, how do we prepare our students for giving that feedback, and how do we use it productively?

The Challenge

Research addresses issues of team cohesiveness as well as individual and team accountability (Michaelsen, Jones, & Watson, 1993). The literature also suggests that student participation in practical classroom team projects significantly predicts increased job performance (Millis & Cottell, 1998). However, in the area of student peer evaluation in student learning teams, research is limited. As instructors, we must not only be clear with our reasons for conducting such evaluation and our allowing it to impact students' grades, but we must be aware of the implications of timing and procedure.

The authors of this collaborative study represent mathematics, English, agribusiness, instructional design, theology, and communication. We identified shared interests in teaching effectively with learning teams, following a learning teams workshop conducted by Larry Michaelsen of the University of Oklahoma. We found adaptations of Michaelsen's model for learning teams helpful, though problematic in some areas. While we resolved many problems through our discussions, we all encountered challenges that we couldn't easily resolve, centered on rubrics for evaluation and the use of the evaluation data for assigning student grades. As a result of these mutual challenges, we began working collaboratively to solve these problems.

LITERATURE REVIEW

Learning Teams: An Overview

Before exploring these areas further, we will describe our terms and the general learning team process on which we base our classes. Learning teams, as an active learning strategy, draw from several theory bases: nonfoundational social construction theory, group dynamic theory, management sciences, and psychology (see especially Bruffee, 1993; Smith, 1996). Each of these disciplines differentiates between more loosely structured groups and semester-long teams. In a learning teams classroom, the class is restructured so that students participate in semester-long teams limited to four to seven participants in which each member individually assumes responsibility for his or her own learning and hones application skills through cooperative learning experiences (Michaelsen & Black, 1994; Michaelsen, Black, & Fink, 1996; Michaelsen, Fink, & Knight, 1997; Michaelsen, Knight, & Fink, 2002). In group work that is not grounded in learning team theory, a common expectation among professors is that the groups meet outside of class to complete group projects. While some class time might be devoted to a discussion of project parameters, often little class time is devoted to project generation. In contrast, a key component of learning teams supported in the literature is the professor's expectation that students learn course principles inside class and complete individual projects outside of class. Thus, work on team projects occurs *during* the class period under the instructor's guidance.

The value of learning teams for students' intellectual and social development can be found in discussions of student development theory. Chickering and Reisser (1993) suggest that the value of learning teams for students lies in their development of interpersonal skills, group management skills, inquiry skills, conflict prevention, mediation and resolution skills, and presentation skills. Students work together to identify and utilize different team members' abilities, to learn to analyze and assign tasks, to apply principles in accomplishing tasks, and to write and/or report collaboratively on findings.

Bruffee (1993) explains that the difference between teams and groups can be described as a difference between cooperation and collaboration. The latter is a loose interaction in which students work together to submit a group project generated with the "divide and conquer" method, lacking cohesive revision needed for a quality project and frequently lacking total team input. Conversely, in a cooperative environment, students interact to complete a task in which they are concerned both about the quality of the performance (as well as with) and about each other's learning processes.

After leaving the academy, students should find that they have matured in their ability to make connections between theory and practice, as well as maturing in competence, management of emotions, movement from autonomy to interdependence, and maturing in the development of personal identity and integrity (Chickering & Reisser, 1993). While growth and interconnectedness sound good, to actualize it, students must be held accountable for their performance as individuals and as team members.

Peer Evaluation Literature

Though much literature can be found on cooperative learning and learning teams, fewer studies actually address issues of peer evaluation. Chickering and Ehrmann (1996) advocate structuring cooperative teams to provide a basis for peer evaluation so that all teams and team members can succeed. The process, however, is complex. In discussing this complexity, Woods (1994, 1997) advocates examining the degree to which students are equipped in task and social skills to perform well in a team. He suggests using a form that reflects qualities that would characterize a valued team member. For example, students are asked about various behaviors of their peers, such as whether or not a teammate attended to both morale and task components, helped the chairperson be effective, assumed the roles the team needed, and informed others of complications.

The use of characteristics as criteria for evaluation is supported by Ohland and Layton's (2000) research. They compared the reliability of two different evaluation procedures. One procedure adapted a rubric from Brown (1995) that used general behavioral descriptors as criteria ("excellent," "very good," and "satisfactory") to evaluate each individual's contributions to the team's projects. With this procedure, the labels were assigned numerical values. When all evaluations were completed, the professor translated the descriptor feedback into a numerical total. The individual student's weighting factor was the individual's average rating as determined by his or her peers, divided by the team average rating. The individual student grade would be the team grade multiplied by this weighting factor.

The second procedure involved using a rubric from Ohland and Layton (2000) that provided ten categories of contribution. Students were asked to assign a numerical rating from 0 to 5 for each category of each teammate's behavior. Some of the behavioral characteristic categories included attending meetings regularly, contributing to decisions, having good communication skills, taking responsibilities seriously, and completing tasks on time. Results from both rubrics were normalized to a common 0–100 scale for comparison. Results modestly supported Ohland and Layton's conclusion that focusing students on behavioral characteristics as opposed to Brown's behavioral descriptors (excellent, good, etc.) provided more useful feedback and thus could improve the meaningfulness of peer evaluation.

Zigon (1998) asserts that criteria should be known to the team and individuals, and that criteria should be linked to organizational measures or objectives. Clary (1997) and Foster et al. (1999) agree, explaining that students take evaluation more seriously when they assume the role of judging individual contributions of their peers—a role they can more logically fill than can their professor. Clary further points out the additional benefit of the evaluation process affords in students learning how to be accountable as well as learning valuable lessons about the learning process and teamwork efforts, which can transfer into useful job skills.

Based on the literature, we began our examination of possible rubrics and methods for using the feedback.

The Evaluation Process: Instruments for Fair Evaluation

To adequately determine the degree to which each student participated in the team activity, both individual and team performance must be measured.

Rubric 1: Team Evaluation With Differentiation and Comments; No Self-Evaluation

"Oh brother!" a student in the back muttered. He slouched further into his seat upon hearing the announcement of the use of teams. When asked about his reaction, he replied, "All group work is the same: one works, two help some, and one totally slacks, but all get the 'A.' The teacher never has a clue." In an attempt to "have a clue" and assess student performance, the authors—only one of us had previously sought to evaluate team effectiveness as a means to give grade percentages—used the rubric from Michaelsen's workshop. This rubric asks students to assess their group members and reward those who worked hard. The rubric offers the caveat to the students' evaluation process that assigning similar scores to everyone hurts those who worked hard and helps those who did not. Ideally, the evaluator is to distribute an average of ten points to each team member, with no two members having the exact same score (forced differentiation). For example, the five-member teams distribute 40 points, the six-member teams distribute 50 points, the seven-member teams distribute 60 points, and so on. As the student evaluators differentiate somewhat in their ratings, they give more points to those who contributed more. Specifically, students are instructed to give at least one score of 11 or higher (with a maximum of 15) and one score of nine or lower.

The rubric has several problems. First, it is structured as a reward/punishment system. Clary (1997) explains that this reward/punishment system is oriented more toward academe; thus, students don't view this evaluation experience as giving them practice in personnel evaluation, which they will be called on to do in the work place. Clary's research states that when students see the connection between team evaluation and work place evaluation, they participate more willingly and thoughtfully in the process). Additionally problematic in this rubric is the failure to include self-evaluation points in the point distribution. Thus, the distribution might be misleading. Finally, the mathematical formula actually privileges larger teams: on average, members of larger teams will receive a higher score than members of smaller teams.

As we reviewed this rubric, we were concerned about student reaction to the process. One colleague was confronted by a student who tearfully complied with the differentiation process, explaining that it undermined the team's previous efforts to bond. In other words, a team might not want to differentiate because of exemplary performance of all members. However, even when problems occur in team performance, team members may still resist differentiation. Clary's (1997) research explains this reaction, noting that even though students dislike and complain about free riders, they are often unwilling to penalize them, suggesting that this is, in part, due to the presentation of peer review as "punishment."

To address these problems, we worked toward increasing student buy-in of peer assessment, developing a rubric with self-evaluation, and understanding the mathematical impact of peer evaluation data on the student's individual grades.

Rubric 2: Team Evaluation, Inclusive of Self-Evaluation and Differentiation

During this time, we discovered additional colleagues who were also wrestling with student evaluation issues. They introduced us to the idea that peer evaluation could first be formative before being used for summative data. Like Michaelsen, they argued that teams should be encouraged to work out differences rather than being reconstituted throughout the semester (Cooke, Drennan, & Drennan, 1997). At this point, we began using an evaluation rubric for both formative and summative purposes.

Our colleagues' rubric, or sociogram (Cooke et al., 1997), called for differentiation in the point distribution, but did not ask for self-evaluation. Building on their work, we created a rubric that asked students to include themselves in the evaluation process to ensure fairness; thus, if student A "pads" his or her scores, the padding will be evident when compared with the scores assigned by other team members. This rubric asks students to rank each team member and themselves on factors specific to team coherence, using a Likert scale (1–5). The factors include such items as a fair share of the work load, shared responsibility rather than taking charge of every activity, and respect for the ideas of other team members. Other factors include attendance, preparation for the quizzes and tests used to determine individual knowledge of course principles, etc.

Additionally, we adapted an academic hiring model for evaluating job candidates. In this model, students are asked to differentiate pair-wise between all team members, themselves included. The rubric is formatted as a grid with all team members' names in alphabetical order along both the X and Y axis. As the evaluator considers the pairings of peers, he or she must decide which of the two in each pairing performed more efficiently.

This rubric was not as effective as desired because it was lengthy, the students hated such overt differentiation, and the Likert scale used in the first part could easily be completed without being taken seriously. Students themselves pointed out during the formative peer evaluation that using the forced differentiation model tended to create antagonism between team members rather than foster greater team cohesion. Consequently, we still struggled with the use of the evaluation data in determining individual grades.

Rubric 3: Team Evaluation With Individual Comments; No Self-Evaluation

"So, Professor, exactly how do our evaluations affect our grades? Do they affect the project grade or the class grade? What if someone in my team doesn't like me? What if someone who didn't really work is afraid of being graded down by the team and gives herself a really high score?" The student folded his arms and leaned back in his seat with an air of "Let's see you get out of this one, Professor." The students waited expectantly.

To address these questions while shifting more toward evaluation as a job skill, we continued searching for evaluation rubrics. The next one we used was designed by Dee Fink (1998), director of the instructional development program at the University of Oklahoma and a colleague of Larry Michaelsen. This rubric asked for assessment of team members based on each member's contribution to the group. The student evaluator was to base this assessment on such areas as preparation, contribution, respect for others' ideas, and flexibility. Instructions to students stated that the assessment would be determine the number of the group's points to be given to each member. The evaluator was to distribute 100 points among the team members, assigning points to each team member for each assessment criterion, giving more points to those who contributed more to the team.

This rubric differed from the others we had tried in ways we believed significant. Each evaluator had to justify the point distribution for *each* individual in the team, by adding comments about the points they assigned to each team member on each criterion. Responses remained confidential, but the form had to be validated with a signature.

Yet even with these significant differences, we found that this rubric had the same problems as the first rubric we tested—problems of being presented as a reward/punishment system as well as mathematical problems when using the data to determine grade percentages.

Rubric 4: Differentiation, Self-Evaluation, and Lessened Resistance—Our Solution

"Well, I think it's important for everyone to get here prepared. I mean groups make it too easy to say, 'I don't have time to read tonight, but I'm sure someone in the group will have done the homework.' And the teacher never knows. Only the group knows." The student sits back, satisfied with her revelation.

"Okay, your team should put that down as a criterion. If you other teams think it works for you, you can add this to your list of criterion, also," responds the professor. "Another area for accountability?"

While the rest of us wrestled with versions of team evaluation instruments, one colleague ensured student feedback in the evaluation process—both formative and summative—by asking each team to articulate its own criteria for evaluation (cf. Clary, 1997). At the beginning of the course, he guided students in considering areas they should evaluate and in framing evaluation in a real-world, job-related context. Each team began with the generic rubric template designed by the instructor, including ten suggestions for evaluation criteria. From the generic template, each team established its own distinct criteria for evaluating team members, thus increasing team buy-in and reducing resistance to the process. Two times during the semester, the teams performed formative evaluation, and at the end of the semester, teams performed summative evaluation using their team's rubric. Evaluation involved distribution of 100 points among team members, excluding the evaluator. After completing an evaluation of his or her team members, the evaluator also self-evaluated, relative to his or her distribution of points to the other team members. We experimented with this approach and collaboratively designed the rubric we have all adapted to be discipline-specific for our respective courses (see Appendix 16.1). Self-evaluation scores provide an introspective opportunity for team members and indicate evaluation anomalies to the instructor.

Formative peer evaluation is imperative, because it aids in the norming of team members' feedback. The formative evaluation process gives teams experience in conducting peer evaluation and helping them identify and address problems of cohesion and individual responsibility toward the goal of all members participating fully. Our experience demonstrates that teams who have learned how to evaluate their peers through the formative evaluation process are more effective when they complete summative peer evaluation.

We advocate this last rubric (see Appendix 16.1) because it can be used for both formative and summative evaluation, requires self-evaluation, and allows for differentiation. However, it also permits teams that performed equitably to distribute peer evaluation scores evenly. Several of us also distribute the peer evaluation via email, thus ensuring confidentiality. The next section describes a mathematical formula for accurately determining individual grade percentages on team projects.

The Evaluation Process: Using the Data in Determining Grades

If the instructor decides to use the summative peer evaluation data for determining a percentage of the final grade or team project grades, a mathematically sound formula is critical. In the case of using the summative peer evaluation data to impact a course grade, the data would be allotted a percentage of the final grade. The instructor would simply use the rubric (Appendix 16.1) to develop a chart (see Figure 16.1). Each team member's total peer score would be divided by the highest individual total peer score and that percentage would be utilized in final course grade computations as a percentage of the final grade. Since many professors utilize a spreadsheet, this procedure is relatively simple. Applying this procedure to determine the percentage of the team project grade that the individual will receive is more complex.

After working with the different mathematical formulas that accompanied each of the four rubrics we tried, we made adjustments and devised a formula for our current rubric that can be used with or without including self-evaluation scores.

Using our suggested rubric, students are asked to distribute 100 points among all team members, excluding themselves. Figure 16.1 illustrates a possible point distribution for Team 1 in a specific class. Team 1 has five members: Susan, Yukiko, Jon, Lavonne, and Ian. Figure 16.1 illustrates points awarded by all team members without self-evaluation scores.

FIGURE 16.1

Points Awarded by All Team Members Without Self-Evaluation Scores

Name of Team Member	Scores Given by Susan	Scores Given by Jon	Scores Given by Lavonne	Scores Given by Ian	Scores Given by Yukiko	Team Members' Total Peer Scores
Susan		26	25	27	27	105
Jon	28		25	30	27	110
Lavonne	18	22		15	19	74
Ian	25	26	25		27	103
Yukiko	29	26	25	28		108

This team scored 85% on its team project. Logically, the team member with the highest total peer score should receive the entire 85% as a grade. Those with lower total peer scores should receive a lower final team project grade. How much lower is determined proportionally.

First, the instructor determines the maximum deduction allowed between the highest and lowest grades within a team. In essence, how much can peer evaluations negatively impact an individual's grade on the team project? The highest grade anyone on this team can make is 85%, because the team project grade is 85%. The instructor decides that the lowest team project grade anyone on this team can make is 60% (minimum passing grade). Thus, the 85% team project grade minus the 60% gives a 25-point maximum deduction. Susan's individual team project score is calculated below:

25 (maximum number points deductible)
x .95 (This is 105/110; Susan's total peer score/the highest individual score)
23 (Susan's peer proportion score)

To figure Susan's percentage of the team grade, subtract the maximum score deductible from the team project grade, and add back Susan's individual group score:

85 (team project score) – 25 (maximum deductible) + 23 (Susan's peer proportion score) = 83 (Susan's individual team project score is 83)

In the case of Lavonne, her scores indicate that all team members perceived her to be the weakest member. Her assigning equal scores to all individuals is typical of weaker students who often make end-of-project/semester attempts to persuade the other team members that everyone deserves the same grade. Lavonne's individual team project score is figured below:

25 (maximum number of points deductible)
x .67 (74/ 110: Lavonne's total peer score/the highest individual total)
16 (Lavonne's peer proportion score)

The percentage of the team project score Lavonne would receive is figured below:

85 (team project score) – 25 (maximum deductible) + 16 (Lavonne's peer proportion score) = 76 (Lavonne's individual team project score is 76)

The project grades now reflect the students' perception of each individual's level of participation. If the instructor guided them carefully through the process of evaluation, using formative feedback first, the professor can feel secure about the equity of these grades.

To determine the individual score with self-evaluation scores included, the process would be the same except that the team members' total peer scores would be higher because of the additional self-evaluation number.

Final Thoughts

We have offered information on rubric design, process, and use of peer evaluation data. In a future article, we will examine factors in ensuring student buy-in to the evaluation process. However, many other areas still remain to be studied about peer assessment. For example, in combined undergraduate/graduate level courses, how would graduate learning teams differ from undergraduate learning teams in evaluation issues? What happens to the mathematical validity of evaluation data when attrition drops the number of team members to three—two strong students and one weak—and how can this be compensated for? To what degree can principles of peer evaluation be useful for faculty peer evaluation? As we address these and other issues sparked by peer assessment in learning teams, our goal is optimally effective and equitable learning teams that are excellent cooperative learning experiences for students and provide meaningful feedback to faculty concerning the team experience.

References

Brown, R. W. (1995). Autorating: Getting individual marks from team marks and enhancing teamwork. *Proceedings of the Frontiers in Education Conference.* Pittsburgh, PA: ISEE/ASEE.

Bruffee, K. (1993). *Collaborative learning: Higher education, interdependence, and the authority of knowledge.* Baltimore, MD: The Johns Hopkins University Press.

Chickering, A. W., & Ehrmann, S. C. (1996). Implementing the seven principles: Technology as lever. *AAHE Bulletin, 49*(2), 3–6.

Chickering, A. W., & Reisser, L. (1993). *Education and identity* (2nd ed.). San Francisco, CA: Jossey-Bass.

Clary, C. R. (1997). Using peer review to build project teams: A case study. *NACTA Journal, 42*(3), 25–27.

Cooke, J. C., Drennan, J. D., & Drennan, P. (1997, October). Peer evaluation as a learning tool. *The Technology Teacher,* 23–27.

Fink, L. D. (1998). *Improving the peer evaluation process in learning teams.* Presentation to Abilene Christian University, Abilene, TX.

Foster, D., Green, B., Lakey, P., Lakey, R., Mills, F., Williams, C., & Williams, D. (1999, March). *Why, when and how to conduct student peer evaluations in learning teams: An interdisciplinary exploration.* Paper presented at the annual convention of the American Association for Higher Education, Washington, DC.

Michaelsen, L. K., & Black, R. H. (1994). Building learning teams: The key to harnessing the power of small groups in higher education. In S. Kadel & J. Keehner (Eds.), *Collaborative learning: A sourcebook for higher education* (Vol. 2, pp. 65–81). Syracuse, NY: National Center on Postsecondary Teaching, Learning, and Assessment.

Michaelsen, L. K., Fink, L. D., & Black, R. H. (1996). What every faculty developer needs to know about learning groups. In L. Richlin & D. DeZure (Eds.), *To improve the academy: Vol. 15. Resources for faculty, instructional, and organizational development* (pp. 31–58). Stillwater, OK: New Forums Press.

Michaelsen, L. K., Fink, L. D., & Knight, A. (1997). Designing effective group activities: Lessons for classroom teaching and faculty development. In D. DeZure & M. Kaplan (Eds.), *To improve the academy: Vol. 16. Resources for faculty, instructional, and organizational development* (pp. 373–398). Stillwater, OK: New Forums Press.

Michaelsen, L. K., Jones, C. F., & Watson, W. E. (1993). Beyond groups and cooperation: Building high performance learning teams. In D. L. Wright & J. P. Lunde (Ed.), *To improve the academy: Vol. 12. Resources for faculty, instructional, and organizational development.* Stillwater, OK: New Forums Press.

Michaelsen, L. K, Knight, A. B., & Fink, L. D. (2002). *Team-based learning: A transformative use of small groups.* Westport, CT: Praeger.

Millis, B. J., & Cottell, P. G. (1998). *Cooperative learning for higher education faculty* (ACE Series on Higher Education). Phoenix, AZ: Oryx Press. [Now distributed through Greenwood Press].

Ohland, M., & Layton, R. (2000). Comparing the reliability of two peer evaluation instruments. *Proceedings of the American Society of Engineering Education.* Washington, DC: ASEE.

Smith, K. A. (1996). Cooperative learning: Making "groupwork" work. In C. Bonwell & T. Sutherlund (Eds.), *Using active learning in college classes: A range of options for faculty* (pp. 71–82). New Directions for Teaching and Learning, No. 67. San Francisco, CA: Jossey-Bass.

Woods, D. R. (1994). *Problem-based learning: How to gain the most from PBL.* Waterdown, Ontario, Canada: D. R. Woods.

Woods, D. R. (1995). *Problem-based learning: Resources to gain the most from PBL.* Waterdown, Ontario, Canada: D. R. Woods.

Zigon, J. (1998). *Measuring the hard stuff: Teams and other hard-to-measure work.* Retrieved March 25, 2003, from http://www.zigonperf.com/articles/hardstuff.html

Contact:

Debbie Williams
Department of English
Abilene Christian University
ACU Box 28252
Abilene, TX 79699
Voice (915) 674-2405
Fax (915) 674-2408
Email Debbie.Williams@engl.acu.edu

Doug Foster
Graduate School of Theology
Abilene Christian University
ACU Box 29429
Abilene, TX 79699
Voice (915) 674-3795
Fax (915) 674-6180
Email foster@bible.acu.edu

Bo Green
Department of Mathematics and Computer Science
Abilene Christian University
ACU Box 28012
Abilene, TX 79699
Voice (915) 674-2008
Fax (915) 674-6753
Email bo.green@csmath.acu.edu

Paul Lakey
Department of Communication
Abilene Christian University
ACU Box 28156
Abilene, TX 79699
Voice (915) 674-2292
Fax (915) 674-6966
Email lakeyp@acu.edu

Raye Lakey
Adams Center for Teaching Excellence
Abilene Christian University
ACU Box 29201
Abilene, TX 79699
Voice (915) 674-2880
Fax (915) 674-2834
Email raye.lakey@cte.acu.edu

Foy Mills
Department of Agriculture and Environment
Abilene Christian University
ACU Box 27986
Abilene, TX 79699
Voice (915) 674-2276
Fax (915) 674-6936
Email f.mills@agenv.acu.edu

Carol Williams
Graduate School
Abilene Christian University
ACU Box 29140
Abilene, TX 79699
Voice (915) 674-2354
Fax (915) 674-6717
Email williamsc@acu.edu

Debbie Williams is Assistant Professor of English at Abilene Christian University. Her PhD is from Purdue University. She is a leader in the utilization of learning teams and learning communities. Her specialties include rhetoric and composition theory and pedagogy.

Doug Foster is Professor of Bible and Director of the Center for Restoration Studies at Abilene Christian University. A PhD from Vanderbilt University, he is a church history scholar, particularly American and Stone-Campbell studies.

Bo Green is Professor of Mathematics at Abilene Christian University. His doctorate is from Purdue University. He is known for his development of mathematical problems and brain challenges. He has made numerous presentations concerning peer evaluation and teams.

Paul Lakey is Professor of Communication and Scholar-in-Residence in the area of faculty development at Abilene Christian University. His PhD is from the University of Oklahoma with emphases in organizational and intercultural communication. His research interests include conflict management, leadership, and active learning.

Raye Lakey is Director of Instructional Development and Faculty Development and Associate Director of the Adams Center for Teaching Excellence at Abilene Christian University. Her research interests include active learning, cultural diversity, and quality assessment.

Foy Mills is Professor and Chair of Agriculture and Environment at Abilene Christian University. A PhD from Texas Tech University, his interests include peanut quality and marketing, team-based learning in the classroom, and experimental economics in the classroom.

Carol Williams is Professor of Mathematics and Acting Assistant Provost for Research and Acting Dean of the Graduate School, Abilene Christian University. Her PhD is from the University of California, Santa Barbara. She specializes in the use of learning teams and mathematics education.

Appendix 16.1

Student Peer Evaluation

Peer evaluation serves several essential purposes in a team-based or collaborative learning classroom. The evaluation provides a measure of team accountability (i.e., how each member participates in group processes). It also allows the professor to judge how well the group is actually working together as a team.

As you evaluate your peers, your judgment should presumably reflect each team member's contribution to group activities, such as:

Attendance: Were team members present and on time for class?
Preparation: Were team members prepared for assignments?
Contribution: Did they contribute productively to team discussion and assignments?
Respect: Did they respect others' ideas and encourage participation?
Cooperation: Were they willing to work through disagreements for the good of the team?
Attitude: Did they demonstrate a positive attitude towards the team and its work?

Please take this responsibility seriously. This evaluation will be a factor in your grade. Evaluating the work of your team members should not be done in haste or carelessness. Please be honest in your appraisal. This evaluation will be kept confidential.

I. Based on these suggested criteria, distribute 100 points among the members of your team. Give more points to those who contributed more to the team efforts. You must write a brief explanation of why you gave each person the number of points you did. If you believe that all members participated equally, divide the points equally and explain your decision.

List each team member	Points
1.__________________	_____
Comments:	
2.__________________	_____
Comments:	

3. ____________________ ____
Comments:

4. ____________________ ____
Comments:

5. ____________________ ____
Comments:

II. Assess your personal contribution to the team. Give yourself a score in comparison to the scores you gave your peers. Then write a brief explanation of why you assigned this number of points. Your self-evaluation will be compared to your peers' evaluation of your contribution.

__________________ (your name)
(points) ____
Comments:

17

An International Perspective on Assessing Group Projects

Deborah Willis
Victoria University of Wellington

Barbara J. Millis
U. S. Air Force Academy

The value of group work for enhancing learning is well documented. However, to maximize the impact of group work on student learning, faculty should carefully consider course design and assessment. This chapter draws on research, policy, and practice from the US, Canada, Australia, and New Zealand to emphasize the importance of adopting an integrated approach to group work through careful planning. Guidelines emphasize ways to provide for the responsive, responsible assessment of group projects.

Looking at Group Work, Including Its Value

Human beings are social animals who have banded together from their earliest evolution to meet common needs such as the procurement of food, shelter, and protection. Not surprisingly, for many years, groups have been used in higher education around the world as a teaching-learning strategy. However, the widespread assessment of group work is a more recent phenomenon growing out of the impetus for accountability and a growing awareness of the complexity of fair and ethical evaluation. Both group work and its assessment (including self and peer assessment) have been the subject of considerable research and discussion in the higher education literature (e.g., Boud, Cohen, & Sampson, 1999; Johnson & Johnson, 1996; Millis & Cottell, 1998).

In a wide variety of teaching contexts group work has been shown to enhance student learning. For example, cooperative learning, a highly structured form of group work emphasizing the positive interdependence of students, their individual accountability (no undifferentiated group grades) and attention to their group processing, and social skills, has a well-established research base at the higher education level. Cuseo (1992) finds cooperative learning to be "the most researched and empirically well-documented form of collaborative learning in terms of its positive impact on multiple outcome measures" (p. 3). Such outcomes include not only increased academic achievement, but also affective outcomes important to faculty around the globe: increased self-esteem, more harmony in multi-ethnic classrooms, higher attendance, and greater liking for the subject matter. Support for cooperative learning emerges from virtually all areas of educational research. For example, Astin's (1993) comprehensive longitudinal study of the impact of college on US undergraduate students determined the significance of two factors in particular—student-student interaction and student-faculty interaction—both of which are also important attributes of structured group work. He declares, "Classroom research has consistently shown that cooperative learning approaches produce outcomes that are superior to those obtained through traditional competitive approaches . . ." (pp. 425–427).

The international literature (e.g., Boud, Cohen, & Sampson, 2001; Millis & Cottell, 1998) documents a range of academic and social benefits of group work. These include improved student performance; the development of cooperation and planning skills; opportunities for leadership and shared leadership; active participation and involvement; the promotion of student autonomy by transferring some of the responsibility for teaching and learning to students; the opportunity to critique personal understanding and receive peer feedback, fostering students' ability to think critically about their learning and to determine what criteria should be used in judging their work. Few of these desirable outcomes will occur, however, if the group-related elements of the course are disconnected from the objectives.

Effective Design and Assessment

Linking Group Projects to Course Objectives

Learning objectives provide the starting point for the course or the section of the course taught. To determine these objectives, faculty members can ask themselves key questions: What topic am I teaching? Is it substantive knowledge, a skill, or a process? What do I want my students to take away from the course or this portion of it? What do I want them to remember or be able to apply ten years down the academic road?

McKeachie (1994) and many other scholars (e.g., Biggs, 1999) emphasize the need to develop clear course objectives from which "all the decisions in course planning should derive . . ." (p. 9). Assessment should also be carefully linked to the course objectives. Astin et al. (1992) note:

> Assessment is a goal-oriented process. It entails comparing educational performance with educational purposes and expectations—these derived from the institution's mission, from faculty intentions in program and course design, and from knowledge of students' own goals. . . . Clear, shared, implementable goals are the cornerstone for assessment that is focused and useful. (p. 2)

Well-thought-out group projects, which are also carefully and responsibly assessed, can help students learn both skills and content germane to many disciplines.

Deciding When to Use Group Projects

Most researchers and practitioners agree that group work should be considered when one or more of the following criteria are met:

- Some goals are best achieved through students working in groups.
- The task can only be carried out by a group (e.g., where students work as a management team or are required to assign roles to group members).
- The task is too large or too complex for one person.
- Resource limitations require group work (limited equipment, limited number of "real" clients).

Michaelsen, Fink, and Black (1996) emphasize that to become cohesive, groups need well-designed assignments. "The critical variable," they claim, "is the degree to which the activities involved in completing the assignment require a high volume and intensity of group interaction" (p. 36). When group projects are either too easy or require too much writing; students tend to delegate rather than cooperate. Delegation is basically an independent task. Thus, these authors do not recommend group term papers.

Faculty must establish and maintain grading policies for group projects that clearly further the course objectives, and they must be equally careful about how they explain their grading system to students. Loacker, Cromwell, and O'Brien (1986) remind us:

> Assessment requires [faculty] to articulate... explicit and public statements of criteria of performance. By doing so, faculty refine their own understanding of expected abilities, clarify for their colleagues the basis of their judgment, and enable students to understand what performance is required. (p. 51)

Michaelsen, Fink, and Black (1996) advocate grading systems for group projects that provide frequent, meaningful feedback and reward group performance.

Determining Strategies for Assessing Group Projects

A number of methods are available for assessing aspects of group work, including allocating a shared group mark or individual marks based on product alone, or on a combination of product, group process, and individual effort. In addition, assessment may involve peer and/or self-assessment as well as assessment by faculty members. Faculty members should answer a number of critical questions before finalizing their assessment approach for group projects.

- Should I give students all the same mark or a mark based on each person's contribution to the group performance?
- If I assess each student's contribution, how will I know what each person has contributed?
- What proportion of a student's course mark should be allocated to a group project?
- Is it appropriate to include an "opt-out" clause for students who do not want to work on the project?
- What do I do if a group member leaves, thus leaving the group with a gap in the allocation of duties to members?
- What do I do if a group falls apart? Or if a member fails to do his or her share?

Specific issues related to group work. Possible problems and pitfalls are associated with group projects and their equitable assessment. As with any form of teaching, a number of potential problems may arise. Staff and students at the University of Technology, Sydney (n.d.) identified the following concerns related to group work:

- Poor internal group dynamics
- Exclusion or marginalization of individual group members
- Inappropriate tasks or assessment criteria for the subject or the range of students
- Less than desired levels of academic support or intervention
- Assessment of group work where there is no acknowledgement of differences in individual contributions
- Excessive amounts of group work when compared with individual work in a program or course

International practitioners agree (e.g., Webb, 1994) that appropriate use of group work, careful planning, support, and monitoring will reduce the likelihood of these problems adversely affecting student learning. Furthermore, faculty members meeting regularly with groups can access progress, provide feedback, and head off disruptive behaviours.

Many of the problems with "difficult" groups or students can be reduced if detected and discussed early on. However, students reluctant to reveal problems should have opportunities to raise concerns in confidence. There needs to be a clear procedure concerning who can help if there is a group problem and what students should do. Scheduling group consultation times and providing confidential email access to the lecturer can help identify and eliminate problems. However, these avenues need to be made clear in course documentation and reinforced in class time. Making class time available to work on the group project provides opportunities for faculty who monitor student progress to identify any group that is, or is in danger of becoming, dysfunctional.

Where problems are detected, students can be asked to respond in writing to the following questions:

- What is the main problem in this group?
- What could be done about it?
- What is your most immediate concern?
- What messages would you like to send to the group?

Lecturers should discuss the results with the group and negotiate a way of working to achieve the groups' learning goals. Alternatively, if student management teams (Nuhfer, 2001) or quality circles (Angelo & Cross, 1993) have been established in a classroom, then other students in the class will actually become involved in the problem-solving efforts. Both of these approaches involve designated class members who serve as a liaison between teachers and students. The overall goal is to optimize the success of students' experiences in a course.

Most groups work quite well with little intervention if clear roles and criteria have been established (see Appendices 17.1 and 17.2 for sample group assessment instruments). Problems may arise if a group member becomes ill or has other personal problems, stops communicating with others, does not contribute equitably or if political alliances arise. An insightful discussion of recommended classroom management approaches appears in Millis (2002). Even after addressing some of these project-specific issues, faculty members need to step back to review their overall assessment philosophy and subsequent strategy.

Fundamental issues related to assessment. University education is based on an assumption that final grades reflect individual student achievement. This approach clearly presents difficulties when the process and/or product of a group project are attributed collectively to group members. To operate group work within a system of individually allocated marks, one response has been to encourage students to enhance their learning through collaboration and assess students on the basis of individual assignments. Individual marks allow outstanding performance to be rewarded and freeloading to be penalized. No competition need be introduced provided marks are allocated based on the standard reached by each student rather than the performance of groups. Thus, students might collaborate on the research aspect of a given project but submit individual papers for which they receive independent grades. The University of Otago's (2001) assessment guidelines, however, conclude that while this method of assessment "preserves the individual character of final grades, [it] tends to undermine motivation for collaboration" (Assessment of Group Work section, ¶ 3). Thus, students who perceive themselves as more capable may think that collaboration on a group project will undermine their advantage on the subsequent individual assessments, especially if the grading is substantially norm-referenced.

International experts agree (e.g., Little & Wolf, 1996) about the practice of norm-referenced grading, particularly when it involves grading on the curve. They urge, "Don't do it!" Grading on the curve is essentially a quota system. Regardless of the class composition, instructors often announce at the beginning of the term, "Only the top X percent of you will earn A grades. Those in the next X percent will receive B's, and so forth."

Another option when assigning grades individually is to allow students to identify a specific part of the project for which they can be responsible and on which they will receive an individual mark. This approach, however, requires faculty members to pay attention to the task of coordinating and integrating the parts to determine who is responsible for what parts (University of Queensland, n.d.).

Instead of awarding individual grades, an alternative approach is to allocate undifferentiated group marks for a project that counts equally toward individual student's grades. Uniform marks encourage collaboration by removing any rationale for competition. The University of Otago's guidelines comment, however, that

> this approach can lead to concern, from teacher or students, that some students are getting good marks based largely on the work of other members of the team, or that capable students would have gained better marks if they had not been handicapped by their weaker partners. (Assessment of Group Work section, ¶ 4)

Teachers using a variation of this approach assign a collective mark (usually a set number of points) to the group for the overall project. One group might receive, for example, 90 points for their overall project, another group 70. The group must then decide whether to divide these points evenly or unevenly among the group members. This approach, however, invites inequity issues and ill will. Too often personality clashes or intercultural misunderstandings occur. Unless specifically tied to course content such as performance appraisal, these frictions do little to promote course objectives.

Most assessment experts recommend an approach that looks at both process and product issues with peer, self, and faculty input. Students work collaboratively to complete the required group project. However, the allocation of individual grades takes into account the contribution of each member. Information on contributions can be provided in a variety of ways (e.g., use of oral tests, individual summaries of contribution and achievements, notes from group meetings, the use of peer assessment to evaluate the contribution of self and other members, group processing forms, group interviews, etc.). Information gained in this way can be used by the faculty member to determine a student's final mark. Most faculty members are comfortable with their own grading standards and approaches, but may be more uncertain with students conducting peer and self-assessments.

Peer assessment. Many faculty members committed to group projects build in peer assessment as a component of the final grade (see Appendix 17.3 for a sample instrument allowing peers to assess group members' contribution). There are many justifications for this practice even though students, unless properly trained and similarly committed to the practice, may be hesitant about passing judgment on their peers. Allowing student input into the process of evaluation sends several signals consistent with a group oriented philosophy:

- Teachers, because they are not the sole arbitrators of success or failure, play less of a gate keeper role responsible for weeding out the unfit and the unworthy. The process of evaluation is shared.
- Students are in a logical position to be able to judge, far more effectively than an instructor, the individual contributions of their peers.
- Peer feedback is usually directed toward an individual within the context of a specific task. Besides being context-specific, it tends to be delivered promptly when feedback is most effective.
- Peer evaluation builds in accountability: Students realize that they are held accountable for their academic achievements and group contributions. They may be able to "psych out" a teacher, but they can rarely hide from their peers.
- Students benefit from the process of peer review. They learn valuable skills about the learning process and about teamwork efforts.

Because of accountability and equity issues, teachers should monitor carefully any peer review process. Students must be assessing peers on attainable course objectives based on carefully specified criteria. They must offer concrete evidence. Woods (1996) advocates training students to do such assessments and providing an environment where peers can give accurate feedback.

Peer assessment becomes even more meaningful when students have input and ownership over the process. For example, in business courses where performance appraisal is a topic of study, teams can develop their own criteria for individual grades for contributions toward a group project. As a first step, they can brainstorm the criteria for evaluation and then group them into broad areas, such as attendance, participation, preparation, cooperation, and attitude. The criteria can then be defined through a rubric with performance standards that are finally weighted. Accompanying such an instrument can be the ground rules for its use.

Peer review is obviously complex. Woods (1996) integrates peer review into virtually every aspect of his problem-based learning engineering classes. Feedback, whether given by the student himself or herself or by peers, typically addresses five strengths for every two things that could be worked on. After all group meetings, students complete a feedback form that looks at both their task performance and their group skills. This approach emphasizes not only accountability to the group, but also self-assessment.

Self-assessment. Researchers involved in determining how to promote deep learning have focused on students engaged in learning within specific contexts by observing, listening, and probing. As Rhem (1995) concludes, "In the end, they have focused on metacognition as the heart of learning and view it as a phenomenon more influenced by the demands of particular learning environments than by predispositions of personality" (p. 2). Similarly, Bransford, Brown, & Cocking (2000) consider metacognition essential to learning. With a solid research base and clear implications for teaching, they conclude that "a 'metacognitive' approach to instruction can help students learn to take control of their own learning by defining learning goals and monitoring their progress in achieving them" (p. 18). This recognition of the role metacognition plays in learning makes it desirable for teachers to include self-assessment opportunities in courses. Woods (1996) places self-assessment at the heart of learning. Students should learn to evaluate:

- The subject knowledge
- The problem solving skills used
- The group process used
- The chairperson skills displayed
- The acquisition of self-directed, interdependent, life-time learning

With assessment comes accountability for both students and the teachers. Assessments must be conducted responsibly based on measurable criteria, evidence, and objectivity.

When self or peer assessment forms part of the assessment requirements for a project, faculty members should do everything possible to ensure that the outcomes are equitable and credible. For example, as mentioned earlier, there may be differences, associated with culture and gender, in the extent to which students are prepared to promote themselves. Following recommended practices for responsive, responsible group projects can alleviate a lot of the stressors for students and faculty alike.

Guidelines for Assessing Group Projects

All forms of student assessment should conform to principles of good practice. The following guidelines apply specifically to the assessment of group work. Faculty members should:

1) Clearly identify the purpose and function of the group project, including why it is appropriate for the project to be completed in groups and how the process and content of the project will help to achieve the stated learning objectives. This information should be communicated to students from the outset.

2) Ensure that the marking practices encourage and reinforce effective group work.

3) Give students, in writing, a full explanation of the requirements for the project, including the usual assessment information (weighting, due date, penalties, etc.). The explanation should also include full details of procedures relating to:

    - The project to be undertaken
    - The basis for group membership
    - Rules that cover the functioning of the group
    - Suggested task allocation within the group
    - The criteria for assessing the group report/project, including how marks will be allocated between the collaborative process (i.e., the way individuals collaborated during the project) and the project content
    - The procedure for assessing individual contributions, if such contributions are to be assessed
    - Who will carry out the assessment (e.g., individual faculty, panel of experts)
    - The fallback position if a group loses a member or in some way falls apart

- The conduct of group meetings—expectations regarding frequency and timing and group contact outside of scheduled class times
- Feedback stages during the assignment period to report group progress and final outcomes
- How the contribution of each member to the group project will be assessed (e.g., using individual process diaries, external assessment of collaborative process and project content; peer, self, and group assessment instruments; group interview, etc.)

4) Define any appropriate group process skills—these may include communication skills such as clarifying questions, asking open questions, including all members (turn-taking, sharing talk time), consensus building, giving encouragement/praise/positive motivation to members, giving and receiving feedback, summarizing discussions and decisions reached, goal setting, planning, evaluating progress, dealing with conflict—that are to be developed during the completion of the project.
5) Give students practice in tutorials or workshops in the skills of group work.
6) Involve students, whenever possible, in devising a combination of teacher and student developed assessment criteria for the project. The criteria should be crystal clear to all parties. Student involvement will likely produce greater buy-in and a greater depth of understanding.
7) Use tutorials or workshops as a basis for further clarifying requirements. These should be circulated in writing to all students.
8) Develop a process for providing the group with detailed feedback to assist the ongoing work of the group and to provide specific feedback on all aspects of the activity and its outcome upon completion. A high standard of timely feedback on assessment tasks is critical to students' development of understanding the relationship between the quality of their work and the assessment criteria. On longer group projects, interim feedback points are useful: brief presentations, one-page outlines of group progress or plans, or submission of different task components in stages can all be useful.
9) Assign grades carefully. Graded group project marks should not be assigned to all members of the group without some moderation—whether by the inclusion of an individual component used to moderate

the collective component by a rating of the contribution of individuals to the collective.

10) Require students to keep a log of the activities that they undertook as part of a group project. These lists of tasks can form the basis for a group discussion on how marks for a project might be divided.

11) Assign an additional piece of written work in which students analyze how their group worked, what they contributed to it, and how its effectiveness might have been increased. Ask group members to evaluate their own and others' contributions to the group effort. These should include task, ideas, and group management functions. The combined evaluation of each individual's performance can be used to moderate the mark for the project, if desired.

Teachers also should model reflective practice. At the end of every group project, they can provide a review of the original plan and the reality. To what extent have improvements been made in:

- The nature and quality of the task.
- The social setting of the collaborative activity and the behavior of students during the execution of the task.
- The teacher's behavior during the execution of the task.
- The teacher's role in group composition and management.
- The nature and quality of the reports made by each group.
- The teacher's performance as a synthesizer and as representative of the academic learning community.
- The relation of the collaborative activity to the design of the course.
- Student satisfaction with the group work.

Conclusion

Group projects can greatly enhance learning experiences when they are appropriately designed and assessed. Probably no aspect of teaching has a greater impact on student learning than the grading system. Just within a single classroom, grades affect students' motivation to learn, their perceptions about the teacher's integrity, and their relationships with one another. Lowman (1984) calls grades "an unpleasant and unavoidable reality" (p. 185) for both teachers and students. Thus, faculty members must take the responsibility of ensuring that group projects do not turn into a counterproductive nightmare for students who may otherwise face interpersonal conflicts, negative learning experiences, and feelings of frustration or inequity. Universities in Australia and New Zealand take this responsibility so seriously that faculty have both policies and resources to guide their decisions. At Victoria University in Wellington (VUW), New Zealand, for example, the University Teaching Development Centre (UTDC) provides a pamphlet in the *Improving Teaching and Learning* series titled "Group Work and Group Assessment." Besides offering detailed guidelines, the pamphlet also contains appendixes with university-wide recommendations and policies from the Group Work and Peer Assessment Working Party report and from the 2002 VUW Assessment Handbook. Additionally, workshops—generic ones for all faculty and ones specifically tailored to departments—are available. One-on-one consultations also provide helpful guidelines and peer coaching. The best practices for assessing group projects are known. Faculty developers (called "academic staff developers" in many parts of the world) have, in turn, the responsibility and the challenge to make faculty aware of these best practices and capable of implementing them.

References

Angelo, T. A., & Cross, K. P. (1993). *Classroom assessment techniques: A handbook for college teachers* (2nd ed.). San Francisco, CA: Jossey-Bass.

Astin, A. W. (1993). *What matters in college? Four critical years revisited.* San Francisco, CA: Jossey-Bass.

Astin, A. W., Banta, T. W., Cross, K. P., El-Khawas, E., Ewell, P. T., Hutchings, P., Marchese, T. J., McClenny, K. M., Mentkowski, M., Miller, M. A., Moran, E. T., & Wright, B. D. (1992). *Principles of good practice for assessing student learning.* Washington, DC: American Association for Higher Education.

Biggs, J. B. (1999). *Teaching for quality learning at university.* Buckingham, England: Society for Research on Higher Education and the Open University.

Boud, D., Cohen, R., & Sampson, J. (1999). Peer learning and assessment. *Assessment and Evaluation in Higher Education, 24*(4), 413–426.

Boud, D., Cohen, R. & Sampson, J. (2001). *Peer learning in higher education: Learning from each other.* London, England: Kogan Page.

Bransford, J. D., Brown, A. L., & Cocking, R. R. (Eds.). (2000). *How people learn: Brain, mind, experience, and school.* Commission on Behavioral and Social Sciences and Education National Research Council. Washington, DC: National Academy Press.

Cuseo, J. (1992, Winter). Collaborative and cooperative learning in higher education: A proposed taxonomy. *Cooperative Learning and College Teaching, 2*(2), 2–4.

Diamond, R. M. (1998). *Designing and assessing courses and curricula: A practical guide.* San Francisco, CA: Jossey-Bass.

Johnson, D. W., & Johnson, R. T. (1996). *Meaningful and manageable assessment through cooperative learning.* Edina, MN: Interaction Book Company.

Little, A., & Wolf, A. (1996). *Assessment in transition: Learning, monitoring and selection in international perspective.* New York, NY: Pergamon Press.

Loacker, G., Cromwell, C., & O'Brien, K. (1986). Assessment in higher education: To serve the learner. In C. Adelman (Ed.), *Assessment in American higher education* (pp. 47–62). Washington, DC: U. S. Department of Education, Office of Educational Research and Improvement.

Lowman, J. (1984). *Mastering the techniques of teaching.* San Francisco, CA: Jossey-Bass.

McKeachie, W. J. (1994). *Teaching tips: Strategies, research, and theory for college and university teachers* (9th ed.). Lexington, MA: D. C. Heath.

Michaelsen, L. K., Fink, L. D., & Black, R. H. (1996). What every faculty developer needs to know about learning groups. In L. Richlin & D. DeZure (Eds.), *To improve the academy: Vol. 15. Resources for faculty, instructional, and organizational development* (pp. 31–58). Stillwater, OK: New Forums Press.

Millis, B. J. (2002). *Enhancing learning—and more!—through cooperative learning.* Retrieved March 25, 2003, from http://www.idea.ksu.edu/papers/Idea_Paper_38.pdf

Millis, B. J., & Cottell, P. G. (1998). *Cooperative learning for higher education faculty* (ACE Series on Higher Education). Phoenix, AZ: Oryx Press. [Now distributed through Greenwood Press].

Nuhfer, E. B. (2001). *A Handbook for student management teams.* Denver, CO: The Office of Teaching Effectiveness. Retrieved March 25, 2003, from http://www.isu.edu/ctl/

Rhem, J. (1995). Deep/surface approaches to learning: An introduction. *The National Teaching & Learning Forum, 5*(1), 1–3.

University of Otago. (2001). *Senate policy on assessment of student performance: Principles and guidelines.* Retrieved March 12, 2003, from http://policy01.otago.ac.nz/rdbase/FMPro?db=policies.fm&format=viewpolicy.html&-lay=viewpolicy&-sortfield=Title&-max=2147483647&-recid=32842&findall=#5

University of Queensland. (n.d.). *Group assessment—Assessment of students on group-based tasks—issues and options.* Retrieved May 25, 2001, from http:www.tedi.uq.edu.au/assess/Assessment/groupwork.html

University of Technology, Sydney. (n.d.). *Students groups: Issues for teaching and learning.* Retrieved May 25, 2001, from http://www/clt.uts.edu.au/Student.Groupwork.html

Webb, N. (1994). *Group collaboration in assessment: Competing objectives, processes, and outcomes* (CSE Technical Report No. 386). Los Angeles, CA: University of California, Los Angeles, National Center for Research on Evaluation, Standards and Student Testing (CRESST).

Woods, D. R. (1996). *Problem-based learning: How to gain the most from PBL* (2nd ed.). Retrieved December 14, 2002, from http://chemeng.mcmaster.ca/pbl/pbl.htm

Contact:
Deborah Willis
Assistant Vice Chancellor (Academic)
Victoria University of Wellington
PO Box 600
Wellington
New Zealand
Voice 04-463-5340
Fax 04-463-5328
Email Deborah.willis@vuw.ac.nz

Barbara J. Millis
Director of Faculty Development
HQ USAFA/DFE
2354 Fairchild Drive, Suite 4K25
USAF Academy, CO 80840-6220
Voice (719) 333-2549
Fax (719) 333-4255
Email Barbara.millis@usafa.af.mil

Deborah Willis is Assistant Vice Chancellor (Academic) at Victoria University of Wellington. Until recently, she was director of the University Teaching Development Centre at Victoria. Her research interests include student assessment and its relation to effective learning and relationships between teaching and research. Other activities include the provision of pre- and in-service training to Cook Islands teachers and professional development to staff at the National University of Samoa in the areas of assessment and curriculum design. She recently led a team that carried out a comprehensive review of the Cook Islands education system.

Barbara J. Millis, Director of Faculty Development at the U. S. Air Force Academy, frequently offers workshops at professional conferences (American Association of Higher Education (AAHE), Lilly Teaching Conferences, Association of American Colleges and Universities (AAC&U), etc.) and for various colleges and universities. She publishes articles on a range of faculty development topics, and co-authored with Philip Cottell, *Cooperative Learning for Higher Education Faculty* (Oryx Press [now Greenwood]) and with John Hertel, *Using Simulations to Promote Learning in Higher Education* (Stylus Press). Appearing shortly from Stylus Press will be *Using Academic Games to Enhance Learning in Higher Education.* Barbara's interests include cooperative learning (see *Enhancing Learning—and More!—Through Cooperative Learning*: http://www.idea.ksu.edu/papers/Idea_Paper_38.pdf), peer review, academic games, classroom observations, microteaching, classroom assessment/research, critical thinking, how students learn, and writing for learning. After the Association of American Colleges and Universities selected the U. S. Air Force Academy as a Leadership Institution in Undergraduate Education, she began serving as the liaison to the AAC&U's Greater Expectations Consortium on Quality Education.

Appendix 17.1

Assessing Group Effectiveness

(all group members to complete)

NB: Questions can be modified to be used at the end of the group work

Please answer all questions from your own perspective. If you cannot answer a question, please state briefly why the information is unavailable.

1) What specific goal(s) is this group trying to accomplish? Please list the goal(s) in your priority order. Do you think the group basically agrees on the contents of this list?

2) What activities has the group specifically chosen to undertake or assign in order to achieve its goal(s)? Indicate which activities, if any, are particularly effective?

3) Does each group member have specific—even unique—responsibilities that help the group attain its goal(s)? Y/N
List all group members by name and their individual responsibilities.

4) The work of your group is stimulating and worth your time.
Strongly agree______________________________strongly disagree

5) How many hours (on average) do you spend working with this group?
____

6) This group has the resources (e.g., organization, communication, leadership, talents, time) to achieve its goals?
Strongly agree______________________________strongly disagree

7) What additional resources are needed for real effectiveness?

(Modified version of the Classroom Assessment Technique designed by Walker) (cited in Diamond, 1998).

Appendix 17.2

Group Processing Form

Group Name: _______________

1) Overall, how effectively did your group work together in learning the course subject matter? (circle the appropriate response)

not at all	**poorly**	**adequately**	**well**	**extremely well**
1	2	3	4	5

2) How many of the group members participated actively most of the time? (circle the appropriate number)

1 2 3 4 5

3) How may of the group members were fully prepared for group work most of the time? (circle the appropriate number)

1 2 3 4 5

4) Give one specific example of something you have learned from the group that you probably would not have learned on your own.

5) Give one specific example of something the other group members learned from you that they probably would not have learned without you.

6) Suggest one specific, practical change the group could make that would help improve everyone's learning.

(This form was adapted by Philip Cottell from one developed by Angelo, T. A. (1994). Using assessment to improve cooperative learning. *Cooperative Learning and College Teaching, 4*(3), 5–7.)

APPENDIX 17.3

GROUP MEMBER CONTRIBUTION

Your Name ____

Group members' names (including your own) in alphabetical order

1)______________________________________

2)______________________________________

3)______________________________________ etc

Evaluation of group member participation involves peer and self-assessment. This information will be used by the paper coordinator to moderate individual student marks.

Scale: 1 = minimal contribution, 2 = minor contribution, 3 = satisfactory contribution, 4 = substantial contribution, 5 = very substantial contribution

Group Member	**1**	**2**	**3**	**4**	**5**
Contribution at meetings (do they attend, participate, and share ideas)					
Commitment to common goal (do they keep on task and show concern for doing things right)					
Skill input (do they show an understanding of ideas and apply them)					
Reliable completion of tasks (do they show a responsibility to the group and the tasks they have to do)					

(From VUW *Group Work and Group Assessment* UTDC Guidelines)

18

The Hesburgh Certificate and Portland State University's Faculty Development Approach to Supporting Service Learning and Community-University Partnerships

Kevin Kecskes
Amy Spring
Devorah Lieberman
Portland State University

Service learning now has a prominent home in hundreds of diverse campuses across the nation. Developing service-learning expertise and other community-campus partnership enhancement strategies for faculty requires innovation. Recently, Portland State University's Center for Academic Excellence received the Theodore M. Hesburgh Certificate of Excellence for Community-University Partnerships. This chapter outlines the center's three-tiered approach to supporting and sustaining civic engagement practices that are sensitive to individual needs on campus and in the community, while also working toward ongoing departmental and institutional transformation.

Service learning, once the occasional activity of a small cadre of community-minded professors in the 1970s, now has a prominent home in hundreds of diverse campuses across the nation. Although service-learning pedagogy (or community-based learning, as it is known at Portland State University) intrigues many faculty, these new, community-connected learning environments can be challenging to navigate. The development, support, and sustainability of community-university partnerships—the collaborative relationships from which service learning must emerge—can seem overwhelming. Despite significant national efforts to move emerging forms of scholarship, such as the scholarship of teaching and the scholarship of community engagement, from the margins to the mainstream in the academy, some faculty continue to view service learning as ancillary to their core work. Therefore, developing faculty for service-learning and other community engagement strategies requires a multifaceted approach, sensitive to individual needs on campus and in the community while simultaneously working toward ongoing institutional transformation.

Given Portland State University's (PSU) institutional mission—essentialized by the university motto, *Let Knowledge Serve the City*—PSU has piloted several efforts over the past decade that work to effect change on multiple levels in favor of institutionalizing and sustaining service learning and community-university partnerships. The Center for Academic Excellence (CAE), PSU's university-wide faculty development center, implements several traditional faculty development activities as well as expands on those initiatives to intentionally integrate dynamic community engagement opportunities into the professional lives of its faculty, staff, and students. For this exemplary community partnership-building work, PSU recently received two national recognitions: the Theodore M. Hesburgh Certificate of Excellence for Community-University Partnerships and a national ranking of forth in *U.S. News & World Report*'s 2003 America's Best Colleges, for the Academic Service Learning category. These recognitions were based largely on PSU's extensive service-learning efforts. Faculty development initiatives at CAE have directly contributed to the growth and sustainability of service learning and civic engagement at PSU.

This chapter articulates how and why PSU and the surrounding community have embraced civic engagement. Also highlighted are the specific faculty development practices facilitated by the Center for Academic Excellence to support and sustain civic engagement within and among the campus and broader community.

Portland State University's Motivation for Engagement

Community-based research, scholarship, and teaching can help to deeply connect Portland State University to its metropolitan area host and to communities world-wide. PSU, now recognized as a national leader in the renewal of higher education, in part due to innovative teaching and learning and community engagement strategies, has not always enjoyed such recognition.

During the early 1990s, PSU faced a morale and funding crisis. The university deeply felt the long-term reductions in funding for higher education from the Oregon State Legislature. The university was also suffering from poor freshman retention rates and widespread frustration with the existing undergraduate general education requirements. Many students reported a feeling of isolation from campus life, with approximately 75% leaving higher education or transferring to other institutions to complete their coursework.

Campus faculty and administrative leaders responded to this crisis by creating an undergraduate education program that was both interdisciplinary and connected to the community. Because PSU is located in the center of Oregon's largest urban community, it had the fortunate opportunity to embrace new approaches to teaching and learning, including those that intentionally enhance the surrounding community. PSU's general education curriculum takes an interdisciplinary approach to student coursework; content from the social sciences, natural sciences, and arts is combined into thematic clusters of courses. The model, designed by a committee of faculty and administrators with the specific goal of creating a new approach to teaching, learning, and research at PSU, emphasizes both collaboration and engagement with community. Indeed, a new "PSU identity" has emerged based on this work.

The late Ernest L. Boyer, and the Boyer Commission at the Carnegie Foundation, produced three national reports on the state of higher education in America: *Scholarship Reconsidered* (Boyer, 1990), *Scholarship Assessed* (Glassick, Huber, & Maeroff, 1997), and *Reinventing Undergraduate Education: A Blueprint for America's Research Universities* (Boyer Commission on Educating Undergraduates in the Research University, 1998). These documents called on higher education to reconsider its definitions of teaching, research, and scholarship to improve the state of higher education. Employing a campus-wide integrated approach to teaching and learning while expanding community-based learning programs was how the PSU campus responded to Boyer's concerns. Transformation occurs through the engagement of skills and experience from members of the university community with those of the surrounding community.

Infrastructure for Institutional Engagement

As an urban university, part of PSU's mission is to provide quality education shaped by, and relevant to, the urban community. The general education reforms of the 1990s helped the university move closer to actualizing this mission. PSU has become an institution that uses its resources to find solutions to the kinds of problems uniquely impacting urban areas.

Connecting curricula, research, and scholarship to community can create a transformation within the academy. These connections demand new ways of thinking about teaching, new ways of identifying research projects, new ways of assessing student learning, and new ways of evaluating scholarship. These are a few of the modifications the academy must undergo if community-campus engagement is to be fully integrated into colleges and universities. These new approaches to faculty work are not realized quickly, nor can they occur without significant and consistent infrastructural assistance.

In an effort to pioneer new approaches teaching and learning, the PSU administration and faculty founded the Center for Academic Excellence (1995). CAE's stated mission is to "support and promote academic excellence in teaching, assessment, and community-university partnerships in order to enhance faculty scholarship, improve student learning outcomes, and contribute to the Portland metropolitan community." The CAE mission, consistent in many respects with most teaching and learning centers around the country, provides faculty with resources to assist with teaching, research, and scholarship. See the CAE web site (http://www.oaa.pdx.edu/cae/) for the activities that support teaching assistant development, assessment, teaching and learning with technology, scholarship, new faculty development, engaged department development, and administrative leadership development. CAE's annual report is also available online: http://www.oaa.pdx.edu/cae/annual report/2001-2002.phtml.

A unique element of CAE, however, is the support it offers to faculty engaged with community-based teaching, research, and scholarship. It was these community-university support efforts that earned CAE the Theodore M. Hesburgh Certificate of Excellence Award.

PSU is unique in its community-based learning support effort because it is one of the few institutions in the country that has centralized support in its Office of Academic Affairs. The CAE office, physically located adjacent to the provost's office, is directed by the vice provost and special assistant to the president. The Community-University Partnerships (CUP) program, a formal division of the CAE, is supported by the general budget, and recognized as an integral part of the faculty development efforts that enhance teaching, learning, and community engagement at PSU. Institutional need for faculty development, specifically focused on community-university partnerships, is evidenced by the fact that the community-based senior capstone is a graduation requirement for all seniors. Each year, over 160 senior capstone courses, serving 175 community partners and well over 2,000 students, are offered at PSU. Because there are resources to support, facilitate, and sustain students, faculty, and community partners in these community-based courses, the capstone program element of PSU's undergraduate curriculum continues to develop and expand with increasing quality.

The centralized nature of CAE programs promotes the efficient use of campus resources. For faculty, technical assistance and consistent, fiscal support, even if limited, is available. For potential community partners, CAE provides the entry point of access to PSU faculty. Additionally, grant writing efforts for community-based learning have been quite effective. Since CAE's inception, over $1,500,000 in grant dollars have supplemented community-based learning and faculty development initiatives at PSU.

Faculty Development Strategies for Community-University Partnership Development

A civically engaged campus must model the values it hopes to carry into its community-university partnerships. Therefore, CAE activities are designed to encourage a spirit of community and collaboration within the university. CAE initiatives promote faculty collaborations across disciplines, establish mentor-mentee relationships, and support diverse faculty networks. PSU's faculty programs are based on collectively developed learning outcomes, and share best practices in support of the goals of the group.

Unlike many faculty development centers around the country, CAE's charge is not only to support faculty in traditional ways such as pedagogical enhancement and professional portfolio development, but also to integrate assessment and community engagement strategies into the core of university life. The faculty development efforts of CAE, therefore, support the ongoing transformation of PSU into an engaged campus. This role presents CAE's professional staff with considerable opportunities for creativity. Through tested and modified strategies, CAE presents an integrated approach to pedagogy, assessment, and community engagement that supports faculty, students, and community partners on multiple levels simultaneously. These levels can best be organized into three distinct stages.

- Stage I programming initiatives focus on supporting university transformation at the macro level.
- Stage II activities are typically more modest in scope and center on work at the small group, or meso, level.

- Stage III activities focus on support and transformation largely directed at the micro level, that is, focus on the individual faculty member or community partner.

Stage I: Macro-Level Programming

Many of the center's CUP programs and activities are designed to support institutional transformation at the macro level. These activities are referred to as Stage I Programming. Events such as the quarterly Civic Engagement Breakfast Series, the year-long Carnegie Campus Conversations, and the annual President's Community Scholars Awards are primarily designed to create and support institutional momentum for innovation (see Appendix 18.1 for a brief description of faculty development activities; see the CAE web site for complete description of activities: http://www.oaa.pdx.edu/cae/). These university-wide events invite the campus and community constituents to think and imagine how they might partner with one another. At these events, nationally recognized speakers are often invited to campus to discuss topics related to community engagement. Participants in Stage I Programs self-select. Conversations and dialogue that support the growth of individual participants in relation to university transformation outcomes are expected from Stage I Programs. See Table 18.1 for a list of the faculty development activities that represent Stage I Programming, and Appendix 18.1 for specific descriptions of these activities.

TABLE 18.1
Stage I Programming

- The Civic Engagement Breakfast Series
- The Civic Engagement Celebration
- Carnegie Campus Conversations
- Focus on Faculty
- The Annual Capstone Fair
- The Teaching and Learning Excellence (TLE) Listserv
- The Faculty Focus Newsletter
- Student Leaders for Service Program
- The President's Community Scholars Award

Stage II: Meso-Level Programming

Stage II Programming supports university transformation primarily via the mechanism of small group work. This level of programming is developed to engage campus constituents who have already indicated interest in community-university partnerships. Therefore, initiatives focus on developing specific skills and techniques that are necessary for effectively connecting campus and community constituents. These programs are generally offered in a seminar format over a period of months. Perhaps the best example of a middle-range programmatic activity indicative of this type of support is CAE's Engaged Department Program. This program currently supports 12 academic units for one year to participate in an in-depth process to encourage department-wide community-university engagement. Utilizing funding from the Corporation for National and Community Service, the strategy of this initiative is to shift the focus of support from individual faculty members to collective teams in departments where they are located in order to increase the collaborative integration of community-based learning (CBL) into their respective units. Stage II Program topics are developed based on requests made by community partners and faculty. See Table 18.2 for a list of the faculty development activities that represent Stage II Programming and Appendix 18.1 for specific descriptions of these activities.

TABLE 18.2
Stage II Programming

- The Engaged Department Program
- The Civic Engagement Study Circle
- Mini Grants Funding
- The Focus on Diversity Series
- The Teaching Excellence Series
- The Scholarship of Teaching Resource Team (STRT)
- The Annual Capstone Fair
- Scholarly Work in Progress (SWIP)
- The Leadership Series
- The New Faculty Series

Stage III: Micro-Level Programming

CAE's Stage III faculty development efforts focus at the micro level, that is, primarily on the development of the individual faculty or community partner. Stage III Programming is comprised of one-on-one development activities such as syllabus revision, in-class observation, discussions concerning service-learning pedagogy, and so on. This level of programming is meant to provide particular and specific resources in response to a very explicit individual concern. Typically, faculty or community partners involved in Stage III Programming are already involved in a community-university partnership. Often, participants turn to CAE for ideas on how to enhance a specific course or community element, or they may be experiencing some challenge with the partnership and are seeking resources to address the concern. This level of support requires individual meeting, classroom visitation, and personal attention. See Table 18.3 for a list of the faculty development activities that represent Stage III Programming and Appendix 18.1 for specific descriptions of these activities.

TABLE 18.3
Stage III Programming

- One-on-One Consultations
- Faculty in Residence
- Promotion-Tenure Portfolio Assistance
- The Faculty Resource Library
- The Annual Capstone Fair
- The Leadership Series
- Focus on Faculty

CONCLUSION

The Theodore M. Hesburgh Certificate of Excellence recognized Portland State University and the university-wide faculty development Center for Academic Excellence as an exemplar in the facilitation of deep undergraduate learning. Over the past decade, Portland State University's Center for Academic Excellence has developed a three-stage approach to support and sustain community-university partnerships. Stage I programming initiatives focus on supporting university transformation at the macro level. Stage II activities are more modest in scope, and center on work at the small group, or meso, level.

Stage III activities focus on support and transformation largely directed at the micro level of the individual faculty member or community partner. All of these faculty development activities ultimately support the realization of the university's motto, Let Knowledge Serve the City. Each activity attempts to support faculty and other campus and community constituents to be effective and responsive to the diverse needs and roles of a large, public, urban institution of higher learning and to the communities that comprise them in the 21st century.

References

Boyer Commission on Educating Undergraduates in the Research University. (1998). *Reinventing undergraduate education: A blueprint for America's research universities.* Menlo Park, CA: The Carnegie Foundation for the Advancement of Teaching.

Boyer, E. L. (1990). *Scholarship reconsidered: Priorities of the professoriate.* San Francisco, CA: Jossey-Bass.

Glassick, C. E., Huber, M. T., & Maeroff, G. I. (1997). *Scholarship assessed: Evaluation of the professoriate.* San Francisco, CA: Jossey-Bass.

Contact:

Kevin Kecskes
Director for Community-Based Learning
Center for Academic Excellence
Portland State University
PO Box 751
Portland, OR 97207
Voice (503) 725-5642
Fax (503) 725-5262
Email kecskesk@pdx.edu

Amy Spring
Assistant Director for Community-Based Learning
Portland State University
PO Box 751-CAE
Portland, OR 97207-0751
Voice (503)725-5582
Fax (503) 725-5262
Email springa@pdx.edu

Devorah Lieberman
Vice Provost and Special Assistant to the President
Center for Academic Excellence
Portland State University
Box 751
Portland, OR 97207
Voice (503) 725-5642
Fax (503) 725-5262
Email Liebermand@pdx.edu

Kevin Kecskes serves as Director for Community-Based Learning at Portland State University. In this capacity he overseas faculty and departmental development for community engagement as well as institutional civic engagement initiatives and events. His research and scholarship interests include community-university partnership development, faculty development for civic engagement, and institutional transformation in higher education.

Amy Spring serves as Assistant Director for Community-Based Learning. In this capacity she facilitates campus-community partnership development and delivers training and technical assistance to faculty, departments, students, and community-based organizations on service-learning pedagogy and other civic engagement strategies. Her research and scholarly interests include student leadership development, assessing service-learning impact, and the scholarship of engagement.

Devorah Lieberman serves as Vice Provost and Special Assistant to the President at Portland State University. In these capacities she is Director for the Center for Academic Excellence and also facilitates the president's four campus wide initiatives: diversity, assessment, student advising, and internationalizing the campus. She continues her discipline-based scholarship in Intercultural Communication as well as research and scholarship on institutional transformation in higher education.

APPENDIX 18.1

SERVICE-LEARNING FACULTY DEVELOPMENT ACTIVITIES

Stage I Programming

- The Civic Engagement Breakfast Series
- The Civic Engagement Celebration
- Carnegie Campus Conversations
- Focus on Faculty
- The Annual Capstone Fair
- The Teaching and Learning Excellence (TLE) Listserv
- The Faculty Focus Newsletter
- Student Leaders for Service Program
- The President's Community Scholars Award

The Civic Engagement Breakfast Series is a monthly discussion meant to inform PSU's work in community-university partnerships. All faculty are invited to join campus and community partner colleagues in discussions that help increase understanding of civic engagement in higher education and community contexts. Examples of past discussion topics include, "Diversity and Multiculturalism—Challenges for Civic Engagement," "Community Coalitions Partnering with the University to Promote Civic Engagement," and "Developing Civic Capacity for the Good of Communities: What Counts for Successful Civic Engagement?"

The Civic Engagement Celebration was held May 17, 2001, and sponsored by PSU and the Kellogg Civic Engagement Cluster to honor Portland State University and its faculty for their exemplary civic engagement. Elizabeth Hollander, Executive Director of National Campus Compact, Mike Kenefick, Senior Program Officer for the Corporation for National Service, and a representative from the Urban League of Portland were present to recognize PSU, Dilafruz Williams, President Bernstine, and Charles White for outstanding civic engagement work. Ten PSU faculty were also recognized for their exemplary civic engagement efforts and awarded the PSU Civic Engagement Award.

Carnegie Campus Conversations supported with funds from Portland General Electric, offers faculty a venue to gather together one afternoon each month and address issues of teaching and learning.

Focus on Faculty is an annual one-day event sponsored by the CAE that joins together faculty from across campus to participate in a variety of activities showcasing the talents and knowledge of faculty and staff at PSU. Faculty participate in discussions and mini-workshops facilitated by their peers that are focused on teaching, learning, advising, and campus life. Past themes include "Who are our students and how do they learn?" and "Enriching the Undergraduate Experience at PSU."

The Annual Capstone Fair is a campus-wide event that highlights new capstones and many of Portland State's community partners. The fair serves as an opportunity for faculty to interact with those involved in capstones and to explore a variety of ways to design and implement a capstone.

The Teaching and Learning Excellence (TLE) Listserv is a means by which faculty can communicate with each other on topics ranging from specific problems or concerns related to teaching and learning to more general discussions related to pedagogy and higher education. Weekly announcements of upcoming events sponsored by the CAE are also provided on the TLE listserv.

The Faculty Focus Newsletter is a PSU in-house newsletter published by the CAE that offers faculty an opportunity to share information with others about teaching and learning. Past articles include "Portland State University's Civic Engagement Celebration," "Water in the Environment—A Science in the Liberal Arts Community-Based Learning Course," and "Integrating Diversity into the Classroom."

Student Leaders for Service is a program meant to provide students with the opportunity to represent PSU in community service initiatives. Once selected, students are placed with a community partner agency and serve as volunteer coordinators for the many PSU students fulfilling community-based learning course requirements. Student Leaders for Service meet weekly with a member of CUP staff to receive ongoing training and support in issues relevant to volunteer management and to provide information about their community-based learning placement site.

The President's Community Scholars Award is jointly sponsored by CUP and the Office of Student Affairs. Seven awards are given annually to students who have made contributions through their community-based learning and capstone experiences. The awards also recognize students who have distinguished themselves in terms of realizing the goals of community-based learning programs at PSU.

Stage II Programming

- The Engaged Department Program
- The Civic Engagement Study Circle
- Mini Grants Funding
- The Focus on Diversity Series
- The Teaching Excellence Series
- The Scholarship of Teaching Resource Team (STRT)
- The Annual Capstone Fair
- Scholarly Work in Progress (SWIP)
- The Leadership Series
- The New Faculty Series

The Engaged Department Program provides resources to 12 academic units for one year to participate in an in-depth process to encourage department-wide community-university engagement. This initiative focuses on shifting the support of individual faculty members to collective teams to increase the collaborative integration of community-based learning into their respective units. The Engaged Department uses community-based learning to facilitate the integration of community work and reflection into students' academic study while providing support for collaborative community engagement activities and encouraging the scholarship of engagement.

Civic Engagement Study Circles/Small Group Faculty Development Seminars meet on a monthly basis each term to examine some of the theoretical frameworks that inform the work of community-university partnerships and community-based learning in a democracy. Faculty and staff from various disciplines meet with their colleagues for lively discussions.

Mini Grants Funding is offered each year through a campus-wide RFP process. Mini grant funds can be used for the development of community-based learning in courses or curricula and are used by faculty to support professional development including, but not limited to travel to professional conferences, subscriptions to relevant professional journals, purchase of books and/or other material, or activities that enhance faculty teaching and scholarship. Funds may also be used to support the special needs of community-based learning courses, such as hiring a student assistant to work with community partners, preparations of "readers" or other curriculum materials for students, and/or production of any course final product.

The Focus on Diversity Series includes programs intended to address research findings and recommendations relating to diversity, teaching, and student learning. Faculty, students, and staff are invited to participate in these monthly sessions that promote dialogue on race and other diversity issues. Additionally, this series focuses on helping faculty to redesign a syllabus so that diversity issues are integrated into course curriculum and integrate a community-based learning component into the course curriculum so that students connect with diverse populations in the community in completing their student learning outcome.

The Teaching Excellence Series provides faculty with an organized, exciting, easily accessed format for building community, gaining strategies for enhancing classroom teaching, and raising the visibility of teaching at PSU.

The Scholarship of Teaching Resource Team (STRT) is made up of PSU faculty who are particularly interested in scholarship of teaching, scholarship of community outreach, and research design. Participants get feedback on a scholarship of teaching project they envision or provide support to those working on projects.

Scholarly Work in Progress (SWIP) sessions provide a monthly venue that encourages faculty to share their work in progress, get feedback from others, hear about research support from experts on campus, and access one-on-one assistance from the CAE Faculty-in-Residence for Scholarship. The first hour of each meeting involves a presentation or discussion of resources available to faculty to assist them with their research and/or other projects. The remainder of the meeting is devoted to faculty sharing and assisting each other.

The Leadership Series offers directors, chairs, and deans a venue to address topics of leadership. Topics included diversity, hiring and retention, collaboration, assessment and program review, defining and documenting the scholarship of teaching and community outreach, enhancing faculty vitality while improving student learning, and more.

The New Faculty Series offers opportunities for first year, tenure-track faculty to gather once a month in a common setting, gaining new knowledge about teaching and learning, learning more about the mission and vision of the university, discussing their scholarly agenda, and using one another as a resource to acclimate to the university. Session topics include syllabus design, setting and managing a scholarly agenda, assessment of teaching and learning, and more.

Stage III Programming

- One-on-One Consultations
- Faculty in Residence
- Promotion-Tenure Portfolio Assistance
- The Faculty Resource Library
- The Annual Capstone Fair
- The Leadership Series
- Focus on Faculty

One-on-One consultations are available with CAE and CUP staff for support in designing and teaching community based-learning and interdisciplinary courses. This includes, but is not limited to, designing new curriculum, crafting a syllabus, developing instructional strategies, grading collaborative and group learning projects, conceptualizing a new interdisciplinary capstone, and other CBL courses, and collaborating with community partners.

Three Faculty-in-Residence are appointed on a yearly basis to deliver services to faculty related to community-based learning, scholarship of teaching and/or community outreach, technology, and assessment. Each Faculty-in-Residence works closely with the CAE staff but takes the primary lead on supporting individual faculty and academic departments through one-on-one consultation, facilitating workshops, and sponsoring CAE groups such as the Scholarship of Teaching Resource Team.

Promotion-Tenure Portfolio Assistance. The promotion-tenure portfolio is a document designed and completed by faculty in universities across the United States. Portfolios can be used for both teaching enhancement and personnel purposes, such as promotion and tenure. The CAE assists faculty in focusing on the process and format of portfolios, including ways faculty can document their own scholarship of teaching, research, and community-university partnerships. CAE provides support by offering ways to design a scholarly agenda, collect the best teaching practice documentation, and use peer consultation.

The Faculty Resource Library is available to all PSU faculty. Faculty members are encouraged to drop by the CAE office to review various faculty development resources including books, videos, publications, and journals. The CAE library contains material on community-based learning, chair leadership, assessment, diversity, and more.

Section VI

Faculty Development With Part-Time Instructors

19

Making Adjunct Faculty Part of the Academic Community

Karen R. Krupar
Metropolitan State College of Denver

Hundreds of adjunct faculty in four-year colleges and universities teach over 45% of the courses, especially in the general education programs, but few institutions have chosen to construct adjunct faculty development programs that integrate these faculty into the instructional community. Metropolitan State College of Denver, recipient of a Title III grant to build an adjunct development program received a TIA-CREF Hesburgh Award of Excellence in 2001 for its innovative adjunct support activities. This chapter articulates the features of this successful program and its effect on the adjunct faculty cohort at the college.

Adjuncts teach over 48% of the coursework in the first two years of college and university education nationally (Leatherman, 2001), and their numbers have increased 15% since 1998 (American Federation of Teachers, 2002). With only 38% of the instructional staff in four-year colleges and universities in the United States as full-time, tenure track/tenured faculty (National Education Association Research Center, 2001; Shapiro, 2002), the remaining faculty are full-time temporary (nontenure track) or part-time faculty (National Center for Educational Statistics, 2001). Although community colleges confronted this adjunct faculty issue more than ten years ago (Gappa, 2002), only recently have four-year colleges and universities faced the same instructional dilemma—limited funds for hiring tenure-track faculty and burgeoning enrollments of high school students and nontraditional adults returning for alternative education and new careers. To handle these enrollment increases, four-year colleges and universities initially depended on graduate assistants (Syverson & Tice, 1993), but this did not sufficiently meet their needs, especially in institutions with limited numbers of graduate programs and graduate assistants (Fogg, 2001). Instead, four-year colleges and universities hire larger numbers of contracted adjunct faculty to fill their instructional quotas (Cox, 2000; Leatherman, 2000). As Lieberman and Guskin (2002) report, "If this trend continues, the non-tenure track faculty will far surpass the tenure-track faculty across higher education" (p. 269).

Not only are these numbers alarming, but despite their need for adjunct instructors, many four-year colleges and universities have not integrated these faculty into their institutions. In 2002, Gappa reported that adjunct faculty (both full-time temporary faculty and part-time adjuncts) are still marginalized by regular faculty, provided limited compensation, and ignored by administrations. Adjuncts are often criticized as incompetent by faculty groups such as the American Association of University Professors (Benjamin, 2002). While some universities have invested in elaborate programs of instructional training for their graduate assistants (Lambert & Tice, 1993; Marincovich, Prostko, & Stout, 1998), there is no national trend or policy regarding adjunct faculty (Gappa & Leslie, 1993). A preconference summary at the 2002 American Association for Higher Education (AAHE) Forum on Faculty Roles and Rewards in Phoenix, Arizona, in which 50 universities and four-year colleges attended, revealed that,

> Part-time faculty are a well-qualified and valuable resource, if properly used. The most serious threats to academic quality come from casual, inconsistent employment practices and a lack of institutional support, rather than from the quality of the part-time faculty themselves. It is therefore crucial for institutions of higher learning to develop systems of institutional support for part-time faculty and to engage in fair, consistent and mutually beneficial employment practices and policies regarding adjunct faculty. (Lucke, 2002, p. 1)

Despite the interest generated in finding solutions to the adjunct issue at four-year colleges and universities, no specific institution or organization has provided national leadership in addressing this concern (with the exception of administrators and faculty developers at Indiana University–Purdue University Indianapolis who initiated the preconference in Phoenix, 2002). Assisting adjunct faculty to create curriculum, advise students, facilitate students' learning, and build a community of scholar-teacher-practitioners that will guarantee quality learning experiences for students enrolled in their course programs remains problematic nationally for higher education.

Like many other colleges and universities confronted with growing evidence of its transformation into ever larger numbers of adjunct (both full-time temporary and part-time faculty) instructional staffing, Metropolitan State College of Denver (Metro) designed a program of faculty development for its 555 part-time faculty, 78 lecturers, and 78 full-time temporary faculty. This college (an urban, four-year, undergraduate-only institution in downtown Denver, Colorado) enrolls 20,000 students. To assist its efforts in managing its large adjunct teaching staff, the college received a U.S. Department of Education Title III grant in 1998; one activity of which is devoted to the professional development and management of adjunct faculty.

Objectives

This chapter describes an award-winning adjunct faculty development program (the 2001 Hesburgh Award of Excellence) that can be instituted at other four-year colleges and universities. Features of the program address

- Orientation program implementation
- Classroom management coaching
- Communications options
- Technology enhancement training
- Team-building experiences
- Reward/recognition systems
- Professional development opportunities: research
- Increased compensation
- Improved resource support efforts
- Assessment

Orientation

A major problem facing adjunct faculty, whether part-time or full-time temporary, is their enculturation in the academic community (Annable, 1996). As Arden (1994) stated,

> What adjuncts sorely need are the same opportunities tenured faculty enjoy—to mix with one's colleagues, to learn from one another, to consider new course materials, to discuss academic issues, and to function in every sense of the term as professionals. (p. 5)

One of the difficulties in including adjuncts into the academic community of the college lies in the varied nature of the adjuncts themselves. Some adjuncts (44%), according to the National Education Association Higher Education Research Center (2001), have other full-time positions. One-third of the adjuncts consider their current position to be their primary employment. Thirty-one percent of the adjuncts receive earnings from other institutions. These represent the migrant adjuncts described by Gappa and Leslie (1993) and Gappa (2002). For all three sets of adjuncts, "Part-time employees do not normally participate in departmental decisions" (Burnstad, 1996, p. 1). Further, in a presentation at the AAHE Faculty Roles and Rewards Conference, Leslie (2002) said that adjunct faculty "are excluded from several important faculty functions, such as curricular development, student advising and professional growth opportunities." To address these needs, Metropolitan State College of Denver (Metro) created a "MENU" of opportunities from which department chairs may choose to use full-time temporary and part-time faculty to perform teaching duties such as advising or creating special course work in their area of expertise. Faculty are paid the same rate for these functions as their teaching assignments. To make it easier to perform these additional faculty options on the MENU, three forms of enculturation are used:

1) An orientation session is held at the beginning of each academic period. Hosted by the Office of Academic Affairs, this orientation (for example, one half-day on August 13, 2002) addresses academic issues such as student diversity, advising options, syllabi construction, library resources, and other professional development opportunities (including training workshops for faculty). Seventy-five faculty have attended this orientation in the past three years.

2) The college provides each adjunct with a *Handbook on Adjunct Instruction.* The adjunct faculty receive either the part-time or the full-time temporary versions of the handbook. In addition, the handbooks are encoded on the Academy for Teaching Excellence web site. The handbooks spell out the college's expectations for adjunct faculty instruction, provide a synopsis of college regulations and procedures as they affect the classroom, and offer suggestions for instructional best practices. Five

hundred fifty-five part-time faculty and 78 lecturers have received the 2002 handbooks.

3) The Academy for Teaching Excellence web site (www.mscd.edu/~academy) contains three other web-based sets of materials for adjunct faculty:

   - One includes an interactive document on student advising. Departments encourage their adjuncts to examine this resource for suggestions and ideas for successfully advising students in a variety of advising formats. In addition, the program developers created a CD-ROM with an interactive element that provides scenarios of various advising problems and can be downloaded to their computers. Faculty pick appropriate strategies for responding to these advising problems which are recorded on paper and sent to the academy for validation. The academy director meets with each adjunct, providing opportunity for discussion and assessment of the faculty member's choice of response to each scenario. To date, 70 adjunct faculty have evaluated their advising practices.

   - A second document contains information about mentoring and coaching. It provides discussions about teaching practices, classroom management techniques, and resources available to the adjunct instructor.

   - The third web-based document provides procedural instructions on how to use media and other technical enhancements in *the technologically smart classrooms* in which the adjunct faculty will be teaching.

In all three web offerings, full-time and part-time faculty work to assimilate the information and construct the web-based data themselves for their own use.

Classroom Management Coaching

Increasing incidences of academic dishonesty (Ashworth, Bannister, & Thorne, 1997) and classroom incivility (e.g., talking that disturbs the classroom, the use of cell phones, students' inattention, students' failure to turn in assignments, etc.) pose problems for adjunct faculty who frequently need assistance in managing their classroom climates. Again, the varied nature of the adjuncts themselves contributes to the problem—many of them bring expertise from their employment experiences but have never taught students. They lack knowledge of instructional methods including classroom management strategies. To assist its adjunct faculty with this issue, the college constructed a web-based classroom management interactive site on the Academy for Teaching Excellence web page. Department chairs encourage their adjuncts to access the site and review the information and note the contact staff (director of counseling, the judicial staff officer, the dean of students, etc.) whose messages provide information about what and how to manage difficult student or faculty incidences in the classroom. Individual questions from adjuncts about the student handbook, procedures, and policies that affect the climate in their classrooms are addressed in group training sessions (three per semester) and individually (coaching) by department chairs or coordinators of specific course programs such as the Freshman Communication Program coordinator or the Mathematics–Statistics 1250 Coordinator. Approximately 73 adjunct faculty have availed themselves of this information since its development in 2001.

Communication Options

One of the most frequently mentioned issues among surveys of adjuncts is their feelings of isolation from other parts of the institution, especially other faculty in the instructional program. Gappa and Leslie (1993) described this phenomenon in their earlier surveys of adjuncts. Leslie reiterated these findings in another survey of 18,000 adjuncts that he reported in 2002: "Institutions by and large have not recognized that part time faculty can be a major asset to their academic programs. Part-timers are painfully aware that administrators and full-time faculty see them as second class citizens" (p. 1). Unger (1995) writes, "There is a marginalizing of adjunct faculty, both economically and professionally" (p. 119). A contributor to this professional marginalizing is the lack of communication mechanisms with which to distribute information and share ideas, teaching strategies, and research concepts among adjuncts. The situation is compounded because adjunct faculty often appear on campus just to teach their specific courses. Many have professional employment elsewhere and bring their particular expertise to students within limited time frames. Others (the migrant part-time faculty) instruct at many institutions as an economic necessity. These adjuncts have no time or incentives to attend department meetings in one institution—their efforts focus on fulfilling their instructional commitments of teaching on a circuit at multiple institutions in the area.

Finding ways to communicate with all three types of adjuncts (full-time temporary, part-time but employed full-time elsewhere, and migrant part-time faculty) presents a significant challenge to the academy. Although labor intensive (even with the use of work study students), the academy provides five types of communication strategies to reach the adjuncts at the college:

- First, all faculty are issued an accessibility (code) to the institution's technology system which they can access through the Internet at home or on campus.
- Second, all faculty are issued a post office box in their departments.
- Third, the academy maintains an elaborate web site for workshop advertisements. It also maintains a portion of the All Campus Training Calendar supported on the institution's home page.
- Fourth, the academy sends emails to all faculty and specifically targets faculty, like the adjuncts, with special information about relevant professional development opportunities, training, grant opportunities, etc.
- Fifth, the academy hand delivers to faculty mail boxes individual information on training opportunities (fliers), professional development grant requests, conference notices, and service options to all faculty.

More than 1,064 faculty receive these materials that identify what is available for faculty development, both on campus as well as regionally and nationally. In some cases (upon request) this data is sent to the adjunct faculty member's other full-time employment mailing address and upon occasion, this data is sent to the home addresses of the adjuncts.

Technology Enhancement Training

Few would argue that adjuncts give departments and programs a degree of flexibility and often bring a special level of expertise into the classroom (Shapiro, 2002). However, as the National Education Association Higher Education Research Center (2001) reports, adjuncts have fewer doctorates or terminal degrees in their disciplines (25% compared with 71% of the full-time faculty. Note that over half of these adjuncts are employed by community colleges that do not require a terminal degree to instruct their students). This group of faculty are also less likely to bring sound instructional methods to the classroom and participate in professional development opportunities, especially technology training that can be used to enhance student learning (Shapiro, 2002).

Responding to this need for instructional technology to enhance student learning, Metro has developed a series of both skill-based and software application training workshops for adjunct faculty. Initially, faculty were paid for the time spent in 15 hours of such professional development. Approximately 165 faculty (of which 120 were adjuncts) attended these workshops on advising online: PowerPoint for classroom enhancement, use of the browsers for research, web page creation, course design for online delivery, Dreamweaver, and Photoshop. In successive years of the grant, the academy has offered Illustrator for the Classroom and Advanced Dreamweaver applications for adjunct training among other types of software applications to improve learning in the classroom.

Since 2001, over 300 adjunct faculty have taken advantage of this free instruction, even though it required their unpaid presence in the faculty instructional laboratory on campus.

Since lack of time to attend workshops on the campus represents a hardship for many adjuncts, the academy is developing web-based workshops that adjunct faculty can access from their home computers. These training sessions are interactive and require the adjunct to register (online) and download worksheets. When completed, the worksheets are emailed to the academy for verification. If the worksheet is completely correct, the adjunct faculty member is issued a certificate of completion. At a later date, the adjunct is contacted to see if the information provided in the workshop training session actually has been implemented into the instructor's class. Twenty-five faculty are registered for two of these workshops for spring semester 2003 in Web Style Design and Syllabi Construction. Four additional workshops have been designed. The entire set of online workshops is the basis of a Certificate for Online Instruction program supported by grant funds.

Team-Building Experiences

The vastly limited contracts and time commitments of adjunct faculty means that they often conduct their work separately from those structures through which the curriculum, department and institution are sustained and renewed (AAUP, 1993). Academic programs require high levels of faculty investment in the architecture of new curricula and the maintenance of older curricula. Adjunct faculty are often excluded from this involvement because they are marginalized from the process, or because the time commitments to engage in departmental and college governance is beyond that which adjuncts can sustain in their role as part-time faculty.

Since Metro relies so heavily on adjunct faculty, it has begun to incorporate adjunct faculty into its curricula renewal process at the departmental level. This is accomplished by creating curricular teams—matching a full-time faculty member with an adjunct to renew, revise, or reconstruct old curricular courses/programs or develop new courses. This teaming of adjuncts and full-time faculty has occurred in seven programs (mathematics, technical communication, psychology, English, history, communication, and biology) and has resulted in the creation of eight new or revised courses. Thirty-six faculty (adjuncts and full-time) will have participated in these teams at the end of the five-year grant period.

Rewards and Recognition

Even community college systems, with 65% of the teaching faculty as part-time adjuncts, demonstrate a minimal reward and recognition program for adjunct faculty. Andrews (2001) reported in 1994 that only 13.2% of community colleges had any merit reward programs for their adjuncts. In 2001 this figure had grown in community colleges to 34%. On the other hand, four-year colleges and universities rarely provide any recognition or compensation for outstanding adjunct instruction (Gappa, 2002).

Realizing the value of the adjunct instructional base, Metro designed several opportunities for public recognition and rewarding of adjunct instructional excellence. First, the college president funds the recognition of two outstanding adjunct faculty selected by the Golden Key Honor Society. The results of this selection are announced at fall convocation. Each recipient is given a cash award equivalent to that given to each outstanding full-time faculty instructor.

Every fall, the academy hosts a Fall Faculty Conference. All adjunct faculty are invited to attend. In 2002, the Fall Conference Committee (composed of full-time and adjunct faculty) designed a competition for the best ideas and best instructional practices and provided awards for the instructional strategies. The best instructional practices from two adjuncts were selected and awarded prizes at the conclusion of this very successful faculty designed and managed conference supported with institutional funds.

Professional Development Opportunities: Research

In addition to building curriculum, adjunct faculty are often precluded from research development opportunities. Despite this exclusion, data from the National Education Association Higher Education Research Center (2001) indicates that one-third of the adjunct faculty (in four-year college and university environments) completed a research publication in the past two years. Their production has been only slightly less than the production of their full-time counterparts. This means that given the opportunity, adjunct faculty will engage in research efforts to increase their professional development.

To assist this process of professional development, Metro instituted the Faculty Research Team concept. The academy provides full-time faculty and adjuncts the opportunity to identify areas of research in which they want to concentrate their efforts as a team of researchers. The academy supplies funding for a professional reference librarian to conduct the literature survey for each research team (adjunct and full-time faculty member) that applies for support. So far, eight teams have engaged in this support in a variety of disciplines including art, management, accounting, teacher education, biology, and physical education. The result of this research is the submission of an article or presentation of the research at a regional or national conference by each team.

Increased Compensation

Low compensation for adjunct instruction remains one of the most glaring inequities in higher education (American Federation of Teachers [AFT], 2002; Marklein, 2001). The AFT report indicates that more than 80% of part time faculty do not have health coverage funded by their institution or a subsidized plan for retirement (Marklein, 2001). Receipt of benefits is dependent upon whether or not the faculty member is allowed to teach at least half time at the institution. Many adjuncts are prohibited from half-time employment at their primary institution. As Murrell (1998) states, "But when calculating budgets and course contracts for part-time faculty, to save money, administrators adopt policies that limit course offerings for part-time faculty members who are eligible for benefits and hire additional part-timers who do not qualify for benefits" (p. 25). The AAUP (1993) reports some institutions prorate benefits for adjunct faculty members who have half-time appointments (20 hours). Approximately 42% of part-time faculty who work more than 20 hours per week indicate that benefits were available to them. Only 11% of those part-timers who teach less than 20 hours per week had accessibility to those benefits enjoyed by other members (AAUP, 1993).

To assist its large adjunct population, particularly its part-time faculty, Metro instituted a new category of faculty. They are the lecturers, who teach a full teaching load, have the stability of year-long contracts, have the benefits of full-time faculty members, but who are paid as part-time instructors. The pay per course is on a sliding scale so that part-time faculty enjoy the same raise percentages that full-time faculty receive each year. Part-time faculty/adjunct funding is now one line-item budget feature of the college, instead of money secured from various unspent funds for projects or programs abandoned or not completed. This provides more security for part-time instructors (year-long contracts) and guarantees annual increases in compensation commensurate with those of the full-time faculty.

Improved Resources

Adjunct faculty at many institutions have no access to faculty resources such as office space, technology equipment, and instructional support (Gappa & Leslie, 1993). To provide for this resource support, the academy director approached each dean and each department chair seeking office space for adjunct faculty. Each time a department physically moves from one space on campus to another building, department chairs and deans promise to configure office space (even if it is a "bullpen") for adjunct faculty use. So far, half of the departments, especially those with large numbers of adjuncts such as mathematics, psychology, English, communications, and history, have found office space for adjunct faculty.

Providing computer accessibility proved more problematic. However, since the entire college instituted a computer replacement program last year in which student laboratory computers are replaced annually from student technology fees and the old student lab computers are given to departments for faculty usage, adjunct faculty needs have been included in the computer replacement process. For those adjunct offices that lack computers, the academy (through the Title III grant) provided new computers for adjunct faculty use. In addition, the academy constructed two laboratories (one a Mac lab and the other a PC lab) for adjunct/full-time faculty training. The academy schedules free time for faculty to use these computer labs when they are not occupied for training. Adjuncts, as well as other faculty, are invited to schedule usage of the labs to meet their personal/professional computing needs.

Each semester, the academy offers between 37 and 60 workshops on a variety of topics on teaching effectiveness (active learning strategies) and technology. In those years when the institution is implementing a new course management system for online instruction, the Academy offers more training workshops in the new course management software. In general the workshops focus on managing large class sections, critical thinking projects, case studies for enhanced learning, advising skills (handling the advising process), professional development options (PowerPoint presentations, conducting research, managing student service learning, issues involving intellectual property rights, etc.), and technology enhancements to the classroom. All faculty are invited to enroll in these workshops. Over 700 faculty participated in these workshops during 2002, and half of these faculty were adjuncts. Fully one-third of these adjuncts attended more than one workshop in 2002.

Assessment

Faculty evaluation is one of the most powerful means of assisting colleges and universities in maintaining quality control over instructional programs, especially those taught by adjunct faculty. But implementing such a practice requires the commitment of the full-time staff and considerable resources. As Moser (2001) wrote,

> For adjuncts to be professionally evaluated and mentored it would take an enormous commitment of resources from the full-time staff. Instead, they are only evaluated by students. It is reasonable to expect that such a system of evaluation would make adjuncts vulnerable to student pressure for better grades or reluctant to teach controversial subjects or engage in stressful disputes over plagiarism. (p. 3)

Because the expenditure of time and resources is large, most four-year colleges and universities do not assess the performance of their adjunct faculty as instructors. However, a study conducted by Andrews (2001) indicates that 77% of all community colleges have instituted evaluation processes of their significantly large numbers of adjunct faculty. These are not just student-based but also peer-based. From this data the college has summarized over a four-year period the performance assessment of its adjunct faculty instructors. In general, adjunct faculty have improved their student evaluations an average of over 30% during the past four years. Beginning with a baseline score in 1998 adjuncts' instructional excellence as perceived by students was 4.10 on a Likert Scale of 1–6 on the criterion of instructional excellence. By the end of the grant period, the average score of all adjuncts on instructional excellence as perceived by their students was 5.389 on a Likert Scale of 1–6. Peer observations that were assessed on a Likert Scale of 1–5 began in the baseline year with a fairly high 4.02 for adjuncts and improved 10% to over 4.42 on a Likert Scale of 1–5. Much of this can be attributed to the increased efforts that the academy has spent developing and supporting this faculty cohort through the Title III grant activities in faculty development. In addition, 10% of the adjunct faculty have been promoted from part-time to full-time temporary faculty or lecturer status. One of the persistent recommendations of AAUP, as well as other professional disciplinary organizations, is the conversion of adjunct faculty positions into tenure-track positions (AAUP, 1993; Benjamin, 2002; Moser, 2001). The college has hired one-third of its new full-time tenure track faculty since 2000 from the ranks of the adjunct instructors (many of whom have participated in academy and Title III programs). Previously, Metro hired very few new tenure-track faculty from the adjunct faculty pool.

Conclusion

The emerging pattern of hiring adjunct faculty as contingency faculty in four-year colleges and universities represents a shift in the instructional staffing of all higher education institutions. It implies changes in the funding strategies, faculty roles and responsibilities, faculty governance of the institution, and a fragmentation of the professorial workforce. Recognizing its dependence on these adjunct faculty, Metropolitan State College of Denver with the help of Title III funds, addressed many of the problems associated with large numbers of nontenure-track faculty as the institution provides quality education for its large urban student population.

References

American Association of University Professors. (1993, June). *The status of non-tenure track faculty.* Retrieved November 18, 2002, from http://www.aaup.org/statements/Redbook/Rbnonlen.htm

American Federation of Teachers. (2002, July). *Standards of good practice in the employment of part-time/adjunct faculty.* Retrieved February 28, 2002, from http://www.aft.org/about/resolutions/2002/standards_ptadjunct.html

Andrews, H. (2001, January). Mainstreaming part-time faculty. *Teaching Professor,* 8.

Annable, T. (1996). Adjunct faculty orientation and mentoring at the department level. *Adjunct Info, 5*(1), 1–2.

Arden, E. (1994). Let's do it for the students. *Adjunct Info, 3*(1), 3–5.

Ashworth, P., Bannister, P., & Thorne, P. (1997). Guilty in whose eyes: University students' perceptions of cheating and plagiarism in academic work and assessment. *Studies in Higher Education, 22*(2), 187–203.

Benjamin, E. (2002, January 24). *Diversity.* Paper presented at the preconference assembly on part-time faculty at the AAHE Forum on Faculty Roles and Rewards Conference, Phoenix, AZ.

Burnstad, H. (1996). Adjunct faculty orientation and mentoring at the department level. *Adjunct Info, 5*(2), 3–5.

Cox, A. M. (2000, December 1). Study shows colleges dependence on their part-time instructors. *The Chronicle of Higher Education,* p. A12.

Fogg, P. (2001, November 2). Colleges cut proportion of full-time faculty members, study finds. *The Chronicle of Higher Education,* p. A17.

Gappa, J. (2002, January 24). *Employment policies and practices.* Paper presented at the preconference assembly on part-time faculty at the AAHE Forum on Faculty Roles and Rewards Conference, Phoenix, AZ.

Gappa, J., & Leslie, D. (1993). *The invisible faculty.* San Francisco, CA: Jossey-Bass.

Lambert, L. M., & Tice, S. E. (Eds.). (1993). *Preparing graduate students to teach: A guide to programs that improve undergraduate education.* Washington, DC: American Association for Higher Education.

Leatherman, C. (2000, January). Part-timers continue to replace full-timers on college faculties. *The Chronicle of Higher Education,* p. A18.

Leatherman, C. (2001, April). Growing use of part-time professors prompts debates and calls for action. *The Chronicle of Higher Education,* p. A14.

Leslie, D. (2002, January 24). *Survey of 18,000 adjunct faculty.* Paper presented at the preconference assembly on part-time faculty at the AAHE Forum on Faculty Roles and Rewards Conference, Phoenix, AZ.

Lieberman, D., & Guskin, A. (2002). The essential role of faculty development in higher education. In C. Wehlburg & S. Chadwick-Blossey (Eds.), *To improve the academy: Vol. 21: Resources for faculty, instructional, and organizational development* (pp. 257–271). Bolton, MA: Anker.

Lucke, J. (2002, January). *Summary.* Paper presented at the preconference assembly on part-time faculty at the AAHE Forum on Faculty Roles and Rewards Conference, Phoenix, AZ.

Marincovich, M., Prostko, J., & Stout, F. (Eds.). (1998). *The professional development of graduate teaching assistants.* Bolton, MA: Anker.

Marklein, M. B. (2001, October 30). Part-time instructors march for better pay. *USA Today,* p. 11D.

Moser, R. (2001). *The new academic labor system, corporation and the renewal of academic citizenship.* Retrieved November 20, 2002, from http://www.aaup.org/Issues/part-time/cewmose.htm

Murrell, G. (1998). *Adjunct faculty: An injury to one is an injury to all.* Retrieved May 9, 2003, from http://www.evergreen.edu/washcenter/resources/spring2002/25-26.pdf

National Center for Educational Statistics. (2001). *The condition of education 2001. Indicator 50: Part-time Instructional Faculty and Staff.* Washington, DC: U.S. Government Printing Office.

National Education Association Higher Education Research Center. (2001). Part-time faculty. *Update, 7*(4), 1–4.

Shapiro, M. (2002). Irreverent commentary on the state of education in America today. Retrieved November 20, 2002, from http://irascibleprofessor.com/comments_11_05_02.htm

Syverson, P. D., & Tice, S. L. (1993). The critical role of the teaching assistantship. In L. M. Lambert & S.E. Tice (Eds.), *Preparing graduate students to teach: A guide to programs that improve undergraduate education and develop tomorrow's faculty.* Washington, DC: American Association for Higher Education.

Unger, D. (1995). Academic apartheid: The predicament of part-time faculty. *NEA Education Journal,* 117–120.

Contract:

Karen R. Krupar
Director, Academy for Teaching Excellence
Metropolitan State College of Denver
PO Box 173362
Denver, CO 80217-3362
Voice (303) 556-3922
Fax (303) 556-6484
Email krupark@mscd.edu

Karen R. Krupar is Director of the Academy for Teaching Excellence and Co-director of a Title III U.S. Department of Education grant (Activity Two) of $508,000 that addresses professional development and retention of adjunct faculty. She received her PhD (1967) in Communication at the University of Denver. She is a full Professor in the Department of Communication Arts and Sciences at Metropolitan State College of Denver. At the Academy for Teaching Excellence, she directs all aspects of faculty enhancement training, coaching/mentoring, faculty orientation, and designs and produces the Fall Faculty Conference each year for the provost of the college. Recently, she has administrated the development of faculty online workshops and currently is part of a writing team for a new Title III collaborative grant that will include other colleges. She wrote the college's submission to the Hesburgh Foundation that gave her college one of the prestigious Awards of Excellence for 2001.

20

Graduate Student Mentors: Meeting the Challenges of the Ongoing Development of Graduate Student Instructors

Chris O'Neal
University of Michigan

Jennifer Karlin
South Dakota School of Mines and Technology

Training and mentoring Graduate Student Instructors (GS Instructors) at large institutions presents three challenges to instructional developers: 1) training numerous GS Instructors from multiple departments, 2) the vast array of duties GS Instructors need training in, and 3) the continual sophistication of GS Instructors. Here we describe how the College of Engineering at the University of Michigan has met these challenges through the use of Graduate Student Mentors (GS Mentors). GS Mentors are experienced GS Instructors who are trained to mentor and advise their peers. We discuss how the GS Mentors are selected, trained, and supervised, and how they have helped to meet the challenges outlined above.

The training and development of Student Instructors (GS Instructors; otherwise known as teaching assistants) presents a number of challenges to large, research-oriented institutions that must employ numerous GS Instructors to teach laboratories and recitations, provide office hours, and even deliver some lectures. These challenges include 1) the logistics of training, supporting, and monitoring a large number of GS Instructors from multiple departments and backgrounds, 2) providing adequate training time and coverage of the many duties that any given GS Instructor may have, and 3) accommodating the changing needs of these GS Instructors as they gain experience and begin to teach more advanced courses with more involved duties. While these challenges are by no means unique to large, research-oriented institutions, this context makes them very visible. In this chapter we discuss the ways in which one institution, the College of Engineering at the University of Michigan (UM) (hereafter referred to as CoE), has met these challenges through the use of a centrally organized group of Graduate Student Mentors (GS Mentors).

Graduate Student Mentors: Helping to Meet the Challenge

In order to address the challenges of preparing GS Instructors, CoE trains and supervises a group of experienced GS Instructors who serve as Graduate Student Mentors to the rest of the GS Instructor population. The GS Mentors are centrally organized through the Office of the Associate Dean for Graduate Education, and are trained and supervised by staff from UM's Center for Research on Learning and Teaching (CRLT). This is in contrast to other models of peer mentoring used at UM which are typically departmentally based. Currently, there are ten GS Mentors each term, with each GS Mentor being accountable for 20 to 30 GS Instructors. While centrally organized, GS Mentors are responsible for GS Instructors in only one to three departments; this allows GS Mentors to get to know one cadre of GS Instructors very well, instead of having their time and energy used to coordinate logistics within multiple departments.

The GS Mentor program in CoE was founded on the belief that developing CoE GS Instructors could benefit from the unique guidance, support, and expertise that peer mentors provide. While all GS Instructors have access to mentoring from their advisors or other professors in their department, the peer mentor relationship provides a safe venue for exploration of teaching strategies and discussion of teaching problems that is absent of fear of judgment from one's professorial superiors. GS Mentors in CoE are trained to mentor in a facilitative way, a model that appeals to their own sense of their role and approaches the collegial style of supervision preferred by most GS Instructors (Prieto, 1999). Additionally, the nature of the peer mentor-mentee interaction is such that it allows both individuals to give and receive benefits (Bollis-Pecci & Walker, 1999), so that it is a valuable learning experience for the GS Mentors themselves.

Roles of the Graduate Student Mentor

GS Mentors serve a number of roles in CoE. They may serve as mentors, evaluators, trainers, and other roles as the GS Mentor encounters unexpected situations within their departments that require support and expertise. This multiplicity of roles calls for a wide set of skills and abilities in the GS Mentor, and presents challenges for their preparation and training.

First and foremost, GS Mentors serve as confidential mentors to GS Instructors in their assigned departments. GS Mentors consult on issues ranging from classroom management challenges, implementation of new teaching and learning strategies, and professor/GS Instructor conflicts. Unless required as part of a GS Instructor's initial training, consultation with a GS Mentor is always at the behest of the GS Instructor. GS Mentors contact their GS Instructors to offer these services either via email or face-to-face contacts at multiple points throughout the term.

GS Mentors also offer valuable classroom feedback services to their GS Instructor clients. GS Mentors may observe a class and share their observations with the GS Instructor afterwards, they may film the class and then conduct a video observation consultation afterwards, or they may conduct a midterm student feedback (also known as a small group instructional diagnosis) in which the GS Instructor leaves the classroom and the GS Mentor talks to the students about how the class is going, then shares the students' feedback with the GS Instructor. As with general consultation, all of these feedback services are confidential to ensure the comfort and engagement of the GS Instructor. Because GS Mentors are peers of the GS Instructors they serve, they are able to present feedback in a nonthreatening way that is easily implementable by the instructors.

GS Mentors also participate in the GS Instructor Teaching Orientation that all new CoE GS Instructors are required to attend. This 12-hour orientation is centrally coordinated and run by the university's Center for Research on Learning and Teaching. The orientation involves GS Mentor-led sessions on organizing and teaching lab and discussion sections, teaching problem solving techniques, multicultural teaching and learning issues, grading/assessment issues, and practice teaching, among others. Besides presenting training sessions in which they share their expertise on particular teaching and learning topics, the GS Mentors use orientation to meet with their new GS Instructors and to lay the groundwork for future mentoring. GS Mentors are also often called on to staff workshops and discussions on teaching throughout the term and often organize get-togethers for their assigned GS Instructors. Using the GS Mentors in this role provides CoE with a trained, organized group of committed and experienced teachers who share a common background and disciplinary perspective with the instructors they are training.

Selection and Training of Graduate Student Mentors

The GS Mentor selection process is competitive. Applicants are selected based on teaching experience, demonstrated dedication to teaching, and demonstrated interest in helping their peers with teaching and learning issues. The current group of GS Mentors for the 2002–2003 academic year has over 17 years of collective teaching experience and 26 combined terms of GS Mentor experience. Hiring of the GS Mentors is coordinated so that new GS Mentors are working with experienced mentors each term. Additionally, the college makes every effort to hire a GS Mentor pool that reflects the diverse ethnic and multicultural makeup of the GS Instructor population the GS Mentors will be serving.

CoE attempts to hire GS Mentors from every department within the college, but this is not always possible. Because more GS Mentors are recruited from some departments than others, GS Mentors are often serving in a department other than their own. This can be seen as a drawback of the centralized model of organizing teaching mentors, since GS Mentors outside their own departments spend much of their time establishing trust with their client base before they can begin their work as instructional developers. CoE attempts to overcome this situation by organizing early and frequent interactions between GS Mentors and their GS Instructors (e.g., at new GS Instructor orientation) and by emphasizing the role of the GS Mentors as facilitators on thinking about pedagogy, rather than content experts. Experience from the CoE GS Mentor program suggests that it is better to hire GS Mentors based on their promise as consultants and mentors, rather than based on their departmental affiliation.

Because the nature of instructional development calls on skills that even experienced instructors may not have mastered, all GS Mentors go through a series of training workshops at the beginning of their tenure. New GS Mentors attend workshops on observing classes and giving feedback, and are specifically trained in observing classes and giving feedback through the use of midterm student feedbacks and videotape observation. This training lasts approximately ten hours and emphasizes the skills that the GS Mentors are most likely to employ during their tenure. This training also teaches the GS Mentors how to build the bonds of respect and communication that are necessary for peer mentoring relationships (Bollis-Pecci & Walker, 1999). Additionally, all of the GS Mentors meet as a group twice monthly for continual staff development and to discuss issues that have come up in their own consulting.

Staff development topics include sessions on promoting retention of underrepresented groups in engineering, instructional technology, discussing case studies to practice consulting skills, and recent advances in engineering education. Throughout the entire term, GS Mentors are mentored to recognize which issues they can comfortably consult on (teaching and learning issues, classroom problems, interactions with students) and which issues should be referred to a campus professional (emotional issues, issues of harassment or abuse, etc.).

The one-on-one, peer mentoring nature of the GS Mentor-GS Instructor interaction directly addresses many of the challenges described above. In the next three sections, we discuss these challenges in detail and highlight how the GS Mentor program has addressed them.

Challenge One: Training Large Numbers of GS Instructors From Multiple Departments

Training GS Instructors at large institutions often represents a logistical challenge, due to the large numbers and varying disciplinary backgrounds of the GS Instructor population. For example, in CoE, there are approximately 225 GS Instructors spread across 13 departments. This presents a particularly diverse pool of instructors to train and develop, an issue which is complicated by the fact that at any time, 70% or more of the GS Instructors in the college are in their first or second term in the classroom (see Table 20.1). This means that a sizable segment of the GS Instructor population is in dire need of basic training that is no longer appropriate for the other segment of more experienced instructors. Data presented in all tables is from a bi-annual survey given to all GS Instructors in the College of Engineering. As of the fall 2002 term, the survey has been administered five times.

TABLE 20.1
Percentage of CoE GS Instructors Arranged by Number of Terms of Experience

Number of Terms	Fall 2000	Winter 2001	Fall 2001	Winter 2002	Fall 2002
1–2	77%	82%	79%	72%	73%
3–6	19%	18%	21%	28%	24%
7+	4%	0%	0%	0%	3%

Data is from a voluntary survey presented to GS Instructors each term and does not account for the total GS Instructor population of CoE.

Expecting departments to train their own GS Instructors is not always feasible in CoE, where one department contains one-third of the college's total GS Instructor population and other departments have only one or two GS Instructors total. Some of these smaller departments do not have the resources to carry out departmentally based training for their own GS Instructors, even though they have small numbers of GS Instructors to train. Instead, CoE centrally organizes GS Instructor training so that all GS Instructors, regardless of their home department, receive the same level and quality of training. This centralized training model includes the New GS Instructor Orientation described earlier, and the GS Mentors themselves. This centralized model allows the college to set a strong, minimum training standard; assure quality in the preparation and presentation of that standard; and maintain programs for continuous improvement.

This centralized approach allows CoE to offer basic training to new GS Instructors (in the form of the orientation) and continual support to more advanced GS Instructors (through the GS Mentors) without the logistical and financial burden of continued large-scale training. Because GS Mentors are assigned to one, or at most a few, departments, they represent a particularly flexible and personalized model of continual training that allows us to reach GS Instructors in all departments equally, in a way that large-scale one-size-fits-all efforts like the orientation cannot. Because interaction with the GS Mentors is voluntary, they allow CoE to provide continual training and support to those GS Instructors who desire it. This efficient model of instructional development is particularly relevant at a time when many instructional development efforts are facing budget cuts.

Challenge Two: Providing Training for GS Instructors With Multiple Duties

While often presented as fairly simple assignments, graduate teaching assistantships at large institutions are actually complicated, involved positions that require a number of skills (an assertion supported in general studies of GS Instructor duties) (Gappa, 1993). Duties GS Instructors perform range from leading discussions to grading papers to running labs and even giving lectures in large classes (see Table 20.2 for a complete listing of GS Instructor duties in CoE). Seventy-five percent of GS Instructors in CoE report having at least four separate and unique duties associated with their teaching assignment every term. Some GS Instructors report having as many as ten duties each term.

Table 20.2
List of Duties Performed by GS Instructors in CoE

1) Hold office hours	7) Teach a discussion section	Maintain web site
2) Grade exams	8) Attend class	Write exams
3) Grade labs or projects	9) Give lectures	Write labs
4) Hold review sessions	Answer student emails	Proctor exams
5) Grade homework or papers	Write homework	Determine grading schemes
6) Write homework solutions	Teach a lab	

Duties are ordered from most common to least common. Duties without a corresponding number were listed only occasionally by GS Instructors.

It is difficult for a single orientation event (such as the one described earlier) to adequately train all of these duties in a single day. GS Instructor orientation in CoE offers GS Instructors their choice of a number of concurrent sessions, but even so, GS Instructors inevitably leave orientation with only a modicum of training in some of the duties they will have to perform. Again, the personalized, one-on-one services that the GS Mentors offer helps to meet this challenge. GS Mentors are often called on after the term has begun to work with GS Instructors who need more help with their specific duties. Because they are able to work in-depth with instructors, GS Mentors can deliver training and support in context, something that the orientation cannot.

Challenge Three: Continual Training for a Maturing Population

The continual development of GS Instructors also presents a conceptual challenge to trainers, as the basic training that proves sufficient for a novice instructor is rarely appropriate for GS Instructors who have progressed to the level of junior colleagues with more advanced duties. Even though CoE has very high turnover of its GS Instructor population, there is a fairly stable core of returning, experienced GS Instructors each term (approximately 30%) who need more advanced training and support. For example, in CoE a first term GS Instructor is sometimes asked to teach a lab section where their duties may include running labs and grading lab reports, and then be asked to be a grader in their next term. GS Instructors returning for a second year of teaching may even be asked to teach a discussion section or their own lecture in some cases. Since GS Instructors are only required to attend one orientation event at the very beginning of their tenure, they face these new duties with no additional training or preparation beyond that which they have independently sought out from peers and other campus resources. In an extension of their role as advanced trainers of specific duties, GS Mentors can help an experienced GS Instructor adjust to a new teaching position, identify areas for growth, and work with that GS Instructor to fill in those areas. This model is time effective for the GS Instructors and they seem more willing to meet for one-on-one with a GS Mentor than to attend large-scale retraining events.

Experienced GS Instructors are also constantly changing in the way they think about teaching. Nyquist and Sprague (1998) describe a model of GS Instructor development that conceptualizes GS Instructor progression from senior learners to colleagues-in-training to junior colleagues. This model sheds light on the changes that GS Instructors may go through in terms of their basic concerns, discourse level, approach to authority, and approach to their students. Accommodating these changes presents a challenge to GS Instructor trainers. Experienced GS Instructors require a different kind of training and support than novice GS Instructors, and this is complicated by the fact that progression through the Nyquist-Sprague model is highly individualized. As with their attention to changing GS Instructor duties, GS Mentors can address the changing perspectives of maturing instructors in a one-on-one environment in a way that large-scale training cannot. By having GS Mentors provide this consultation, CoE is able to offer a service to instructors that is flexible to the varying needs and developmental levels of the GS Instructors. The bond of trust that is needed for GS Mentors to work effectively with GS Instructors establishes the groundwork for GS Mentors to deliver their support in a way that makes the most sense for GS Instructors at certain stages of development.

Evaluation of the Current GS Mentor Program

As seen in Table 20.3, the current GS Mentor program has been very successful. The majority (91%–100%) of CoE GS Instructors are aware of the program, even if they have not yet taken advantage of their GS Mentor's services. The 40% or more of the GS Instructors in each term who have used their GS Mentor have rated their GS Mentor highly (94%–98% rated their GS Mentor as excellent or good), and report that they learned a variety of skills and knowledge from the interaction, such as learning of a peer group with whom to share experience; awareness of new resources; improvement of their skills; and the knowledge that, as one respondent stated, "I'm not alone, fumbling through the world of teaching." Even those GS Instructors who have not actively pursued engagement with their GS Mentor have reported appreciation for their GS Mentors' presence, knowing that the GS Mentor is there as a resource should he or she be needed.

TABLE 20.3
Evaluation of the Current Program

	Fall 2000	**Winter 2001**	**Fall 2001**	**Winter 2002**	**Fall 2002**
Aware of program?	91.2%	98.0%	100%	100%	98.9%
Had contact?	42.1%	45.1%	66.1%	53.3%	43.0%
Rated GS Mentor excellent or good (of those who rated their GS Mentor)	93.8%	95.0%	95.7%	97.9%	97.6%

"Aware of program" indicates what percentage of GS Instructors polled reported knowing about the GS Mentor program. "Had contact" indicates what percentage of GS Instructor polled reported having contact of some sort with their GS Mentor. "Rated GS Mentor..." indicates what percentage of those GS Instructors reporting contact with their GS Mentor rated their performance as excellent or good.

CHALLENGES AND OPPORTUNITIES FOR PROGRAM GROWTH

While a centrally managed mentorship group like the GS Mentors has a number of advantages over departmentally based ones, it does present some challenges (see Mintz, 1998, for a complete review of centralized training programs). First and foremost, communicating and publicizing the value of the GS Mentors is a continual, difficult process. Despite a steady stream of emails from the program managers and the associate dean's office, a number of graduate students are uncertain of the role of the GS Mentors, and some faculty, mistrustful of faculty development efforts, discourage their GS Instructors from taking advantage of this service. In the College of Engineering, we have attempted to rectify these constraints in several ways. For new and experienced GS Instructors, we heavily advertise the GS Mentors at the centralized new GS Instructor orientation and at the various departmental welcomes at the beginning of the year. For faculty, we do a number of presentations on the value of the GS Mentor program in departmental and higher level meetings across campus. For both groups, we continually emphasize the confidential nature of the GS Mentors in all our communications and presentations.

Second, because some departments are not represented in the GS Mentor group, it is often a struggle for mentors outside of those departments to reach GS Instructors within those departments. As mentioned earlier, we have attempted to recruit GS Mentors from all departments, but some are too small to furnish GS Mentors, and others, while large, have not had enough graduate students interested in the position. This imbalance has hampered our efforts at impacting CoE's largest department, Electrical Engineering and Computer Science (EECS), which has four GS Mentors assigned to it, only one of which is currently enrolled in EECS. Recruitment of GS Mentors from EECS is also complicated by the fact that most EECS graduate students are well funded. Additionally, there are some programs (e.g., the first year design classes) which have no graduate students, but are instead served by GS Instructors from many departments. We continue to aggressively recruit for GS Mentors in EECS and the other large departments, but until the culture of teaching changes substantially in these departments, it is likely that we will always have to draw on GS Mentors from other departments to serve them.

Third, quality control is a constant priority for the program. Considering that the GS Mentors are relatively new to teaching themselves and may, therefore, not be qualified to give others teaching advice is important to consider. However, as with the peer consulting programs described in Petrulis, Carroll, and Skow (1993), the GS Mentors primarily facilitate their clients' thinking about their own teaching; they do not prescribe a "correct" way of teaching and thus need not be experts on all potential pedagogical issues their GS Instructors might encounter. Bimonthly meetings with the GS Mentor group and Center for Research on Learning and Teaching staff provide an opportunity to share opinions and feedback on how consultations should be handled and skills that can be implemented to handle them. Furthermore, delicate situations are directly supervised by the CRLT staff who manage the group. A survey evaluating the GS Mentors' performance is sent out every term, and GS Mentors receive that feedback along with guidance on how they might improve their own consulting. To further our quality control efforts, in future academic years the program is instituting more frequent individual check-ins with the GS Mentors, as well as issuing satisfaction surveys to "clients" within weeks of their interaction with a GS Mentor.

Conclusion

This chapter documented one way that a peer mentoring program can be implemented, that is, via a centralized model. It is not the only way that a peer mentoring group can work, and there are numerous examples of departmentally based models. UM's own College of Literature, Science, and the Arts is one example of a successful departmentally based system where peer mentors are organized by their home department and serve only the GS Instructors of that department. Departmentally based models of peer mentoring exceed their centralized counterparts in at least one dimension: The training/mentoring is delivered in the context of the department and is therefore more in line with the culture and goals of the department than a centralized model ever could be. Centralized models, on the other hand, maintain a minimum level of quality of training/mentoring in all departments and benefit from inter-departmental exchange between the trainers/mentors.

The decision to institute a centralized or departmentally based model of peer mentoring hinges on a number of issues. Administrators must consider the costs of each model, the level to which resources are already shared between departments, the presence or absence of a shared vision between departments of how much teaching is valued, and the importance of a shared disciplinary context. The decision to implement a centralized model of peer mentoring in CoE was largely based on concern over some departments' ability to adequately commit to and support peer mentors and the comparatively low cost of managing them centrally. Regarding costs, we have found that we get exceptionally high quality service from our GS Mentors without the intensive, long-term training that other peer mentoring programs have used. We ascribe this to excellent selection of the GS Mentors and extensive mentoring of them by professional staff during the term.

The Graduate Student Mentor group at the University of Michigan's College of Engineering has been extremely effective at meeting the instructional development needs of a large, diverse GS Instructor population. It can be seen as a good model for similar centralized efforts at comparable institutions with large numbers of GS Instructors from very different departments. However, perhaps more important than the many roles described earlier, the GS Mentor group serves as a visible reminder that teaching is valued and important in CoE. By modeling a culture that "teaching is OK," (as discussed in Winternitz & Davis, 2000), the GS Mentors give graduate students in CoE the chance to value and take pride in their own teaching efforts, opportunities that are all to often lacking at large research institutions.

As a final note, let us emphasize that the GS Mentor position is not simply a service role. The GS Mentors receive valuable advanced training in teaching which places them at the vanguard of the next generation of higher education instructors. Consulting and mentoring build a host of additional skills that will complement their teaching and make them valuable commodities to institutions that are emphasizing teaching more and more (Petrulis et al., 1993). The GS Mentors are an advanced group of outstanding teachers who take pride and joy in the opportunity to share their experience and wisdom with their peers.

Acknowledgments

This chapter, and the entire GS Mentor program, would not have been possible without the strong support of Deans Stella Pang and James Bean in the College of Engineering. Their commitment to graduate student instruction is a model for leadership in this area. We would also like to thank the numerous cohorts of GS Mentors who have worked tirelessly to improve teaching and learning at the University of Michigan.

References

Bollis-Pecci, T. S., & Walker K. L. (1999). Peer mentoring perspectives in GTA training: a conceptual road map. *The Journal of Graduate Teaching Assistant Development, 7*(1), 27–37.

Gappa, L. (1993). The teaching associate program: A collaborative approach. *The Journal of Graduate Teaching Assistant Development, 1*(1), 25–32.

Mintz, J. A. (1998). The role of centralized programs in preparing graduate students to teach. In M. Marincovich, J. Prostko, & F. Stout (Eds.), *The professional development of graduate teaching assistants* (pp. 19–40). Bolton, MA: Anker.

Nyquist, J. D., & Sprague, J. (1998). Thinking developmentally about TAs. In M. Marincovich, J. Prostko, & F. Stout (Eds.), *The professional development of graduate teaching assistants* (pp. 61–88). Bolton, MA: Anker.

Petrulis, R., Carroll, S., & Skow, L. (1993). Graduate students as instructional consultant: case studies from two universities. *The Journal of Graduate Teaching Assistant Development, 1*(2), 85–93.

Prieto, L. R. (1999). Teaching assistants' preferences for supervisory style: Testing a developmental model of GTA supervision. *The Journal of Graduate Teaching Assistant Development, 6*(3), 111–118.

Winternitz, T., & Davis, W. E. (2000). Lessons learned during five years of the UC Davis program in college teaching. *The Journal of Graduate Teaching Assistant Development, 7*(2), 69–75.

Contact:

Chris O'Neal
3300 School of Education Building
University of Michigan
610 E. University Street
Ann Arbor, MI 48109--1259
Voice (734) 763-4418
Fax (734) 647-3600
Email coneal@umich.edu

Jennifer Karlin
South Dakota School of Mines and Technology
501 East St. Joseph Street
Rapid City, SD 57701
Voice (605) 394-1271
Fax (605) 394-2409

Chris O'Neal is an Instructional Consultant at the Center for Research on Learning and Teaching at the University of Michigan. A PhD in biology, he works with sciences, math, and engineering instructors, and runs numerous workshops and seminars on active learning and engaging students. He is the coordinator of the Graduate Student Mentors group at UM's College of Engineering as well as the team leader for the Center for Research on Learning and Teaching's Graduate Student Instructor Team.

Jennifer Karlin recently completed her PhD in industrial engineering at the University of Michigan. While there, she taught as both a teaching assistant and as primary instructor. She also worked for the Center for Research on Learning and Teaching as a Graduate Teaching Consultant (GTC). As a GTC, she co-coordinated the Graduate Student Mentor program and the new Graduate Student Instructor Orientation. She is now an Assistant Professor of Industrial Engineering at the South Dakota School of Mines and Technology

Bibliography

Allen, R. R. (1991). Encouraging reflection in teaching assistants. In J. D. Nyquist, R. D. Abbott, D. H. Wulff, & J. Sprague (Eds.), *Preparing the professorate for tomorrow to teach: Selected readings in TA training* (pp. 323–317). Dubuques, IA: Kendall/Hunt.

Alley, M. (1996). *The craft of scientific writing.* New York, NY: Springer-Verlag.

American Association of University Professors. (1993, June). *Report on the status of non-tenure track faculty.* Retrieved November 18, 2002, from http://www.aaup.org/statements/ Redbook/Rbnonlen.htm

American Federation of Teachers. (2002, July). *Standards of good practice in the employment of part-time/adjunct faculty.* Retrieved February 28, 2002, from http://www.aft.org/highered/part-time/history.html

Andrews, H. (2001, January). Mainstreaming part-time faculty. *Teaching Professor,* 8.

Angelo, T. A., & Cross, K. P. (1993). *Classroom assessment techniques: A handbook for college teachers* (2nd ed.). San Francisco, CA: Jossey-Bass.

Annable, T. (1996). Adjunct faculty orientation and mentoring at the department level. *Adjunct Info, 5*(1), 1–2.

Anson, C. (2002). *A WAC casebook: Scenes for faculty reflection and program development.* New York, NY: Oxford University Press.

Arden, E. (1994). Let's do it for the students. *Adjunct Info, 3*(1), 3–5.

Ashworth, P., Bannister, P., & Thorne, P. (1997). Guilty in whose eyes: University students' perceptions of cheating and plagiarism in academic work and assessment. *Studies in Higher Education, 22*(2), 187–203.

Astin, A. W. (1993). *What matters in college: Four critical years revisited.* San Francisco, CA: Jossey-Bass.

Astin, A. W., Banta, T. W., Cross, K. P., El-Khawas, E., Ewell, P. T., Hutchings, P., Marchese, T. J., McClenny, K. M., Mentkowski, M., Miller, M. A., Moran, E. T., & Wright, B. D. (1992). *Principles of good practice for assessing student learning.* Washington, DC: American Association for Higher Education.

Astin, A. W., & Colleagues. (2001, July). *Toward a theory of institutional transformation in higher education.* Paper presented at the annual meeting of the AAC&U Institute on Campus Leadership for Sustainable Innovation, Leesburg, VA.

Baker, P. (1980). Inquiry into the teaching-learning process: Trickery, folklore, or science? *Teaching Sociology, 7*(3), 237–245.

Baker, P. (1985). Does the sociology of teaching inform *Teaching Sociology? Teaching Sociology, 12*(3), 361–375.

Baker, P. (1986). The helter-skelter relationship between teaching and research. *Teaching Sociology, 14*(1), 50–66.

Baker, P. (2002, July). *Teacher-scholars and the scholarship of teaching in the research-intensive university: reflections on a slow revolution.* Paper presented at Mission, Values, and Identity: A National Conference for Carnegie Doctoral/Research Intensive Institutions, Normal, IL.

Baron, D. (2002). *ASTD ROI network.* Retrieved November 11, 2002, from http://roi.astd.org/index.aspx

Bass, R. (1999, February). The scholarship of teaching: What's the problem? *Invention: Creative Thinking about Learning and Teaching, 1*(1), 1–10.

Baxter-Magolda, M. (1992). *Knowing and reasoning in college.* San Francisco, CA: Jossey-Bass.

Baxter-Magolda, M. (2001). *Making their own way: Narratives for transforming higher education to promote self-development.* Sterling, VA: Stylus.

Beach, J. (1993, Summer). *Address to faculty.* Department of Behavioral Sciences and Leadership, West Point, NY.

Bean, J. (1996). *Engaging ideas: The professor's guide to integrating writing, critical thinking and active learning in the classroom.* San Francisco, CA: Jossey-Bass.

Bellas, M. L., & Toutkoushian, R. K. (1999). Faculty time allocations and research productivity: Gender, race, and family effects. *The Review of Higher Education, 22(4),* 367–390.

Benjamin, E. (2002, January 24). *Diversity.* Paper presented at the preconference assembly on part-time faculty at the AAHE Forum on Faculty Roles and Rewards Conference, Phoenix, AZ.

Bennett, W. E. (1987). Small group instructional diagnosis: A dialogic approach to instructional improvement for tenured faculty. *The Journal of Staff, Program, and Organization Development, 5,* 100–104.

Biggs, J. B. (1999). *Teaching for quality learning at university.* Buckingham, England: Society for Research on Higher Education and the Open University.

Black, B. (1998). Using the SGID method for a variety of purposes. In M. Kaplan & D. Lieberman (Eds.), *To improve the academy: Vol. 17. Resources for faculty, instructional, and organizational development* (pp. 245–262). Stillwater, OK: New Forums Press.

Boice, R. (1987). Is released time an effective component of faculty development programs? *Research in Higher Education, 26*(3), 311–326.

Boice, R. (1989). Procrastination, busyness, and bingeing. *Behavior Research Therapy, 27*(6), 605–611.

Boice, R. (1997). What discourages research-practitioners in faculty development? *Higher Education: Handbook of Theory and Research, 12*, 371–435.

Boice, R., & Turner, J. L. (1989). The FIPSE-CSULB mentoring project for new faculty. In S. Kahn (Ed.), *To improve the academy: Vol. 8. Resources for faculty, instructional, and organizational development* (pp. 117–141). Stillwater, OK: New Forums Press.

Bollis-Pecci, T. S., & Walker K. L. (1999). Peer mentoring perspectives in GTA training: a conceptual road map. *The Journal of Graduate Teaching Assistant Development, 7*(1), 27–37.

Border, L. L. B. (1997). The creative art of effective consultation. In K. T. Brinko & R. J. Menges (Eds.), *Practically speaking: A sourcebook for instructional consultants in higher education* (pp. 17–24). Stillwater, OK: New Forums Press.

Border, L. L. B., & Chism, N. V. N. (1992). The future is now: A call for action and a list of resources. In L. L. B. Border & N. V. N. Chism (Eds.), *Teaching for diversity* (pp. 103–115). New Directions for Teaching and Learning, No. 49. San Francisco, CA: Jossey-Bass.

Bordo, S. (1997). *Twilight zones: The hidden life of cultural images from Plato to O.J.* Berkeley, CA: California University Press.

Boud, D., Cohen, R., & Sampson, J. (1999). Peer learning and assessment. *Assessment and Evaluation in Higher Education, 24*(4), 413–426.

Boud, D., Cohen, R., & Sampson, J. (2001). *Peer learning in higher education: Learning from each other.* London, England: Kogan Page.

Boyer Commission on Educating Undergraduates in the Research University. (1998). *Reinventing undergraduate education: A blueprint for America's research universities.* Menlo Park, CA: The Carnegie Foundation for the Advancement of Teaching.

Boyer, E. (1990). *Scholarship reconsidered: Priorities of the professoriate.* San Francisco, CA: Jossey-Bass.

Bransford, J. D., Brown, A. L., & Cocking, R. R. (Eds.). (2000). *How people learn: Brain, mind, experience, and school.* Commission on Behavioral and Social Sciences and Education National Research Council. Washington, DC: National Academy Press.

Braxton, J. M., Bray, N. J., & Berger, J. B. (2000). Faculty teaching skills and their influence on the college student departure process. *Journal of College Student Development, 41,* 215–227.

Braxton, J. M., Luckey, W., & Helland, P. (2002). *Institutionalizing a broader view of scholarship through Boyer's four domains* (ASHE-ERIC Higher Education Report, 29 [2]). San Francisco, CA: Jossey-Bass.

Braxton, J. M., & Toombs, W. (1982). Faculty uses of doctoral training: Consideration of a technique for the differentiation of scholarly effort from research activity. *Research in Higher Education, 16*(3), 265–282.

Brinko, K. (1997). The interactions of teaching improvement. In K. T. Brinko & R. J. Menges (Eds.), *Practically speaking: A sourcebook for instructional consultants in higher education* (pp. 3–8). Stillwater, OK: New Forums Press.

Brinko, K. T., & Menges, R. J. (1997). *Practically speaking: A sourcebook for instructional consultants in higher education.* Stillwater, OK: New Forums Press.

Brookfield, S. D. (1995). *Becoming a critically reflective teacher.* San Francisco, CA: Jossey-Bass.

Brookfield, S. D. (2001). Teaching through discussion as the exercise of disciplinary power. In D. Lieberman & C. Wehlburg (Eds.), *To improve the academy: Vol. 20. Resources for faculty, instructional, and organizational development* (pp. 260–273). Bolton, MA: Anker.

Brown, R. W. (1995). Autorating: Getting individual marks from team marks and enhancing teamwork. *Proceedings of the Frontiers in Education Conference.* Pittsburgh, PA: ISEE/ASEE.

Brown, S. (1990). Strengthening ties to academic affairs. In M. J. Barr, M. L. Upcraft, & Associates, *New futures for student affairs.* San Francisco, CA: Jossey-Bass.

Bruffee, K. (1993). *Collaborative learning: Higher education, interdependence, and the authority of knowledge.* Baltimore, MD: The Johns Hopkins University Press.

Burnstad, H. (1996). Adjunct faculty orientation and mentoring at the department level. *Adjunct Info, 5*(2), 3–5.

Cambridge, B. (2001). Fostering the scholarship of teaching and learning: Communities of practice. In D. Lieberman & C. Wehlburg (Eds.), *To improve the academy: Vol. 19. Resources for faculty, instructional, and organizational development* (pp. 3–16). Bolton, MA: Anker.

Cambridge, B. (2002). Linking change initiatives: The Carnegie Academy for the Scholarship of Teaching and Learning in the company of other national projects. In D. Lieberman & C. Wehlburg (Eds.), *To improve the academy: Vol. 20. Resources for faculty, instructional, and organizational development* (pp. 38–48). Bolton, MA: Anker.

Campbell, W. E., & Smith, K. A. (1997). *New paradigms for college teaching.* Edina, MN: Interaction.

Carroll, K. (2002, Fall). Faculty design courses to engage students—University Writing Program Annual Workshop. *Virginia Tech Center for Excellence in Undergraduate Teaching Newsletter,* 6.

Cashin, W. E. (1999). Student ratings of teaching: Uses and misuses. In P. Seldin & Associates, *Changing practices in evaluating teaching: A practical guide to improved faculty performance and promotion/tenure decisions* (pp. 25–44). Bolton, MA: Anker.

Chickering, A. W., & Ehrmann, S. C. (1996). Implementing the seven principles: Technology as lever. *AAHE Bulletin, 49*(2), 3–6.

Chickering, A. W., & Gamson, Z. F. (1987, June). Seven principles for good practice in undergraduate education. *AAHE Bulletin, 39,* 3–7.

Chickering, A. W., & Reisser, L. (1993). *Education and identity* (2nd ed.). San Francisco, CA: Jossey-Bass.

Chin, J. (2002). Is there a scholarship of teaching and learning in *Teaching Sociology? Teaching Sociology, 30*(1), 53–62.

Chism, N. V. N., Lees, N. D., & Evenbeck, S. (2002). Faculty development for teaching innovation through communities of practice. *Liberal Education, 88*(3), 34–41.

Chism, N. V. N., & Szabó, B, (1996). Who uses faculty development services? In L. Richlin & D. DeZure (Eds.), *To improve the academy: Vol. 15. Resources for faculty, instructional, and organizational development* (pp. 115–128). Stillwater, OK: New Forums Press.

Clark, D., & Redmond, M. (1982). *Small group instructional diagnosis: Final report.* Washington, DC: Fund for the Improvement of Postsecondary Education. (ERIC Document Reproduction Service No. ED217954)

Clary, C. R. (1997). Using peer review to build project teams: A case study. *NACTA Journal, 42*(3), 25–27.

Cohen, P. A. (1980). Effectiveness of student-rating feedback for improving college instruction: A meta-analysis of findings. *Research in Higher Education, 13*, 321–341.

Collett, J., & Serrano, B. (1992). Stirring it up: The inclusive classroom. In L. L. B. Border & N. V. N. Chism (Eds.), *Teaching for diversity* (pp. 35–48). New Directions for Teaching and Learning, No. 49. San Francisco, CA: Jossey-Bass.

Commander, N. E., Hart, L., & Singer, M. (2000). Preparing tomorrow's faculty: An assessment model to determine institutional needs. *The Journal of Graduate Teaching Assistant Development, 7*(2), 93–111.

Cook, C. E., & Sorcinelli, M. D. (1999). Building multiculturalism into teaching development programs. *AAHE Bulletin, 51*(7), 3–6.

Cooke, J. C., Drennan, J. D., & Drennan, P. (1997, October). Peer evaluation as a learning tool. *The Technology Teacher*, 23–27.

Cox, A. M. (2000, December 1). Study shows colleges dependence on their part-time instructors. *The Chronicle of Higher Education,* p. A12.

Cranton, P. (1994). *Understanding and promoting transformative learning: A guide for educators of adults.* San Francisco, CA: Jossey-Bass.

Cranton, P. (1996). *Professional development as transformative learning: New perspectives for teachers of adults.* San Francisco, CA: Jossey-Bass.

Creswell, J. W. (2002). *Educational research: Planning, conducting, and evaluating quantitative and qualitative research.* Upper Saddle River, NJ: Merrill/Prentice Hall.

Cross, K. P., & Steadman, M. H. (1996). *Classroom research: Implementing the scholarship of teaching.* San Francisco, CA: Jossey-Bass.

Cubeta, J. F., Travers, N. L., & Sheckley, B. G. (2001). Predicting the academic success of adults from diverse populations. *Journal of College Student Retention, 2*, 295–311.

Cuseo, J. (1992, Winter). Collaborative and cooperative learning in higher education: A proposed taxonomy. *Cooperative Learning and College Teaching, 2*(2), 2–4.

Darling, A. L. (2003). Scholarship of teaching and learning in communication: New connections, new directions, new possibilities. *Communication Education, 52*(1), 47–49.

Diamond, N. A. (2002). Small group instructional diagnosis: Tapping student perceptions of teaching. In K. H. Gillespie (Ed.), *A guide to faculty development: Practical advice, examples, and resources* (pp. 82–91). Bolton, MA: Anker.

Diamond, R. M. (1998). *Designing and assessing courses and curricula: A practical guide.* San Francisco, CA: Jossey-Bass.

Dick, W., Carey, L., & Carey, J. (2001). *The systematic design of instruction* (5th ed.). Boston, MA: Addison, Wesley, & Longman.

Duch, B. J., Groh, S. E., & Allen, D. E. (2001). Why problem-based learning? A case study of institutional change in undergraduate education. In B. J. Duch, S. E. Groh, & D. E. Allen (Eds.), *The power of problem-based learning* (pp. 3–11). Sterling, VA: Stylus.

Duffy, K., & Jones, J. (1995). *Teaching within the rhythms of the semester.* San Francisco, CA: Jossey-Bass.

Eisenberg, A. (2002, August). *Educational praxis: Linking the practice of teaching with the scholarship of teaching and learning.* Paper presented at the American Sociological Association annual meeting, Chicago, IL.

Engleberg, I. N. (1991). Needs assessment: The first step in staff development. *Journal of Staff, Program, and Organizational Development, 9*(4), 215–222.

Engstrom, C. M., & Tinto, V. (2000). Developing partnerships with academic affairs to enhance student learning. In M. J. Barr, M. K. Desler, & Associates (Eds.), *The handbook of student affairs administration* (2nd ed., pp. 425–452). San Francisco, CA: Jossey-Bass.

Eyler, J., & Giles, D. E., Jr. (1999). *Where's the learning in service-learning?* San Francisco, CA: Jossey-Bass.

Faculty Teaching Excellence Program, University of Colorado at Boulder. (1990). *Compendium of good teaching ideas.* Retrieved March 12, 2003, from www.colorado.edu/ftep/publications

Farquhar, R. (2001). Faculty renewal and institutional revitalization in Canadian universities. *Change, 33*(4), 12–20.

Feldman, K. A. (1989). The association between student ratings of specific instructional dimensions and student achievement: Refining and extending the syntheses of data from multisection validity studies. *Research in Higher Education, 30*(6), 583–645.

Ferren, A., & Geller, W. (1993). Faculty development's role in promoting an inclusive community: Addressing sexual orientation. In D. L. Wright & J. P. Lunde (Eds.), *To improve the academy: Vol. 12. Resources for faculty, instructional, and organizational development* (pp. 97–108). Stillwater, OK: New Forums Press.

Fink, L. D. (1998). *Improving the peer evaluation process in learning teams.* Presentation to Abilene Christian University, Abilene, TX.

Fogg, P. (2001, November 2). Colleges cut proportion of full-time faculty members, study finds. *The Chronicle of Higher Education,* p. A17.

Foster, D., Green, B., Lakey, P., Lakey, R., Mills, F., Williams, C., & Williams, D. (1999, March). *Why, when and how to conduct student peer evaluations in learning teams: An interdisciplinary exploration.* Paper presented at the annual convention of the American Association for Higher Education, Washington, DC.

Foucault, M. (1980a). Prison talk. In C. Gordon (Ed. & Trans.), *Power/knowledge: Selected interviews and other writings, 1972–1977* (pp. 37–54). New York, NY: Bentham.

Foucault, M. (1980b). Two lectures. In C. Gordon (Ed. & Trans.), *Power/knowledge: Selected interviews and other writings, 1972–1977* (pp. 78–108). New York, NY: Bentham.

Foucault, M. (1983). On the genealogy of ethics. In H. L Dreyfus & P. Rabinow (Eds.), *Michel Foucault: Beyond structuralism and hermeneutics* (pp. 231–232). Chicago, IL: The University of Chicago Press.

Foucault, M. (1995). *Discipline and punish: The birth of the prison* (A. Sheridan, Trans.). New York, NY: Vintage Books. (Original work published 1977).

Franklin, J. (2001). Interpreting the numbers: Using a narrative to help others read student evaluations of your teaching accurately. In K. G. Lewis (Ed.), *Techniques and strategies for interpreting student evaluations* (pp. 85–100). New Directions for Teaching and Learning, No. 87. San Francisco, CA: Jossey-Bass.

Fried, J. (1995). Border crossings in higher education: Faculty/student affairs collaboration. In J. Fried & Associates, *Shifting paradigms in student affairs: Culture, context, teaching and learning* (pp. 171–188). Washington, DC: American College Personnel Association.

Furr, S. R., & Elling, T. W. (2002). African-American students in a predominantly White university: Factors associated with retention. *College Student Journal, 36,* 188–199.

Fullan, M. (1993). *Change forces: Probing the depths of educational reform.* Bristol, PA: Farmer Press.

Gappa, J. (2002, January 24). *Employment policies and practices.* Paper presented at the preconference assembly on part-time faculty at the AAHE Forum on Faculty Roles and Rewards Conference, Phoenix, AZ.

Gappa, J., & Leslie, D. (1993). *The invisible faculty.* San Francisco, CA: Jossey-Bass.

Gappa, L. (1993). The teaching associate program: A collaborative approach. *The Journal of Graduate Teaching Assistant Development, 1*(1), 25–32.

Glassick, C. E., Huber, M. T., & Maeroff, G. I. (1997). *Scholarship assessed: Evaluation of the professoriate.* San Francisco, CA: Jossey-Bass.

Goldsmid, C. A., & Wilson, E. K. (1980). *Passing on sociology: The teaching of a discipline.* Belmont, CA: Wadsworth.

Gordon, R. (2000). Problem based service learning: The power of learning through service. In R. Gordon (Ed.), *Problem based service learning: A fieldguide for making a difference in higher education* (2nd ed., pp. 1–13) Keene, NH: Education by Design.

Graf, D. L., & Wheeler, D. (1996). *Defining the field: The POD membership survey.* Ames, IA: The POD Network.

Gray, T., & Birch, J. (2001). Publish, don't perish: A program to help scholars flourish. In D. Lieberman & C. Wehlburg (Eds.), *To improve the academy: Vol. 19. Resources for faculty, instructional, and organization development* (pp. 268–284). Bolton, MA: Anker.

Green, M. (2002). Joining the world: The challenge to internationalizing undergraduate education. *Change, 34*(3), 12–21.

Grunert, J. (1997). *The course syllabus: A learning-centered approach.* Bolton, MA: Anker.

Harnish, D., & Wild, L. A. (1992). Faculty speak: A way to assess the impact of professional development on instruction. *Journal of Staff, Program, and Organizational Development, 10* (1), 5–12.

Healey, M. (2000). Developing the scholarship of teaching and learning in higher education: A discipline-based approach. *Higher Education Research and Development, 19*(2), 167–187.

Henscheid, J. M. (1999). *Washington State University freshman seminar program research findings.* Retrieved November 17, 2002, from http://salc.wsu.edu/freshman/details/research_findings.htm

Henscheid, J. M. (2001). Peer facilitators as lead freshman seminar instructors. In J. E. Miller, J. E., Groccia, & M. S. Miller (Eds.), *Student-assisted teaching: A guide to faculty-student team work* (pp. 21–26). Bolton, MA: Anker.

Hicks, O. (1999). A conceptual framework for instructional consultation. In C. Knapper & S. Piccinin (Eds.), *Using consultants to improve teaching* (pp. 9–18). New Directions for Teaching and Learning. No. 79. San Francisco, CA: Jossey-Bass.

Hjortshoj, K. (2001). *The transition to college writing.* Boston, MA: Bedford-St. Martin's.

Howard, J. (2001). *Michigan Journal of Community Service Learning: Service-learning course design workbook.* Ann Arbor, MI: OCSL Press, The University of Michigan.

Hu, S., & St. John, E. P. (2001). Student persistence in a public education system: Understanding racial and ethnic differences. *The Journal of Higher Education, 72,* 265–286.

Huber, M. T. (2001). Balancing acts: Designing careers around the scholarship of teaching and learning. *Change, 33*(4), 21–29.

Huber, M. T., & Morreale, S. P. (Eds.). (2002). *Disciplinary styles in the scholarship of teaching and learning: Exploring common ground.* Washington DC: American Association for Higher Education.

Hutchings, P. (2002a, March). *Informal handout and remarks at the SoTL community of practice.* Annual meeting of the American Association for Higher Education, Chicago, IL.

Hutchings, P. (2002b). *Ethics of inquiry: Issues in the scholarship of teaching and learning.* Menlo Park, CA: The Carnegie Foundation for the Advancement of Teaching.

Hutchings, P., & Shulman, L. S. (1999, September/October). The scholarship of teaching: New elaborations, new developments. *Change, 31*(5), 10–15.

Ingram, K. (2001). The effects of reflective thinking training on TAs' reflective thinking, use of instructional activities, instructional effectiveness, motivation to teach and their students' attitudes toward instruction. (Doctoral Dissertation, Florida State University, 2001). *Dissertation Abstracts International, 62*(2), 486.

Jackson, B., & Hardiman, R. (1994). Multicultural organizational development. In E. Cross, H. Katz, F. Miller, & E. Seashore (Eds.), *The promise of diversity* (pp. 231–239). Chicago, IL: Irwin Professional Publishing.

Jackson, B., & Holvino, E. (1988). Developing multicultural organizations. Creative change. *The Journal of Religion and the Applied Behavioral Sciences, 9*(2), 14–19.

Jenkins, A. (1996). Discipline-based educational development. *The International Journal for Academic Development, 1*(1), 50–62.

Jenson, J. D. (2002). If I knew then what I know now: A first-year faculty consultant's top ten list. In K. H. Gillespie (Ed.), *A guide to faculty development: Practical advice, examples, and resources* (pp. 92–98). Bolton, MA: Anker.

Johnson, D. W., & Johnson, R. T. (1996). *Meaningful and manageable assessment through cooperative learning.* Edina, MN: Interaction Book Company.

Johnson, D. W., Johnson, R. T., & Smith, K. A. (1998). *Active learning: Cooperation in the college classroom.* Edina, MN: Interaction.

Johnson, J. L. (1997). Commuter college students: What factors determine who will persist and who will drop out? *College Student Journal, 31,* 323–333.

Jones, D. (2001). *Technology costing methodology project.* Retrieved November 19, 2002, from http://www.wcet.info/projects/tcm/TCM_Handbook_Final.pdf

Kardia, D. (1998). Becoming a multicultural faculty developer. In M. Kaplan & D. Lieberman (Eds.), *To improve the academy: Vol. 17. Resources for faculty, instructional, and organizational development* (pp. 15–33). Stillwater, OK: New Forums Press.

Katz, J. (1978). *White awareness: Handbook of anti-racism training.* Norman, OK: University of Oklahoma Press.

Keller, J. M. (1987a). Strategies for stimulating the motivation to learn. *Performance & Instruction, 26,* 1–7.

Keller, J. M. (1987b). The systematic process of motivational design. *Performance & Instruction, 26,* 1–8.

Kezar, A. (2002). Assessing community service learning: Are we identifying the right outcomes? *About Campus, 7,* 14–20.

Kirkpatrick, D. L. (1996). *Evaluating training programs: The four levels.* San Francisco, CA: Berrett-Koehler.

Knapper, C., & Piccinin, S. (1999). Consulting about teaching: An overview. In C. Knapper & S. Piccinin (Eds.), *Using consultants to improve teaching* (pp. 3–7). New Directions for Teaching and Learning, No. 79. San Francisco, CA: Jossey-Bass.

Knowlton, L. M., & Ratliffe, S. A. (1992). Statewide staff development survey reveals trends and outcomes in California. *Journal of Staff, Program and Organizational Development, 10*(2), 111–116.

Kreber, C. (Ed.) (2001a). Scholarship revisited: Perspectives on the scholarship of teaching and learning. *New Directions for Teaching and Learning, No. 86.* San Francisco, CA: Jossey-Bass.

Kreber, C. (2001b). The scholarship of teaching and its implementation in faculty development and graduate education. In C. Kreber (Ed.), *Scholarship revisited: Perspectives on the scholarship of teaching and learning* (pp. 79–88). New Directions for Teaching and Learning, No. 86. San Francisco, CA: Jossey-Bass.

Kreber, C., & Cranton, P. A. (2000). Exploring the scholarship of teaching. *The Journal of Higher Education, 71* (4), 476–495.

Kuh, G. D. (1993). *Cultural perspectives in student affairs work.* Lanham, MD: University Press of America.

Lacey, P. A. (1983). *Revitalizing teaching through faculty development.* San Francisco, CA: Jossey-Bass.

Lambert, L. M., & Tice, S. E. (Eds.). (1993). *Preparing graduate students to teach: A guide to programs that improve undergraduate education.* Washington, DC: American Association for Higher Education.

Lang, M. (2001). Student retention in higher education: Some conceptual and programmatic perspectives. *Journal of College Student Retention, 3,* 217–229.

Langer, J. A., & Applebee, A. N. (1987). *How writing shapes thinking.* Urbana, IL: National Council of Teachers of English.

Leatherman, C. (2000, January). Part-timers continue to replace full-timers on college faculties. *The Chronicle of Higher Education,* p. A18.

Leatherman, C. (2001, April). Growing use of part-time professors prompts debates and calls for action. *The Chronicle of Higher Education,* p. A14.

Leibowitz, K. (2002). *Higher Education Research Institute Faculty Survey 2001–2002.* Philadelphia, PA: University of the Sciences in Philadelphia.

Lenze, L. F. (1997). Small group instructional diagnosis (SGID). In K. T. Brinko & R. J. Menges (Eds.), *Practically speaking: A sourcebook for instructional consultants in higher education* (pp. 143–146). Stillwater, OK: New Forums Press.

Leslie, D. (2002, January 24). *Survey of 18,000 adjunct faculty.* Paper presented at the preconference assembly on part-time faculty at the AAHE Forum on Faculty Roles and Rewards Conference, Phoenix, AZ.

Lewis, K. G. (2001). Making sense of student written comments. In K. G. Lewis (Ed.), *Techniques and strategies for interpreting student evaluations* (pp. 25–32). New Directions for Teaching and Learning, No. 87. San Francisco, CA: Jossey-Bass.

Lewis, K. G. (2002). The process of individual consultation. In K. H. Gillespie (Ed.), *A guide to faculty development: Practical advice, examples, and resources* (pp. 59–73). Bolton, MA: Anker.

L' Hommedieu, R., Menges, R., & Brinko, K. (1990). Methodological explanations for the modest effects of feedback. *Journal of Educational Psychology, 82,* 232–241.

Lieberman, D., & Guskin, A. (2002). The essential role of faculty development in higher education. In C. Wehlburg & S. Chadwick-Blossey (Eds.), *To improve the academy: Vol. 21: Resources for faculty, instructional, and organizational development* (pp. 257–271). Bolton, MA: Anker.

Little, A., & Wolf, A. (1996). *Assessment in transition: Learning, monitoring and selection in international perspective.* New York, NY: Pergamon Press.

Loacker, G., Cromwell, C., & O'Brien, K. (1986). Assessment in higher education: To serve the learner. In C. Adelman (Ed.), *Assessment in American higher education* (pp. 47–62). Washington, DC: U. S. Department of Education, Office of Educational Research and Improvement.

Lovett, C. (2002). Cracks in the bedrock: Can U. S. higher education remain number one? *Change, 34*(2), 10–15.

Lowman, J. (1984). *Mastering the techniques of teaching.* San Francisco, CA: Jossey-Bass.

Lucke, J. (2002, January). *Summary.* Paper presented at the preconference assembly on part-time faculty at the AAHE Forum on Faculty Roles and Rewards Conference, Phoenix, AZ.

Marincovich, M., Prostko, J., & Stout, F. (Eds.). (1998). *The professional development of graduate teaching assistants.* Bolton, MA: Anker.

Marklein, M. B. (2001, October 30). Part-time instructors march for better pay. *USA Today,* p. 11D.

Martin, E., Benjamin, J., Prosser, M., & Trigwell, K. (1999). Scholarship of teaching: A study of the approaches of academic staff. In C. Rust (Ed.), *Improving student learning: Improving student learning outcomes* (pp. 326–331). Oxford, England: Oxford Brookes University, Oxford Centre for Staff Learning and Development.

Mauksch, H. O., & Howery, C. B. (1986). Social change for teaching: The case of one disciplinary association. *Teaching Sociology, 14*(1), 73–82.

Maxwell, W. E., & Kazlauskas, E. J. (1992). Which faculty development methods really work in community colleges? A review of research. *Community Junior College Quarterly, 16,* 351–360.

McCarthy, J. D., & Zald, M. N. (1977). Resource mobilization and social movements: A partial theory. *American Journal of Sociology, 82*(6), 1212–1241.

McDonough, K. (1993). *Overcoming ambivalence about Foucault's relevance for education.* Retrieved March 23, 2003, from http://www.ed.uiuc.edu/eps/pes-yearbook/93_docs/mcdonoug.htm

McKeachie, W. J. (1994). *Teaching tips: Strategies, research, and theory for college and university teachers* (9th ed.). Lexington, MA: D. C. Heath.

McKeachie, W. J. (1997). Student ratings: The validity of use. *American Psychologist, 52,* 1218–1225.

McKenna, J., Bickle, M., & Carroll, J. B. (2002). Using scholarship to integrate teaching and research. *Journal of Family & Consumer Sciences, 94*(3), 39–45.

Menges, R. J. (1996). Experiences of newly hired faculty. In L. Richlin & D. DeZure (Eds.), *To improve the academy: Vol. 15. Resources for faculty, instructional, and organizational development* (pp. 169–183). Bolton, MA: Anker.

Mezirow, J. (1991). *Transformative dimensions of adult learning.* San Francisco, CA: Jossey-Bass.

Mezirow, J. (2000). Learning to think like an adult: Core concepts of transformation theory. In J. Mezirow & Associates (Eds.), *Learning as transformation: Critical perspectives on a theory in progress* (pp. 3–33). San Francisco, CA: Jossey-Bass

Michaelsen, L. K., & Black, R. H. (1994). Building learning teams: The key to harnessing the power of small groups in higher education. In S. Kadel & J. Keehner (Eds.), *Collaborative learning: A sourcebook for higher education,* (Vol. 2, pp. 65–81). Syracuse, NY: National Center on Postsecondary Teaching, Learning, and Assessment.

Michaelsen, L. K., Fink, L. D., & Black, R. H. (1996). What every faculty developer needs to know about learning groups. In L. Richlin & D. DeZure (Eds.), *To improve the academy: Vol. 15. Resources for faculty, instructional, and organizational development* (pp. 31–58). Stillwater, OK: New Forums Press.

Michaelsen, L. K., Fink, L. D., & Knight, A. (1997). Designing effective group activities: Lessons for classroom teaching and faculty development. In D. DeZure & M. Kaplan (Eds.), *To improve the academy: Vol. 16. Resources for faculty, instructional, and organizational development* (pp. 373–398). Stillwater, OK: New Forums Press.

Michaelsen, L. K., Jones, C. F., & Watson, W. E. (1993). Beyond groups and cooperation: Building high performance learning teams. In D. L. Wright & J. P. Lunde (Eds.), *To improve the academy: Vol. 12. Resources for faculty, instructional, and organizational development.* Stillwater, OK: New Forums Press.

Michaelsen, L. K, Knight, A. B., & Fink, L. D. (2002). *Team-based learning: A transformative use of small groups.* Westport, CT: Praeger.

Millis, B. J. (2002). *Enhancing learning—and more!—through cooperative learning.* Retrieved March 25, 2003, from http://www.idea.ksu.edu/papers/Idea_Paper_38.pdf

Millis, B. J., & Cottell, P. G. (1998). *Cooperative learning for higher education faculty* (ACE Series on Higher Education). Phoenix, AZ: Oryx Press. [Now distributed through Greenwood Press].

Mintz, J. A. (1998). The role of centralized programs in preparing graduate students to teach. In M. Marincovich, J. Prostko, & F. Stout (Eds.), *The professional development of graduate teaching assistants* (pp. 19–40). Bolton, MA: Anker.

Mintz, J. M. (1999, Spring). Faculty development and teaching: A holistic approach. *Liberal Education, 85*(2), 32–37.

Morrison, D. E. (1997). Overview of instructional consultation in North America. In K. T. Brinko & R. J. Menges (Eds.), *Practically speaking: A sourcebook for instructional consultants in higher education* (pp. 121–129). Stillwater, OK: New Forums Press.

Moser, R. (2001). *The new academic labor system, corporation and the renewal of academic citizenship.* Retrieved November 20, 2002, fromhttp://www.aaup.org/Issues/part-time/cewmose.htm

Murray, J. P. (1995). Faculty (mis)development in Ohio two-year colleges. *Community College Journal of Research and Practice, 19*, 549–563.

Murray, J. P. (1999). Faculty development in a national sample of community colleges. *Community College Review, 27*(3), 47–64.

Murrell, G. (1998). *Adjunct faculty: An injury to one is an injury to all.* Retrieved May 9, 2003, from http://www.evergreen.edu/washcenter/resources/spring2002/25-26.pdf

Narum, J. (2002). *Science for all students.* Paper presented at the American Council on Education conference on Fostering Innovation in Undergraduate Science, Technology, Engineering, and Mathematics for all students, Washington, DC.

National Center for Educational Statistics. (2001). *The condition of education 2001. Indicator 50: Part-time Instructional Faculty and Staff.* Washington, DC: U.S. Government Printing Office.

National Education Association Higher Education Research Center. (2001). Part-time faculty. *Update, 7*(4), 1–4.

Nelsen, W. C. (1980). Faculty development: Perceived needs of the 1980's. In W. C. Nelsen & M. E. Siegel (Eds.), *Effective approaches to faculty development* (pp. 145–149). Washington, DC: Association of American Colleges.

Newman, F., & Couturier, L. (2001). The new competitive arena: Market forces invade the academy. *Change, 33*(5), 10–17.

Noonan, J. F. (1980). An institute on teaching and learning for new faculty. In W. C. Nelsen & M. E. Siegel (Eds.), *Effective approaches to faculty development* (pp. 49–70). Washington, DC: Association of American Colleges.

Nuhfer, E. B. (2001). *A Handbook for student management teams.* Denver, CO: The Office of Teaching Effectiveness. Retrieved March 25, 2003, from http://www.isu.edu/ctl/

Rhem, J. (1995). Deep/surface approaches to learning: An introduction. *The National Teaching & Learning Forum, 5*(1), 1–3.

Nyquist, J. D., & Sprague, J. (1998). Thinking developmentally about TAs. In M. Marincovich, J. Prostko, & F. Stout (Eds.), *The professional development of graduate teaching assistants* (pp. 61–88). Bolton, MA: Anker.

Office of Educational Development, University of California at Berkeley. (2002). *Compendium of good ideas on teaching and learning.* Retrieved March 12, 2003, from http://teaching.berkeley.edu/goodteachers/index.html

Ohland, M., & Layton, R. (2000). Comparing the reliability of two peer evaluation instruments. *Proceedings of the American Society of Engineering Education.* Washington, DC: ASEE.

Ory, J. C. (2001). Faculty thoughts and concerns about student ratings. In K. G. Lewis (Ed.), *Techniques and strategies for interpreting student evaluations* (pp. 3–15). New Directions for Teaching and Learning, No. 87. San Francisco, CA: Jossey-Bass.

Ouellett, M. L., & Sorcinelli, M. D. (1995). Teaching and learning in the diverse classroom: A faculty and TA partnership program. In E. Neal & L. Richlin (Eds.), *To improve the academy: Vol. 14. Resources for faculty, instructional, and organizational development* (pp. 205–217). Stillwater, OK: New Forums Press.

Ouellett, M. L., & Sorcinelli, M. D. (1998). TA training: Strategies for responding to diversity in the classroom. In M. Marincovich, J. Prostko, & F. Stout (Eds.), *The professional development of graduate teaching assistants* (pp. 105–120). Bolton, MA: Anker.

Palmer, P. J. (1998). *The courage to teach.* San Francisco, CA: Jossey-Bass.

Pascarella, E. T., & Terenzini, P. (1991). *How college affects students.* San Francisco, CA: Jossey-Bass.

Paulsen, M. B., & Feldman, K. A. (1995). Toward a re-conceptualization of scholarship: A human action system with functional imperatives. *Journal of Higher Education, 66*(6), 615–640.

Pellino, G. R., Blackburn, R. T., & Boberg, A. L. (1984). The dimensions of academic scholarship: Faculty and administrator views. *Research in Higher Education, 20*(1), 103–115.

Petrulis, R., Carroll, S., & Skow, L. (1993). Graduate students as instructional consultant: case studies from two universities. *The Journal of Graduate Teaching Assistant Development, 1*(2), 85–93.

Phillips, J. J. (1997a). *Return on investment in training and performance improvement programs.* Woburn, MA: Butterworth-Heinemann.

Phillips, J. J. (1997b). *Handbook of training evaluation and measurement methods.* Houston, TX: Gulf Publishing.

Phillips, J. J. (2000). *The consultant's scorecard: Tracking results and bottom-line impact of consulting projects.* New York, NY: McGraw-Hill.

Pierce, G. (2001). Developing new faculty: An evolving program. In D. Lieberman & C. Wehlburg (Eds.), *To improve the academy: Vol. 19. Resources for faculty, instructional, and organizational development* (pp. 253–267). Bolton, MA: Anker.

POD Network. (2002). *Ethical guidelines for educational developers.* Retrieved March 23, 2003, from http://www.podnetwork.org/development/ethicalguidelines.htm

Prieto, L. R. (1999). Teaching assistants' preferences for supervisory style: Testing a developmental model of GTA supervision. *The Journal of Graduate Teaching Assistant Development, 6*(3), 111–118.

Redmond, M. V., & Clark, D. J. (1982). Student group instructional diagnosis: A practical approach to improving teaching. *AAHE Bulletin, 34,* 8–10.

Reiser, R., & Dick, W. (1996). *Instructional planning: A guide for teachers* (2nd ed.). Boston, MA: Allyn and Bacon.

Rice, R. E. (1992). Toward a broader conception of scholarship: The American context. In T. G. Whiston & R. L. Geiger (Eds.), *Research and higher education in the United Kingdom and the United States* (pp. 117–129). Lancaster, England: Society for Research on Higher Education.

Richlin. L. (Ed.). (1993). Preparing faculty for the new conception of scholarship. *New Directions for Teaching and Learning, No. 54.* San Francisco, CA: Jossey-Bass.

Richlin, L. (2001, Summer). Scholarly teaching and the scholarship of teaching. In C. Kreber (Ed.), *Scholarship revisited: Perspectives on the scholarship of teaching and learning* (pp. 57–68). New Directions for Teaching and Learning, No. 86. San Francisco, CA: Jossey-Bass

Romer, A. (1980). The role of a faculty committee in facilitating faculty development. In W. C. Nelsen & M. E. Siegel (Eds.), *Effective approaches to faculty development* (pp. 77–83). Washington, DC: Association of American Colleges.

Santanello, C., & Eder, D. (2001). Classroom assessment techniques. *Thriving in academe, 19,* 5–8.

Schmitz, B., Paul, S., & Greenberg, J. (1992). Creating multicultural classrooms: An experience-derived faculty development program. In L. L. B. Border & N. V. N. Chism (Eds.), *Teaching for diversity* (pp. 75–87). New Directions for Teaching and Learning, No. 49. San Francisco, CA: Jossey-Bass.

Schön, D. A. (1983). *The reflective practitioner: How professionals think in action.* New York, NY: Basic Books.

Schön, D. A. (1987). *Educating the reflective practitioner: Toward a new design for teaching and learning in the professions.* San Francisco, CA: Jossey-Bass.

Schön, D. A. (1995). The new scholarship requires a new epistemology. *Change, 27*(6), 26–34.

Schroeder, C. C. (1998). *Collaboration and partnerships.* Retrieved April 6, 2002, from http://www.acpa.nche.edu/seniorscholars/trends/trends7.htm

Seaman, R. (2000). Project design. In R. Gordon (Ed.), *Problem based service learning: A fieldguide for making a difference in higher education* (2nd ed., pp. 15–23). Keene, NH: Education by Design.

Seldin, P. (1999). Current practices—good and bad—nationally. In P. Seldin & Associates, *Changing practices in evaluating teaching: A practical guide to improved faculty performance and promotion/tenure decisions* (pp. 1–24). Bolton, MA: Anker.

Senge, P. (1990). *The fifth discipline: The art and practice of a learning organization.* New York, NY: Doubleday.

Shapiro, M. (2002). Irreverent commentary on the state of education in America today. Retrieved November 20, 2002, from http://irascibleprofessor.com/comments_11_05_02.htm

Shulman, L. S. (1987). Knowledge and teaching: Foundations of the new reform. *Harvard Educational Review, 36*(1), 1–22.

Shulman, L. S. (1993, November/December). Teaching as community property: Putting an end to pedagogical solitude. *Change, 25*(6), 6–7.

Shulman, L. S. (1999). *Visions of the possible: Models for campus support of the scholarship of teaching and learning.* Retrieved April 28, 2003, from http://www.carnegiefoundation.org/elibrary/docs/Visions.htm

Shulman, L. S. (2001). Remarks at the teaching symposium for the Cross Endowed Chair for the Scholarship of Teaching and Learning, Illinois State University.

Siegel, M. E. (1980). Empirical findings on faculty development programs. In W. C. Nelsen & M. E. Siegel (Eds.), *Effective approaches to faculty development* (pp. 131–144). Washington, DC: Association of American Colleges.

Smelser, N. J. (1963). *Theory of collective behavior.* New York, NY: Free Press.

Smith, K. A. (1996). Cooperative learning: Making "groupwork" work. In C. Bonwell & T. Sutherlund (Eds.), *Using active learning in college classes: A range of options for faculty* (pp. 71–82). New Directions for Teaching and Learning, No. 67. San Francisco, CA: Jossey-Bass.

Smith, R. (2001). Expertise and the scholarship of teaching. In C. Kreber (Ed.). *Scholarship revisited: Perspectives on the scholarship of teaching and learning* (pp. 69–78). New Directions for Teaching and Learning, No. 86. San Francisco, CA: Jossey-Bass.

Sorcinelli, M. D. (1988). Satisfactions and concerns of new university teachers. In J. G. Kurfiss (Ed.), *To improve the academy: Vol. 7. Resources for faculty, instructional, and organizational development* (pp. 121–131). Stillwater, OK: New Forums Press.

Sorcinelli, M. D., & Elbow, P. (Eds.). (1997). Writing to learn: Strategies for assigning and responding to writing across the disciplines. *New Directions for Teaching and Learning, No. 69.* San Francisco, CA: Jossey-Bass.

Speck, B. W. (2000). Grading students' classroom writing: Issues and strategies (ASHE-ERIC Higher Education Report, 27[3]). Washington, DC: George Washington University, Graduate School of Education and Human Development.

Stanley, C. A. (2001). A review of the pipeline: The value of diversity in staffing teaching and learning centers in the new millennium. *The Journal of Faculty Development, 18*(2), 75–85.

Stanley, C. A., & Chism, N. V. N. (1991). Selected characteristics of new faculty: Implications for faculty development. In K. J. Zahorski (Ed.), *To improve the academy: Vol. 10. Resources for faculty, instructional, and organizational development* (pp. 55–63). Stillwater, OK: New Forums Press.

Stanley, C. A., & Ouellett, M. L. (2000). On the path: POD as multicultural organization.. In M. Kaplan & D. Lieberman (Eds.), *To improve the academy: Vol. 18. Resources for faculty, instructional, and organizational development* (pp. 38–54). Bolton, MA: Anker.

Swail, W. (2002). Higher education and the new demographics: Questions for policy. *Change, 34*(4), 14–23.

Syversen, P. D., & Tice, S. L. (1993). The critical role of the teaching assistantship. In L. M. Lambert & S.E. Tice (Eds.), *Preparing graduate students to teach: A guide to programs that improve undergraduate education and develop tomorrow's faculty.* Washington, DC: American Association for Higher Education.

Taylor-Way, D. (1988). Consultation with video: Memory management through stimulated recall. In K. G. Lewis (Ed.), *Face to face: A sourcebook of individual consultation techniques for faculty/instructional developers* (pp. 159–191). Stillwater, OK: New Forums Press.

Tharp, J. (1998). Predicting persistence of urban commuter campus students utilizing student background characteristics from enrollment data. *Community College Journal of Research and Practice, 22,* 279–294.

Theall, M., & Franklin, J. (2001). Looking for bias in all the wrong places: A search for truth or a witch hunt in student ratings of instruction? In M. Theall, P. C. Abrami, & L. A. Mets (Eds.), *The student ratings debate: Are they valid? How can we best use them?* (pp. 45–56). New Directions for Institutional Research, No. 109. San Francisco, CA: Jossey-Bass.

Tiberius, R. (1997). Small group methods for collecting information from students. In K. T. Brinko & R. J. Menges (Eds.), *Practically speaking: A sourcebook for instructional consultants in higher education* (pp. 53–63). Stillwater, OK: New Forums Press.

Travis, J. E., Hursh, D., Lankewicz, G., & Tang, L. (1996). Monitoring the pulse of the faculty: Needs assessment in faculty development programs. In L. Richlin & D. DeZure (Eds.), *To improve the academy: Vol. 15. Resources for faculty, instructional, and organizational development* (pp. 95–113). Stillwater, OK: New Forums Press.

Unger, D. (1995). Academic apartheid: The predicament of part-time faculty. *NEA Education Journal,* 117–120.

University of Otago. (2001). *Senate policy on assessment of student performance: Principles and guidelines.* Retrieved March 12, 2003, from http://policy01.otago.ac.nz/rdbase/FMPro?db=policies.fm&format=viewpolicy.html&-lay=viewpolicy&-sortfield=Title&-max=2147483647&-recid=32842&findall=#5

University of Queensland. (n.d.). *Group assessment—Assessment of students on group-based tasks—issues and options.* Retrieved May 25, 2001, from http:www.tedi.uq.edu.au/assess/Assessment/groupwork.html

University of Technology, Sydney. (n.d.). *Students groups: Issues for teaching and learning.* Retrieved May 25, 2001, from http://www/clt.uts.edu.au/Student.Group work.html

University of the Sciences in Philadelphia. (2002). *The University of the Sciences in Philadelphia: A self-study report.* Submitted to the Commission on Higher Education of the Middle States Association and the American Council on Pharmaceutical Education, Philadelphia, PA.

USMA Academic Board and Office of the Dean. (1998). *Educating army leaders for the 21st century.* West Point, NY: United States Military Academy.

Walvoord, B. E. (1986). *Helping students write well: A guide for teachers in all disciplines.* New York, NY: The Modern Language Association.

Walvoord, B. E., & McCarthy, L. P. (1990). *Thinking and writing in college: A naturalistic study of students in four disciplines.* Urbana, IL: National Council of Teachers of English.

Webb, N. (1994). *Group collaboration in assessment: Competing objectives, processes, and outcomes* (CSE Technical Report No. 386). Los Angeles, CA: University of California, Los Angeles, National Center for Research on Evaluation, Standards and Student Testing (CRESST).

Weimer, M. (1990). *Improving college teaching: Strategies for developing instructional effectiveness.* San Francisco, CA: Jossey-Bass.

Weimer, M. (1996). Why scholarship is the bedrock of good teaching. In R. J. Menges & M. Weimer (Eds.), *Teaching on solid ground: Using scholarship to improve practice* (pp. 1–12). San Francisco, CA: Jossey-Bass.

Weimer, M. (1997). Exploring the implications: From research to practice. In R. P. Perry & J. C. Smart (Eds.), *Effective teaching in higher education: Research and practice* (pp. 411–435). New York, NY: Agathon.

Weimer, M. (2002). *Learner-centered teaching: Five key changes to practice.* San Francisco, CA: Jossey-Bass.

Wenger, E. (1999). *Communities of practice: Learning, meaning, and identity.* Cambridge, England: Cambridge University Press.

Wenger, E., McDermott, R., & Snyder, W. M. (2002). *Cultivating communities of practice: A guide to managing knowledge.* Cambridge, MA: Harvard Business School Press.

Weston, C. B., & McAlpine, L. (2001). Making explicit the development toward the scholarship of teaching. In C. Kreber (Ed.), *Scholarship revisited: Perspectives on the scholarship of teaching and learning* (pp. 89–98). New Directions for Teaching and Learning, No. 86. San Francisco, CA: Jossey-Bass.

Wilbee, J. (1997). Instructional skills workshop program: A peer-based model for the improvement of teaching and learning. In K. T. Brinko & R. J. Menges (Eds.), *Practically speaking: A sourcebook for instructional consultants in higher education* (pp. 147–156). Stillwater, OK: New Forums Press.

Wilber, K. (2000). The four corners of the known universe. In K. Wilber (Ed.), *The collected works of Ken Wilber* (Vol. 8, pp. 135–148). Boston, MA: Shambhala.

Winternitz, T., & Davis, W. E. (2000). Lessons learned during five years of the UC Davis program in college teaching. *The Journal of Graduate Teaching Assistant Development, 7*(2), 69–75.

Woods, D. R. (1994). *Problem-based learning: How to gain the most from PBL.* Waterdown, Ontario, Canada: D. R. Woods.

Woods, D. R. (1995). *Problem-based learning: Resources to gain the most from PBL.* Waterdown, Ontario, Canada: D. R. Woods.

Woods, D. R. (1996). *Problem-based learning: How to gain the most from PBL* (2nd ed.). Retrieved December 14, 2002, from http://chemeng.mcmaster.ca/pbl/pbl.htm

Wright, S. P., & Hendershott, A. (1992). In D. H. Wulff, & J. D. Nyquist (Eds.), *To improve the academy: Vol. 11. Resources for Faculty, Instructional, and Organizational Development* (pp. 87–104). Stillwater, OK: New Forums Press.

Wulff, D. H. (1996, Fall). *Small group instructional diagnosis (SGID).* Training workshops conducted at the U. S. Air Force Academy.

Wulff, D. H., Staton-Spicer, A. Q., Hess, C. W., & Nyquist, J. D. (1985). The student perspective on evaluating teaching effectiveness. *Association for Communication Administration Bulletin, 53,* 39–47.

Zahorski, K. J. (Ed.). (2002). Scholarship in the postmodern era: New venues, new values, new visions. *New Directions in Teaching and Learning, No. 90.* San Francisco, CA: Jossey-Bass.

Zigon, J. (1998). *Measuring the hard stuff: Teams and other hard-to-measure work.* Retrieved March 25, 2003, from http://www.zigonperf.com/articles/hardstuff.html